# Desktop Publis  with Adobe® PageMaker® 6.5 for Windows
## Includes Publishing for the Web

**James Shuman**
**Marcia Williams**
Bellevue Community College

**COURSE**
TECHNOLOGY

ONE MAIN STREET, CAMBRIDGE, MA 02142

*an International Thomson Publishing company* I(T)P®

Cambridge • Albany • Bonn • Boston • Cincinnati • London • Madrid • Melbourne • Mexico City
New York • Paris • San Francisco • Singapore • Tokyo • Toronto • Washington

**Desktop Publishing with Adobe PageMaker 6.5** is published by Course Technology.

| | |
|---|---|
| Managing Editor: | Kristen Duerr |
| Product Managers: | Robin Geller, Jennifer Normandin |
| Developmental Editor: | Robin Geller |
| Production Editor: | Nancy Shea |
| Text Designer: | GEX, Inc. |
| Cover Illustrator: | Douglas Goodman |

© 1998 by Course Technology.
A Division of International Thomson Publishing—I(T)P®

**For more information contact:**

**Course Technology**
One Main Street
Cambridge, MA 02142

**ITP Europe**
Berkshire House 168-173
High Holborn
London WCIV 7AA
England

**Nelson ITP, Australia**
102 Dodds Street
South Melbourne, 3205
Victoria, Australia

**ITP Nelson Canada**
1120 Birchmount Road
Scarborough, Ontario
Canada M1K 5G4

**International Thomson Editores**
Seneca, 53
Colonia Polanco
11560 Mexico D.F. Mexico

**ITP GmbH**
Königswinterer Strasse 418
53227 Bonn
Germany

**ITP Asia**
60 Albert Street, #15-01
Albert Complex
Singapore 189969

**ITP Japan**
Hirakawacho Kyowa Building, 3F
2-2-1 Hirakawacho
Chiyoda-ku, Tokyo 102
Japan

**Trademarks**
Course Technology and the Open Book logo are registered trademarks and CourseKits is a trademark of Course Technology. The ITP logo is a registered trademark of International Thomson Publishing.

Some of the product names and company names used in this book have been used for identification purposes only and may be trademarks or registered trademarks of their respective manufacturers and sellers.

**Disclaimer**
Course Technology reserves the right to revise this publication and make changes from time to time in its content without notice.

ISBN 0-7600-4956-4

Printed in the United States of America

2 3 4 5 6 7 8 9 BM 02 01 00 99 98

To Barbara and Bruce for their support and
encouragement throughout this project.

# CONTENTS

# PREFACE

This text provides a practical, hands-on approach to developing skills in the use of the most popular desktop publishing program, Adobe PageMaker 6.5 for Windows. After completing this text, students will be able to use PageMaker to develop professional-looking publications, including newsletters, advertisements, stationery, flyers, business cards, and announcements. The text requires active participation as the students develop these real-world applications. The emphasis is on learning by doing. The learning process becomes exciting and motivating for students as they create a portfolio of their work.

## Text Organization

This text is presented as a self-paced tutorial, designed to be used in a lab setting. A concept, such as resizing a graphic, is presented. The process is explained, followed by the actual steps so students learn the "why" along with the "how." In each chapter, students work through examples so that new commands are practiced as they are presented. End-of-chapter questions and projects are used to reinforce learning by requiring students to apply skills as they are learned. Screen shots guide students through the operations involved in completing a particular exercise. This approach allows you to determine your level of involvement—from providing presentations that supplement the text material to acting as a resource person.

Chapters are organized as follows:

- Chapter objectives
- Self-paced tutorials to teach new commands and techniques
- Exercises to reinforce learning
- End-of-chapter Questions and Projects

## Features and Benefits of This Text

*Explanation of underlying concepts:* Students gain an understanding of desktop publishing using PageMaker.

*Sequential instruction:* Step-by-step instructions allow students to progress at their own pace. They learn the basic commands first and then move to more advanced features. This approach allows students to redo a section for reinforcement or review. Chapters may be completed in an open lab setting where the instructor need not be present and where students can aid one another in the learning process.

*Extensive use of figures:* Students can check what is displayed on the monitor with more than 370 screens reproduced in the text. These figures guide students through the sequential instruction.

*Exercises:* Once a command is learned, students are challenged to use the skill to complete a practical exercise.

*Realistic examples:* This text uses actual publications developed by companies using PageMaker.

*Case study:* The Inn at Portage Bay is used as a comprehensive case study throughout the text. This case provides a realistic example of how desktop publishing can be used in a business setting.

*Numerous projects:* In addition to the case study, end-of-chapter projects provide practical applications to stimulate interest and reinforce learning.

*Help questions:* Students are encouraged to use the PageMaker Help feature, both within the chapters and for the end-of-chapter review questions and projects.

*Student-tested approach:* Students familiar with word processing are able to complete this text with minimal guidance. Students like the self-paced tutorial approach and the comprehensive case study.

*Data disk:* The data disk (bundled with the Instructor's Manual) used with this text has 60 files, including publications, templates, graphics, word processing documents, and spreadsheets. These files are used by the students to complete the tutorials, exercises, and projects. Use of the data disk simulates a business environment. In addition, students are able to work with more complex and larger publications without having to spend time entering text.

*Most popular desktop publishing program:* Students learn advanced features of the most widely used desktop publishing program, the same program that is used for business, government, and personal applications.

*Separate chapter on design concepts:* Chapter 8 emphasizes the importance of design as a part of desktop publishing. It includes several examples by professional designers.

*Internet and Web chapter:* In Chapter 9, students learn about the Internet and how PageMaker can be used to create publications for the World Wide Web. They create a home page with text, photos, and hyperlinks that is exported as an HTML document and viewed in a browser.

*Appendix:* The appendix provides a quick reference to the PageMaker menus and shortcut keys.

## TO THE STUDENT

The average business spends 8 percent of its operating costs on printing and publishing. To reduce these costs and to maintain control over the printing process, more and more companies are turning to desktop publishing.

This text provides a practical, hands-on approach to developing skills in the use of the most popular desktop publishing program, Adobe PageMaker. After completing this text you will be able to use PageMaker to develop professional-looking publications, such as newsletters, advertisements, flyers, announcements, stationery, and business cards.

The text allows you to work at your own pace through step-by-step tutorials. A concept is presented, such as resizing a graphic. The process is explained, followed by the actual steps. Throughout the text, figures show appropriate screen displays to help keep you on track. Examples, exercises, and projects will reinforce your learning. A case study, The Inn at Portage Bay, provides a real-world application of how desktop publishing can be used in a business setting.

To learn the most from the use of this text, you should:

- Proceed slowly: Accuracy is more important than speed.

- Understand what is happening with each step before you continue to the next step.

- After finishing a process, ask yourself: Can I do the process on my own? If the answer is no, review the steps.

- Check your screen display with the figures in the text. Be aware that sometimes the text figure might not exactly match your screen display—usually because of the font (type style and size) used.

Enjoy learning PageMaker!

## ACKNOWLEDGMENTS

The authors would like to thank the following individuals and organizations for their support in the development of this text: Daniela Birch of Adobe Systems Inc. for her invaluable support; Jenna Ashley, Jarod Brown and Anistatia Miller; Mitch Curren, OverLake Hospital Medical Center, Bob and Lula Cusack, Sheila Hoffman, Mithun Partners, Lari Power, and Ken Trimpe for providing design materials; and our spouses, Bruce and Barbara, the artistic ones, for their drawings: Bruce created the Portage, Cottages, Crab, Spinnaker, and Golf graphics, and Barbara created the Fort graphic. The authors would also like to thank the reviewers who were so important to the development of this text: Marjorie Obrist, Columbus State Community College and Judith Scheeren, Westmoreland County Community College. In addition, we would like to thank the team at Course Technology who helped in the development and production of this book: Kristen Duerr, Jennifer Normandin, Lisa Ayers, Nancy Shea, Brian McCooey, and Chris Hall. Special thanks to Robin Geller of Pale Moon Productions, an important partner in the development of this text through her generous encouragement and creative editorial skills.

# CHAPTER 1

# Introduction to Desktop Publishing

**Upon completion of this chapter you will be able to:**

- Define the term *desktop publishing*
- Trace the development of desktop publishing
- Specify the tools used in page description
- Compare traditional and desktop publishing methods of page design and printing
- Explain the advantages and disadvantages of desktop publishing
- Specify the components of a desktop publishing system
- Understand different ways companies use desktop publishing

The term *desktop publishing* was coined in 1984 by Paul Brainerd to describe his product, PageMaker. Brainerd was the founder and CEO of Aldus until it was purchased by the Adobe Corporation. Now Adobe manufactures **PageMaker,** currently the country's most popular desktop publishing program. Since the term was first used, a billion-dollar industry has grown up around desktop publishing that includes computer-related equipment, software programs, training companies, trade associations, specialty magazines, and thousands of jobs. As has been typical in the computer field, a new industry arose from a few major technological advances, including the creation of personal computers that could produce graphics, the development of **desktop publishing programs,** and the invention of the **laser printer.** This chapter introduces desktop publishing, presents its history, and describes how companies use it.

## WHAT IS DESKTOP PUBLISHING?

**Desktop publishing** is the process of using a personal computer and a software program to merge **text** (words, headings, titles, and so forth) and **graphics** (pictures, illustrations, graphs, and so forth) into printed material. Companies typically use desktop publishing to produce documents such as newsletters, advertisements, price lists, and brochures. Before desktop publishing, a company could either send its work to outside typesetting and printing firms or use a computer, word processing program, and printer to create its work in-house. The typesetting house produced high-quality type for the printing firm, but the finished product was very expensive and time-consuming to create. The computer and word processing program, although cheaper and in the right hands faster, produced poorer-quality documents and, until recently, could not incorporate graphics (a graphic designer added such images in both processes). Desktop publishing picks up where word processing ends; it enables a company to create high-quality, modestly priced documents in-house that utilize illustrations, borders, multiple columns, and different type styles and sizes.

## DEVELOPMENT OF DESKTOP PUBLISHING

To understand how desktop publishing has developed, it is useful to look at the broader field of publishing. **Publishing** involves the creation, production, and distribution of printed material. The page, such as a newsletter, advertisement, or flyer, is the most common form of printed material. Some of the creative and production aspects of publishing describe how a page will look, that is, what will be placed on a page and where it will be placed—a process called **page description**. What will be placed on a page falls into one of two broad categories: text or graphics. The selection and placement (also called **layout**) of the text and graphics are limited by the tools used to produce the page and, of course, by the skills of the persons doing the work.

## TOOLS USED IN PAGE DESCRIPTION

The tools used in page description can be classified as manual, mechanical, and electronic. The pen, printing press, and computer, respectively, are the most common tools fitting these classifications. Some questions you could ask to help evaluate these tools are:

- Does the tool enhance creativity? That is, does the tool allow you to use different type styles—such as script or block—and type sizes? Can you easily change the size of the graphics and rearrange the layout of the page?

- How effectively does the tool merge text and graphics? Can the text be developed and then the graphics easily incorporated into the page?

- Who controls the process? That is, can a company use this tool to create and produce the printed material in-house?

- What will be the quality of the printed material?

- What will the process cost?

- How long will the process take?

The oldest and least complex tool used for page description is the pen. A skilled craftsperson can use this tool to create text in various styles and sizes, as well as illustrations. In the right hands, the pen permits an almost endless number of ways to arrange (or lay out) text and graphics on a page. This manual process enhances the creative process, increases quality, and leaves control of the finished product with one person. However, the manual process can be very slow, and even minor changes might require rewriting the entire page.

The invention of the printing press (a machine with movable type) by Johannes Gutenberg in the mid-1400s was revolutionary. As a page description tool, it dramatically reduced the amount of time required to produce printed material. This mechanical process also made possible the mass distribution of books, which contributed to a higher literacy rate and the spread of knowledge. However, the craftsperson lost creative flexibility in the page description process because the style and size of type as well as the kind of graphics were limited. Control over the process was also reduced because production was done in the print shop instead of at the craftsperson's desk.

With the twentieth-century development of **phototypesetting** equipment, a computer was used to generate text and send it electronically to a typesetting machine. However, until recently these computers were dedicated machines (not used for other purposes), whose programs linked directly with the typesetting equipment. Specialists were needed to operate these computers and insert text codes to control the typesetter's operations. Also, the input was limited to text. No graphics could be developed or incorporated into the page design using the computer.

From the time the printing press appeared until recently, the publishing process had become increasingly specialized. Each new technological advance, such as phototypesetting, required specialists. The publishing process, once done at the desk by a craftsperson with pen and paper, now required writers, editors, illustrators, graphic designers, and typesetters. With the rise of the personal computer, page description software, and the laser printer, control over many aspects of the publishing process have returned to one person.

The following is a simplified view of the steps involved in producing a printed page using the traditional method. The desktop publishing method is then compared to the traditional method. Figure 1.1 illustrates this comparison.

**Figure 1.1**
Comparison of traditional and desktop publishing methods of producing a printed page

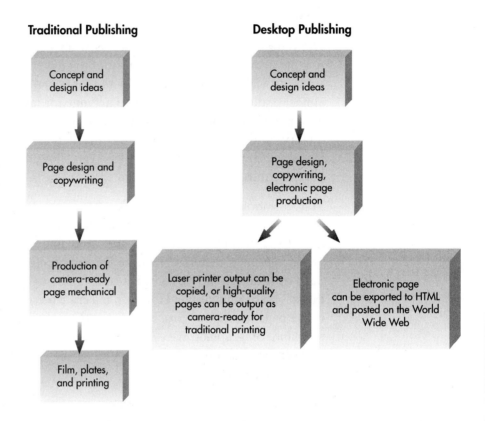

**Traditional Publishing**

Concept and design ideas

Page design and copywriting

Production of camera-ready page mechanical

Film, plates, and printing

**Desktop Publishing**

Concept and design ideas

Page design, copywriting, electronic page production

Laser printer output can be copied, or high-quality pages can be output as camera-ready for traditional printing

Electronic page can be exported to HTML and posted on the World Wide Web

**Traditional Method of Page Design and Printing**

The traditional method of page design and printing can be divided into four distinct steps, as outlined here.

1. **Developing the concept.** This process generates ideas for elements to be included on the page. For example, a company working on a direct-mail advertising campaign would hold a brainstorming session to generate a theme and other ideas for the campaign. This step also involves determining the objective of the finished piece. Every publication communicates a message not only by what is said, but also by how it is said. For example, an advertising objective might be to have the reader make a phone call. To accomplish this, a phone number could be typeset in bold type to draw the reader's attention.

2. **Creating a preliminary page design.** A rough layout of the elements included on the page would be developed. For example, an advertisement might contain a headline, copy, illustrations, a logo, and so on. A copywriter would write the text and an artist would sketch the illustrations. An editor and those involved in the advertising campaign, such as marketing personnel, would review this preliminary work. Rewrites and redesigns would follow this review.

3. **Preparing the page for printing.** Depending on time, cost, quality, and quantity considerations, the page could be prepared for printing in several ways. If the ad, for example, were to be high-quality, color, and include photographs, a manual pasteup process would be needed, although individual pieces might be prepared on a computer or using other tools. A computer could be used to lay out the text, leaving blank areas where the photos would be placed (pasted). After the pasteup, the camera-ready page would be photographed and printing plates made.

4. **Printing.** If high quality is wanted, a printing process called offset lithography would be used. This process uses light to expose a photo-sensitive emulsion on a metal plate, which is then placed around the rollers of a printing press. The image area of the plate, created by the exposure to light, is coated with a material that accepts ink. The plate is inked and paper is fed through the rollers, creating the printed page.

---

**Desktop Publishing Method of Page Design and Printing**

Overall, the desktop publishing method provides greater ease and flexibility in creating a page design and printing. Although the steps for desktop publishing are similar to those of the traditional method, some steps can be combined.

1. The concept development step in the desktop publishing environment is the same as in the traditional method.

2. & 3. Creating a preliminary page design and preparing the page for printing can be combined. One person could incorporate both text, written by a copywriter using a word processing program, and illustrations, created by an artist, into the page design. Alternately, one person could write the text, draw the illustrations electronically, and scan in photographs to be used in the page design. Editing text and rearranging elements could be done quickly. Additionally, the finished page design can be viewed before printing. This feature is called **WYSIWYG** (What You See Is What You Get) and is not available in traditional methods of page design.

4. Printing could be accomplished with a desktop laser printer and a copier. Or a quick-print shop could produce a printing plate from the laser printer output. If higher quality is wanted, the desktop publishing page design could be sent electronically to a high-end laser printer, producing type of greater visual clarity and definition.

The primary advantage of desktop publishing is greater control over the publishing process. Desktop publishing provides the opportunity for a company, depending on its needs and resources, to do some or all of its publishing in-house. This method enables the company to determine its own time lines. If a project has a high priority, it is not delayed by being sent outside the company. Projects previously spread over several weeks can now be completed in a few days. Furthermore, fewer specialists are needed, and less time is taken for rewriting and redesigning.

On the other hand, as desktop publishing systems become more and more common, the potential for misuse increases. Placing such a powerful tool in the hands of a novice can result in poor-quality documents. It is very easy for a person lacking design skills to get carried away, using too many type styles and sizes, and produce something resembling a ransom note instead of an effective communication. In addition, companies are concerned with image. Some companies want to be thought of as conservative, others as caring or innovative. Advertisements, catalogs, annual reports, and so on can reinforce or contradict the desired image. For example, a company trying to portray itself as tough and assertive might not want to use a script type in its publications. Yet if the marketing, public relations, product development, and accounting departments can all create their own publications, the possibility increases of someone using a script font that contradicts the intended image.

## THE DESKTOP PUBLISHING SYSTEM

Once a company determines that the advantages of using a desktop publishing system outweigh the disadvantages, it must decide on a system—the computer, printer, software, and other options. Figure 1.2 shows a typical system with a Windows-based personal computer (PC) and a laser printer. A scanner, which transfers photographs, drawings, and other printed material into the computer, is on the left. Not visible is the software package for a desktop publishing program.

**Figure 1.2**
Typical desktop
publishing system

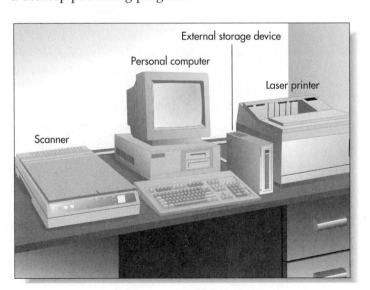

Depending on the power of the computer, the quality of the printer, the sophistication of the program, and the need for options, desktop publishing systems generally cost between $3,000 and $10,000.

## The Computer

When choosing a computer, consider the programs you'll be using. These programs will determine the minimum processing speed and amount of memory you need. Desktop publishing works with graphics, which take longer for a computer to manipulate than text. Graphics also require a great deal of computer memory. A minimum configuration is a model 486 computer, with 8 megabytes of memory, a graphics card, a graphics monitor, a floppy disk drive, a hard disk drive, and a CD-ROM drive. The model 486 computer provides the minimum necessary processing speed. Computers with faster processing speeds, such as the Pentium, and more memory (24 megabytes) are more desirable for desktop publishing. The graphics card and monitor allow you to work with illustrations, graphs, and drawings. The hard disk drive stores the software program and can be used for saving and revising your work. A CD-ROM drive reads compact discs, which can store more than 650 megabytes of data, such as illustrations and photographs.

## The Printer

Although desktop publishing programs will work with ink-jet printers, laser printers provide higher quality output. A measurement of printer quality is dots-per-inch (dpi): the more dots, the higher the quality. Figure 1.3 shows the same heading printed on two laser printers, one with 300 dpi and the other with 1,200 dpi. Notice the difference in quality between the two headings.

**Figure 1.3**
Comparison of output from laser printer and high-resolution imagesetter

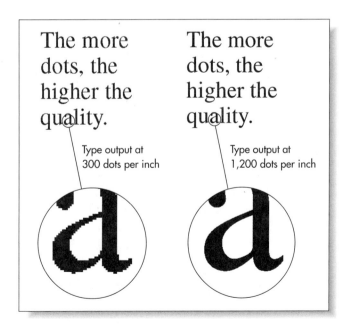

The more dots, the higher the quality.

Type output at 300 dots per inch

The more dots, the higher the quality.

Type output at 1,200 dots per inch

The computer and printer can be used for different applications, such as word processing and database management. What turns this **hardware** (computer and printer) into a desktop publishing system is a set of instructions called a **software** program.

## The Program

A variety of desktop publishing programs are available, ranging in price from $100 to $1,000 or more. The less expensive programs lack the advanced features—especially the ease in merging text and graphics—of the more expensive programs. The cheaper programs with fewer options are best suited for in-house, text-based publications, such as newsletters and announcements. The following capabilities are common in more powerful desktop publishing programs.

- Insert graphics into the page and have text flow around the graphics automatically
- Rotate text and graphics
- View the page as it will be printed (WYSIWYG)
- Develop book-length documents that include a table of contents and an index
- Adjust spacing between characters and lines of text
- Enlarge or reduce graphic images
- Develop publications that use color
- Utilize text and graphics frames as placeholders
- Work with document-wide layers
- Export documents to HTML file format for display on the World Wide Web
- Link files created using other programs and automatically update a publication using revised versions of these files

Recently, the more sophisticated word processing programs have added features comparable to those of the low-end desktop publishing programs.

The decision about which program to buy should be based primarily on your anticipated needs, hardware considerations, and budget. If your company plans to produce only newsletters, announcements, posters, and other simple internal documents, a sophisticated word processing program might be adequate. If a company plans to produce brochures, product specification sheets, annual reports, book-length documents, and other materials that will be seen outside the organization, or will use color, a high-end desktop publishing program would be more appropriate.

In deciding which program to purchase, a company should answer these questions: How much are we currently spending on publishing? How much of our publishing could we realistically do ourselves? Do we have the expertise to publish in-house or will we need to hire new personnel and/or train existing employees? What are the start-up expenses, such as those for hardware, software, and training? What are the time considerations? And, ultimately, what are the net savings of doing part or all of our publishing in-house?

## The PageMaker Program

As mentioned at the beginning of this chapter, PageMaker is currently the country's most popular desktop publishing program. It offers extremely sophisticated features, yet is relatively easy to learn. If you have worked with a personal computer and a word processing program, you have valuable skills that are transferable to the desktop publishing environment. Knowing how to use the keyboard, mouse, and disk drives, as well as how to save and retrieve work, will speed up the process of learning PageMaker.

## The Options

Although desktop publishing can be accomplished with a computer, a program, and a laser printer, numerous options, both in hardware and software, can enhance the basic desktop publishing system. Among these options are scanners to transfer in graphics, drawing programs for free-hand illustration, **clip art** that contains predesigned illustrations, and additional fonts that will give you more flexibility in the text design. A useful option for a computer system is an external storage device such as a Zip or Jaz drive that holds 100 megabytes and 1 gigabyte, respectively. These allow you to store and transport large files, such as graphics.

## DESKTOP PUBLISHING IN PRACTICE

A company bases its decision about whether to purchase a desktop system by determining how best to supplement its current publishing activities, not replace them. The following four examples show how desktop publishing is being used in some businesses.

**ROI** is a one-person accounting service. Sandra Gilbert, the owner, uses a personal computer, laser printer, and sophisticated word processing program—Microsoft Word—to create simple documents. She publishes a quarterly newsletter (see Figure 1.4) to inform her clients of changes in tax codes and pending tax legislation. She also produces promotional flyers to send to prospective clients. These documents include both text and graphics. She incorporates borders, shading, and various type sizes to enhance the documents. Because the documents are relatively simple, Sandra does not need to supplement Word with any other software packages, such as drawing programs.

Figure 1.4
ROI Newsletter

## R O I

### N E W S L E T T E R
First Quarter

*Capital Gains Tax*

Representative Griffey of Washington State has proposed a reduction in the Capital gains tax. Her proposal would set the maximum tax rate at 15%, down from the current maximum of 36%. Her intent is to stimulate investment in hopes that this will give a boost to our stagnant economy. She faces some stiff opposition from Democrats, who see this as a tax break for the rich.

*Quarterly Tax payments*

For those of you who make quarterly tax payments, your next installment is due at the end of March.

*New Employee (Intern)*

I am happy to announce that Ann Grey will be joining ROI as an intern. She is a senior at City University and will complete her degree (BS Accounting) in June. Her arrival is very timely because tax return season is quickly approaching.

*Property Tax Assessment*

All property in King County was reassessed beginning on January 1. You will receive a valuation notice by June 1. As you know, property values have been skyrocketing the past 18 months. However, the price of residential property has increased at a higher rate than commercial property. Therefore, homeowners will find that their taxes will increase while commercial investors may actually see a tax decrease. You may appeal your reevaluation up to 30 days after receiving the notice. The most important evidence to support an appeal is comparables — prices of properties that are comparable to yours and have sold recently. If you would like help with your appeal, call me.

*Vacation*

I am planning a two-week trip to Hawaii to visit my brother and the office will be closed from May 15 – 30.

Remember April 15 is coming soon.

**World Trade Network** is an international marketing firm that employs 12 people. The company specializes in athletic equipment and sells more than 80 products worldwide, primarily through trade shows. The company uses a personal computer, laser printer, scanner, and desktop publishing program—PageMaker—to create several kinds of documents, including product specification sheets, price lists, promotional brochures, and sales reports. The company scans photographs of its products to create electronic graphic images, which are combined with text to create its product specification sheets. The company uses a drawing program for freehand artwork and clip art to enhance its promotional brochures and sales reports. Also, the company produces a product catalog and annual report with the help of an electronic publishing service. This service provides high-resolution printing, color printing, and binding using equipment too expensive for World Trade Network to purchase. Figure 1.5 shows a **template** (a predesigned document) that contains a standard page layout. Whenever World Trade Network acquires a new product, an employee uses the template to create a product specification sheet. Blank areas of the template indicate where a graphic of the product and data (such as the description and price, which vary from product to product) can be inserted.

**World Trade Network**

100 East 35th Street
San Francisco, CA 95222
(415) 555-4397
Fax (415) 555-4822
www.wtn.com

"The Key to International Markets"

PRODUCT SPECIFICATION SHEET

Product Name:

Product Description:

List Price U.S. $:

Quantity Discounts:

Terms:

Shipping Weight:

**Cusack's Alaska Lodge** is a family-owned lodge that caters to hunters and fishers. The lodge is located on Iliamna Lake in southern Alaska between Lake Clark National Park and Katmai National Monument. The lodge is accessible only by floatplane. The company works with a graphic designer to develop various publications. Figure 1.6 shows several of the publications, including a general information sheet, a sheet of company stationery, a business card, and a brochure. The designer developed these publications using PageMaker on a personal computer. He created text with a word processing program and used a scanner to incorporate photographs. The brochure, which includes color maps and photographs, was printed using an offset printer. This is a good example of how a company can tie together a variety of publications to produce a consistent image. Notice, for instance, how the company name, Cusack's, and the logo, a fly-type hook, appear on each document.

**Figure 1.6**
Various publications of
Cusack's Alaska Lodge

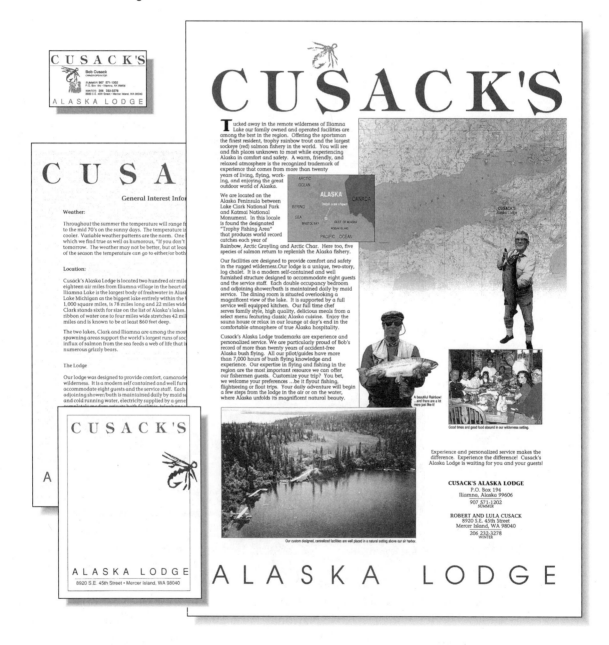

**Seafirst Bank** is a large regional bank with more than 6,000 employees. The company creates several publications, including brochures, bulletins, and forms. The Administrative Services department oversees three publishing areas—Forms Management, Graphic Services, and Publications—that provide publishing services to the entire company. For example, a specialist in the Forms Management area might work with the Marketing department to create a credit card application. The specialist would provide expertise in layout and design as well as ensure quality and continuity with other corporate publications. In addition to the basic desktop publishing system—computer, laser printer, and PageMaker program—the company uses a high-resolution printer called an **imagesetter**. In essence, Seafirst has its own in-house publishing service. Figure 1.7 shows an application form created by Seafirst personnel using a desktop publishing system and printed on a high-resolution printer.

Figure 1.7
Seafirst Bank application form

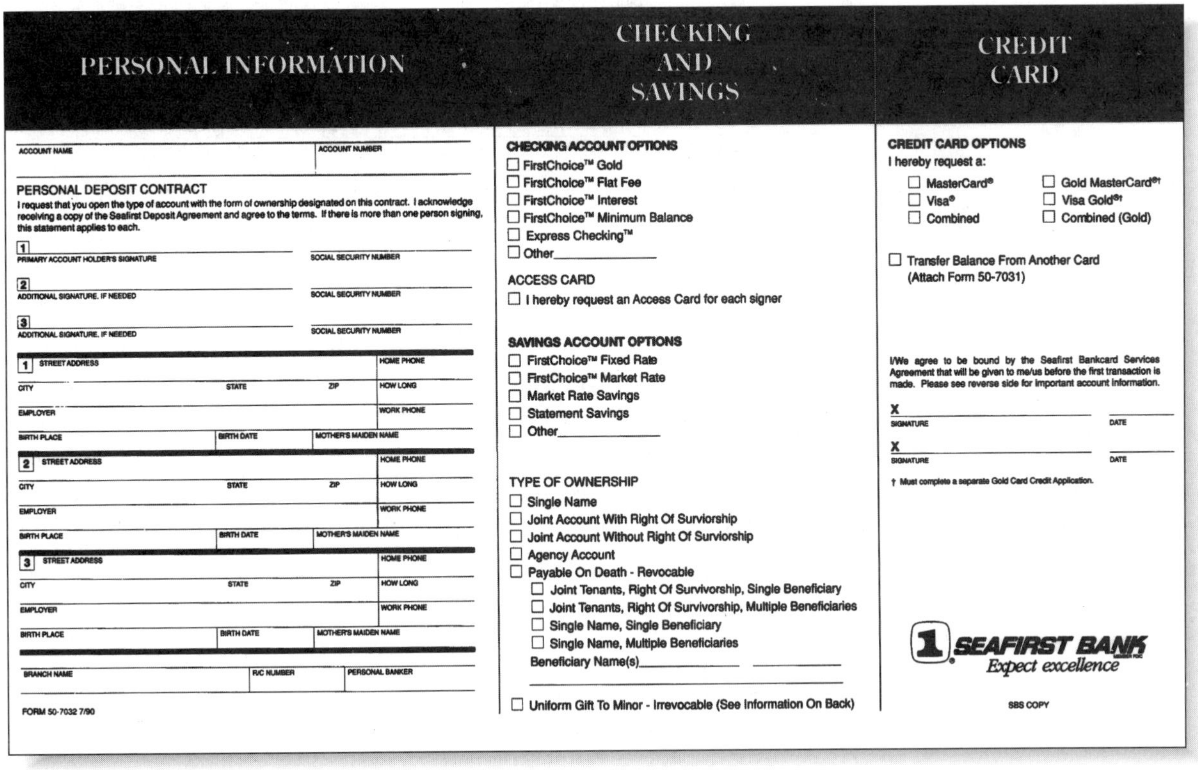

PERSONAL INFORMATION

ACCOUNT NAME | ACCOUNT NUMBER

PERSONAL DEPOSIT CONTRACT
I request that you open the type of account with the form of ownership designated on this contract. I acknowledge receiving a copy of the Seafirst Deposit Agreement and agree to the terms. If there is more than one person signing, this statement applies to each.

1 PRIMARY ACCOUNT HOLDER'S SIGNATURE | SOCIAL SECURITY NUMBER
2 ADDITIONAL SIGNATURE, IF NEEDED | SOCIAL SECURITY NUMBER
3 ADDITIONAL SIGNATURE, IF NEEDED | SOCIAL SECURITY NUMBER

1 STREET ADDRESS | HOME PHONE
CITY | STATE | ZIP | HOW LONG
EMPLOYER | WORK PHONE
BIRTH PLACE | BIRTH DATE | MOTHER'S MAIDEN NAME

2 STREET ADDRESS | HOME PHONE
CITY | STATE | ZIP | HOW LONG
EMPLOYER | WORK PHONE
BIRTH PLACE | BIRTH DATE | MOTHER'S MAIDEN NAME

3 STREET ADDRESS | HOME PHONE
CITY | STATE | ZIP | HOW LONG
EMPLOYER | WORK PHONE
BIRTH PLACE | BIRTH DATE | MOTHER'S MAIDEN NAME

BRANCH NAME | R/C NUMBER | PERSONAL BANKER

FORM 50-7032 7/90

CHECKING AND SAVINGS

CHECKING ACCOUNT OPTIONS
☐ FirstChoice™ Gold
☐ FirstChoice™ Flat Fee
☐ FirstChoice™ Interest
☐ FirstChoice™ Minimum Balance
☐ Express Checking™
☐ Other________

ACCESS CARD
☐ I hereby request an Access Card for each signer

SAVINGS ACCOUNT OPTIONS
☐ FirstChoice™ Fixed Rate
☐ FirstChoice™ Market Rate
☐ Market Rate Savings
☐ Statement Savings
☐ Other________

TYPE OF OWNERSHIP
☐ Single Name
☐ Joint Account With Right Of Surviorship
☐ Joint Account Without Right Of Surviorship
☐ Agency Account
☐ Payable On Death - Revocable
☐ Joint Tenants, Right Of Survivorship, Single Beneficiary
☐ Joint Tenants, Right Of Survivorship, Multiple Beneficiaries
☐ Single Name, Single Beneficiary
☐ Single Name, Multiple Beneficiaries
Beneficiary Name(s)________ ________

☐ Uniform Gift To Minor - Irrevocable (See Information On Back)

CREDIT CARD

CREDIT CARD OPTIONS
I hereby request a:
☐ MasterCard® ☐ Gold MasterCard®†
☐ Visa® ☐ Visa Gold®†
☐ Combined ☐ Combined (Gold)

☐ Transfer Balance From Another Card (Attach Form 50-7031)

I/We agree to be bound by the Seafirst Bankcard Services Agreement that will be given to me/us before the first transaction is made. Please see reverse side for important account information.

X SIGNATURE | DATE
X SIGNATURE | DATE

† Must complete a separate Gold Card Credit Application.

SEAFIRST BANK
Expect excellence

SBS COPY

The way these four companies use desktop publishing ranges from the very simple to the very sophisticated. The common thread is the use of a personal computer, laser printer, and software program that allow the merging of text and graphics to create a serviceable, attractive publication.

In response to the incredible growth of the World Wide Web, desktop publishing programs have been enhanced to enable a user to create **Web pages,** which are documents that can be displayed on the Internet using a Web browser such as Netscape Navigator or Microsoft Internet Explorer. Figure 1.8 shows a Web page with text, graphics, and hyperlinks. PageMaker 6.5 provides a feature that enables you to create a single document that you can use as a printed publication or display on the Web.

**Figure 1.8**
PageMaker publication exported as an HTML document

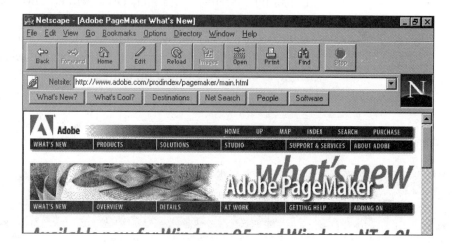

## SUMMARY

This chapter introduced desktop publishing and traced its development. You learned how desktop publishing can be used as a tool in page description and how it compares with traditional methods of page design and printing. You examined the components of a desktop publishing system and some of its advantages and disadvantages. Keep in mind that desktop publishing will not allow you to eliminate printing situations that require typeset- or photographic-quality documents, but it can be used to enhance the documents.

In Chapter 2 you will begin to learn the PageMaker program. The steps to start the program can vary, and you should check with your instructor or lab assistant before beginning. You will also need access to the student files for this book in order to complete the following chapters. These files include publications that were developed using PageMaker, documents developed using a word processing program, graphs developed using a spreadsheet program, and graphics developed using a drawing program. In Chapter 2 you will also be introduced to The Inn at Portage Bay, a fictional company for which you will create publications throughout this book.

1. Define *desktop publishing*.

2. Explain when it is appropriate to use a word processing program and when it is appropriate to use a desktop publishing program.

3. Briefly trace how desktop publishing developed.

4. What does the phrase "Desktop publishing is a tool used in page description" mean?

5. Compare the traditional and desktop publishing methods of page design and printing.

6. Explain the advantages and disadvantages of desktop publishing.

7. List and explain the functions of the components of a desktop publishing system.

8. List four features common in more powerful desktop publishing programs.

## PROJECTS

1. Visit a company or organization and obtain a publication its staff developed using desktop publishing. Then determine:
   - the basic hardware and software program being used
   - other equipment and programs used in the publishing process
   - the steps taken to create the publication
   - the people involved and the skills each must have to do the job properly
   - the time needed to produce the publication
   - the outside services, if any, being used

2. Through library research, write a review of a magazine or newspaper article that deals with desktop publishing. The article should be at least three pages in length. Include:

- the name and date of the publication, the name and page length of the article, and the author, if specified

- a one-page summary of the article, covering two or three main points

3. Obtain a direct mail document and write a one- to two-page summary of your evaluation of the document. Include:

- your opinion about the attractiveness or unattractiveness of the piece, and why you feel that way

- your opinion of the effectiveness of the document's design and text (does the document grab your attention, get you to read the copy, and/or cause you to perform some action such as purchasing a product or calling a number?)

- an evaluation of the document's readability

- any other design-related comments you feel are relevant

Be prepared to share your evaluation with the class.

4. Describe the desktop publishing features of the word processing program you use.

5. Visit the Adobe company World Wide Web site (http://www.adobe.com) and review the information about the PageMaker 6.5 program.

# CHAPTER 2

# The PageMaker Environment

**Upon completion of this chapter you will be able to:**

- Use the mouse pointer, pull-down menus, and shortcut keys

- Use a dialog box

- Understand the components of the PageMaker screen

- Start a new publication

- Open an existing publication

- Describe the tools of the Toolbox

- Print a publication

- Obtain Help

This chapter presents an overview of how PageMaker works. In order to complete this chapter, you must know how to start the PageMaker program and have access to the student files used with this text. The chapter walks you through the PageMaker environment and teaches you how to use the menu system. A **menu** is a list of related options or commands. For example, the File menu includes the Save command and the Print command. You will learn how to select a menu and execute a command later in this chapter.

The chapter also introduces you to The Inn at Portage Bay, a luxury resort hotel located near the ocean in Washington State. The Inn is known for its quality service and dramatic views of the ocean, distant islands, and the Olympic Mountains. The Inn at Portage Bay needs many documents that can be produced using a desktop publishing system: newsletters, employee benefit booklets, brochures, menus, advertisements, price lists, and stationery, to name a few. Some of these you will create by following specific directions within the chapters, and others you will create as part of projects at the end of each chapter.

## SELECTING COMMANDS IN PAGEMAKER

In PageMaker, you select commands and perform actions using the mouse pointer, pull-down menus, or shortcut keys. Before you begin working on a PageMaker publication, you'll review each method.

### Using the Mouse Pointer

Although a mouse can have one, two, or three buttons, PageMaker actions require only one button—the left. However, you can use the right mouse button to open a shortcut menu from which you can change the size of the image displayed onscreen or perform common text commands, such as Copy and Paste.

In PageMaker, you'll use five mouse techniques: **click, double-click, press, drag**, and **right-click**. Each technique requires a different action and has a specific function, as indicated in Figure 2.1.

**Figure 2.1**
Techniques for using a mouse

| Technique | Action | Function |
|---|---|---|
| Click | Press and release the left mouse button. | Selects a menu or activates a menu command, such as Print. |
| Double-click | Quickly click and release the left mouse button twice. | Shortcuts a process. For example, to open a file, you can double-click its file name instead of typing the file name. |
| Press | Press and hold the left mouse button. Release when done. | Causes a continuous action, such as scrolling a list of options. |
| Drag | Press and hold the left mouse button while moving the mouse in any direction. | Moves an object, such as a drawing, around the screen, selects a screen area, or draws graphics. |
| Right-click | Press and release the right mouse button. | Opens a shortcut menu. |

You will use all five mouse techniques to execute PageMaker instructions.

In the following sections you will start the PageMaker program and learn about the PageMaker environment. Throughout the chapter you will be directed to carry out specific actions, such as pointing and clicking the mouse. All actions are numbered in color. Carefully work through the steps, pausing to study each figure presented. Make sure you understand what is happening as you proceed through the exercise. If you are unsure of what is happening, return to the last point you understood, or return here and start again.

1. Start the PageMaker program according to the procedure for your computer. (A copyright statement will appear briefly onscreen.)

Depending upon which options were selected previously, one or more objects, such as the Toolbox shown in Figure 2.2, might appear on your screen. For now, don't worry about anything extra that appears; you'll learn how to close and move those objects later.

2. Find the mouse pointer ▶ onscreen.

3. Take a moment to move the pointer around the screen. (Do not click the mouse button.)

When you first start the program, the PageMaker window should be enlarged to its maximum size. If yours is not, you can click on the maximize button in the upper-right corner of the window (see Figure 2.2).

**Figure 2.2**
Pointing to the maximize button

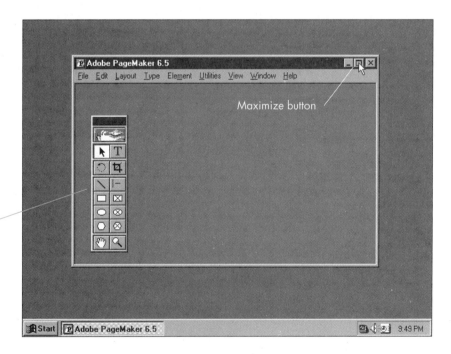

1. If necessary, move the mouse pointer to the maximize button in the upper-right corner of the window.

2. Click the mouse button. (Remember, click means to press and release the left mouse button.)

Figure 2.3 shows the PageMaker menu bar. When you click a word in the menu bar, PageMaker displays a pull-down menu. A **pull-down menu** is a list of related options, called **commands**, that you can select to perform an action. PageMaker has nine pull-down menus in the menu bar: File, Edit, Layout, Type, Element, Utilities, View, Window, and Help. Above the File menu is the Control-menu box, which is also a pull-down menu. The Control-menu box has options to resize, move, and close the PageMaker program window.

Figure 2.3
Menu bar

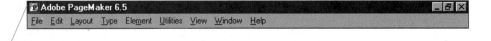

Control-menu box

First, you need to understand some features that are common to all the pull-down menus. Using the mouse, select the File menu as follows:

1. Point to File in the menu bar.

2. Click the mouse button.

Several features are notable in the File menu. Some commands—such as Open, Document Setup, Preferences, and Exit—are in black; other commands—such as Save, Place, and Print—are in gray. Black options are active and available for you to select. Gray options are inactive; clicking on them will have no effect. PageMaker "knows" which options are appropriate at any time in your session. For example, because you have not yet opened a document this session, there is nothing to print, so the Print command is in gray. Try clicking a gray command. Notice that nothing happens.

1. Point to Save.

2. Click the mouse button.

Many commands, including Open and Document Setup, are followed by an **ellipsis** (three periods). Clicking such a command will display a new window, called a **dialog box**, with additional choices for you to make before the command is executed. For example, selecting the Document Setup command displays a dialog box from which you can change the page size, margins, and model of printer you are using. Commands without an ellipsis, such as Close and Save, usually require no additional choices and will execute immediately after you click them.

There are four ways to choose a command from a pull-down menu. First, you can point to and click its name. Second, you can hold down the mouse button, point to the command, and release the mouse button. Third, you can press the key corresponding to the underlined letter in the command name. (Notice that each command has a different letter underlined, which identifies that command. For example, with the File menu displayed, you can press $\textcircled{O}$, the underlined letter, to select the Open command.) Fourth, you can press the down-arrow key to highlight a command and press (←ENTER) to select any highlighted option. To remove a pull-down menu from the screen, simply click anywhere outside the menu or point to and click the menu name in the menu bar.

**Using Shortcut Keys**

Some commands can be selected by pressing a combination of keys directly from the PageMaker window instead of clicking the menu name to display the pull-down menu. Menu options that have an entry to the far right, such as:

New...        ^N

can be selected by holding down (CTRL) (represented by the ^ symbol) while you press (N). These are called **shortcut keys**.

Throughout this book, the directions will have you use the first method to select commands, that is, selecting pull-down menus and commands with the mouse. Starting in Chapter 4, after you're familiar with the pull-down menus, the shortcut keys for commands will be listed. Then you can choose the selection method you prefer.

For the remainder of the chapter, you will familiarize yourself with the commands in the menu bar by pointing and clicking the mouse to display the various menus. Each section contains a short overview of the commands available in that pull-down menu. Then you are directed to point to and click different options. Don't be concerned now with the details of each command—they will be explained when you use them in a publication. This practice is intended only to show you how to use pull-down menus and what is contained in each.

## FILE MENU

Figure 2.4 shows the File menu, from which you open (start), save, close, and print publications; place text and graphics developed using another program in a PageMaker publication; and exit PageMaker.

**Figure 2.4**
**File menu**

To start a new publication, you must tell PageMaker about the publication. How many pages does the publication have? What size is the page? How wide are the margins? You can specify these and other settings in the Document Setup dialog box, before or after you place text and graphics on a page.

For this practice you will select the New command from the File menu to start a new publication, and use the Document Setup dialog box to change the top margin setting. In Chapter 3 you will take this process one step further by entering text into the publication window. *Note:* The New command in the File menu starts a new publication, while the Open command opens a previously saved publication.

   1. Point to New.

   2. Click the mouse button.

The Document Setup dialog box appears, as shown in Figure 2.5.

**Figure 2.5**
Document Setup
dialog box

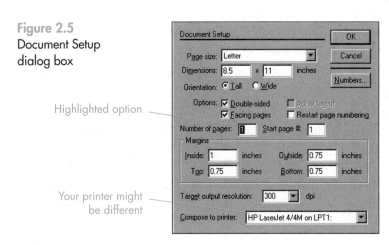

Highlighted option

Your printer might
be different

## WORKING WITH DIALOG BOXES

A dialog box enables you to issue instructions to the program or specify characteristics about a publication. For example, when you are just beginning a publication, you use the Document Setup dialog box to specify the margin settings and the number of pages in the publication. If you want to retrieve a previously saved publication, you use the Open Publication dialog box to specify which disk drive holds the file and the file name. Each dialog box has a name that specifies its function, such as Document Setup, Preferences, or Open Publication. Also, most dialog boxes contain two buttons—OK and Cancel. You click the OK button after you've made changes in the dialog box that you want to apply to the publication and are ready to continue. You click the Cancel button if you displayed the dialog box accidentally or don't want to apply your changes to the publication. Clicking the Cancel button returns you to the publication window or to another dialog box.

Study the Document Setup dialog box shown in Figure 2.5. Several predetermined settings, called **default** settings, are specified. For example, the default Page size is Letter with Dimensions of 8.5 × 11 inches; and the Margins settings in inches are Inside (left), 1; Outside (right), 0.75; Top, 0.75; and Bottom, 0.75. Other settings in the Page size section include Legal, Magazine, and Browser (used when developing documents to be displayed on the World Wide Web). Any setting in this and other dialog boxes can be changed in two ways. First, if the setting is simply a choice among options, such as Letter versus Legal versus Browser, you can use the point-and-click method. If a setting requires you to enter text or numbers, such as changing a margin setting, you must first select the option and then type the new entry from the keyboard.

Notice that the 1 in the Number of pages option is highlighted, indicating that this setting is selected. Typing another number replaces the 1. There are three methods to select an option in a dialog box.

Method 1—TAB

By pressing the Tab key you can move the highlight from one option to the next.

1. Press TAB three times.

The highlight moves through three options to the Outside margin setting. To change this setting, you would type another number.

Method 2—ALT plus a Letter

Notice how the label for each option contains one underlined letter (for example, o for Top margin and B for Bottom margin). To select an option, hold down ALT while you press the appropriate underlined letter. You can use either uppercase or lowercase letters, such as pressing the lowercase letter b for B.

2. Hold down ALT and press B.

The highlight moves to the Bottom margin setting.

Method 3—Drag

You use the mouse pointer to highlight an option by pointing the arrow at the setting and dragging the pointer to the right.

3. Point to the left of the 0 (zero) in the Top margin setting.

Notice that the pointer changes from an arrow ➤ to an **I-beam** Ɪ (Figure 2.6), which indicates that you can enter or edit text.

Figure 2.6
Pointer changed to
I-beam, indicating that
you can select and
edit text

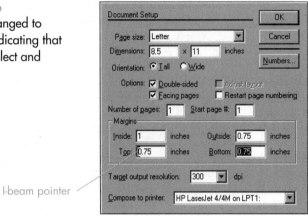

I-beam pointer

**4.** Drag (hold down the left mouse button) the I-beam ‡ to the right.

The setting 0.75 is highlighted and you can enter a new number.

**5.** Release the mouse button.

**6.** Type 2.

The 0.75 changes to 2. Now you will leave the dialog box and display the publication with these new settings.

**7.** Click OK.

The dialog box closes and you return to the publication window.

## THE PUBLICATION WINDOW

Figure 2.7 shows the **publication window** with the document setup in the middle.

Figure 2.7
Publication window with
the document setup

Title bar
Rulers

Toolbox

Pasteboard

Scroll bars

Menu bar

Document setup

Top margin at 2"

Margin guides

The window components are listed in the table shown in Figure 2.8.

| Component | Function |
|---|---|
| Document setup | Displays the publication's layout, including page size, orientation, and margins. |
| Title Bar | Displays the current publication's file name. Because this is a new publication, the word "Untitled-1" appears. You can have more than one open publication at a time. If you were to start another new publication its default name would be "Untitled-2." |
| Menu bar | Displays the available menu names. |
| Toolbox | Displays the tool icons (symbols Pagemaker uses to suggest functions) to enter and edit text and to draw and manipulate graphics. |
| Rulers | Displays the measurement scales you use to align text and graphics within the publication. |
| Scroll bars | Used to reposition the window and publication on the screen. |
| Pasteboard | Area outside the document setup where you can store text and graphics for later use. |

The Pasteboard is similar to a desktop in that you can move items onto it for storage and remove them as needed. For example, you can lace text and graphics in the empty spaces on either side of the document setup, and then, when needed, bring them inside the document.

The publication you are working with has standard dimensions, 8½ inches wide × 11 inches high, which are bound by a solid line. The dotted lines within the page are called margin guides and indicate the margin settings. Notice that the top margin is at the 2-inch mark, the number you specified earlier in the Document Setup dialog box. At this point you can add text or graphics to the page or change its design. Guides make placing text and graphics easier and more precise.

## CREATING GUIDES

In addition to margin guides, you can display ruler and column guides. **Ruler guides** help you align text and graphics on the page. **Column guides** appear when you specify that the publication will have more than one column, such as in a newsletter.

All guidelines are nonprinting, which means you see them onscreen but they don't appear in the printed document. The table in Figure 2.9 shows how you create the three types of guides.

Figure 2.9
How to create guides

| Type | How Created | Menu and Command |
|------|-------------|------------------|
| Margin | Document Setup dialog box | File/New |
| | | File/Document Setup |
| Column | Column Guides dialog box | Layout/Column Guides |
| Ruler | Drag from horizontal or vertical ruler | None |

## Ruler Guides

Figure 2.10 shows a document setup with ruler guides. You can display both vertical and horizontal ruler guides. To display a vertical ruler guide, point anywhere on the left ruler, press, and while you hold down the mouse button, drag the line to the desired location on the page. *Note:* Point to the ruler, but do not point at the ruler's left edge.

Figure 2.10
Document setup
with ruler guides

Horizontal ruler

Horizontal ruler guide

Vertical ruler guide

Vertical ruler

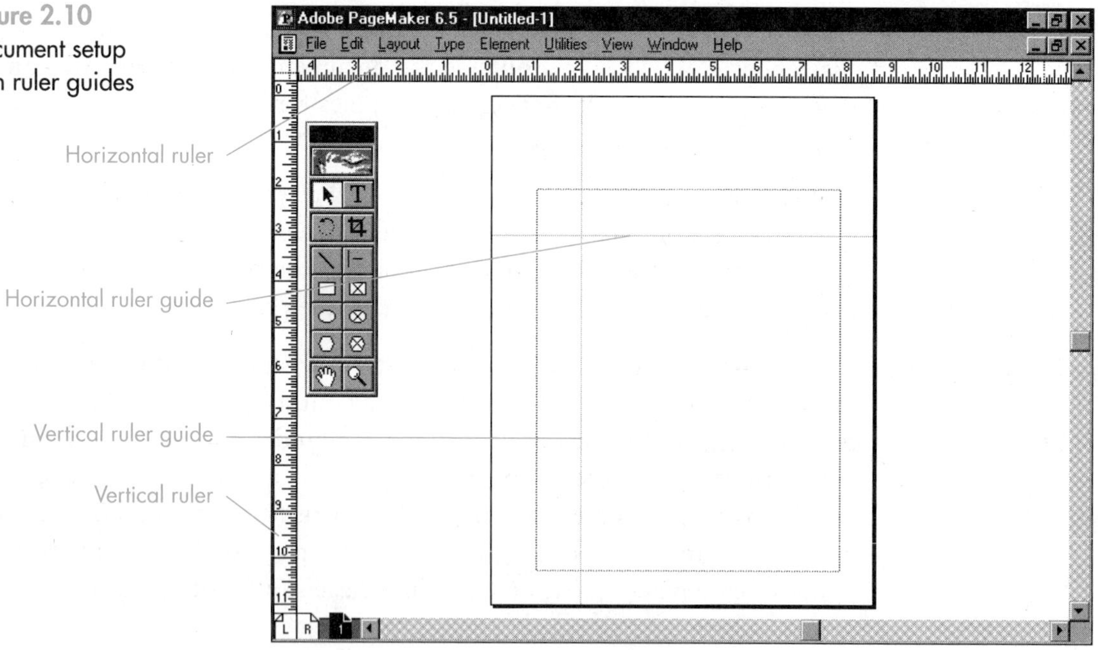

Complete the following to duplicate Figure 2.10.

1. Point to the left ruler.

The pointer changes to a larger single arrow.

2. Press and hold the mouse button.

The pointer changes to a double arrow ↔, as shown in Figure 2.11, which indicates the directions in which you can move the guide.

Figure 2.11
Pointer changed
to double arrow

Drag guide to here

Double-arrow pointer

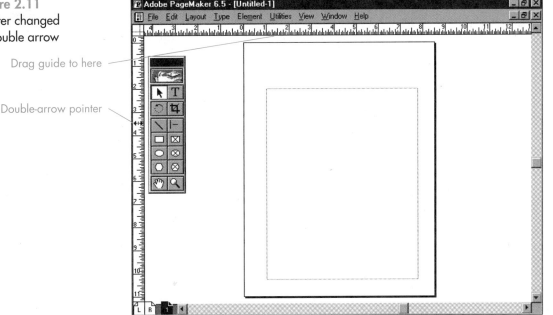

3. Drag the line to the 2-inch mark on the top ruler.

4. Release the button.

5. Point to the top ruler.

6. Drag the line down to the 3-inch mark on the left ruler. Notice that this time the pointer changes to ↕.

7. Release the button.

To clear a ruler guide, you simply drag it back to the ruler. Clear the ruler guides as follows:

1. Point to the horizontal ruler guide on the page.

2. Press and hold the mouse button.

The pointer changes to a double arrow ↕.

3. Drag the line to the top ruler.

4. Release the button.

5. On your own, drag the vertical ruler guide back to the left ruler.

## Column Guides

Figure 2.12 shows a document setup with column guides for a two-column layout.

**Figure 2.12**
Document setup for a two-column layout

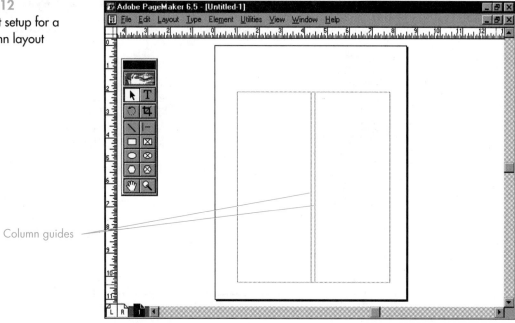

Column guides

You'll use the Column Guides command from the Layout menu to display the dialog box in which you specify the number of columns.

1. Click Layout in the menu bar.

2. Click Column Guides.

The Column Guides dialog box appears with the Number of columns default set at 1. Notice that the number is highlighted.

3. Type 2.

4. Click OK.

The publication window now appears with the document setup divided into two columns.

## EDIT MENU

Figure 2.13 shows the Edit menu, which allows you to undo your last action and make content changes to a publication, such as copying paragraphs and graphics or deleting (Clear) text. You can also use the Edit menu to insert charts or drawings into a publication and to switch to

Story Editor—the PageMaker word processor. Many of the Edit options are inactive (gray) because there are no graphics or text in the publication yet. However, you will use the Undo command on the Edit menu to remove the column guides from the document setup.

Figure 2.13
Edit menu

1. Click Edit in the menu bar.

2. Click Undo Guide Move.

The column guides disappear from the publication. The Undo command is useful when you change your mind about an action you have just taken. Keep in mind that Undo can be used to reverse only your most recent action, and it is not available for all actions.

## LAYOUT MENU

Figure 2.14 shows the Layout menu, which you just used to display the column guides for a two-column document setup. You can also use the commands in this menu to insert, remove, and sort pages as well as to go to a particular page in a multipage document.

Figure 2.14
Layout menu

Figure 2.15 shows the Utilities menu, which allows you to search for words in a publication, check for spelling errors, and create an index and table of contents. The Utilities menu also includes Plug-ins, which are commands that enable you to automate various tasks, such as capitalizing the first letter in each word of a selection of words.

**Figure 2.15**
Utilities menu

You'll close the current publication using the Close command from the File menu.

1. Click File in the menu bar.

2. Click Close.

A message dialog box appears asking if you want to save the publication before closing. If you click Yes, a dialog box will appear, allowing you to enter a file name and location to save to. If you click No, the publication will disappear from the screen and not be saved. If you click Cancel, you will return to the publication window.

3. Click No.

The document setup disappears from the screen and the PageMaker window replaces the publication window.

## OPENING A SAVED PUBLICATION

Before looking at the rest of the menus, you will open a file named Promotion. As Figure 2.16 shows, this publication is a promotion for The Inn at Portage Bay.

Figure 2.16
Promotion—a
promotional piece for
The Inn at Portage Bay

# The Inn at Portage Bay

R E S O R T

Beachwalkers have been exploring the shoreline of Portage Bay for decades. Walking its beaches. Watching the orca whales frolic in the afternoon sun. Harvesting the clams. Enjoying the unspoiled beauty of deserted coastlines. Marvelling at the views of islands and mountains in the distance. Portage Bay is a unique blend of all that the Pacific Northwest is known for.

Now you have an opportunity to share the beauty of Portage Bay by scheduling a conference or merely spending a relaxing weekend in our newly completed world-class resort. Guests will be treated to luxury accommodations, breathtaking views, and service fit for royalty.

We are located on Sunset Hill Road in Portage Bay, Washington, a short ride from nearby airports. For help arranging your next meeting, or just to make a vacation one to remember, please call on us. We look forward to serving you.

RESERVATIONS:         1-800-555-PORT
GROUP COORDINATOR:  Elizabeth Loudon

You will use the Open command from the File menu to open this publication.

1. Specify the disk drive and folder where the files are located.

It is recommended that you work with files that are stored on your computer's hard drive, not on a floppy disk. In this case the files are opened from a folder on the C drive called The Inn. If the files on your computer are in a different folder or on a different drive, use that location whenever the directions tell you to open or save a file.

2. Click File in the menu bar.

3. Click Open.

The Open Publication dialog box appears so you can specify the name of your publication and the disk drive holding it. The components of this dialog box are:

- a Look in box where you specify the drive and/or folder containing the file you want

- a box listing the names of the files and folders that appear in the current Look in folder

- a File name box where you type in a file name (and, if needed, a drive letter and folder name)

- a Files of type box where you specify the type of files to list, in this case, PageMaker files

- the Open as settings which allow you to open the original file or a copy of the original file

You can use the dialog box to locate a file or type in the file's location and name in the File name box. Figure 2.17 shows the completed Open Publication dialog box set up to open the Promotion publication from The Inn folder on the C drive.

**Figure 2.17**
Open Publication
dialog box

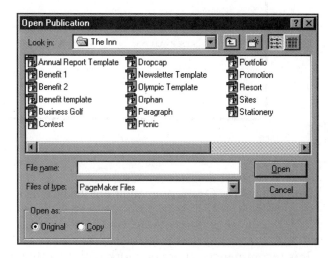

The dialog box lists all the files stored in The Inn folder. Select the Promotion file and then click the Open button to open the publication.

4. On your own, open the Promotion publication.

At this point a message dialog box might appear, telling you the publication was not composed for your printer. This means you are not using the same printer as was used when the document was created. If so, you can still print the document by clicking OK, but the printed document might look slightly different than the document you see onscreen.

Figure 2.18 shows the publication layout as it appears onscreen.

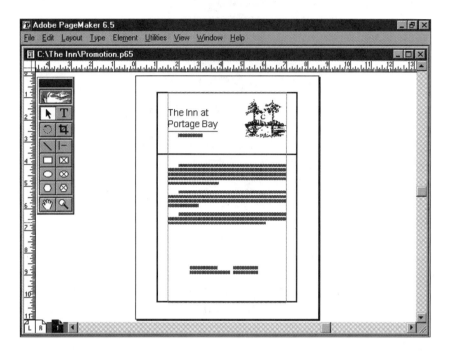

Figure 2.18
Promotion publication
displayed in Greeked text

Compare the screen view of the publication with Figure 2.16, which shows the printed publication. All of the text, except for the top heading lines, is simulated and illegible in the screen view because the screen is too small to display the entire publication in a type size large enough to read. **Greeked text** is the term used to describe simulated text. Despite its limitations, the Fit in Window view lets you see the exact position of the publication's paragraphs and heading lines. (The heading lines are legible because they are in larger type sizes.) As you make changes in a publication, PageMaker might need to redraw the publication onscreen. Using Greeked text speeds up this process in addition to allowing you to see the design of an entire page. In the following section you will see how to change the screen view of the publication so all the text is legible.

Figure 2.19 shows the View menu, which you use to show and hide the ruler and column guides and to specify how much of the publication you see onscreen.

**Figure 2.19**
**View menu**

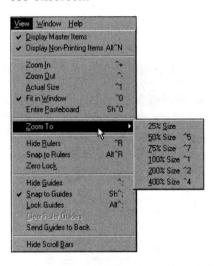

1. Click View in the menu bar.

2. Point to Zoom To.

The commands that control the size of the publication view are described in the table shown in Figure 2.20.

**Figure 2.20**

Commands that control the size of the publication view

| Command | Displays Document Setup |
|---|---|
| Zoom In | at the next higher magnification. |
| Zoom Out | at the next lower magnification. |
| Actual Size | at the size it will be when printed. |
| Fit in Window | at the size it will fit in the publication window (this is the default setting). |
| Entire Pasteboard | with the complete Pasteboard, including all text and graphics stored there. |
| 25% Size | at 25% of its actual size. |
| 50% Size | at 50% of its actual size. |
| 75% Size | at 75% of its actual size. |
| 100% Size | at its actual size. |
| 200% Size | at twice its actual size. |
| 400% Size | at four times its actual size. |

Next you'll look at the publication in five of these views. Examine each view before moving to the next one.

**3.** Click Actual Size.

This view is similar to what you would see onscreen if you were using a word processing program.

**4.** Point to Zoom To from the View menu.

**5.** Click 75% Size.

You can see more of the publication with this view than with the Actual Size view; however, the type is smaller.

**6.** Point to Zoom To from the View menu.

**7.** Click 50% Size.

You see even more of the publication at 50% Size. However, the type appears as Greeked text.

**8.** On your own, select 200% Size.

Only a small part of the document setup is displayed because the text is enlarged to twice the actual size.

**9.** On your own, select Fit in Window.

The entire publication appears onscreen with Greeked text.

In PageMaker you can use the right mouse button as a shortcut to switch between Fit in Window and Actual Size. You click the right mouse button to display a menu and then click the view size you want. Which part of the publication stays in view depends on the pointer's location. If the pointer is at the top of the page, then the upper part of the publication is displayed.

**10.** Move the pointer to above the word Inn.

**11.** Click the right mouse button.

**12.** Click Actual Size.

The top of the document setup appears in actual size. Now return to the Fit in Window view.

**13.** Click the right mouse button.

**14.** Click Fit in Window.

The right mouse button is also useful for working with text, as you'll see in a later chapter.

When you use any view, except for Fit in Window, 25% Size, and Entire Pasteboard, only part of the publication is visible. However, you can use the scroll bars or grabber hand to reposition the publication on the screen.

## Using the Scroll Bars

The scroll bars are located on the bottom and right sides of the screen, and you can use them to view any part of an open publication. The scroll bars move the publication window up, down, left, and right while the page stays fixed in place. There are four ways to scroll the publication window: (1) click an arrow at either end of the scroll bars, (2) click in the gray area of the scroll bars, (3) drag a box in the scroll bars, and (4) point to an arrow and hold down the mouse button.

First, you'll use the click method to scroll up the window.

1. Point to the down arrow in the lower-right corner of the screen.

2. Click the mouse button six times.

Notice that the window moves down to display the ending lines. Before continuing, reset the view to Fit in Window.

1. On your own, select Fit in Window.

Notice that although the size of the window didn't change, the page repositioned to the center of the publication window.

## Using the Grabber Hand

The **grabber hand** is an icon in the shape of a hand. It allows you to "grab" your publication and move it to another place on the Pasteboard. When your view is larger than Fit in Window, the grabber hand enables you to bring another portion of your document into view. To use the grabber hand you'll use both the keyboard and the mouse.

1. Position the pointer in the middle of the document setup.

2. Hold down ⌐ALT⌐ while you press and hold down the mouse button. (Note that the arrow icon changes to a hand icon 🖑.)

3. Release ⌐ALT⌐ but continue to press the mouse button.

4. Drag the mouse to the left.

The grabber hand pulls the publication in that direction as you drag the mouse.

5. Release the mouse button.

After you release the mouse button, the pointer changes back to an arrow. Before continuing, change the view back to its original size.

6. Select Fit in Window from the View menu.

Another way to display the grabber hand is from the Toolbox.

## USING THE TOOLBOX

The Toolbox contains fourteen tools for working with text and graphics in your publication. You use these tools to select, resize, move, and rotate text and graphics; type and edit text; and create drawings. You can crop (trim) graphics and create frames that act as placeholders for text and graphics. You can also change the view and reposition the document on the Pasteboard.

To select a tool in the Toolbox, point to the tool and click the mouse button, and then move the mouse pointer back to the document setup. The pointer changes to the icon that represents the selected tool (see Figure 2.21).

Figure 2.21
Toolbox icons

| Tool | Icon | Function |
| --- | --- | --- |
| Pointer | | Selecting text blocks and graphics |
| Rotating | | Rotating text and graphics |
| Line | | Drawing diagonal lines |
| Rectangle | | Drawing rectangles and squares |
| Ellipse | | Drawing ovals and circles |
| Polygon | | Drawing polygons |
| Grabberhand | | Scrolling the page |
| Text | | Selecting, entering, and editing text |
| Cropping | | Trimming graphics |
| Constrained line | | Drawing perpendicular lines |
| Rectangle frame | | Creating rectangular placeholders for text and graphics |
| Ellipse frame | | Creating elliptical placeholders for text and graphics |
| Polygon frame | | Creating polygonal placeholders for text and graphics |
| Zoom | | Magnifying or reducing view of the page |

You can move the Toolbox by clicking the Toolbox title bar and dragging it to another location in the publication window, which is helpful when the Toolbox covers a portion of the publication you want to work with. You'll move the Toolbox to the upper-right corner of the Pasteboard as shown in Figure 2.22. *Note:* If the Toolbox on your screen is already in the upper-right corner, first move it to the upper-left corner of the screen and then move it back. If the Toolbox is not on your screen, select Show Tools from the Window menu and continue with the steps that follow.

**Figure 2.22**
Moving the Toolbox

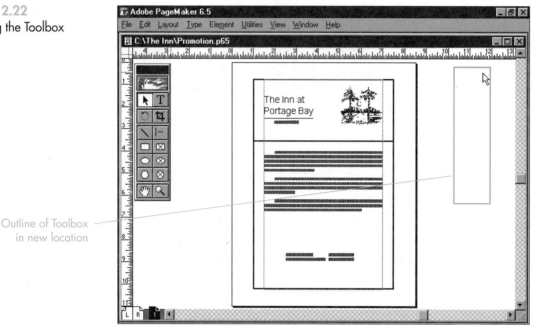

Outline of Toolbox
in new location

1. Point to the top of the Toolbox.

2. Hold down the mouse button while you drag the Toolbox to the upper-right corner of the Pasteboard (refer to Figure 2.22).

3. Release the button.

Now change the view to Actual Size and display the top of the document.

4. On your own, change the view to Actual Size.

5. Use the scroll bar to scroll the window until you can see all the heading lines at the top of the document setup.

To illustrate the use of the Toolbox tools, you will use the text tool to select the word "Inn." Then you will select the Italic command from the Type menu so the word "Inn" appears in italic.

1. Point to the text tool ⊤ in the Toolbox.

2. Click the mouse button.

3. Move the pointer to the document setup.

Notice that the icon changes to an I-beam Ⅰ.

**4.** Place the I-beam on the space before the word "Inn". See Figure 2.23.

**Figure 2.23**
Positioning the I-beam

I-beam

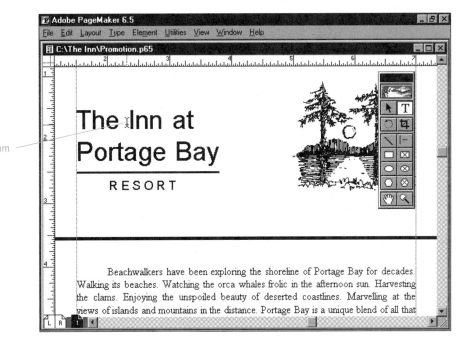

**5.** Hold down the mouse button and slowly drag the I-beam to highlight the word "Inn."

**6.** Release the mouse button.

With the word "Inn" selected, you can change its type style.

## TYPE MENU

Figure 2.24 shows the Type menu, which contains commands that let you specify how text will appear in a publication.

**Figure 2.24**
Type menu

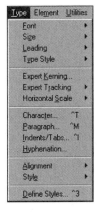

The first two groups of commands allow you to select a font (typeface) and type size and to specify the spacing between characters. You can also indicate the type style, such as bold or italic. The third group of commands allows you to format paragraphs by designating indentation, hyphenation, and type specifications. The last three commands enable you to align text (left, right, center, justify, and force justify) and to define and apply styles. A **style** is a set of specifications that determines how a body of text will look. For example, you could define a headline style in your publication as a large type size, bold, underlined, and centered. You might then define a subhead style as a smaller type size, normal type, and aligned with the left edge of the text.

You'll use the Type menu to change the word "Inn" to italic.

1. Click Type in the menu bar.

2. Click Type Style.

3. Click Italic.

The word "Inn" is now in italic and it is still highlighted, which means that you can perform another action, such as underlining, on this selection. Instead, you'll remove the highlight.

4. Move the I-beam to a blank area of the document setup.

5. Click the mouse button.

Next, change from the text tool ⌶ to the pointer ⬆ :

6. Click the pointer tool ⬆ in the Toolbox.

## ELEMENT MENU

Figure 2.25 shows the Element menu. Figures 2.26 and 2.27 show the Element menu with the Fill and Stroke menus.

**Figure 2.25**
Element menu

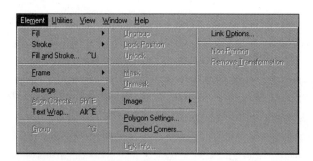

**Figure 2.26**
Fill options

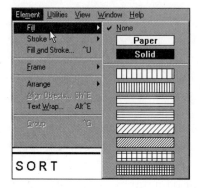

Figure 2.27
Stroke options

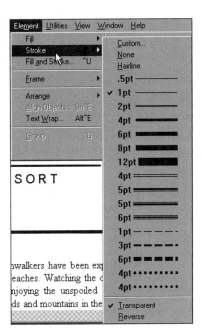

The Fill menu lists eight patterns for filling in shapes drawn in your publication. The Stroke menu lists the widths and patterns available for lines and graphics drawn in PageMaker. You will use the Stroke and Fill options in Chapter 3. Take a moment to view the Stroke and Fill options.

1. Click Element in the menu bar.

2. Point to Fill.

3. Point to Stroke.

Another feature of the Element menu allows you to work with text and graphics that overlap. For example, you could draw two boxes and have them overlap to create a three-dimensional effect. The Bring to Front and Send to Back commands in the Arrange option enable you to change the position of these overlapped boxes.

In addition, the Element menu contains commands to specify how text will wrap around a graphic (such as flowing text around all sides of the graphic or flowing text through the graphic). You can also control the appearance of graphics (such as the lightness and contrast) and round the corners of rectangles drawn in PageMaker. The Element menu also allows you to mask (cover) part of an object (such as a drawing) so that only part of the object appears.

4. Click Element in the menu bar.

The Element menu closes.

Figure 2.28 shows the Window menu, which contains two options to display (Tile, Cascade) all of the open publications in the publication window at one time. You can also show or hide the Toolbox and the palettes from this menu. The **palettes** contain icons that are used as shortcuts for performing many PageMaker functions. For instance, from the Control palette you can change the type style and type size of text. Finally, the bottom of the Window menu shows the drive, folder, and file names of the open publications. You'll use this menu to show the Control palette, which you'll then use to underline the word "Inn." Start by selecting "Inn."

**Figure 2.28**
**Window menu**

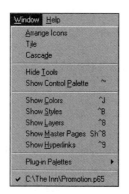

1. Click the text tool **T** in the Toolbox.

2. Point to the left of the word Inn.

3. Drag the I-beam over the word Inn to select it.

4. Click Window in the menu bar.

5. Click Show Control Palette.

The Control palette appears, displaying information about the selected text—Inn. (*Note:* There are several features of this palette that you will be learning later.) Notice that *I* is highlighted on the Control palette, indicating that the selected text is formatted in italic type. You'll underline the word by clicking the underline button on the Control palette.

6. Click the underline button **U**. See Figure 2.29.

Figure 2.29
Control palette

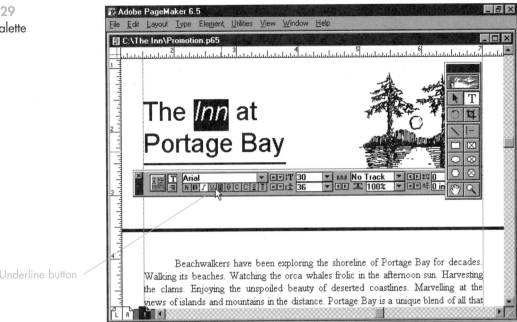

Underline button

Inn becomes underlined. Now remove the Control palette from the screen (although you could also move it out of your way by dragging the title bar on the left edge of the palette).

7. Select Hide Control Palette from the Window menu.

8. Click a blank area of the screen to deselect the word Inn.

## HELP MENU

As you are working on a publication, you might want additional information about a procedure or want a quick review of the steps to perform an action. The Help menu enables you to locate a PageMaker topic and display information about it.

1. Select Help Topics from the Help menu.

The Help Topics dialog box appears with three tabs: Contents, Index, and Find. The Contents tab displays a list of topics, such as step-by-step instructions and commands that you can choose from. The Index tab displays a dialog box that allows you to search for help on a specific topic. For example, if you need help on printing a publication you could type the word "printing," and PageMaker would search for and display the appropriate Help window. The Find tab enables you to search for specific words and phrases by help topics instead of by category.

To illustrate how the Help function works, you will use the Index option to get help on creating a new publication.

2. If necessary, click the Index tab.

The Index dialog box appears.

**3.** Read the information at the top of the dialog box.

**4.** Type *new*.

Notice that as you type, the list changes based on your entry.

**5.** Click New publications: creating, as shown in Figure 2.30.

**Figure 2.30**
**Using Help to search for a topic**

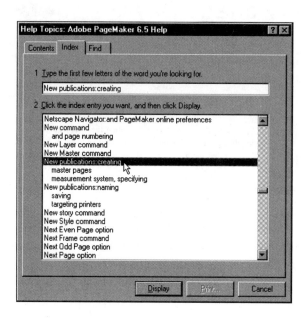

**6.** Click the Display button.

The Topics Found dialog box appears with two topics. The Creating a publication from scratch topic, which you want to look up, is highlighted.

**7.** Click the Display button.

The Creating a publication from scratch Help window appears.

**8.** Read the information.

Notice the buttons near the top of the Help window. The Back button takes you back one window if you have looked at more than one Help window, and the Help Topics button returns you to the Help Topics dialog box.

**9.** Click the Help Topics button.

**10.** Click the Contents tab.

A list of books appears.

**11.** On your own, open the Basic Concepts book.

**12.** On your own, display the Using the toolbox Help window.

**13.** Read the information about using the Toolbox.

**14.** Click the word toolbox, which is colored and underlined. See Figure 2.31.

Figure 2.31
Getting Help on Using
the Toolbox

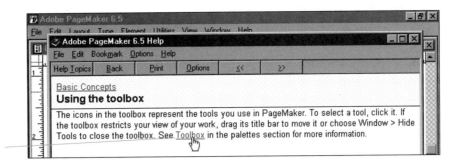

Click underlined word
to jump to a related
Help window

15. Read the information on the Toolbox screen.

16. Click the text tool **T** to display the description.

17. Select Exit from the File menu in the Help window to exit Help.

The Help menu is most useful after you have learned the basics of the PageMaker program. Help is best used to walk you through a process you have already learned but have partially forgotten, rather than to teach you a new process.

## ENDING A PAGEMAKER SESSION

Before quitting PageMaker, you must decide if you want to print and/or save the current publication. Then you're free to close the publication and exit the program. This time, you will print, but not save, the publication.

Printing a
Publication

To print a publication, you click the Print command from the File menu. Before you print, make sure your computer is connected to a printer, the printer is ready, and the paper is aligned.

1. Click File in the menu bar.

2. Click Print.

The Print Document dialog box appears with print settings that you can modify, such as the number of copies and the page range to print. Usually you will not need to change these settings. The name of the printer appears near the top of the dialog box. Make sure the box displays the printer you are using. You might need to check with your lab assistant or instructor to determine which printer you'll be using.

3. Click Print.

In a few moments the publication is printed.

## Closing a Publication and Exiting PageMaker

Earlier you opened the Promotion file using the Open command. Now that you're done with the document, you'll use the Close command from the File menu to close this file.

1. Click File in the menu bar.

2. Click Close.

A message dialog box appears, asking if you want to save changes before closing. Remember, you made a change in the document when you italicized and underlined the word Inn. If you choose Yes, the original Promotion file will be overwritten. You do not want to save the changes you made, so you'll choose No.

3. Click No.

The publication window disappears, leaving only the PageMaker screen visible. Now use the Exit command from the File menu to exit PageMaker.

1. Click File in the menu bar.

2. Click Exit.

After you have finished working on a publication, you should always close any open publications and exit PageMaker.

## SUMMARY

This chapter introduced you to the PageMaker environment. You learned how to use the mouse to select pull-down menus and execute commands. You practiced changing the page view and repositioning the document setup on the Pasteboard. You know how to use dialog boxes, the Toolbox, and the Control palette, as well as how to open and print documents. In Chapter 3 you will create your first PageMaker document.

## QUESTIONS

1. Describe the five techniques for using the mouse.

2. What is a pull-down menu?

3. List and briefly describe each of the pull-down menus.

4. What are commands and how are they chosen?

5. What is the purpose of a dialog box? Give an example.

6. Briefly describe the components of the publication window.

7. How is the Pasteboard used?

8. What is the difference between the margin, ruler, and column guides?

9. Describe the process for opening a file.

10. How is the grabber hand used?

11. Briefly describe the components of the Toolbox.

12. Describe the process for printing a publication.

13. Turn to the Quick Reference section of this book and describe the type of information you find and how it can be used.

14. Using the Index at the end of this book, list the page numbers for the following terms:

    Greeked text _____

    publication window _____

    ruler guides _____

15. Use the Help menu to search for the word Open. Then display the Open command topic and go to Opening an existing publication. Answer the following questions.

    a. PageMaker keeps track of how many of the last publications you have opened?

    b. How would you open a recently saved publication?

## PROJECTS

1. The following project lets you practice many of the commands and techniques you learned in this chapter. Picnic is one of the student files used with this book. Open this one-page publication and complete the following procedures.

   ■ Use the View menu to change the page view to 75% Size. What is the last line of text displayed onscreen?

   ■ Use the scroll bars to move the last sentence of the document to the middle of the screen.

   ■ Use the scroll bars to display the document heading.

   ■ Use the right mouse button to change the view to Actual Size.

   ■ Use the text tool to highlight the top heading line.

   ■ Use the Control palette to underline the selected text.

   ■ Deselect the highlighted text.

   ■ Remove the Control palette from the screen.

- Remove the Toolbox from the screen.

- Print the document.

- Close, but do not save, the document.

2. Throughout this book you will be creating publications for The Inn at Portage Bay. You might want to collect your work in a portfolio. In this project you will create a cover for your portfolio. On your disk is a file called Portfolio. This is a portfolio cover that you will customize by adding your name, the course name, and today's date. Figure 2.32 shows the Portfolio publication. In the upper-left corner of the page there are placeholders for your name, the course name, and the date. To replace one of these, you drag the text tool to highlight it, and then type the appropriate text. Complete the following steps to create your customized portfolio cover.

   - Open the Portfolio publication.

   - Point to the Greeked text in the upper-left corner of the publication page.

   - Use the right mouse button to enlarge the view to Actual Size.

   - Select the text tool from the Toolbox.

   - Drag the I-beam pointer across *your name* to highlight it.

   - Type your name.

   - On your own, replace the course name and date placeholders with the appropriate text.

   - Print the publication.

   - Save the publication using the file name My Portfolio. To save the publication with a new file name, choose Save As from the File menu. Then specify the drive and folder to which you will save, as well as the file name.

**Figure 2.32**
Portfolio publication

3. Stationery, one of the student files used with this book, allows you to customize the stationery by inserting your name and address. The process is the same as for Project 2. Complete the following to customize the stationery.

- Open the Stationery publication.
- Point to the Greeked text at the top of the publication page.
- Use the right mouse button to enlarge the view to Actual Size.
- Select the text tool from the Toolbox.
- Drag the I-beam pointer across Name to highlight it.
- Type your name.
- On your own, enter the address lines.
- Print the publication.
- Save the publication using the file name My Stationery. To save the publication with a new file name, choose Save As from the File menu. Then specify the drive and folder to which you will save, as well as the file name.

# CHAPTER 3

# Creating a Single-Page Publication

**Upon completion of this chapter you will be able to:**

- **Set defaults for PageMaker**
- **Understand the difference between application and publication defaults**
- **Create a publication with multiple columns**
- **Use horizontal and vertical ruler guides**
- **Use the Element menu to select different stroke types**
- **Control text alignment**
- **Create text for a publication**
- **Change the page view with four methods**
- **Create, copy and paste a simple graphic**
- **Save and print a publication**

In this chapter you will create your first complete publication—a telephone directory advertisement for The Inn at Portage Bay. First you will set PageMaker defaults and tell PageMaker about the new publication. Then you will create the publication, save it, and print it. In the process you will learn about typing text, drawing lines and boxes, controlling text alignment, and copying a box. By the end of the chapter you will have been introduced to many more PageMaker features and will have completed a publication.

The Inn at Portage Bay manager plans to place an advertisement in the Yellow Pages and in magazines. A media consultant has developed a simple and readable design, with the headline *The Inn at Portage Bay* featured prominently. Further, the consultant and Inn manager want to include a list of the resort's amenities. To draw the reader's eye and to enhance readability, the ad will contain substantial **white space**, which is area intentionally left empty, or white. The final piece, based on the consultant's layout, is shown in Figure 3.1.

Figure 3.1
Finished design

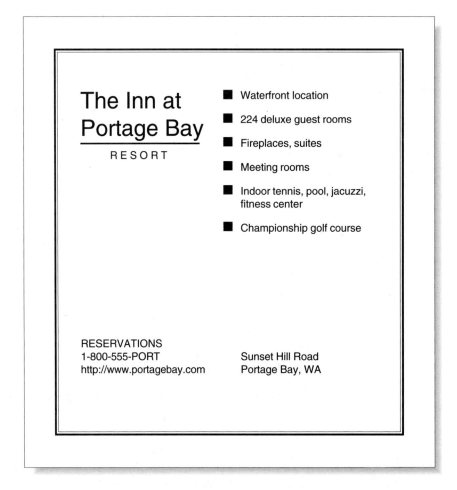

## UNDERSTANDING PAGEMAKER DEFAULTS

When PageMaker is first installed, it contains preset specifications for many aspects of publishing. You can change these default settings to suit your preferences and needs. As a result, it is impossible to predict how the computer you're working on is set up. Before even opening a new publication, you should verify and, if necessary, set some defaults for it. The kinds of defaults you can set include paragraph indentation, type size, line width, and whether or not graphics, such as circles and boxes, are filled.

There are two kinds of defaults: application and publication. **Application defaults** are specifications that you set when all publications are closed and that PageMaker remembers even after you exit and restart the program. **Publication defaults** are specifications that you set when a publication is open but no object is selected and that are applicable to the current publication only. For example, type specifications set before any publication is opened apply to all PageMaker publications created on that computer and are application defaults. Type specifications set when a publication is open and no text is selected apply to only that publication and are publication defaults. You will set both kinds of defaults in this chapter.

Setting Application
Defaults

Why set application defaults? Setting defaults prior to opening a publication makes sense for two reasons. First, you need select the settings only once. For example, suppose most of the publication's text will be set in Arial 12, but the default is set to Times New Roman 36 bold. You open a publication, change the type specifications to Arial 12, and type some text. Then you click on the line tool in the Toolbox and draw a line. Now you want to resume typing in Arial 12. You click on the text tool and continue typing. But this text appears in Times New Roman 36 bold, the earlier default, because PageMaker is designed to return to the type specification set when the publication was first opened. Setting defaults *before* you open a publication makes the process of creating the publication easier.

A second reason to set application defaults is that the process itself requires you to plan *before* opening a publication. Just as a graphic designer will organize the workspace before starting, to make sure all the needed tools are available, you should verify and, if necessary, reset the defaults before opening a new publication. Planning produces better-looking documents, which in turn communicate a message more effectively—the ultimate goal of desktop publishing.

About the Defaults

For the Inn's advertisement, you will verify or, if necessary, set application defaults. First you want to tell PageMaker the kind of type, or characters, you will be using for most of the publication. You'll do this from the Character Specifications dialog box.

Second, you need to indicate how the type will be aligned between the left and right margins. For this publication, most text will be set **left justified**, which means that it is lined up flush to the left margin, while along the right margin the text is uneven, or **ragged**. You specify left justification by selecting the Alignment command from the Type menu and clicking Align Left. Four other Alignment options are available. **Align Center** places text equidistant from the left and right margins. **Align Right** places text flush to the right margin while leaving it ragged along the left margin. **Justify** uses proportional spacing (where various letters require different amounts of space) between words and characters so that a full line of text completely and evenly fills the space between the margins, and is flush to both left and right margins. With Justify, a short (or partial) line, such as the last line of a paragraph, will have normal spacing and be left justified. **Force Justify** is the same as Justify, except that a short line also completely and evenly fills the space between the margins. You would use Force Justify to make a headline or the last line of a paragraph completely fill its allotted space. Figure 3.2 shows text that is left justified, centered, right justified, justified, and force justified.

Figure 3.2
Examples of left, centered, right, justified, and force justified text

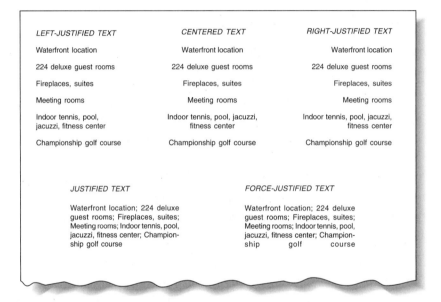

Third, you will look at the commands in the View menu and select those that will help you compose your publication. Some of the commands might already be set the way the directions indicate and you can just verify the selection. In other cases, you will have to make a change.

## Character Specifications Dialog Box

The Character command in the Type menu opens the Character Specifications dialog box, as shown in Figure 3.3. You can select the font name and size from the Character Specifications dialog box. In addition, you make other choices about how the text will appear on the page from this dialog box. The choices are Leading, Horizontal scale, Color, Tint, Position, Case, Track, Line end, and Type style.

Figure 3.3
Character Specifications
dialog box

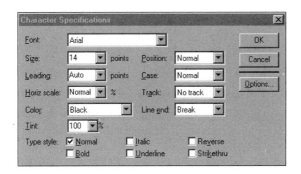

A **font** or **face** is the entire group of letters and other characters of a certain shape, or design, in a particular size. Font includes the weight, width, and style of a typeface. An example of a font or face is Arial 12. Although "font" and "face" are used interchangeably and "font" appears throughout PageMaker, graphic designers prefer the term "face." **Font name** is the label associated with a "family" of fonts or all sizes of a font. Examples of font names include Braggadocio, Helvetica, Goudy Modern, and Times New Roman. **Font size** is measured in points. One **point** equals about ½-inch. Thus, a 72-point font would measure about an inch from the top of the letter b to the bottom of the letter g. Figure 3.4 shows five fonts in two font families. You'll learn more about fonts in Chapter 8.

Figure 3.4

Five fonts in two font families.

Fonts are measured in points from the top of the ascender to the bottom of the descender

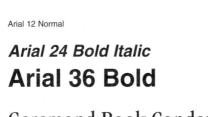

**Leading** (pronounced "ledding") refers to the amount of space between lines of text and is measured in points. Chapter 4 has a more complete discussion of leading, text processing, and the options available in the Character Specifications dialog box.

**Horizontal scale** refers to the proportional width of characters. It allows you to take text, such as a newsletter masthead, and fit it to a particular width. You will use this option in Chapter 6.

**Color** enables you to select a color for text. With the **Tint** option, you can specify a different intensity of a color, which in effect expands the number of colors available in your color palette.

**Position** refers to where on a baseline the text appears. A **baseline** is an imaginary line on which the majority of the characters in a face seem to "rest." Position choices are Normal, Superscript, and Subscript. **Superscript** text appears above the normal baseline, like an exponent. **Subscript** text appears below the line. In this book you will always use **Normal**, which places text on the baseline. You might want to experiment on your own with Superscript and Subscript.

**Case** refers to whether what you type is to be printed in **Normal**, a mix of uppercase and lowercase, in **All caps**, entirely in uppercase, or in a version called **Small caps**, which prints each letter in uppercase but uses a shorter uppercase for letters you type without holding down (SHIFT). When Normal is selected, hold down (SHIFT) for capital letters. Most of the text you will work with will be Normal, but from time to time you will want to use All caps for special emphasis. An alternative to using the All caps option is to press (CAPS LOCK) on the keyboard while you type. Small caps is useful in certain design situations when you want to vary the look of the text.

**Track**, also called letter spacing, is the average space between characters in a block of text. With this average spacing, certain letter combinations, such as "fy," might appear too close together. Tracking enables you to better control the spacing between letters. You will practice using tracking in Chapter 4.

The **Line end** option allows you to control line breaks for selected text. When you set No Break, you specify words that must appear on the same line regardless of where the end of the line falls. Break allows each line to end when the line is full.

**Type style** includes the following options: Normal, Bold, Italic, Underline, Reverse, and Strikethru. Generally, you will use Normal, Bold (heavier or darker text), and Italic (slanted text). Be aware that **Reverse**, white letters on a black background, does not work on every printer.

## Setting Font and Point Defaults

In this section you will learn more about fonts and points. In the publication you're creating you will be using two type sizes: 30 point for the headline (*The Inn at Portage Bay*) and 14 point for the rest of the text. The face used in this project is Arial, chosen for its clean, simple lines.

The available fonts are the ones listed when you point to Font in the Type menu. When Aldus produced PageMaker, the software did not have its own fonts. Since Adobe purchased Aldus, PageMaker comes bundled with Adobe Type Manager. Now when you install the product you also get many Adobe fonts. In addition, Windows comes with True Type fonts, which are fonts associated with Windows 95 or NT (the operating system required by PageMaker 6.5), and which are also available in PageMaker. Other companies, such as Bitstream, make font software that works with PageMaker. Fonts are available in sizes that range from 4 to 650 points.

You can select a size from a list of point sizes or select Other and type a number between 4 and 650 in 0.1 increments. Chapter 8 contains a more detailed discussion of fonts.

Now you'll set the defaults for the Inn's advertisement. To set the default font to Arial 14:

1. Start PageMaker.

2. Click the Type menu.

3. Click Character.

Look at the selected font. If it is not already set to Arial:

4. Click the arrow to the right of Font.

5. Click Arial (use the scroll box to find it, if necessary).

Look at Size. If it is not set to 14:

6. Click the arrow to the right of Size.

7. Click 14.

Compare your dialog box to the one shown in Figure 3.3. Change any settings necessary to make it match the figure.

8. Click OK.

Even though you won't be typing text right away, the type specification for the document you open will be set to Arial 14 as an application default because you made this change before opening a publication.

To verify your selection of Arial 14 and see an alternate method for selecting font name and size, do the following:

1. Click Type.

2. Point to Font. Note that Arial is checked, indicating it is selected.

3. Point to Size. Note that 14 is checked.

Remember that you can change the font and size from either the Character Specifications dialog box or the Type menu.

## Verifying the Align Left Command

Look again at the advertisement in Figure 3.1. The ad is split into two columns, and the text in each column is lined up on the left margin. Thus, you want to specify Align Left as an application default before opening the publication. Verify that the Align Left command is selected:

1. Point to Alignment.

You want to make sure Align Left is checked, as shown in Figure 3.5.

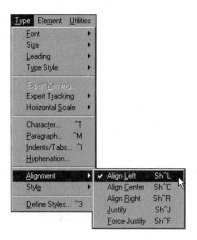

Figure 3.5
Type menu with Align left
selected

If it is, click outside the menu to make the menu disappear. If Align Left is not checked, click Align Left.

## Selecting Pasteboard Options from the View Menu

Next you will select several options to make it easier to work with your publication. First, you want to make sure Show Guides is selected. When Show Guides is on, you will see margin and column guides on your publication and Hide Guides in the View menu. You'll also select Show Rulers, so the rulers appear on your screen. When this option is selected, the View menu displays Hide Rulers. Also, you want to ensure that Snap to Rulers does not have a check next to it. If this command is selected, the guidelines can be placed to align only with a ruler hash mark. You will need more flexibility to draw and place some of the lines in this publication.

You will want the Snap to Guides command checked. Typically, you will draw vertical and horizontal nonprinting guidelines to help you place different elements on the page accurately. Once the guidelines are drawn, you will want graphic elements, such as lines, circles, and squares, to line up with the guidelines, which is one reason you drew them in the first place. When Snap to Guides is checked in the View menu, graphics automatically align on the guidelines. For example, if you wanted to draw three horizontal lines that start and end at the two guidelines you drew, the Snap to Guides command ensures that all the lines will do just that. If you draw the lines without Snap to Guides selected, you'll have no guarantee the lines will align exactly. The critical eye will see the minor difference among the lengths of the three lines and how they are positioned.

You want the Lock Guides option off until you finish drawing the guidelines so you can move the guidelines if necessary. If the Lock Guides option is checked (on) when you create a ruler guide and place it, you cannot adjust that ruler guide. After you have all ruler guides where you want them, you will change this setting to on.

To make these selections:

1. Click the View menu.

**2.** Click the appropriate commands to make your menu match the one shown in Figure 3.6. You might need to select the View menu several times.

Figure 3.6
View menu with correct selections

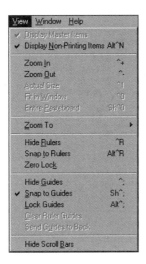

You have established several application defaults. These defaults will remain in effect for the PageMaker program on your computer until you or someone else changes them when no publication is open.

## SETTING UP A NEW PUBLICATION

Before you can put text and graphics on a page, you must first place a piece of paper on your desktop and draw some guides on it. To do this electronically, you will open a new publication in PageMaker. To draw some guides on the "paper," you will use the column guides and the rulers.

### Starting a New Publication

Files must be opened before they can be created, changed, or printed, and they must be closed when you are done with them. There are two ways to open a publication file: New, which creates a new publication, and Open, which opens an existing publication. Because you are creating a new publication for this project you will use New.

To create a new publication:

1. Click File in the menu bar.

2. Click New.

The Document Setup dialog box appears.

The Document Setup dialog box allows you to tell PageMaker about the publication you will create and the paper you will put on the Pasteboard. How many pages will there be? What are the page dimensions? How wide will the margins be?

**3.** With the Document Setup dialog box onscreen, duplicate Figure 3.7 by selecting or verifying the settings listed below.

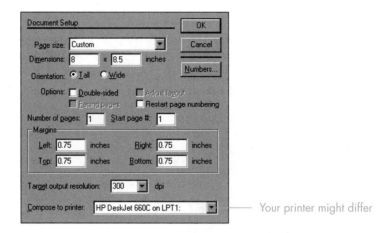

Your printer might differ

Recall that you can use TAB, the mouse, or ALT and the underlined letter in the option name to move from option to option.

| | |
|---|---|
| Page Dimensions: | 8 × 8.5 inches (Custom Page size will appear automatically when you type these dimensions.) |
| Orientation: | Tall |
| Double-sided: | Not selected |
| Number of pages: | 1 |
| Start page #: | 1 |
| Margins in inches: | 0.75 for all margins |

Because this publication is one page, you clicked Double-sided to remove the checkmark. Double-sided documents contain odd- and even-numbered pages (as in a book) with margins that are mirror images of each other, so when you print page 1 and page 2 back-to-back, the text on the two sides of the page will occupy the same part of the paper.

**4.** When your dialog box matches the one in Figure 3.7, click OK.

Now the "piece of paper" is on the desk. In PageMaker terms, you have an empty document setup on the Pasteboard. The next step is to draw guidelines on the paper.

## Creating Columns

As you saw earlier, the ad for the Inn is a two-column layout. Right now, the publication is set for one column, so you need to change the number of columns to two.

To create columns:

**1.** Click the Layout menu.

**2.** Click Column Guides.

**3.** Change Number of columns to 2, as shown in Figure 3.8.

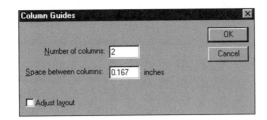

**4.** Click OK.

Column guides, indicating left and right margins for the two columns, appear in the center of the publication, as shown in Figure 3.9. These lines will not show up when you print the publication. The space between the columns, called **gutter space**, is 0.167 inch.

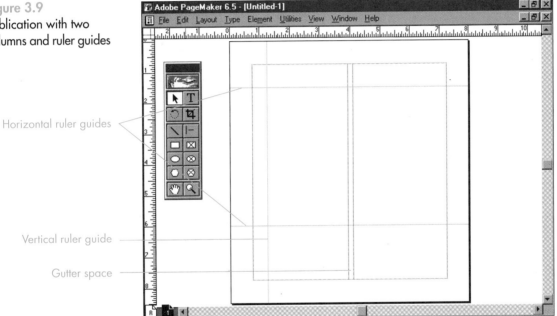

You have set two columns as a publication default, which applies only to this publication. Had you set the column guides prior to opening a publication, every publication created on this computer would open with two columns.

Specifying columns allows you to start text for the second column, in this case *Waterfront location*, without having to press (TAB) or the spacebar to position the I-beam midline. In other words, when you are typing text in the second column and press (↵ ENTER), the I-beam will move automatically to the next line at the beginning of the second column.

**Creating Ruler Guides**

Ruler guides are vertical and horizontal lines that you use to help position text and graphics on the page. Recall from Chapter 2 that to create ruler guides, you drag the lines from the vertical and horizontal rulers. For this project you will need two horizontal ruler guides, 1½ inches and 6 inches, and one vertical ruler guide, 1¼ inches. Figure 3.9 shows the publication with both column and ruler guides.

If you remember from Chapter 2 how to create the ruler guides, create them and proceed to the next section. If you need a reminder of how to create ruler guides, follow these steps:

1. Point to the top (horizontal) ruler.

2. Drag the double-arrow pointer ↕ down until the line intersects 1½ inches on the left (vertical) ruler. Then release the mouse button.

3. Repeat steps 1 and 2 to create a second horizontal ruler guide at 6 inches.

4. Point to the left (vertical) ruler.

5. Press and drag the double-arrow pointer ↔ to the right until the line intersects 1¼ inches on the top (horizontal) ruler.

The ruler guides on your screen should match those in Figure 3.9. If you need to move a line, point to it, press the mouse button, and drag to reposition it.

*Troubleshooting Tip:* If the ruler guide does not move, click the View menu. If a check mark appears to the left of Lock Guides, click Lock Guides to remove the check. Remember that when Lock Guides is selected, once a ruler or column guide is positioned, it can't be moved. This feature prevents you from accidentally changing the guides. Deselecting the Lock Guides option allows you to reposition ruler guides.

Once the column guides on your screen match those in Figure 3.9, you should lock them to prevent inadvertently moving any of them.

6. Click the View menu.

7. Click Lock Guides.

Now that you have set the PageMaker defaults, created a new publication, and set it up, you are ready to actually compose the advertisement for The Inn at Portage Bay.

## CREATING THE PUBLICATION

The first things you'll do for the advertisement are to draw a border around the ad and enter the text in the first column, which includes changing the font size as well as drawing a horizontal line.

You'll create a double-line border around the publication by (1) selecting the pattern, or **stroke**, for the border line, (2) selecting the amount of shading, or **fill**, for the inside of the rectangle, and (3) drawing a rectangle.

To select the line's fill and stroke:

1. Click the Element menu.

2. Click Fill and Stroke.

3. Choose the 5pt double line, as shown in Figure 3.10.

Figure 3.10
Fill and Stroke dialog box

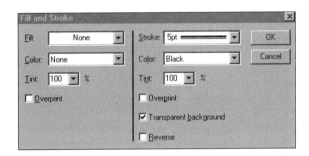

In a moment you will be drawing a double-line border. It might seem unusual to worry about fills when you are only drawing lines. However, from the PageMaker perspective, you will be drawing the exterior of a rectangle, and a rectangle is a graphic, which can have a fill. Graphics shading varies from no fill to partial gray fill to solid black fill. For this rectangle, you want no shading.

To select the amount of fill:

4. Look at Fill. Verify that None is selected.

5. When your Fill and Stroke dialog box matches the one shown in Figure 3.10, click OK.

You have used the Fill and Stroke command from the Element menu to set the specifications for the border. You could have also selected the specifications from the Fill command and the Stroke command separately in the Element menu.

To practice drawing a rectangle, you will draw, resize, delete, and then redraw the rectangle.

6. Click the rectangle tool ▢ in the Toolbox. The rectangle tool becomes highlighted, and the mouse pointer, when moved out of the Toolbox, changes from ▶ to +.

7. Position the pointer at the upper-left corner of the margin guides.

8. Press and drag the mouse to the lower-right corner of the margin guides.

9. Release the mouse button.

The rectangle should be visible as a border around your publication.

Notice that the box has handles at several places on each side. A **handle** is a small rectangle on a graphic that indicates the graphic is selected. You can move, resize, or delete selected items. Pointing to a place other than the handle with the pointer tool allows you to move the graphic. Pointing to a handle with the pointer tool allows you to resize the graphic. In this case, you can drag the handles at the midpoint of a line to change the length or width of the box. You can also drag the corner handles diagonally to resize the length and width of the box simultaneously and proportionally. Experiment now with moving, resizing, and deleting the rectangle.

10. Click the pointer tool in the Toolbox.

11. Select the box by clicking a line in any location.

12. Point to anywhere on the line except a handle.

13. Press the mouse button.

14. Drag the box to a new location.

15. When the box is where you want it, release the mouse button.

Next you'll try changing the size of the box.

16. Point to one of the handles.

17. Press the mouse button.

18. Drag the handle to make the box smaller. (Moving the handle inward reduces the size of the box; moving it outward enlarges the box.)

19. When the box is the size you want, release the mouse button.

20. Repeat steps 16 through 19 to enlarge the box.

Finally, you'll remove the border.

21. Make sure the double-line border is selected (has handles).

22. Press ( DELETE ).

You can also erase the border by (1) selecting the border and (2) pressing ( ← BACKSPACE ).

As you work, you might sometimes perform an action you didn't intend to, such as deleting the box. You can reverse your last action in PageMaker by selecting the Undo command from the Edit menu. The Undo feature works for many, although not all, PageMaker actions. To undo the deletion you just did:

1. Click the Edit menu.

2. Click Undo Clear.

Look at the Undo command again. The Undo feature is context-sensitive, that is, the choices (Undo Clear and Redo Clear) change, depending on what is appropriate with respect to your last action. You can undo your last action, which was restoring the deleted box.

1. Click the Edit menu.

2. Click Redo Clear.

Notice that the box again disappears from the publication. Re-create the border by following the abbreviated set of directions for creating the border listed below. If you need more detailed instructions, refer to the steps starting with "To select the line's fill and stroke" on page 61.

1. Click the rectangle tool ▢ in the Toolbox.

2. Select a Stroke and Fill.

3. Draw the border.

With the appropriate border on the publication, you are ready to enter the text in the first column.

Entering the
Heading

Recall that before you created this new publication, you set the default type specs to Arial 14. Now you will change them to Arial 30 in preparation for typing the heading, the only text in this publication not in Arial 14.

1. Click the text tool ⊤ in the Toolbox.

2. Click the Type menu.

3. Click Size.

4. Click 30. See Figure 3.11.

Figure 3.11
Selecting 30-point type

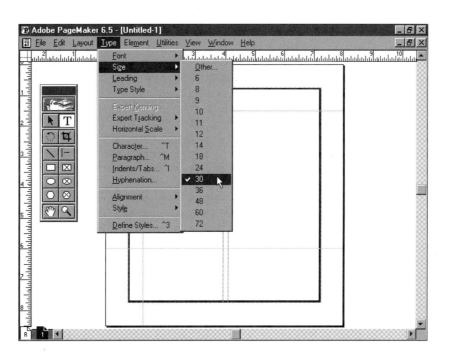

Based on the designer's layout, the words *The Inn at Portage Bay* need to start at the vertical ruler guideline. There are two methods for making this line of type align with the ruler guideline: you could use (TAB) or you could set the paragraph indent. Desktop publishers generally prefer the second method because it gives you more control, you don't have to press (TAB) for each paragraph, and changing the paragraph indent to another value is perceived as being easier.

To set the indent:

1. Click the Type menu.

2. Click Paragraph.

3. Type .5 for the Left Indent. See Figure 3.12.

**Figure 3.12**
Paragraph Specifications
dialog box

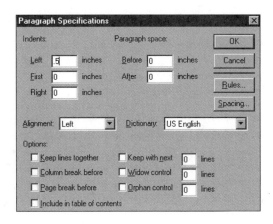

4. Click OK.

Now you're ready to start typing.

5. Position the I-beam as shown in Figure 3.13 and click the mouse button anywhere on that line.

**Figure 3.13**
Positioning the I-beam
for text

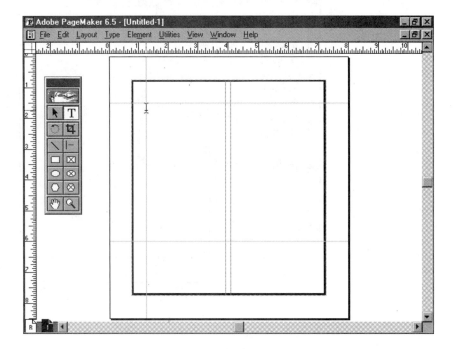

This inserts a vertical bar, called an **insertion point**, which shows where text will be placed. The insertion point is positioned 0.5 inch from the left margin.

6. Type *The Inn at.*

7. Press ⏎ ENTER once.

8. Type *Portage Bay.* Compare your screen to Figure 3.14.

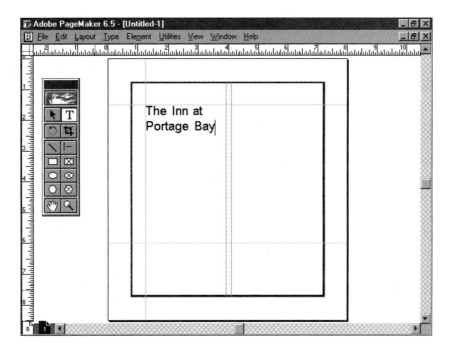

You have now entered the entire name of the Inn. If you need to reposition the text, click the pointer tool in the Toolbox, click the text block to select it, and drag the text to the proper location.

## Drawing the Horizontal Line

Below the resort name in the designer's layout is a horizontal line. To draw it you must select the constrained line tool from the Toolbox, select the correct line width from the Element menu (as seen in Figure 3.15), and then draw the line.

Figure 3.15
Element Stroke options
for drawing the
horizontal line

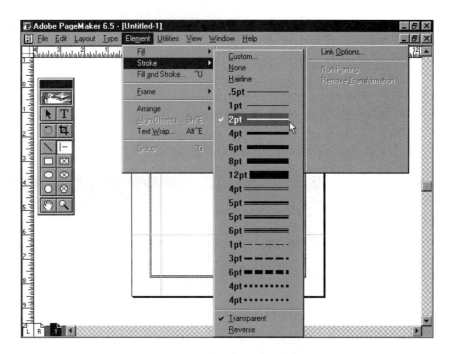

1. Click the constrained line tool |− in the Toolbox.

2. Click the Element menu.

3. Point to Stroke.

4. Click 2pt.

Draw a horizontal line far enough below the words *Portage Bay* so that the line doesn't "crash into" the words. Specifically, you want to avoid the line going through the descenders of the letters *g* and *y*.

5. Point to the left ruler guide.

6. Press and drag the mouse to the end of the word *Bay*.

7. Release the mouse button.

Notice that the line has handles on it, indicating it is still selected. If you want to delete the line, press either (DELETE) or (← BACKSPACE) and redraw the line. If you need to move the line to position it correctly, click the pointer tool in the Toolbox, point anywhere on the line except the handles, and move it to the correct location. If the line is in the correct place, click the mouse button anywhere off the line to deselect it.

8. Click the pointer tool �]k if you haven't already.

This will deselect the constrained line tool and keep you from inadvertently drawing little lines in unwanted places on the page. Clicking the pointer tool after drawing a line or graphic is good practice.

## TYPING THE 14-POINT TEXT

With the horizontal line in place, you are ready to type the rest of the text. First, you will change the page view to enlarge the area of the publication in which you will work. Second, you will select the text tool, verify the type specifications, and type the word *RESORT* in the first column. Third, you will type the list of features in the second column. Finally, you will type the lower part of the publication.

Changing the Page View

Recall from Chapter 2 that PageMaker allows you to adjust the view so you can see the complete publication or focus on a specific part of the page. When the publication is set to Fit in Window, meaning the complete publication can be viewed on the screen, you can't see the details on the page. When you enlarge the document setup so details are visible, you lose the ability to see the complete page layout. Because you can't view both detail and layout at the same time, you must switch between different views as the tasks demand.

For typing in the smaller 14-point type, you will want to change the view from the current Fit in Window to a view that shows more detail. Remember from Chapter 2 that the views range from Fit in Window through 400% Size, and that there are four methods for changing the view. You should choose the view and method that best suits your needs at any time during the creation of a publication. The next steps will review the methods for changing the view, and you should try all four. Later, as you need to change the view, choose the method you prefer.

Method 1—From the Pull-Down Menu

1. Point to Zoom To in the View menu, as shown in Figure 3.16.

Figure 3.16
Using the Zoom To option to select a different viewing size

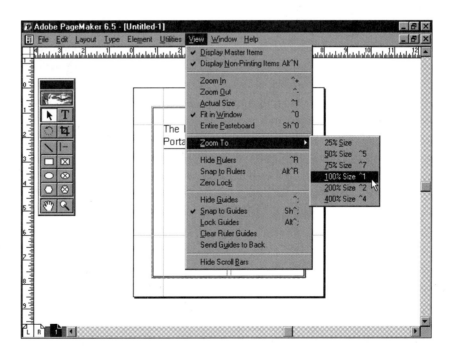

2. Click 100% Size.

3. Click the scroll bars until you can see the horizontal line you have just drawn and some space beneath it.

### Method 2—From the Pasteboard Using Shortcut Keys

1. Press (CTRL) and (0) (zero) at the same time.

Notice the shortcut keys in Figure 3.16 next to most commands. The ^ means to press (CTRL). After you have selected a command in the conventional way, try using the shortcut keys as your comfort level allows.

### Method 3—Using the Right Mouse Button

1. Point to the center of the space you want to see in detail—in this case, to a spot near the middle of where you will type the word *RESORT*.

2. Right-click (click the right mouse button) and then click 75% Size.

To toggle between Fit in Window and Actual Size (100%), press (SHIFT) while you right-click. When switching to Actual Size, the place you right-click becomes centered in the publication window.

### Method 4—Using the Zoom Tool

1. Click the zoom tool 🔍 in the Toolbox.

The pointer changes to ⊕. The + in the magnifying glass means that the zoom tool will increase the size of your image.

2. Click to magnify the area.

Each subsequent click will take you through the options on the zoom list—25%, 50%, 75%, 100%, 200%, and 400%—starting with your present view.

Similarly, to reduce the view, press (CTRL) and click. The magnifying glass pointer changes to ⊖. The – in the magnifying glass indicates that the zoom tool will decrease the size of your image. To toggle between increasing and reducing size, press the (CTRL) key.

You can also magnify a portion of a page:

3. Click the zoom tool 🔍 in the Toolbox.

4. Drag to draw a box around the area you want to magnify.

5. Click the mouse button.

Depending on the size of the space you want to see, your view can enlarge as much as 731%, almost double the 400% Size available from the View menu. The magnifying glass pointer changes to 🔍 when you have reached the maximum magnification or reduction size. Now, zoom to the area below *Portage Bay*, where you will type *RESORT*. Use either 75% Size or 100% Size.

Before you type the word *RESORT*, you will verify that the default type specifications you selected before you opened the publication are active.

1. Click the text tool **T** in the Toolbox.

2. Select Size from the Type menu.

3. Verify that the selected font is Arial 14. Change the size if necessary.

With the font back at Arial 14, you can type the word *RESORT* below the horizontal line.

Typing Centered Text

The word *RESORT* will be centered in the first column below the horizontal line, as shown in Figure 3.17. You'll change the alignment first and then type the word.

Figure 3.17
Typing RESORT

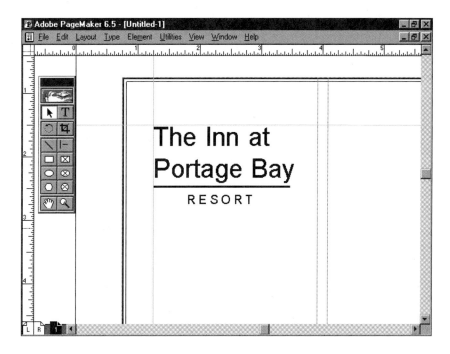

1. Click below the horizontal line to place an insertion point.

2. Select Alignment from the Type menu and click Align Center.

3. Select Paragraph from the Type menu. Make sure Left Indent is set to 0. Change it if it is not.

4. Press ⟨CAPS LOCK⟩ to type in all uppercase letters.

5. Type *R E S O R T* (pressing the spacebar once between each letter).

The next part of the advertisement for the Inn that you will complete is entering the list of the Inn's features in the second column.

To move from one column to the other, simply position the I-beam in the second column and click the mouse button.

1. Click the scroll bars to adjust the view to display the top of column 2.

2. Position the I-beam in the second column on the same line as the words *The Inn at*.

3. Click to insert the I-beam.

Now that the I-beam is in the second column, you will again set Paragraph Specifications. To indent the list of features the proper amount (so there is space between the bullets and the text), you will type *0.15* in Indents, Left, and to avoid double-spacing manually, you will type *0.2* in Paragraph space, After. By specifying paragraph space, rather than double-spacing, you are working less in a "typewriter" mode and more in a "desktop publisher" mode as well as gaining the flexibility to work with less than the space of a full line. You will also change the Alignment to Left, if necessary.

1. Select Paragraph from the Type menu.

2. Enter *0.15* as the Left Indent and *0.2* as the Paragraph space After, and then make sure Left is set as the Alignment, as shown in Figure 3.18.

**Figure 3.18**
Completed Paragraph
Specifications dialog box

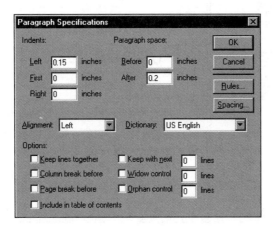

3. When your dialog box matches the one shown in Figure 3.18, click OK.

4. Press (CAPS LOCK) to turn off the uppercase mode.

5. Using Figure 3.19 as a guide, type the list of features. If you make a typing error, press (← BACKSPACE) to erase it, and then retype the text.

Figure 3.19
List of features

Waterfront location

224 deluxe guest rooms

Fireplaces, suites

Meeting rooms

Indoor tennis, pool, jacuzzi, fitness center

Championship golf course

Notice that the phrase *fitness center* appears on two lines and leaves the word *center* all alone, as shown in Figure 3.20.

Figure 3.20
Adjusting the text block to force "fitness" to second line

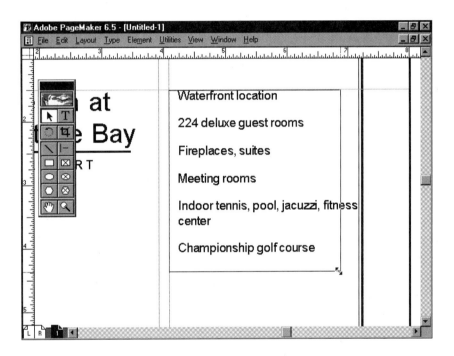

The list would look better and be easier to read if *fitness* and *center* were on the same line. PageMaker gives you the ability to control the size of **text blocks,** which are rectangular areas that contain text. In order to move *fitness* to the second line so the whole phrase is together:

1. Click the pointer tool ▶ in the Toolbox.

2. Click anywhere in the list to select the text block.

3. Drag the lower-right text block handle until the right margin moves into the middle of the word *fitness.* See Figure 3.20.

4. Release the mouse button.

You will learn more about controlling text blocks in Chapter 4, but for now you have improved the appearance of the list.

Before you place the square bullets before each item in the list of features, you'll enter the rest of the text in the advertisement. To type the word *RESERVATIONS* and the telephone number and URL in the first column:

1. Use the grabber hand tool ⬛ to adjust the view until you can see the first column below the 6-inch horizontal ruler guide.

2. Click the text tool **T** in the Toolbox, and then click the I-beam in the first line below the ruler guide to place an insertion point.

3. On your own, verify that the Paragraph Specifications are set to 0.5 for Left Indent.

4. Press (CAPS LOCK) to activate uppercase mode.

5. Type *RESERVATIONS* and press (↵ ENTER).

6. Type *1-800-555-PORT* and press (↵ ENTER).

7. Press (CAPS LOCK) to deactivate uppercase mode.

8. Type *http://www.portagebay.com.*

You will be typing the address in the second column to line up with the last two lines of the Reservations information. Lining up the bottom lines of each section will give the two sides a better balance. To type the address in the second column:

9. Adjust the view so you can see the second column below the 6-inch horizontal ruler guide.

10. Click the I-beam in the second column on the same line as the text *RESERVATIONS*. Press (↵ ENTER) to move to the second line.

11. Set the Paragraph Specifications to 0.15 for Left Indent and Paragraph space After to 0 if necessary.

12. Type *Sunset Hill Road* and press (↵ ENTER).

13. Type *Portage Bay, WA.*

Compare your publication with Figure 3.1. Pull a horizontal ruler guide to the bottom of the text in the two columns and adjust one of the text blocks as necessary so the text in both columns sits on the horizontal ruler guide. Refer to Figure 3.21.

Figure 3.21
Adjusting text for same
bottom alignment

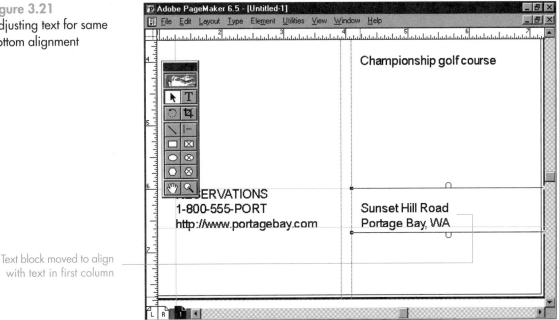

Text block moved to align
with text in first column

Make sure every word is spelled correctly and is positioned in the right place. If you need to make changes, do so before adding bullets to the list of features.

## ADDING SQUARE BULLETS

In order to help emphasize the list of the Inn's features, the design calls for a bullet before each item in the list. A **bullet** is a graphic, such as a filled circle or square, that appears to the left of a line of text.

### Drawing a Square Bullet

The next step is to create one small, solid-black square for the bullet to the left of *Waterfront location* to highlight that feature. Then you will copy the bullet once and paste it five times, once next to each item in the list.

You want to make sure each square bullet lines up evenly with its line of text. To do this, you'll set up horizontal ruler guides that touch the baseline of each line of text. In order to ensure that you place the ruler guides precisely, you'll magnify the page view.

1. Adjust the view to show the list of features enlarged. *Hint:* Use 200% Size.

2. Pull down a horizontal ruler guide to align with the baseline of each line of text in the list. See Figure 3.22.

Figure 3.22
Baseline ruler guides
placed in preparation for
drawing the square
bullets

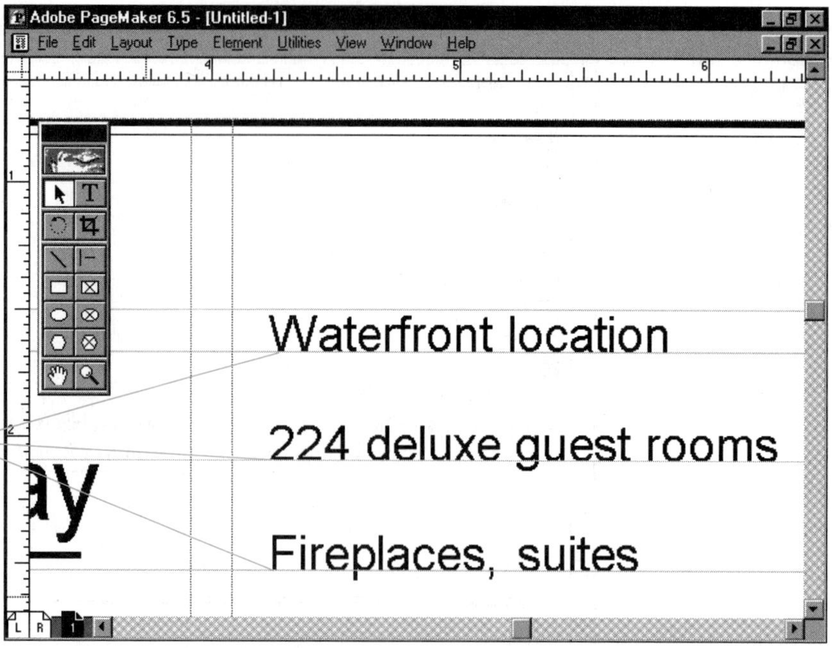

```
Adobe PageMaker 6.5 - [Untitled-1]
File  Edit  Layout  Type  Element  Utilities  View  Window  Help
```

Waterfront location

224 deluxe guest rooms

Fireplaces, suites

Pull horizontal ruler guides
to align with baselines
of text

With the ruler guidelines in place, you can draw the first square bullet next to the first item in the list. To create the filled, square bullet:

1. Select Fill from the Element menu.

2. Click Solid.

3. Select the rectangle tool ▣ in the Toolbox. The pointer changes to a crossbar +.

4. Position the crossbar + at the lower-left corner of the box created by the column guides, and the ruler guides, next to the words *Waterfront location*.

5. Hold down (SHIFT) while you do the next step. This will ensure you draw a square; otherwise, you will draw a rectangle.

6. Drag the crossbar + diagonally to the upper-right corner of where the square will go.

7. Release the mouse button and (SHIFT).

The square is slightly taller than the cap height of the text. Depending on how you drew your guide, the bullet might not fill the guidelines completely. The square bullet has handles on it, indicating it is selected. If the bullet is not positioned correctly or is not sized correctly, press either (DELETE) or (← BACKSPACE) to erase it. Repeat the steps above to create a new square bullet. When the square is correctly positioned and sized, continue with the next section, leaving the square selected.

## Copying the Square Bullet

This advertisement needs six square bullets to highlight the various amenities the resort offers. You could draw five additional bullets, but each could wind up a different size. A better technique is to draw one bullet, as you have already done, copy it once, and paste it five times to guarantee that each bullet will be exactly the same.

1. Click the pointer tool  in the Toolbox.

2. Select the square bullet by pointing to it and clicking.

3. Select Copy from the Edit menu.

This command duplicates the selected item, in this case a bullet, to a holding area called the **Clipboard**.

4. Select Paste from the Edit menu.

This command places the last item (text or graphics) copied to the Clipboard on the PageMaker publication.

Notice that the handles now appear around the pasted square bullet. When you paste, the pasted object will appear either on top of the original object that was copied or in the center of the screen if the original object is not in your screen view.

5. Move the new bullet to the correct location by (1) pointing to the center of the bullet, being careful not to point to a handle, and (2) dragging the bullet to the correct location—to the left of *224 deluxe guest rooms* below the first bullet. See Figure 3.23.

Figure 3.23
Pasting a square bullet

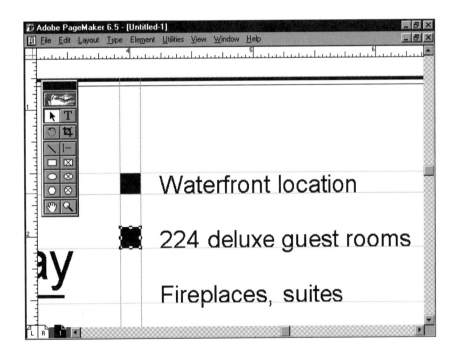

The ruler guides, along with the activated Snap to Guides setting, help anchor the pasted graphic in precise alignment with the original bullet.

Repeat steps 3, 4, and 5 four times to paste a bullet next to each remaining feature on the list. Make sure you use the baseline ruler guides you set earlier to align the bullets with the text.

You have almost finished the advertisement for The Inn at Portage Bay. Save your publication as *Advertisement* using the steps described in Chapter 2, along with any special considerations for your computer. After you return to the PageMaker screen, notice that the title bar now includes your publication's name.

There are four ways to save your publication from the File menu: Close, Save, Save As, and Exit. If your publication is unnamed because it is a new publication, all these selections will open the Save Publication dialog box. The table in Figure 3.24 summarizes the functions of these five commands.

**Figure 3.24**
Save commands from the File menu

| Command | Function |
| --- | --- |
| Close | Prompts you to save if unsaved changes have been made; closes the publication; returns to the PageMaker desktop. |
| Save | Saves the publication with the same name it already has; performs a fast save; for an unnamed publication, opens the Save Publication dialog box; returns to the publication. |
| Save As | Saves the publication; allows you to save with a different name, save on a different drive, or make a copy of the publication; compresses your file, making its file size as small as possible; returns to the publication. |
| Save All | Press Shift and click File, Save All; saves all open publications. |
| Exit | Prompts you if you have not saved changes; for unsaved changes you want to save, opens the Save Publication dialog box; closes the publication and exits PageMaker; returns to Windows. |

## PRINTING YOUR PUBLICATION

Your final step for the advertisement is to print a copy of the finished publication. Then you'll exit PageMaker.

Because the publication is a nonstandard size, it's a good idea to include printer's marks when you print. **Printer's marks** are small lines that indicate the corners of a publication, which are used to align the document for printing and trimming. You should include printer's marks any time your publication is a nonstandard size.

1. Make sure your computer is connected to a printer and the printer is ready.

**2.** Select Print from the File menu.

The Print Document dialog box appears. Follow any special instructions for your installation.

**3.** Click Options.

The Print Options dialog box appears.

**4.** Click the Printer's marks check box.

**5.** Click Print.

Close your publication and exit PageMaker by selecting Exit from the File menu. Do not save your publication again.

## SUMMARY

Congratulations! You have created a complete publication from start to finish. In the process you have used several PageMaker features: drawing a border, using different fonts, setting paragraph specifications, copying, and pasting. You planned the publication, drew guidelines, created the publication, and then saved and printed it. With minimal instruction, you have used many common features. In subsequent chapters, you will explore many of these features in more depth.

## QUESTIONS

1. Use the Help menu to answer the following questions.

    a. Explain multiple pasting. What are the keystrokes for multiple pasting?

    b. There are two choices for saving a file, faster and
    _____.

    c. When you copy text or a graphic, where does it get stored?

    d. What is the maximum number of ruler guides you may have in any one publication?

2. Explain the purpose of white space.

3. Why is it a good idea to set defaults before opening a publication?

4. Explain the difference between an application and a publication default. Give an example of how the same selection will have a different impact, depending on the kind of default it is.

5. Explain the differences between the on and off settings for Lock Guides.

6. Why would you want to have the Snap to Guides option selected?

7. How do the New and Open commands differ?

8. What two commands display the Document Setup dialog box?

9. What is the purpose of column guides?

10. Can column guides be reset? If yes, how?

11. What is the purpose of ruler guides?

12. How can you tell when a graphic is selected?

13. In what ways can you alter a selected graphic?

14. Explain the two ways to erase a graphic.

15. Describe the four methods for changing the page view. Which method do you prefer? Why?

16. Name the four ways to save a publication. Compare and contrast them.

17. Use the Appendix of this book to name the menu in which you find each of the following:

    a. Character

    b. Multiple Paste

    c. Column Guides

    d. Document Setup

    e. Find

## PROJECTS

1. Create a new publication and draw a square-corner rectangle border for a page using a 1-point line and 10% shading. Delete the figure using (DELETE).

2. Create a new publication and draw a square-corner rectangle border using a 6-point line and 40% shading. Delete the figure using (← BACKSPACE).

3. Using Windows Explorer, copy the Advertisement file you created in this chapter. Rename the copied file Project 3-3. Open the Project 3-3 file. Make several changes to the publication, saving the file after each change. Then, use Save As to save the publication with the file name Project 3-3a. Using Windows Explorer, compare the file sizes of Project 3-3 and Project 3-3a. Reread the description of Save and Save As. What conclusions can you draw?

4. Using the specifications in Figure 3.25, create a business reply card.

**Figure 3.25**
Project 3.4—Business
reply card
(4⅛" x 5⅛")
Margins: 0.5 inches
Orientation: wide

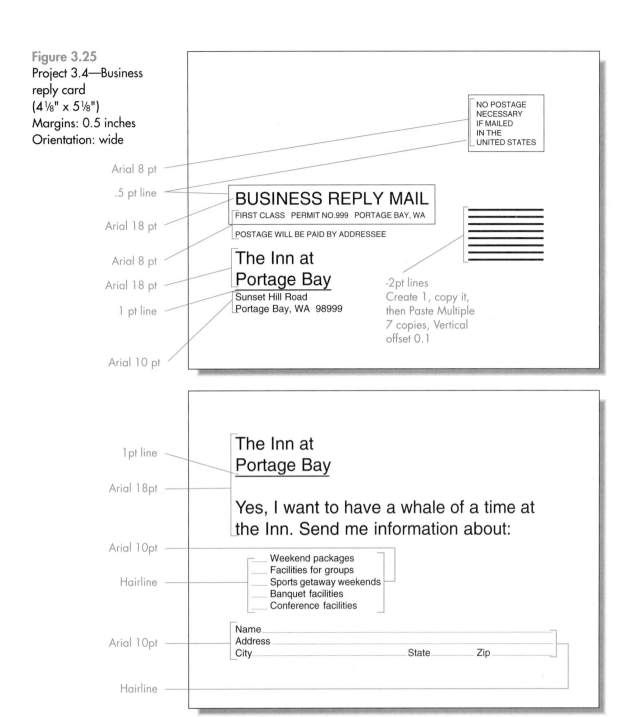

Arial 8 pt

NO POSTAGE
NECESSARY
IF MAILED
IN THE
UNITED STATES

.5 pt line

## BUSINESS REPLY MAIL

FIRST CLASS   PERMIT NO.999   PORTAGE BAY, WA

Arial 18 pt

POSTAGE WILL BE PAID BY ADDRESSEE

Arial 8 pt

## The Inn at
## Portage Bay

Arial 18 pt

Sunset Hill Road
Portage Bay, WA  98999

1 pt line

-2pt lines
Create 1, copy it,
then Paste Multiple
7 copies, Vertical
offset 0.1

Arial 10 pt

---

1pt line

## The Inn at
## Portage Bay

Arial 18pt

## Yes, I want to have a whale of a time at
## the Inn. Send me information about:

Arial 10pt

Weekend packages
Facilities for groups
Sports getaway weekends
Banquet facilities
Conference facilities

Hairline

Arial 10pt

Name
Address
City                                          State          Zip

Hairline

5. The Inn wants a set of stickers to use on items such as the packet of information left in each room. Using the specifications in Figure 3.26, create the generic sticker that can be used on various items at the Inn.

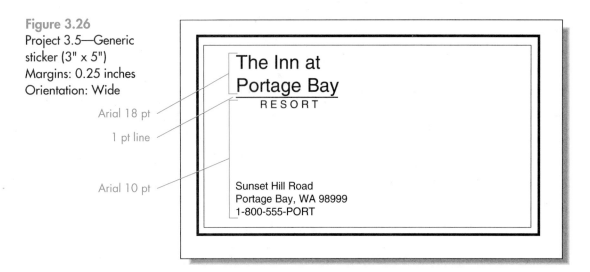

6. Using the specifications in Figure 3.27, create a business card for the Inn. Use the name on the card or your own name. Use two columns; second column is right justified.

7. The Inn needs some stationery and envelopes made. Using the specifications in Figure 3.28, create a letterhead and envelope for the Inn.

**Figure 3.28**
Letterhead
(8½" x 11")
Margins: 0.75 inches
Orientation: Tall
and envelope
(9½" x 4⅛")
Margins: 0.75 inches
Orientation: Wide

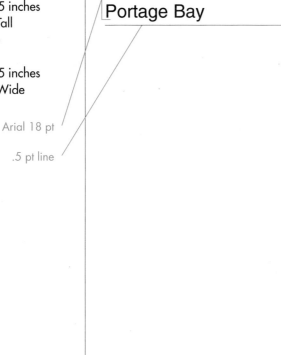

# The Inn at
# Portage Bay

Sunset Hill Road
Portage Bay, WA 98999

1-800-555-PORT

Arial 18 pt

.5 pt line

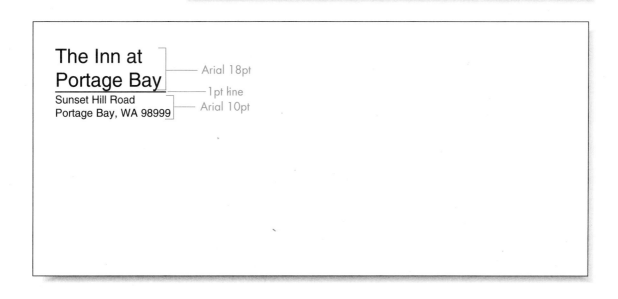

# The Inn at
# Portage Bay

Sunset Hill Road
Portage Bay, WA 98999

Arial 18pt

1pt line

Arial 10pt

8. The Inn leaves a pad of paper on the desk in each room. Using the specifications in Figure 3.29, create the master copy, which the Inn can duplicate. To draw rounded corners, select Rounded Corners from the Element menu, and select the last option in the first row.

**Figure 3.29**
Project 3.8—Pad
of paper
(4½" x 5½")
Margins: 0.05 inches
Orientation: Tall

Arial 18 pt

1 pt line

Arial 10 pt

Rounded Corners
from Element menu

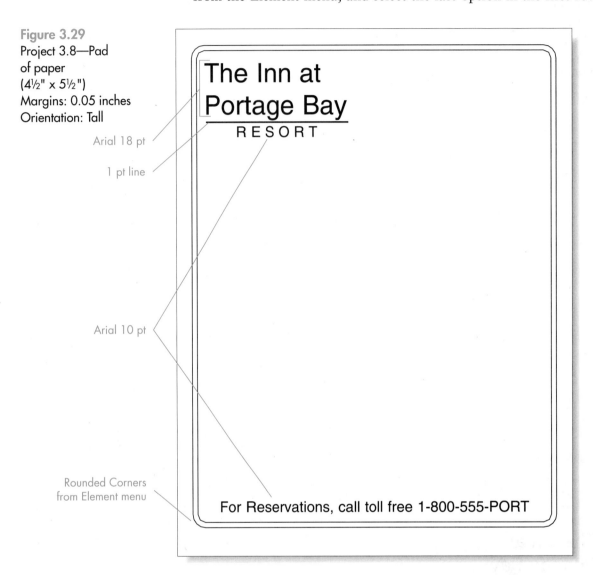

The Inn at
Portage Bay
R E S O R T

For Reservations, call toll free 1-800-555-PORT

9. Create the Ambassador of Service Nomination Card shown in Figure 3.30. The Inn saves money by printing two cards per page and cutting the sheet once.

   a. Create the left half of an 8½" x 11" card.

   b. Save the publication.

   c. Copy the entire card by first choosing Select All from the Edit menu, and then copying and pasting the selection.

   d. Point to the selected object (that you just pasted) and drag the entire pasted group to the right column. Align with the left column. If you make a mistake, close the publication without saving, open the saved publication from part b and try again.

Figure 3.30
Project 3.9—
Ambassador of Service
Nomination Card
(8½" x 11")
Margins 0.5 inches

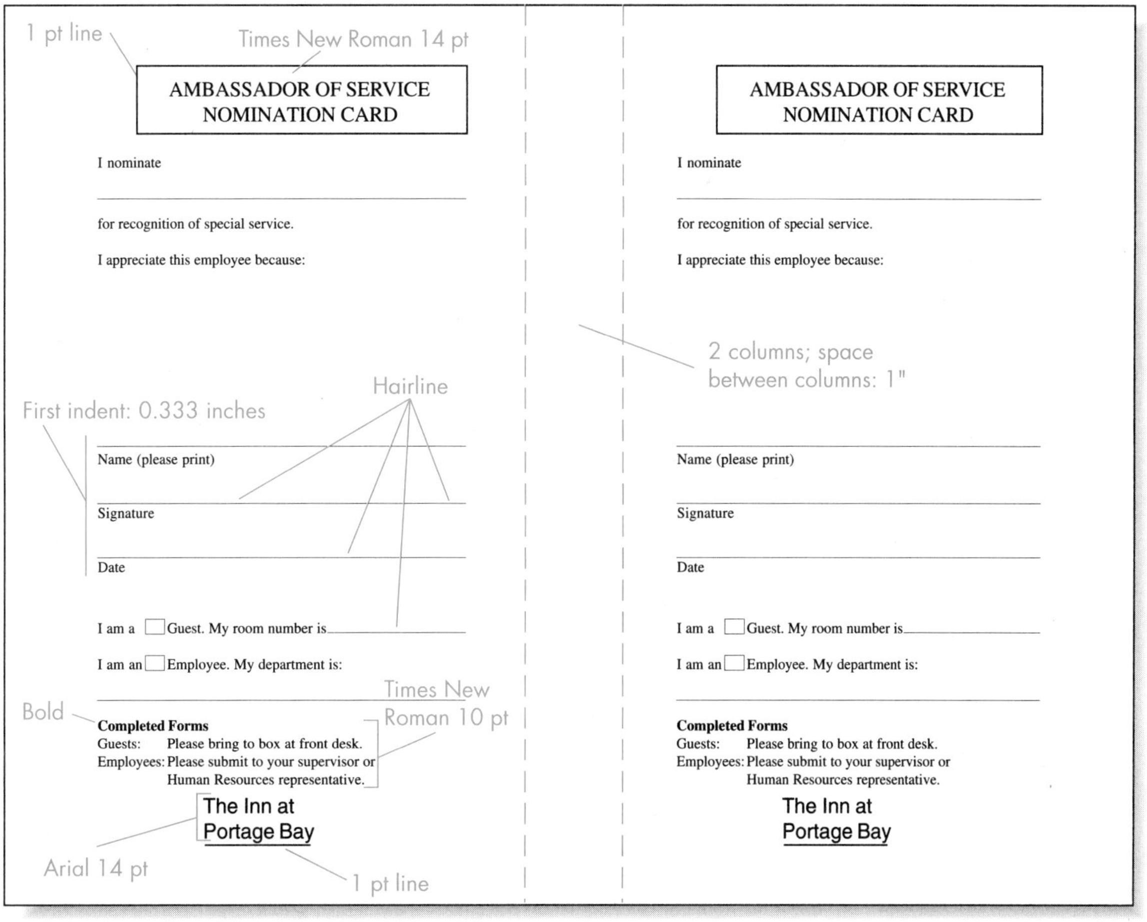

10. Create the Room Service Breakfast Order form shown in Figure 3.31.

11. Create your own business card.

12. Create your own letterhead and envelope.

**Figure 3.31**
Project 3.10—Room
service breakfast
order form
(5" x 11")

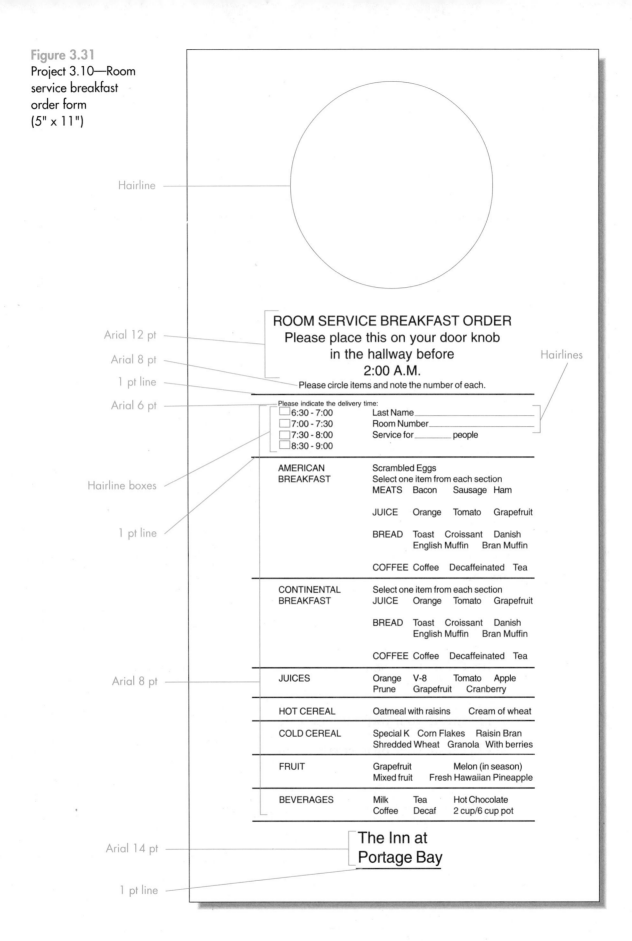

Hairline

Arial 12 pt

Arial 8 pt

1 pt line

Arial 6 pt

Hairline boxes

1 pt line

Arial 8 pt

Arial 14 pt

1 pt line

Hairlines

**ROOM SERVICE BREAKFAST ORDER**
**Please place this on your door knob**
**in the hallway before**
**2:00 A.M.**

Please circle items and note the number of each.

Please indicate the delivery time:
☐ 6:30 - 7:00      Last Name_____
☐ 7:00 - 7:30      Room Number_____
☐ 7:30 - 8:00      Service for_____ people
☐ 8:30 - 9:00

| AMERICAN BREAKFAST | Scrambled Eggs<br>Select one item from each section<br>MEATS   Bacon   Sausage   Ham<br><br>JUICE   Orange   Tomato   Grapefruit<br><br>BREAD   Toast   Croissant   Danish<br>English Muffin   Bran Muffin<br><br>COFFEE   Coffee   Decaffeinated   Tea |
| --- | --- |
| CONTINENTAL BREAKFAST | Select one item from each section<br>JUICE   Orange   Tomato   Grapefruit<br><br>BREAD   Toast   Croissant   Danish<br>English Muffin   Bran Muffin<br><br>COFFEE   Coffee   Decaffeinated   Tea |
| JUICES | Orange   V-8   Tomato   Apple<br>Prune   Grapefruit   Cranberry |
| HOT CEREAL | Oatmeal with raisins   Cream of wheat |
| COLD CEREAL | Special K   Corn Flakes   Raisin Bran<br>Shredded Wheat   Granola   With berries |
| FRUIT | Grapefruit   Melon (in season)<br>Mixed fruit   Fresh Hawaiian Pineapple |
| BEVERAGES | Milk   Tea   Hot Chocolate<br>Coffee   Decaf   2 cup/6 cup pot |

**The Inn at**
**Portage Bay**

# CHAPTER 4

# Working with Text

Upon completion of this chapter you will be able to:

- Import text onto a publication
- Use the text tool and the pointer tool to select a portion of text
- Move, copy, and delete text
- Change the appearance of text and paragraphs
- Work with text blocks
- Draw frames
- Use the Control palette
- Create drop caps
- Rotate, flip, and slant text

In previous chapters you learned how to create a PageMaker publication. You know how to use guides to align objects on a publication and how to type in text. You also know how to save and print a publication. Although you can develop many different kinds of documents using the skills you have learned so far, you will often want more flexibility to edit text and control a publication's appearance. For example, after placing text, you might want to move or delete a large portion of it, or you might want to change the text's appearance by right-justifying each paragraph. In this chapter, you'll learn how to import text onto a publication, and how to modify and manipulate the text after it is placed.

PageMaker provides three ways to add text to a publication. Assuming you have set up the publication page with the desired margins and column and ruler guides, you can enter text onto a page by (1) typing text using the text tool, (2) using the copy/paste process, or (3) importing text from a word processing program.

You learned the first process—typing text directly onto the publication—in Chapter 1. Recall that with this method you select the text tool, position the I-beam at the location where you want the text to appear, click the mouse button to set the insertion point, and type the text. Because PageMaker is not a word processing program, you should use this method only to type small amounts of text, such as titles and headings, and to edit text by inserting and deleting words and correcting spelling errors. For typing large amounts of text, PageMaker has a Story Editor with word processing capabilities, which you will learn more about in Chapter 11.

The second process is similar to the steps for copying and pasting in any word processing program. Because PageMaker is a Windows program, you can copy text from other Windows programs. For example, you could copy a part of a document created in a word processing program, such as Microsoft Word, to a PageMaker publication.

The third process—importing—is a more efficient way to transfer all the text from a file in another program onto a PageMaker publication.

## IMPORTING TEXT

When you import text from a word processing program, you choose the Place command from the File menu and select the file you want to transfer. Then you position the text icon on the document setup or Pasteboard and click the mouse button. All the text from the selected file transfers onto the PageMaker publication. Whenever you import text, you must be concerned with the compatibility between PageMaker and your word processing program. Several word processing programs create files that require no changes when correctly imported into PageMaker. Other programs create files that are incompatible with PageMaker or that must be converted to a format compatible with PageMaker before you import them onto a publication.

In the following steps you will practice importing and editing text. The student files used with this book include a document created in Word and saved with the file name Business Center. Figure 4.1 shows this document, which is an announcement to the employees of The Inn at Portage Bay about the new business center.

Figure 4.1
Business Center
document

Business Center

THE INN AT PORTAGE BAY is proud to announce the opening of our new
Business Center. This facility will be available to our guests starting on Monday
the 15th. The services that will be provided are explained below.

To acquaint you with the center, there will be an orientation on Wednesday the
10th at 9:00am and 3:00pm.

The Business Center will provide a full range of secretarial services, including
taking minutes of meetings; preparing and copying documents, overhead
transparencies, and slides; and desktop publishing. We are linked to
CompuServe, Internet, and Prodigy.

The center has state-of-the-art equipment, including a fax machine, personal
computers (IBM-compatible, Macintosh) equipped with CD-ROM drives and
modems, color laser printers, and scanners. The most popular applications are
available.

Location:  Room 144
Hours:  M-F 7:00am to 5:00pm
Phone ext:  2311

Start the PageMaker program and import this document onto a new page.

1. Start the PageMaker program.

2. Select New from the File menu.

CTRL N

Check the Document Setup dialog box and verify that the settings are:

| | |
|---|---|
| Page size: | Letter |
| Number of pages: | 1 |
| Margins: | Inside 1" |
| | Outside, Top, and Bottom 0.75" |

3. Click OK.

4. If necessary, click the maximize button in the upper-right corner to
enlarge the publication window.

Check the blank page. You should not see any column guides. If there
are multiple columns, select Column Guides from the Layout menu and
change the number of columns to 1.

Before placing this document, you need to select Arial as the font and 12
as the font size—the intended type specifications for this document.

5. Point to Font in the Type menu and click Arial.

6. Point to Size in the Type menu and click 12.

7. Select Place from the File menu.

CTRL D

The Place dialog box appears so that you can select the file you want to
import. The Place command imports a copy of the document, not the
original, onto the publication.

**8.** Click Business Center and click Open.

The pointer changes to the text icon ▤, which represents the text to be placed.

**9.** Position ▤ as shown in Figure 4.2.

Figure 4.2
Positioning the text icon

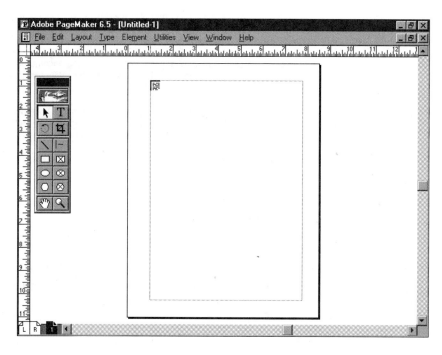

**10.** Click the mouse button.

The imported text is placed on the page. Now use the View menu to switch to 75% Size.

CTRL 7

**11.** Point to Zoom To in the View menu and click 75% Size.

**12.** If necessary, use the scroll bars to duplicate the view shown in Figure 4.3.

Figure 4.3
Viewing the document

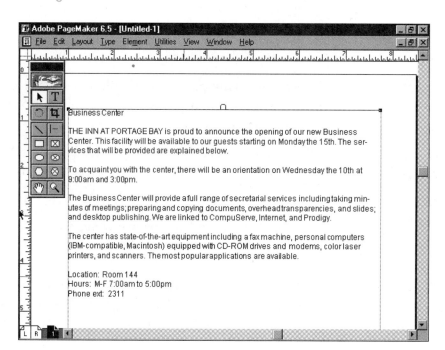

Your document might look slightly different from the one shown in Figure 4.3, because the type size will vary with different kinds of monitors.

## SELECTING TEXT

PageMaker provides several ways to select a portion of text. You can use the pointer tool to select blocks of text, which you will do later in this chapter, or you can use the text tool. Text selected with the text tool is highlighted onscreen.

One method of selecting text is to place the I-beam at the beginning of the text you want to select, hold down the mouse button, and drag the I-beam to highlight the desired text. Complete the following to select the words *Business Center*.

1. Click the text tool **T** in the Toolbox.

2. Position the I-beam to the left of the word *Business*. See Figure 4.4.

Figure 4.4
Selecting text by
dragging the I-beam

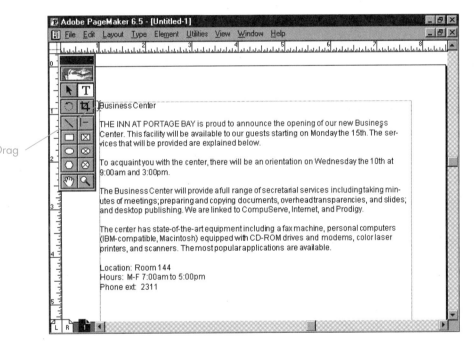

3. Hold down the mouse button and slowly drag the mouse across the words *Business Center*.

4. Release the mouse button.

At this point you could move, copy, replace, or delete the highlighted text. To deselect the text (remove the highlight), simply click a blank area of the screen.

5. Position the I-beam in a blank area and click the mouse button.

You can use this **drag method** to select any portion of continuous text. Complete the following to select the first paragraph.

6. Position the I-beam to the left of the word *THE* in the first paragraph.

7. Hold down the mouse button and drag the mouse to highlight the entire paragraph. Then release the mouse button.

8. Click a blank area to remove the highlight.

Another method for selecting text is to use the text tool to point to a word or paragraph and then double-click to select the word or triple-click to select the paragraph. First try selecting a word using this method.

9. Position the I-beam on the word *BAY* and double-click the mouse button.

The word *BAY* and the space after it are highlighted.

10. Click a blank area to remove the highlight.

Now select the entire paragraph.

11. Position the I-beam on the word *BAY* and triple-click the mouse button.

The entire paragraph is highlighted.

12. On your own, deselect the text.

The previous methods of selecting text use the text tool and allow you to select a part or all of the text. You can also use the Select All command from the Edit menu to highlight all the text at once. To use this command you must first click the text tool on any text.

13. Click any text on the page.

( CTRL )( A )  14. Choose Select All from the Edit menu.

Notice that all the text is highlighted.

15. Deselect the text.

You'll need to select text in order to manipulate it.

## MOVING, COPYING, AND DELETING TEXT

Now that you know how to select text, you can practice using the text editing functions, which include moving, copying, and deleting text.

Moving Text

When you move text, you change its location on the publication by cutting the text you want to move (placing it on the Clipboard) and then pasting it from the Clipboard to a new location. Start by moving the second paragraph of the Business Center file to the end of the document.

**1.** Highlight the second paragraph, including the blank line above it. See Figure 4.5.

**Figure 4.5**
Selecting text to be moved

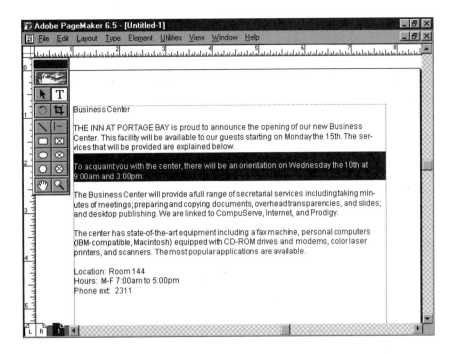

CTRL X **2.** Select Cut from the Edit menu.

**3.** Position the I-beam at the bottom of the document. See Figure 4.6.

**Figure 4.6**
Positioning the I-beam

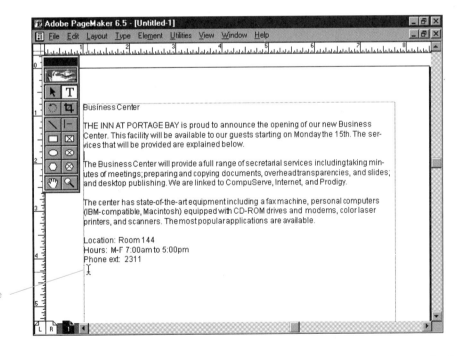

point here

**4.** Click an insertion point. Notice that the vertical bar moves to the left margin.

CTRL V **5.** Select Paste from the Edit menu.

The second paragraph is pasted onto the page at the insertion point.

The **copy** process allows you to place a duplicate of the selected text on the Clipboard and then paste it in two or more locations on the publication. Practice this function by copying the title *Business Center* to the bottom of the page, as shown in Figure 4.7.

Figure 4.7
Copying the title
*Business Center*

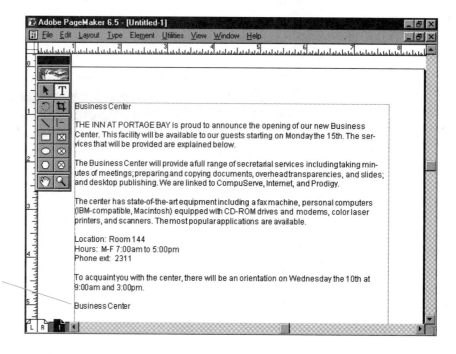

1. Highlight *Business Center* (but not the blank space following the phrase).

2. Select Copy from the Edit menu.

3. Position the I-beam at the bottom of the document, one line below the paragraph you just moved.

4. Click an insertion point. (The vertical bar moves to the left margin.)

5. Select Paste from the Edit menu.

The text is duplicated and the highlight disappears. Notice that the vertical line is at the end of the words *Business Center*. If you continue to select Paste, the text will be copied wherever the insertion point is located. Copy the text three more times.

6. Select Paste from the Edit menu three more times.

| Deleting Text | Sometimes you'll want to remove text that appears on a publication. The Clear command from the Edit menu allows you to **clear**, or delete, selected text. You will practice this function by deleting the line of *Business Center* from the bottom of the publication. |

1. Highlight all four instances of the words *Business Center* at the bottom of the publication.

`DELETE`

2. Select Clear from the Edit menu.

The highlighted text is removed from the page. If you change your mind about deleting text, you can replace it with the Undo command in the Edit menu.

3. Click the Edit menu.

Notice that the first option is Undo Edit. The command name changes to reflect your last action.

`CTRL` `Z`

4. Click the Undo Edit command.

The text reappears in the same location and is still highlighted. The Undo Edit command changes to Redo Edit, which you can use to again clear the selected text. The Undo and Redo commands work with the Cut, Copy, Paste, and Clear commands. Now remove the text permanently.

`CTRL` `Z`

5. Select Redo Edit from the Edit menu.

Besides editing the text on a publication, you can also control how the lines and letters are spaced.

## WORKING WITH LINE AND CHARACTER SPACING

In any publication, you are concerned with how the text appears. That is, you want to ensure that the text is set in an appropriate type style and size, with complementary spacing between characters, words, and paragraphs. Earlier, you used the Character Specifications dialog box to change fonts and type size, and the Type menu to change type styles (bold, italic, and so forth). Now you will change the spacing between lines and between characters.

| Changing Line Spacing | Figure 4.8 shows the Type menu and the Leading command. **Leading** (pronounced "ledding") is the measurement of the vertical spacing between the base of one line (an imaginary line upon which text rests, called the **baseline**) and the base of the following line. Leading is measured in points, and the default setting is 120% of the largest type size on a line. (Remember, you can override any default setting.) For example, if the type size is 10 point, the default leading will be 12 point. |

Figure 4.8

Leading command in the
Type menu

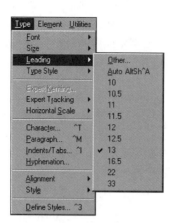

Figure 4.9 shows three examples of 12-point type with different leading values. The first example, 12-point type with 12-point leading, allows the **ascender** (part of a lowercase letter that extends above the body of the letter) and **descender** (part of a lowercase letter that extends below the body of the letter) of individual letters on different lines to touch. Notice how the descender on the *p* touches the ascender on the *T*. Obviously then, if the leading is the same as the type size, characters may touch. The second example shows 12-point type with 14.4-point leading, which is the default spacing, 120%. The third example shows 12-point type with 18-point leading, which leaves a lot of space between the lines.

Figure 4.9

12-point type with
different leading values

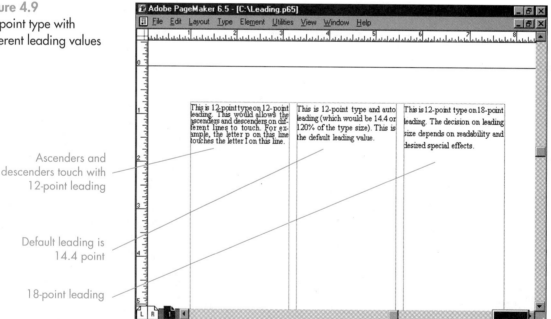

Ascenders and
descenders touch with
12-point leading

Default leading is
14.4 point

18-point leading

The decision on how much leading to use is based on readability as well as on special design effects you want to create. Generally, a larger type size requires less leading. Also, if you are using all uppercase characters, which will have no descenders, you might want to specify a leading smaller than the type size.

To illustrate leading you will change the spacing between the three lines (Location, Hours, Phone ext) near the end of the document we've been working on.

1. Highlight the three lines (Location, Hours, Phone ext).

2. Point to Leading in the Type menu.

A list appears with several leading sizes. The check mark next to Auto indicates that leading is being set automatically.

3. Click 18.

The three lines change to 18-point leading. Now clear the highlight.

4. Click a blank area.

Before continuing, change the view to Actual Size, and scroll the publication so you can see the top of the document.

CTRL 1

5. Select Actual Size from the View menu.

6. If necessary, scroll until you can see the top of the document.

You'll not only want to change spacing between lines of type, but also between specific letters.

## Changing Spacing Between Characters

PageMaker allows you to change the spacing between characters. Each font has built-in spacing for pairs of characters. But certain pairs, such as *WA* and *Yo*, often appear too far apart with this standard spacing. The process of adjusting spacing between pairs of characters is called **kerning**. PageMaker has an automatic pair-kerning function to correct the common kerning problems between certain letters. If you want to adjust the spacing between characters manually, you can use the text tool to select the characters. Then hold down CTRL and ALT while you press ← to reduce spacing or → to increase spacing. Complete the following steps to reduce the spacing between the *A* and *Y* in *BAY*.

1. Drag the I-beam to select the *A* and *Y* in *BAY* in the first paragraph.

2. Hold down CTRL and ALT.

3. Press ← three times.

4. Click in a blank area.

Notice that the spacing between the *A* and *Y* is reduced, and the insertion point is removed. You can also design the appearance of larger sections of text, such as paragraphs.

PageMaker provides several ways for you to change the appearance of paragraphs. You can align and indent them and change the spacing between them. You can also control the hyphenation used to fit lines within margins. These functions are carried out from the commands within the Type menu.

## Aligning Paragraphs

Currently, the open publication consists of text that is left aligned—the alignment set in the word processing program used to create it. To change the alignment, select the text you want to realign and use the Alignment options in the Type menu. Complete the following steps to change the alignment of selected paragraphs. Start by right-aligning the first paragraph.

1. Use the View menu to change the view to 75% Size.

2. If necessary, scroll the page until you can see the entire first paragraph.

3. Drag the I-beam to highlight the first paragraph.

4. Point to Alignment in the Type menu.

5. Select Justify.

6. Click a blank area to remove the highlight.

Notice that the text moves flush to the right margin as well as to the left margin. PageMaker inserts additional spaces between words and letters until the text stretches evenly between the margins. Next, you'll try center alignment for the Location, Hours, and Phone ext lines.

7. Highlight the three Location, Hours, and Phone ext lines.

8. Point to Alignment in the Type menu and click Align Center.

9. Click a blank area to remove the highlight.

Notice that the Alignment command controls an entire paragraph.

## Indenting Paragraphs

You can control how different lines of a paragraph appear. Next, you will learn how to set paragraph indents and tabs. Figure 4.10 shows the Business Center document with various paragraph indents. The first paragraph has a first-line indent, which means that the top line begins at a different indent than the other lines in the paragraph. The second and third paragraphs are indented from both the left and right margins.

Figure 4.10
Business Center
document with different
paragraph indents

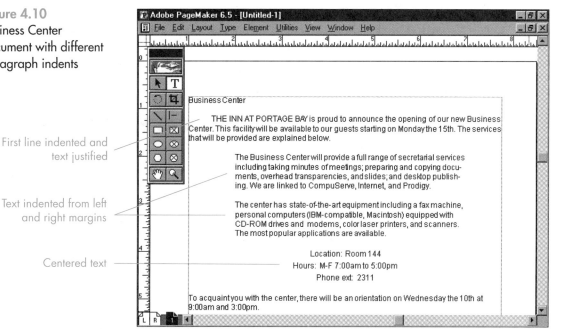

Figure 4.10
Business Center document with different paragraph indents

First line indented and text justified

Text indented from left and right margins

Centered text

Complete the following steps to duplicate this figure.

1. Highlight the first paragraph.

2. Select Indents/Tabs from the Type menu.

Figure 4.11 shows the Indents/Tabs dialog box, from which you set paragraph indents and tabs for moving the vertical insertion bar across the page. The ruler part of the dialog box shows the location of the indent and tab settings and indicates their type.

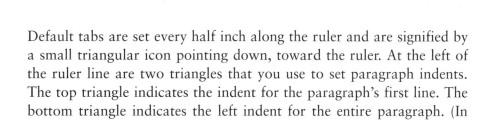

Figure 4.11
Indents/Tabs dialog box

Sets first-line indent

Sets left margin indent for entire paragraph

Default tab settings

Default tabs are set every half inch along the ruler and are signified by a small triangular icon pointing down, toward the ruler. At the left of the ruler line are two triangles that you use to set paragraph indents. The top triangle indicates the indent for the paragraph's first line. The bottom triangle indicates the left indent for the entire paragraph. (In effect, the bottom triangle sets a new left margin for the paragraph.)

You will set a first-line indent for the first paragraph. Then you will set a left and right paragraph indent for the second and third paragraphs. To set these indents, you drag the appropriate triangle to the desired location on the ruler. Figure 4.12 shows the top triangle moved to the 0.5-inch mark.

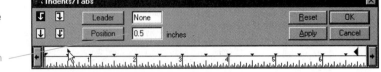

3. Point to the top triangle.

4. Hold down the mouse button and drag the top triangle to the 0.5-inch mark on the ruler.

As you drag the triangle, its location appears in the box next to the word *inches*.

5. Release the mouse button.

6. Click OK.

The first line of the highlighted paragraph is indented a half inch.

7. Click a blank area to remove the highlight.

Now you will indent the second and third paragraphs.

8. Highlight the second and third paragraphs.

9. Select Indents/Tabs from the Type menu.

Because the first line will not be indented any further than the rest of the paragraph, you will move both the triangles to the same position on the ruler.

10. Point to the bottom triangle.

11. Hold down the mouse button and drag the icons to the 1-inch mark. (Both triangles will move together.)

12. Release the mouse button.

13. Click Apply to view the changes. Notice that the paragraphs shift to show the new left indent but the dialog box remains onscreen.

Your next step is to change the right indent, which is similar to a right margin, for the selected paragraphs. Figure 4.13 shows the right indent positioned at the 6.75-inch mark, which is the same as the right margin, as indicated by the vertical dotted line. You will move the right triangle to the 6-inch mark to set the right indent shown in Figure 4.13.

**Figure 4.13**
Setting a right indent

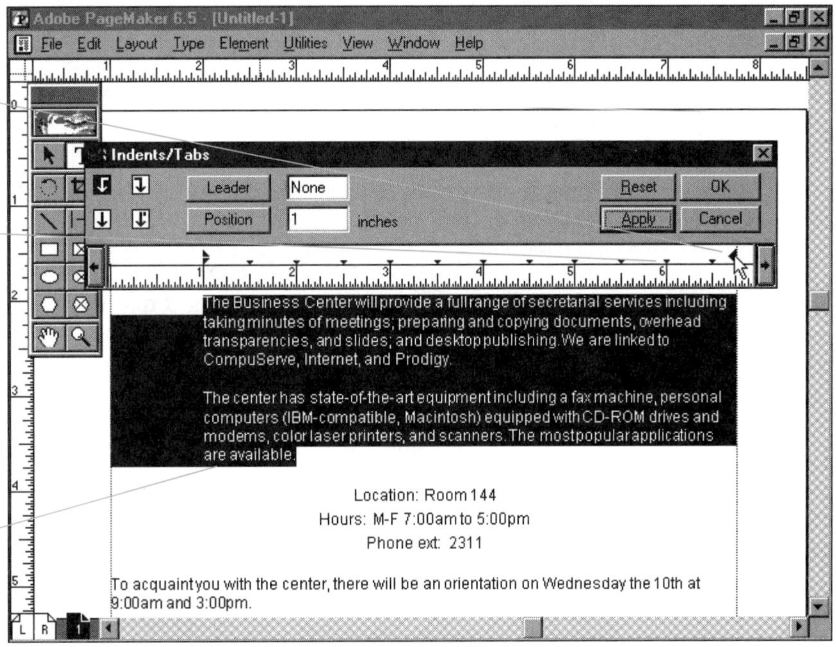

Right indent marker

Drag marker to here

Selected paragraphs
indented one inch

**14.** Point to the right-indent triangle (refer to Figure 4.13).

**15.** Hold down the mouse button and drag the triangle to the 6-inch mark.

The box next to the word *inches* will specify 0.75, which is the distance from the triangle to the right margin.

**16.** Release the mouse button.

**17.** Click Apply.

Take a moment to review your actions. The dialog box shows that you have set a left indent at the 1-inch mark and a right indent at the 6-inch mark for the highlighted paragraphs.

**18.** Click OK.

**19.** Click a blank area to remove the highlight.

The publication shows the paragraphs indented.

So far, while working with paragraph indents, you have used the text tool to drag the I-beam to select the desired paragraph(s). There are two other ways to specify a paragraph for indentation. First, if you want to work with only one paragraph that is already in the publication, just click the I-beam anywhere on the paragraph. Then any indent setting you change will apply to just this paragraph.

Second, if you want to indent a paragraph that has not yet been typed, use the pointer tool instead of the text tool to set an indent. This changes the default paragraph setting so that any new paragraph you enter onto the publication will be formatted according to the new indent setting.

Earlier you learned that PageMaker sets default tabs at half-inch increments. When you press (TAB), the vertical insertion bar moves across the page to the next tab setting. To add tabs, you must specify the location of the tab on the ruler line and the tab type. PageMaker provides four types of tabs: left, right, center, and decimal. If you specify a **left tab**, the tab appears to the left of the text you type. If you specify a **right tab**, the tab appears to the right of the text you type. Specifying a **center tab** centers the text around the tab. Specifying a **decimal tab** aligns the numbers that you type on their decimal point, which is useful for lining up a column of numbers. When you add tabs to the ruler in the Indents/Tabs dialog box, all default tabs to the left of the new tab are erased. Figure 4.14 shows left, center, and decimal tabs used when adding four lines of text to the Business Center document. The tab positions on the ruler line (in inches) are: left, 1.5; center, 3.5; and decimal, 5.

**Figure 4.14**
Left, center, and decimal tabs

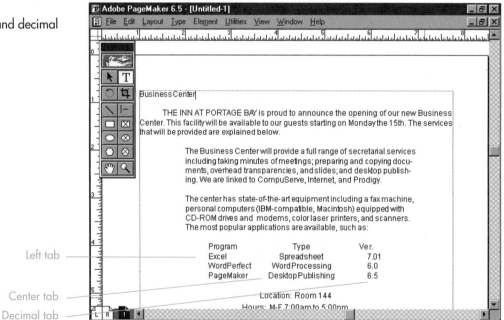

Figure 4.15 shows the Indents/Tabs dialog box with these settings. Each tab has a different icon: ⬇ for left, ⬇ for center, and ⬇ for decimal.

**Figure 4.15**
Indents/Tabs dialog box with tab settings

Tab-type icons

Left tab marker

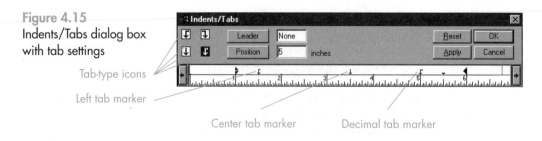

Center tab marker        Decimal tab marker

Before setting these tabs, add the words *such as:* to the end of the third paragraph.

**1.** Position the I-beam to the right of the period after the word *available* and click an insertion point.

**2.** Press ( ← BACKSPACE ) once to erase the period.

**3.** Type , *such as:*

**4.** Press ( ↵ ENTER ) twice.

Now use the Indents/Tabs dialog box to set the tabs.

( CTRL )( I )

**5.** Select Indents/Tabs from the Type menu.

The four tab-type icons are located on the left side of the dialog box. To select a tab type, you click the appropriate icon to highlight it. The first tab setting you need to add is left aligned. The left tab icon is already highlighted, so you do not have to change this setting. But you do have to specify the tab location. To set a tab, point to the location on the ruler and click the mouse button. To move a tab, drag the tab icon to the left or right. To reset all tabs to their original position, click the Reset button. To remove a specific tab setting, drag the icon down off the ruler.

**6.** Point to the 1.5-inch mark on the ruler.

**7.** Click the mouse button.

The left tab icon appears above the ruler, replacing the default tab marker. Before adding the next tab, click a blank area above the ruler in the dialog box to remove the highlight from the current tab-type icon.

**8.** Click a blank area above the ruler in the dialog box.

To set the next tab, first indicate that it will be center aligned.

**9.** Click the center tab icon ⬇.

**10.** Click the 3.5-inch mark.

Notice that all the default tab settings to the left of the added tab disappear.

**11.** Click a blank area in the dialog box to remove the highlight.

The last tab is decimal aligned.

**12.** Click the decimal tab icon ⬇.

**13.** Click the 5-inch mark on the ruler, and then click a blank area.

Check to make sure your settings match those shown in Figure 4.15. If necessary, drag the tab icons to the correct locations.

**14.** Click OK.

Now enter the new lines for the document.

**15.** Press ( TAB ) and type *Program.*

**16.** Press ( TAB ) and type *Type.*

**17.** Press ( TAB ) and type *Ver.* (including the period).

**18.** Press ⏎ ENTER.

**19.** Press TAB and type *Excel.*

**20.** Continue to type the new lines as shown in Figure 4.14, pressing TAB to move from one column to another.

Notice how each column automatically aligns according to the tab type you set.

---

**Setting Leaders**

PageMaker provides a function called Set leader that allows you to specify a string of characters to automatically be placed in front of a tab setting. Figure 4.16 shows the publication with the Location, Hours, and Phone ext lines left aligned.

**Figure 4.16**
**Example of leaders**

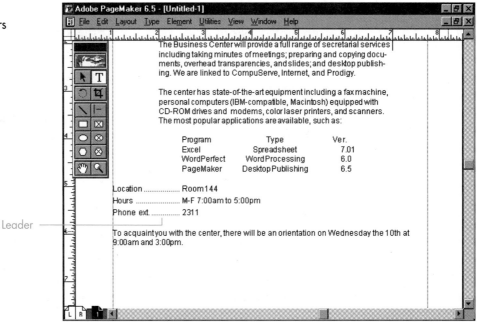

Leader

Notice that there is a series of dots, called a **leader,** that follows each heading and extends to the next tab setting. To create these lines, you use the Indents/Tabs dialog box to specify a leader type (in this case, a series of dots) and then set the tab. Begin by clearing these lines in the publication.

**1.** Highlight the three lines.

**2.** Select Clear from the Edit menu.

DELETE

**3.** Select Indents/Tabs from the Type menu.

CTRL I

**4.** If necessary, click the Reset button to clear all the tabs you set and return to the default tabs.

**5.** Click the Leader button.

A list of options appears with a check mark next to the word None. This indicates that no leader is selected. The option below None is a series of dots. The next two options are a solid line and a solid underscore line. The last option is Custom, which allows you to specify a character to use as a leader.

6. Click the dots.

The word None is replaced by dots. Now set a left-align tab at the 1.5-inch mark.

7. Click the 1.5-inch mark.

8. Click OK.

SHIFT  CTRL  L

9. If necessary, select Align Left from the Alignment command in the Type menu to move the insertion line to the left margin.

10. Type *Location* and press TAB.

The dots fill the line to the tab setting.

11. Type *Room 144* and press ⏎ ENTER.

12. Complete the other two lines on your own.

You'll use a different publication to work with paragraph spacing and hyphenation, so close the document before continuing.

CTRL  W

13. Select Close from the File menu.

A message appears, asking if you want to save your changes.

14. Click No (indicating that you do not want to save the document).

If your study time is up, select Exit from the File menu to quit PageMaker. If not, continue with the rest of the chapter.

## Working with Paragraph Spacing and Hyphenation

Earlier you learned how to change the spacing between lines and between characters. In this section you will learn how PageMaker spaces words and letters within paragraphs and how this affects **hyphenation**. Controlling the spacing within paragraphs is especially important when you are working with justified text in narrow columns, such as in a newsletter. To justify text, PageMaker forces each line to end at the right margin. Because few lines will have the exact number of characters to end exactly at the right margin, PageMaker adjusts the spacing between characters and words and/or hyphenates a word at the end of the line. The amount of spacing is determined by ranges specified in the Spacing Attributes dialog box, which is accessed by selecting Paragraph from the Type menu and then pressing the Spacing button. Figure 4.17, on the next page, shows the Spacing Attributes dialog box with the default spacing values. Remember, you can reset the defaults at any point.

Figure 4.17
Spacing Attributes
dialog box

Default spacing values

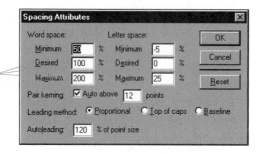

The word and letter spacing values are percentages of the overall font spacing as determined by the font designer. Thus, a spacing value of 50% is one-half of the predetermined font spacing. The default values shown in Figure 4.17 allow PageMaker to use word spacing of between three quarters of (75%) and one and a half times (150%) the font spacing when justifying a line.

An important consideration in word and letter spacing is the relationship between spacing and hyphenation. To justify text, PageMaker first adjusts the spacing between words and letters within the specified ranges. Then, if necessary, PageMaker hyphenates words. Thus, the larger the spacing range, the less hyphenation is needed. However, the larger the spacing range, the larger the gaps between words and letters. In most cases you would leave the spacing at the default values. To change the appearance of the paragraphs, you could turn the hyphenation off and on, and change paragraph alignment from justified to unjustified.

Figure 4.18 shows three paragraphs with the same text and spacing values but with different alignments and hyphenation. Paragraph 1 is justified and the hyphenation is turned on. Paragraph 2 is justified and the hyphenation is turned off. Paragraph 3 is not justified and the hyphenation is turned on. You can change these settings in the Hyphenation dialog box, which you open by selecting Hyphenation from the Type menu.

Figure 4.18
Three paragraphs with the same text and spacing values but different alignments and hyphenation

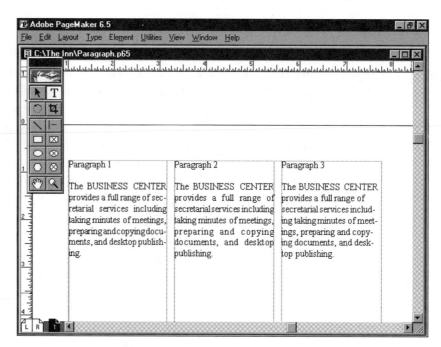

To practice using the Hyphenation dialog box, you will retrieve the file Paragraph, which has three identical paragraphs. You will then change them to duplicate Figure 4.18. Start by opening Paragraph.

CTRL O

1. Open the Paragraph publication.

At this point the paragraphs are identical. They are justified, and the hyphenation is turned on. Change Paragraph 2 by turning off the hyphenation. *Note:* When working with these paragraphs, do not highlight the headings.

2. Use the text tool  to highlight Paragraph 2.

3. Select Hyphenation from the Type menu.

The Hyphenation dialog box appears. This dialog box contains several options that enable you to turn hyphenation on and off, select the type of hyphenation (such as Manual only, which permits PageMaker to hyphenate only words you specify), limit the number of consecutive lines in a paragraph that end in a hyphen, and specify the amount of space at the end of a line in which hyphenation is allowed.

Continue by turning off hyphenation for the selected paragraph.

4. Click the Off radio button and click OK.

5. Click a blank area to deselect the text.

After you turn off the hyphenation, PageMaker inserts additional space between words in order to justify the paragraph, which can create "rivers" of white space in the paragraph. Now change the alignment of Paragraph 3.

6. Highlight Paragraph 3 and point to Alignment from the Type menu.

SHIFT ALT L

7. Click Align Left.

8. Click a blank area to remove the highlight.

Paragraph 3 now displays a ragged right edge.

All three paragraphs have a different appearance due to variations in hyphenation and justification. Track kerning creates another appearance. Earlier you learned about kerning, which adjusts spacing between two characters. **Track kerning** allows you to adjust the space between letters and words in selected text, such as a line or paragraph. This function is useful for creating special effects, such as darkening or lightening a block of text. If you tighten the space between letters and words, the text block will appear darker. If you loosen the space between letters and words, the text will appear lighter. Another use of track kerning is to change the spacing of lines of very small or very large text, such as captions and headlines.

You will use the Track command to change the letter and word spacing for Paragraphs 2 and 3 of the original Paragraph publication. Begin by closing this publication and opening Paragraph again.

CTRL W

9. Select Close from the File menu.

10. Click No (do not save).

11. Point to Recent Publications in the File menu and click Paragraph to reopen the publication.

12. Use the text tool 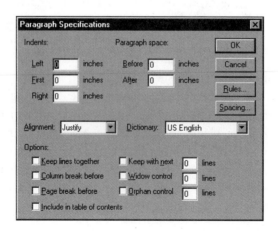 to highlight Paragraph 2.

13. Point to Expert Tracking in the Type menu.

A list of options for the Track command appears with the No Track option checked. This indicates that the selected text has no track kerning. Change the track kerning to Very Tight.

14. Click Very Tight.

15. Use the text tool to select Paragraph 3.

16. On your own, change the track option to Very Loose.

17. Click a blank area to deselect the text.

Paragraph 2 appears darker because it has less space between the letters and words, and Paragraph 3 appears lighter because it has more space between the letters and words. Alignment, hyphenation, and spacing are adjustments that you can control to manipulate the appearance of text.

## Working with the Paragraph Specifications Dialog Box

Thus far you have worked with several PageMaker functions (including indents, tabs, alignment, letter spacing, and hyphenation) that allow you to change the appearance of paragraphs. You can specify several of these functions, and others, in the Paragraph Specifications dialog box shown in Figure 4.19.

Figure 4.19
Paragraph Specifications dialog box

Notice that paragraph indents and alignment settings are in this dialog box. In addition, you can control spaces between paragraphs, as well as column breaks, page breaks, widows, and orphans.

## Controlling Paragraph Spacing

The Paragraph space option allows you to specify (in inches) the amount of additional space before or after selected paragraphs. Try increasing the spacing above Paragraph 1 by 0.25 inch.

1. Highlight Paragraph 1 (do not highlight the heading).

2. Select Paragraph from the Type menu.

CTRL M

3. Highlight the 0 in the Before box and type .25.

4. Click OK.

5. Click a blank area to deselect the text.

Notice that the increased spacing caused the paragraph to shift down.

6. Close the publication without saving it.

Next, you'll learn other ways to control the way text is positioned in a publication.

## Controlling Page and Column Breaks, and Widows and Orphans

The Paragraph Specifications dialog box has several options that control the flow of text from column to column and page to page. When working with these options, you must determine which paragraph will be affected by the option. You can highlight the appropriate paragraph with the text tool and then change the options you want in the Paragraph Specifications dialog box. Refer to Figure 4.19 as you read the following explanation for each option.

■ **Keep lines together** This option allows you to specify that a paragraph will not be split at a column or page break. This is useful if you want to keep a table or list together.

■ **Column break before and Page break before** When working on a publication with multiple pages or columns, you need to watch for page and column breaks. If you want a paragraph to begin a new page or column, you merely select the paragraph and choose the desired option from the dialog box.

■ **Keep with next *x* lines** This option ensures that the last line of a paragraph will be placed with a certain number of lines (1, 2, or 3) of the next paragraph. This is useful for keeping headings connected to their accompanying text.

■ **Widow control** *x* **lines** A **widow** in PageMaker occurs when the beginning line or lines of a paragraph are isolated at the bottom of a column or page. Use this option to specify the maximum number of lines (1, 2, or 3) that make up a widow. Figure 4.20 shows an example of a widow.

**Figure 4.20**
Example of widow

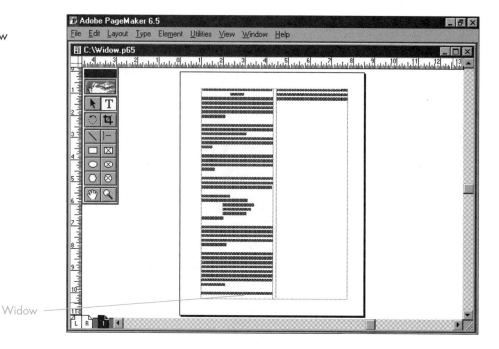

■ **Orphan control** *x* **lines** An **orphan** in PageMaker occurs when the last line or lines of a paragraph is isolated at the top of a column or page. Use this option to specify the maximum number of lines that make up an orphan. Figure 4.21 shows an example of an orphan.

**Figure 4.21**
Example of orphan

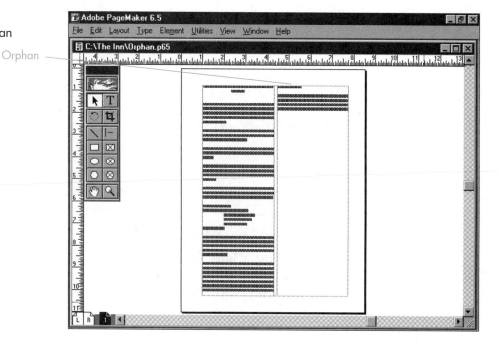

Now take a moment to practice using two of these options: Keep lines together and Orphan control. Begin by opening a publication called Orphan.

CTRL O

**1.** Open the Orphan publication.

Notice that the top of the second column begins with a single line. This is an orphan—the last line of the paragraph that ends the first column. Use the Paragraph Specifications dialog box to set the Orphan control to 3. Start by highlighting the paragraph.

**2.** Select the text tool **T** and triple-click the last paragraph in column 1.

CTRL M

**3.** Select Paragraph from the Type menu.

**4.** Click Orphan control and type 3.

**5.** Click OK.

Three more lines moved from the bottom of the first column to the top of the second column. Now use the Keep lines together option. With the paragraph still highlighted:

CTRL M

**6.** Select Paragraph from the Type menu.

**7.** Click Orphan control to turn it off.

**8.** Click Keep lines together and click OK.

This tells PageMaker not to separate any of these lines, and the entire paragraph moves to the second column. You've seen how you can control page and column breaks, and widows and orphans. Before continuing, close the publication.

CTRL W

**9.** Close the publication without saving it.

The next section shows you how to work with groups of paragraphs.

## WORKING WITH TEXT BLOCKS

Earlier you learned how to use the text tool to select a portion of text that could then be edited—moved, copied, deleted, and so forth. In this section you will learn how to use the pointer tool to select a text block. A **text block** is a rectangular area on the page that contains text. A publication can have one or more text blocks. A text block is created when you place, paste, or type text on a page.

If a publication has more than one text block, the text blocks are often **threaded**, or linked together, so that a change in one text block affects the others. For example, reducing the size of one text block might increase the size of the following text block. Threaded text blocks combine to form a story. A **story** is text that PageMaker recognizes as a unit, such as a document created using a word processing program. Publications can have more than one story.

One advantage of working with a text block is that you can change its shape and easily move it. This allows you to rearrange text on a page to make space for a graphic or to enhance the document's appearance. To work with a text block, you must first select it by clicking the pointer tool inside the text block boundaries.

Figure 4.22 shows a selected text block. After you select a text block, the top and bottom boundary lines, called **windowshades**, appear. The windowshades are used to manipulate a text block. The windowshades have loops, called **handles**, which are either empty or contain a + or ▼ symbol. An empty loop at the top of a text block indicates the beginning of a story. An empty loop at the bottom of a text block indicates the end of a story. The + symbol in a loop indicates that the text block is threaded to the previous or following text block. When there is text that does not appear, the ▼ symbol is displayed in a loop. To display the text, either drag the loop lower or click the loop to display a text icon; then place the text.

**Figure 4.22**
Selected text block

Rectangular handles

Text block

Windowshade

Loop

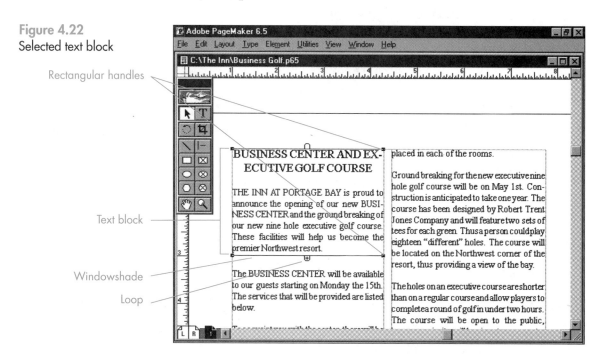

At each corner of the text block is a small rectangular handle, which you can select with the pointer tool and then drag to change the shape (such as the width) of the text block. You also can use the pointer tool to select the text block and drag it to another location on the document setup.

To practice manipulating text blocks, you will open a PageMaker document named Business Golf, which is shown in Figure 4.23. This is a two-column document containing announcements of the business center and a new golf course.

Figure 4.23
Fit in Window view
of Business Golf

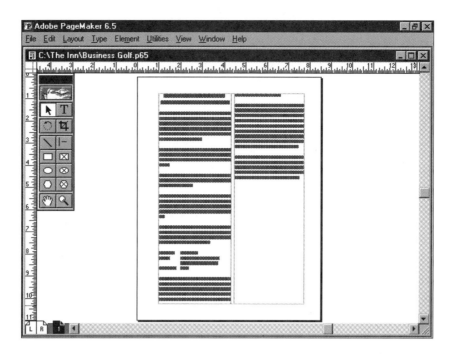

Figure 4.24 shows a printout of this document.

Figure 4.24
Printout of Business Golf
publication

## BUSINESS CENTER AND EXECUTIVE GOLF COURSE

THE INN AT PORTAGE BAY is proud to announce the opening of our new BUSINESS CENTER and the ground breaking of our new nine hole executive golf course. These facilities will help us become the premier Northwest resort.

The BUSINESS CENTER will be available to our guests starting on Monday the 15th. The services that will be provided are listed below.

To acquaint you with the center, there will be an orientation on Wednesday the 10th at 9:00am and 3:00pm.

The BUSINESS CENTER will provide a full range of secretarial services including taking minutes of meetings, preparing and copying documents, and desktop publishing.

The center has state-of-the-art equipment including a fax machine, personal computers (IBM and Macintosh), laser printers and the popular applications programs.

Location:    Room 144
Hours:       M-F 7:00am to 5:00pm
             Sat 9:00am to 3:00pm
Phone ext:   2311

The center will also be open to our local business community on a space available basis. A grand opening of the center will be held on Friday the 19th at 9:00am. Announcements of the grand opening will be

placed in each of the rooms.

Ground breaking for the new executive nine hole golf course will be on May 1st. Construction is anticipated to take one year. The course has been designed by Robert Trent Jones Company and will feature two sets of tees for each green. Thus a person could play eighteen "different" holes. The course will be located on the Northwest corner of the resort, thus providing a view of the bay.

The holes on an executive course are shorter than on a regular course and allow players to complete a round of golf in under two hours. The course will be open to the public, however priority will be given to our guests.

You will revise this document to create the layout shown in Figure 4.25.

Figure 4.25
Revised publication using
text blocks

## BUSINESS CENTER AND EXECUTIVE GOLF COURSE

THE INN AT PORTAGE BAY is proud to announce the opening of our new BUSINESS CENTER and the ground breaking of our new nine hole executive golf course. These facilities will help us become the premier Northwest resort.

The BUSINESS CENTER will be available to our guests starting on Monday the 15th. The services that will be provided are listed below.

To acquaint you with the center, there will be an orientation on Wednesday the 10th at 9:00am and 3:00pm.

The BUSINESS CENTER will provide a full range of secretarial services including taking minutes of meetings, preparing and copying documents, and desktop publishing.

The center has state of the art equipment including a fax machine, personal computers (IBM and Macintosh), laser printers and the popular applications programs.

Location:    Room 144
Hours:       M-F 7:00am to 5:00pm
             Sat 9:00am to 3:00pm
Phone ext:   2311

The center will also be open to our local business community on a space available basis. A grand opening of the center will be held on Friday the 19th at 9:00am. Announcements of the grand opening will be placed in each of the rooms.

Ground breaking for the new executive nine hole golf course will be on May 1st. Construction is anticipated to take one year. The course has been designed by Robert Trent Jones Company and will feature two sets of tees for each green. Thus a person could play eighteen "different" holes. The course will be located on the Northwest corner of the resort, thus providing a view of the bay.

The holes on an executive course are shorter than on a regular course and allow players to complete a round of golf in under two hours. The course will be open to the public, however priority will be given to our guests.

You will recreate the layout using text blocks by:

- changing the size of the text blocks so the amount of text in each column is approximately the same

- dividing a large text block into two smaller ones so you can work with each text block separately

- moving text blocks

- changing the shape of a text block so it flows across both columns

Figure 4.26 shows the Fit in Window view of the revised document.

Figure 4.26
Fit in Window view of the
revised document

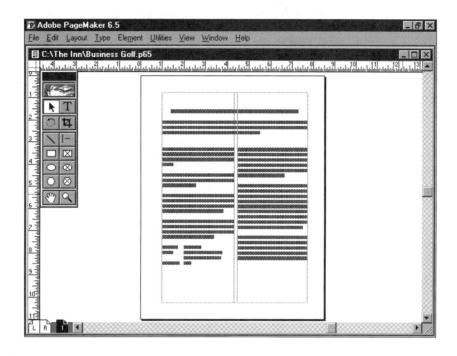

Start by opening Business Golf.

CTRL O

1. Open the Business Golf publication.

Next you will select the text blocks.

## Displaying Text Blocks

When you first open a publication, it might not be clear how many text blocks it contains. A text block can be as short as a single line or as long as the page. Because this document setup is divided into two columns, the publication contains at least two text blocks. To view a single text block, you would click the text. To view all the text blocks on a page, you can use the Select All command from the Edit menu.

CTRL A

1. Choose Select All from the Edit menu.

Figure 4.27, on the next page, shows the publication's windowshades and loops, indicating that there are two text blocks.

Figure 4.27
Windowshades and
loops for two text blocks

Empty loop at top
of text block
indicates beginning
of story

Text block

Empty loop at bottom
of text block indicates
end of story

+ indicates text block
is threaded

The top loop in the left column is empty, signifying the story's beginning. The empty loop in the right column signifies the story's end. The loops with a + signify that threaded text blocks appear before or after that windowshade. Because these two text blocks are threaded, a change in one can affect the other. To remove the windowshades, click an empty area of the publication.

**2.** Move the pointer to an empty area and click the mouse button.

First, you will shorten the text block in the left column. The process is to select the text block, point to the bottom loop, and drag up the window-shade. Figure 4.28 shows this process.

Figure 4.28
Shortening a text block

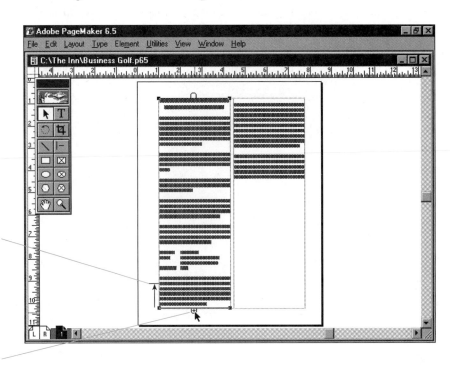

Drag up to the
9-inch mark

Point here

Note that if you make a mistake while working with text blocks and want to start over from this point, you can choose Revert from the File menu. **Revert** removes all changes you made to the active publication since you last saved it. In this case, selecting Revert is the same as closing your publication without saving any changes and reopening the original publication.

3. Click the text in the left column.

4. Point to the + in the lower loop (refer to Figure 4.28).

5. Hold down the mouse button. When the double arrow ↕ appears, drag the windowshade up to the 9-inch mark on the ruler line (refer to Figure 4.28).

The paragraph at the bottom of column 1 shifts to the top of column 2, but the blank line remains at the end of column 1 instead of adding space at the top of the next column.

6. Release the mouse button.

Notice that the text below the windowshade moved to the next text block. Now you will divide the text in the left column into two text blocks. The process is to drag a windowshade to the desired dividing line, and then click the windowshade loop. A text icon appears, representing text covered by the windowshade. You place the icon in the desired location and click the mouse button to place the text as a text block. Figures 4.29 and 4.30 illustrate this process. (This is tricky; before starting, read through the following six steps, referring to the figures. Then go slowly.)

**Figure 4.29**
Process for dividing text blocks

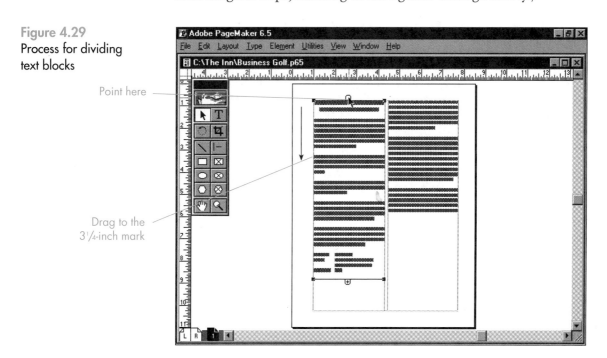

Point here

Drag to the 3¼-inch mark

Figure 4.30
Placing the text icon

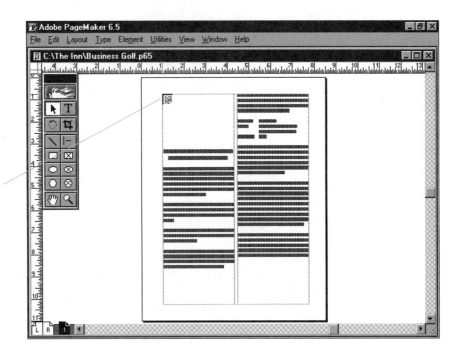

Text icon indicating where the text covered by the windowshade will be placed as a new text block

7. Point to the loop in the top windowshade (refer to Figure 4.29).

8. Hold down the mouse button. When the double arrow ↕ appears, drag the windowshade down to the 3¼-inch mark (refer to Figure 4.29). Again, this leaves the blank line at the bottom of column 1.

9. Release the mouse button.

The amount of text covered by the windowshade flows to the next text block. In addition, the text covered by the windowshade can be placed as a separate text block.

10. Click the loop in the top windowshade.

A text icon appears, representing the text covered by the windowshade.

11. Move the text icon ▦ to the upper-left corner of the publication (refer to Figure 4.30).

12. Click the mouse button.

The text flows back as a text block. Now the document has three text blocks, all of which are threaded.

## Moving Text Blocks

Your next step is to move the two large text blocks down the column. The process is to select a text block, hold down the mouse button, and drag the text block to another location.

1. Point to the text block in the right column.

2. Hold down the mouse button and wait until you see the triangle pointer ▶.

Flowing Text across Columns

Next you will change the shape of the small text block at the top of the page so text flows across both columns.

Notice the corner handles. You will use the lower-right handle to drag the text block across the two columns, as illustrated in Figures 4.31 and 4.32.

Figure 4.31
Flowing text across columns

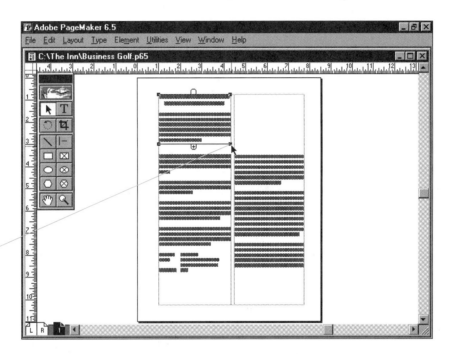

Point to handle

Figure 4.32
Flowing text across columns (continued)

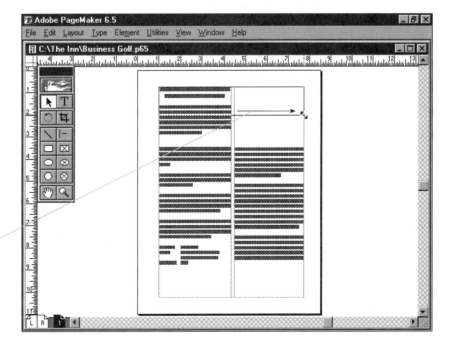

Drag

**2.** Point to the lower-right handle (refer to Figure 4.31).

**3.** Hold down the mouse button and wait until you see the double arrow ↘.

**4.** Drag the handle across the page to the right margin of the second column at the 2-inch mark (refer to Figure 4.32).

**5.** Release the mouse button.

The text, an introductory paragraph, flows across the page to fill the new text block shape. Now move this text block down.

**6.** Point to the text block and hold down the mouse button.

**7.** When the triangle pointer ▶ appears, drag the text block down to the 1½-inch mark.

**8.** Release the mouse button.

**9.** Click an empty area.

With the changes you have made, there is room at the top of the document for the resort's logo and room at the bottom for placing a graphic or other text. The document could be further enhanced by changing the type size of the heading and emphasizing the first paragraph with bold, italic, or another type style.

## Combining Text Blocks

In the previous section you divided a text block into two text blocks. In this section you will combine two text blocks into one. The advantage of combining two text blocks is that the text is easier to work with. For example, you might want to combine two adjacent text blocks so that you can move the text as a single block. The process is to select a text block and use the Cut command. Then, using the text tool, click an insertion point inside the other text block. Finally, use the Paste command to place the cut text into the text block.

To practice combining text blocks, you will first type a line of text at the end of the document. This text will be a separate text block that you will combine with the text block above it. Figure 4.33 shows the sentence you will add.

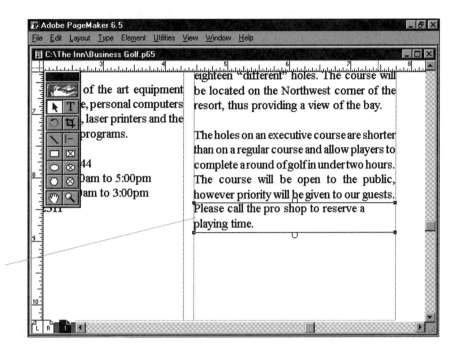

Sentence to add

1. Change the view to Actual Size.

2. Use the scroll bars to display the end of the document.

3. Select the text tool **T**.

4. Point to Size in the Type menu and click 14.

5. Click an insertion point below the end of the document.

*Note:* Clicking an insertion point outside of any text block and typing text creates a new text block.

6. Type the sentence shown in Figure 4.33.

7. Use the pointer tool [▶] to select the sentence.

Your screen should resemble Figure 4.33. Notice the empty loops in the windowshades, indicating that this is a separate story as well as a text block.

8. Select Cut from the Edit menu.

Now use the text tool to set an insertion point.

9. Select the text tool 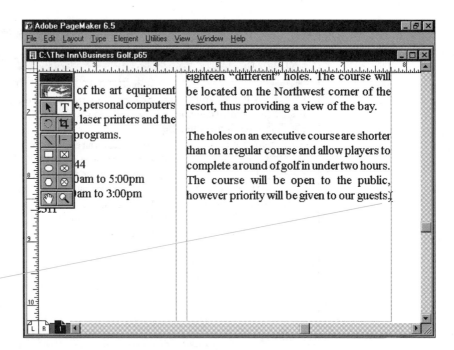 and click an insertion point at the end of the paragraph. See Figure 4.34.

**Figure 4.34**
Setting an insertion point

Insertion point

CTRL V

10. Select Paste from the Edit menu.

11. Click an insertion point before the *P* in *Please* and press ↵ ENTER twice.

12. Select the pointer tool and click the new sentence.

CTRL 0

13. Change the view to Fit in Window.

The screen now shows the sentence as part of the larger text block.

Text blocks, like paragraphs, can be copied, moved, and cleared using the Edit menu options.

14. Close but do not save the publication.

If your study time is up, use the File menu to exit PageMaker.

## WORKING WITH FRAMES

PageMaker provides another way to work with text. A **frame** is an object that acts as a placeholder for text and graphics. The frame object can be in the shape of a rectangle, oval, or polygon. Frames allow you to lay out the publication and then force the text to be displayed within it. Multiple frames, just like text blocks, can be threaded. The process for creating a frame is to use the frame tools in the Toolbox to draw a frame of a particular shape and then place text within the frame.

Next create a publication with the two oval frames shown in Figure 4.35.

Figure 4.35
Two oval frames with text
placed in them

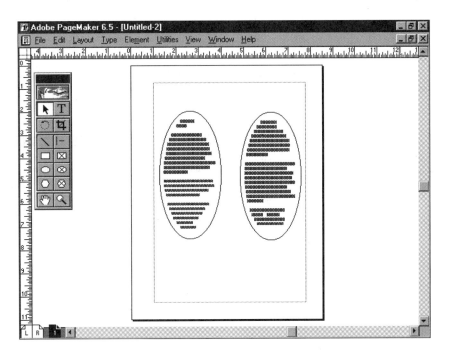

Start by drawing one frame and then copying it to create the other.

CTRL N

1. Open a new publication.

2. Click the ellipse frame tool ⊠ in the Toolbox.

3. Draw an oval similar to the one shown in Figure 4.36. To draw the
   oval, position the crossbar pointer + where you want the upper-left
   part of the oval to appear, hold down the mouse button, and drag the
   pointer + diagonally until the oval is the size you want. You can delete
   the oval by selecting it with the pointer tool ▶ and pressing DELETE.

Figure 4.36
An oval frame

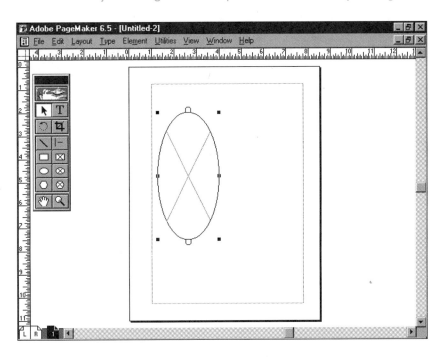

Notice that an X appears in the oval, indicating that it is a frame.

CTRL C

**4.** With the frame selected, select Copy from the Edit menu.

CTRL V

**5.** Select Paste from the Edit menu.

A copy of the frame appears on top of the original.

**6.** Drag the copy to the location shown in Figure 4.37.

**Figure 4.37**
Positioning the copied
oval frame

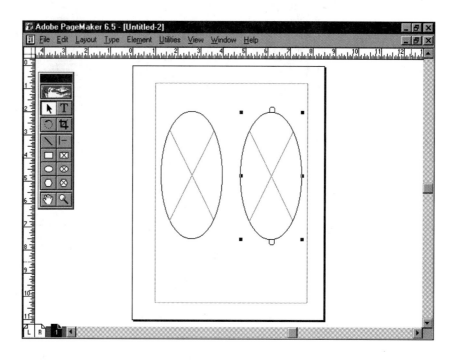

**7.** Click the left frame to select it.

CTRL D

**8.** Select Place from the File menu and open The Center document.

Text is placed in the selected frame. Now thread the text to the other frame.

**9.** Click the bottom loop of the left frame. See Figure 4.38.

**Figure 4.38**
Beginning to thread text
to the next frame

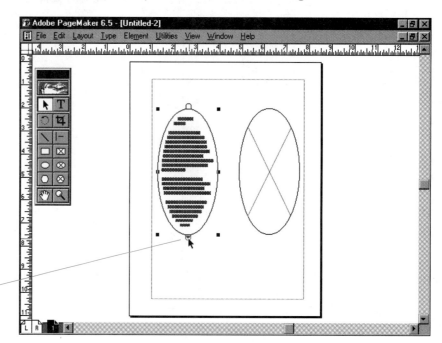

Click here

The pointer changes to ▶🌡.

**10.** Point ▶🌡 to the top of the right frame. See Figure 4.39.

**Figure 4.39**
Location to place the
threaded text icon

Point here

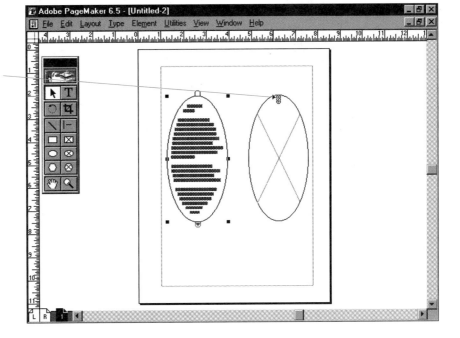

**11.** Click the mouse button.

The rest of the text flows into the right frame. After placing the text you can edit and delete it, as well as move and reshape the frames. Start by center-aligning the text in each frame.

**12.** Click the text tool [T] and drag to select the text in one frame.

**13.** Select Align Center from the Alignment options in the Type menu.

(SHIFT) (CTRL) (C)    **14.** On your own, align the text in the other frame.

Now move the frames to the positions shown in Figure 4.40.

Figure 4.40
Moving the frames

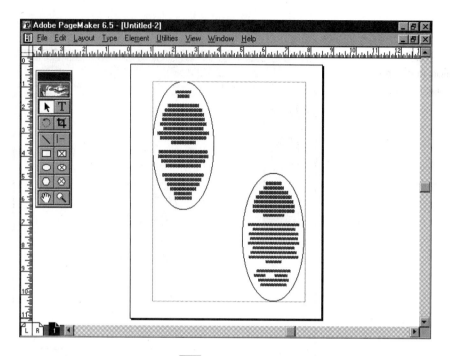

15. Select the pointer tool , and then drag the frames to the positions shown in Figure 4.40.

After moving the frames, you could place or draw other objects such as graphics on the page. Frames are more versatile than text blocks when you are laying out a publication because you can determine exactly how and where text and graphics will appear. You can also change the thickness of the border on a frame and fill the frame with a pattern.

CTRL W    16. Close the publication without saving it.

In the next chapter you will learn more about frames and how they are used with graphics.

## USING THE CONTROL PALETTE

In this chapter you have been learning how to use the Type menu and the Paragraph Specifications dialog box to change the appearance of text and paragraphs by using formatting attributes such as bold and indents. PageMaker provides a shortcut when formatting text and paragraphs called the **Control palette**, which contains most of the commands and options you have tried in this chapter. You will use the Control palette to make changes in the Business Center document you worked with earlier. Start by opening a new publication and placing the Business Center document on it.

CTRL N    1. Select New from the File menu and click OK.

CTRL D    2. Use the Place command to import the Business Center document.

CTRL 7    3. Change the view to 75% Size.

4. Click the text tool [T] and highlight the words *Business Center* at the beginning of the document.

5. Select Show Control Palette from the Window menu.

The Control palette, shown in Figure 4.41, appears onscreen. If necessary, use the colored bar on the left side of the Control palette to drag the Control palette to the bottom of the screen.

**Figure 4.41**
Control palette in character view

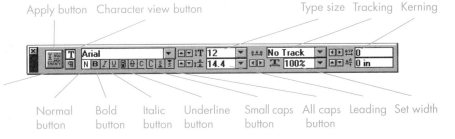

The Control palette has two views, character and paragraph, that are used when working with text. The **character view** allows you to modify the appearance of text, such as changing type styles (bold, italic, etc.), sizes, fonts, and character spacing (kerning and tracking). Figure 4.41 labels many of the buttons in the character view. It also shows the two buttons used to switch between views.

The **paragraph view** allows you to align paragraphs, set indents, and specify spacing. Figure 4.42 labels many of the paragraph-view buttons.

**Figure 4.42**
Control palette in paragraph view

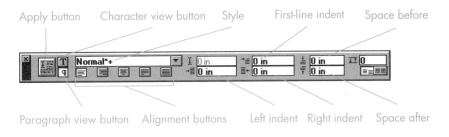

Currently, your Control palette should be in character view.

6. Click the paragraph-view button [¶] to change to paragraph view.

7. Click the character-view button [T] to return to character view.

You will use the Control palette to make several changes to the Business Center publication. Start by changing the *Business Center* heading to Times New Roman font, 18 point.

8. Click the down arrow next to the font box and scroll to display Times New Roman.

9. Click Times New Roman.

10. Click the down arrow next to the size box and click 18.

Now use the type style options. After making each change, notice the effect on the heading. With the *Business Center* heading still selected:

11. Click the bold button **B** .

12. Click the italic button *I* .

13. Click the underline button U .

14. Click the small caps button C .

15. Click the all caps button C .

16. Click the normal button **N** .

The heading is Times New Roman, 18 point, all capital letters.

The spacing options on the Control palette include set-width, kerning, tracking, and leading. The **set-width** option allows you to adjust the horizontal shape of characters in the selected text. You can use the **nudge buttons** to change the width in increments of 1%, type in a percentage, or use the scroll list to choose a preset percentage. Start by trying the nudge buttons.

1. Point to the right arrow next to the set-width option. See Figure 4.43.

**Figure 4.43**
Nudge button for the set-width option

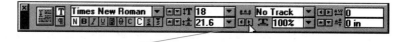

Point here

2. Click the mouse button.

Notice that the percentage changes to 101%.

3. Continue clicking the nudge button and viewing the changes to the BUSINESS CENTER heading until you reach 110%.

4. Use the left-arrow nudge button to return the width to 100%.

Now use the scroll list to change the width.

**5.** Click the down arrow next to 100%.

**6.** Click 80% and notice the change in the heading.

**7.** Use the scroll list to change the width to 130% and view the change.

**8.** Use the scroll list to return the width to normal.

Next use the kerning button to change the spacing between the *A* and *Y* in *BAY*, which is in the first paragraph.

**9.** Click an insertion point between the *A* and *Y* in *BAY*.

**10.** Click the left-arrow nudge button for the kerning option five times.

Notice that the setting changes to – 0.05, indicating that the spacing has been reduced. For the next two options, tracking and leading, you need to select a paragraph.

**11.** Triple-click the second paragraph to select it.

**12.** Click the down arrow for the tracking option.

**13.** Click Very Loose and notice the result.

**14.** On your own, select Very Tight from the tracking options.

The character and word spacing is decreased in the paragraph. However, the words are more difficult to read.

**15.** On your own, change the tracking back to Normal.

Now use the leading option to change the line spacing.

**16.** Click the down arrow next to the leading option.

**17.** Click 11.

Notice that the lines run together because the leading is less than the font size (12 point).

**18.** On your own, change the leading to 18.

**19.** On your own, change the leading to Auto.

Now you will use the paragraph view to make changes to the publication. Start by centering the heading.

**20.** Click the paragraph-view button ▣.

**21.** Select the heading *BUSINESS CENTER*.

**22.** Click the center-align button ▤.

Next indent the first line of the first paragraph. There are no nudge buttons or scroll lists for the indent button, so you will need to drag the mouse pointer to select the option and then type a new setting.

**23.** Click the first paragraph.

**24.** Drag the mouse pointer to select 0, displayed in the first-line indent box. See Figure 4.44.

**Figure 4.44**
Setting the first-line indent

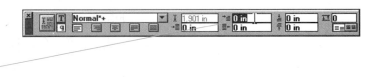

Drag to select

**25.** Type .3.

**26.** Click the Apply button.

The first line of the first paragraph is indented 0.3 inch. Figure 4.45 shows several changes to the second paragraph. The left and right margins of the paragraph are indented 0.3 inch and the spacing above and below the paragraph is increased by 0.2 inch.

**Figure 4.45**
Contol palette with several changes

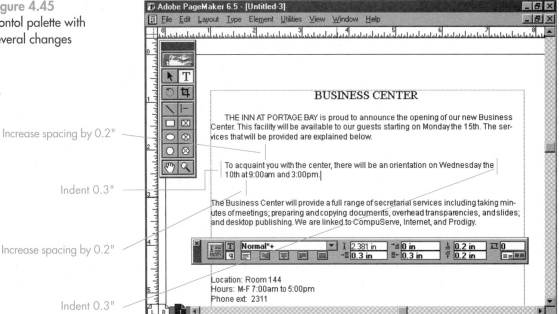

Increase spacing by 0.2"

Indent 0.3"

Increase spacing by 0.2"

Indent 0.3"

**27.** Select the second paragraph.

**28.** On your own, change the settings on the Control palette to match those shown in Figure 4.45. Click the Apply button after each change.

As you can see, the Control palette is a quick way to make several changes to the text on the publication and to view the results immediately. Continue by removing the Control palette from the Pasteboard and closing the publication.

CTRL ' 

**29.** Select Hide Control Palette from the Window menu.

CTRL W

**30.** Use the File menu to close the publication without saving.

In addition to making character and paragraph spacing changes, and changing font type, style, and size, you can format text with special effects.

## SPECIAL TEXT FEATURES

In this section you will learn how to create four special text features: drop caps, and rotated, flipped, and skewed text. All of these provide a different look for a publication.

### Creating Drop Caps

A **drop cap** is the first letter in a paragraph that has been enlarged and dropped below the baseline of the first line of the paragraph, often for two or three lines. A drop cap, as shown in Figure 4.46, helps draw the reader's attention to a particular paragraph. Drop caps often appear at the beginning of a section, such as at the beginning of each chapter in a book.

**Figure 4.46**
A drop cap

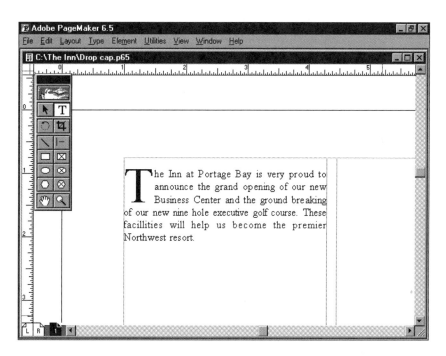

You will use a publication called Drop cap to create the drop cap shown in Figure 4.46.

CTRL O

1. Open Drop cap.

The easiest way to create a drop cap is to use the **Plug-ins,** which are programs that automate and enhance many of the PageMaker features. They are found in the Utilities menu. Start by selecting the letter you want to change to a drop cap.

2. Click the text tool T.

*Plug-in error:
Can't complete Drop Cap
action. Please place
Text Tool in initial paragraph.
(yrs)*

**3.** Click anywhere in the paragraph.

**4.** Point to Plug-ins in the Utilities menu to display a list of plug-ins.

**5.** Click Drop cap.

The Drop cap dialog box appears. You can drag the dialog box to the bottom of the screen to view the text on the publication page.

**6.** Point to the title bar of the dialog box. Hold down the mouse button and drag the dialog box down.

The dialog box allows you to specify the number of lines for the drop cap and to apply the change without leaving the dialog box. Currently, the size is set to 3. *Note:* Your dialog box may be set to a size other than 3.

**7.** If necessary, change the size to 2.

**8.** Click Apply.

The drop cap is created without the dialog box closing. To add a drop of a different size, you must first remove the current drop cap.

**9.** Click Remove.

**10.** Change the size to 3 and click Apply.

A larger drop cap appears at the beginning of the paragraph.

**11.** Click Close to return to the publication.

**12.** Click a blank area to deselect the text.

CTRL W  **13.** Close the publication without saving.

A drop cap is a very effective way to mark the beginning of a section or chapter within a long document.

## Creating Rotated Text

PageMaker allows you to turn selected text at any angle. This can create interesting effects for your publication. This **rotated text** is often placed along the borders of a publication, as shown in Figure 4.47. In this figure, the resort's name was rotated 90 degrees and placed along the left side of the page. When you rotate text, the entire text block turns, so make sure the text you want to rotate is a separate text block.

**Figure 4.47**
Example of rotated text

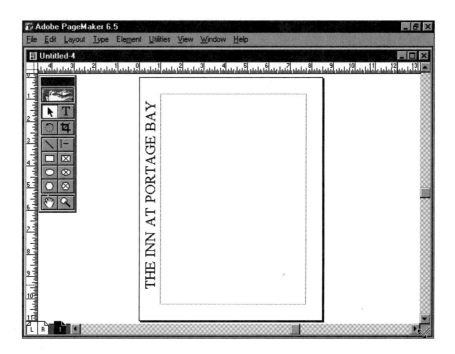

The following steps lead you through the process of rotating a text block (a heading in this case) that you will create. Depending on the configuration of your computer and your printer type, the screen display and printed copy of your publication might vary in quality.

1. Select New from the File menu and click OK.

2. Change the view to 75% Size.

3. Scroll so you can see the upper-left corner of the page.

4. Select the text tool .

5. Click an insertion line in the upper-left corner of the page.

6. Type *THE INN AT PORTAGE BAY.*

7. Select the pointer tool ▲.

8. Click the text block to display the windowshades.

9. Drag the lower-right handle to reduce the size of the text block. See Figure 4.48 on the next page.

Figure 4.48
Dragging the handle to
reduce the size of the
text block

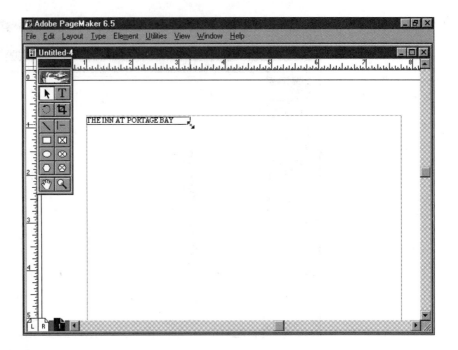

The process to rotate text is to select the rotating tool from the Toolbox
and point to the text block. Then, hold down the mouse button and
slowly move the pointer to create the desired rotation.

10. Click the rotating tool .

11. Point to the *Y* in *BAY*.

Notice that the pointer changes to a star ✳. The location of the pointer
indicates the reference point around which the text rotates.

12. Hold down the mouse button and slowly drag the pointer down a
few inches.

Notice that a line follows the pointer.

13. Slowly rotate the line counterclockwise. When the line is at the
desired rotation (90 degrees), release the mouse button.

The Undo command can be used to return the text to its original orientation.

(CTRL) (Z)

14. Select Undo Rotate from the Edit menu.

The Control palette provides a way to rotate text more precisely.

(CTRL) (`)

15. With the text block still selected, select Show Control Palette from the
Window menu.

Because a text block is selected, the Control palette displays options that
allow you to work with objects (text blocks and graphics).

Figure 4.49 labels several of these options.

**Figure 4.49**
Control palette when an
object is selected

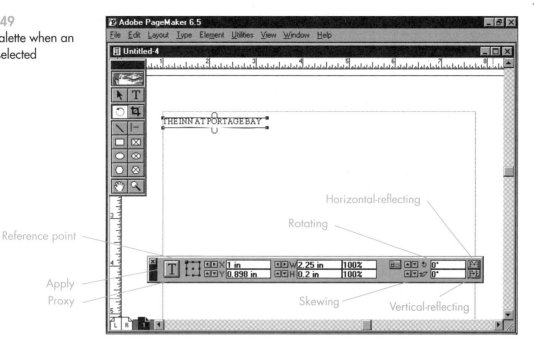

When rotating an object, you need to be concerned with the **reference point;** that is, the point around which the object rotates. The **proxy button** displays the reference point and allows you to change it. Figure 4.49 shows the reference point for the text block. Figure 4.50 shows the result of rotating the text block 30 degrees using the rotation option.

**Figure 4.50**
Text block rotated
30 degrees

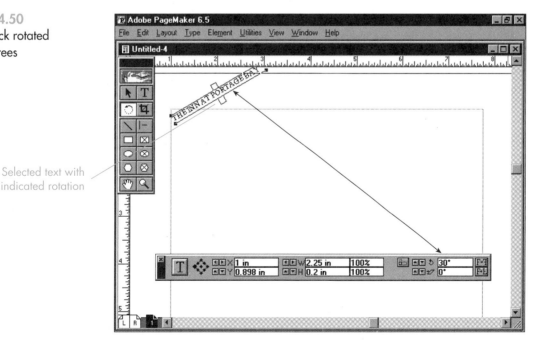

Complete the following to duplicate Figure 4.50.

16. Select the 0 in the rotating option box and type *30.*

17. Click the apply button.

The text block rotates 30 degrees around the reference point. Use the Undo command to return the text block to its original orientation. Then, change the reference point and rotate the object again.

CTRL Z

18. Choose Undo Apply from the Edit menu.

19. Click the upper-right corner of the proxy button ⊞ to change the reference point.

20. Change the rotation to 30 and click the apply button 🔳.

Notice how the text block rotates around the new reference point.

21. On your own, undo the rotation.

In appropriate instances, rotated text can create a very dramatic effect.

## Flipping Text

Two other Control palette options for objects are vertical and horizontal reflecting. These options flip the object vertically and horizontally. **Flipped text** can be used to create mirror images of words. You can also flip graphics.

1. With the text block selected, click the horizontal-reflecting button 🔳.

2. Click 🔳 again to reverse the effect.

3. Click the vertical-reflecting button 🔳.

4. Click 🔳 again to reverse the effect.

In addition to rotating and flipping objects, you can slant them with the skewing option.

## Skewing Text

**Skewed text** can be used to draw attention to a word or phrase. Skewing can also be used to suggest movement in a graphic. Skewing and flipping together can create shadow effects for characters, words, and graphics.

1. With the text block selected, select the 0 in the skewing option box.

2. Type *36* and click the apply button 🔳.

The text slants 36 degrees.

3. Change the skew to –20 degrees and click the Apply button 🔳.

A negative number slants the text to the left, a positive number to the right. The rotating and skewing options on the Control palette also have nudge buttons so you can select very fine increments and immediately view the results. Use the File menu to close the publication.

CTRL W

4. Close the publication without saving.

These four special effects—drop cap, and rotated, flipped, or skewed text—can help add interest to a particular design.

## SUMMARY

In this chapter you learned how to place text on a publication and how to use the pointer and text tools to select a portion of text. You now know how to move, copy, and delete text, and how to work with text blocks. You have also learned how to work with spacing, hyphenation, paragraph alignment, and paragraph indentation. In addition, you have worked with the Control palette, frames, and drop caps and learned to rotate, flip, and skew text.

## QUESTIONS

1. List and explain the three ways to add text to a page.

2. Describe three ways to select text using the text tool.

3. When would you use the text tool to select text? the pointer tool?

4. Explain the process for moving text.

5. Define *leading*. What is its default value?

6. Why would you want to change the leading value?

7. Define *kerning*.

8. PageMaker provides five ways to align paragraphs. List and explain them.

9. List and distinguish between the four types of tabs.

10. When working with paragraphs, why is it important to understand the relationship between spacing and hyphenation?

11. What is a text block; how can it be used?

12. A windowshade loop can be empty or contain a + or ▼. What does each signify?

13. True or False? A frame is an object that acts as a placeholder for text and graphics.

14. What is the value of using the Control palette?

15. What are nudge buttons?

16. Use the Help menu to search for and display the Help window called Using the Control palette to format text. Read the information and then exit the Help function.

1. Attraction is a document developed using Word. Open a new PageMaker publication, place this document on the page, and edit it to duplicate Figure 4.51. When you are done, save the publication as Area Attractions.

Figure 4.51
Completed Attractions
publication

### AREA ATTRACTIONS

Following is a sample of the most popular seasonal attractions found in our area. There is a comprehensive brochure listing all of the parks, museums, tourist attractions, and tours available in our lobby. Tours of the first two attractions can be arranged at the information desk.

The Skagit Valley Tulip Festival is held early in April. Thousands of visitors flock to the Skagit Valley to enjoy the miles and miles of tulips as they bloom into a dazzling array of colors. Hundreds of varieties of daffodils, tulips, and other spring flowers make this a photographer's and artist's paradise. The climate, soil, and rain combined with the care of the Dutch settlers make the bulb and cut-flower industry one of the most important in the region, with sales estimated at over $14 million. After touring the valley, visitors can enjoy a salmon barbecue, patterned after the native Indian recipes, at the nearby town of La Conner. The Skagit Valley is located on Interstate 5 at Mt. Vernon. The drive takes about one hour and 20 minutes from The Inn at Portage Bay.

The Suquamish Museum is dedicated to the study of the Puget Sound Salish Indians, who were the original inhabitants of this area. Chief Seattle, for whom the City of Seattle is named, was from the Suquamish Tribe. The museum's exhibition, which has toured in Europe, depicts the lives of the Puget Sound Indians prior to and after white settlement through photographs, artifacts, and interviews with tribal elders. The Suquamish Museum is located in one of the most beautiful settings in the Northwest, on the shores of Agate Pass, six miles north of Winslow on Highway 305. The hours are Monday through Thursday 10am - 5pm and Friday through Sunday 10am - 8pm. The admission is:

| Adults | 2.50 |
|---|---|
| Senior Citizens | 2.00 |
| Children | .50 |

Located on the United States and Canadian border, this park is dedicated to the friendship of the two countries. The park was opened in 1921 and was built with contributions from the schoolchildren in Washington and British Columbia. The Arch monument, which divides the highway, is a symbolic portal for the citizens who visit each country. The beautifully landscaped park provides a serene setting from which to view nearby Birch Bay. The Peace Arch State Park is located on Interstate 5 at the Canadian border. The drive takes about 45 minutes from The Inn at Portage Bay.

This process involves:

- using the Control palette to change the heading *AREA ATTRACTIONS* to Times New Roman font, size 18, all caps
- centering the heading
- justify-aligning all paragraphs
- setting a left and right indent for the second and third paragraphs at 0.75 inch
- inserting tabs (including a decimal tab) below the third paragraph and typing in the admission prices

2. Contest is a document created using PageMaker. Open this document and, using text blocks, edit it to duplicate Figure 4.52. (This project is similar to one you completed earlier in this chapter.) When you are done, save the publication as Employee Cookoff.

Figure 4.52
Edited Contest
publication

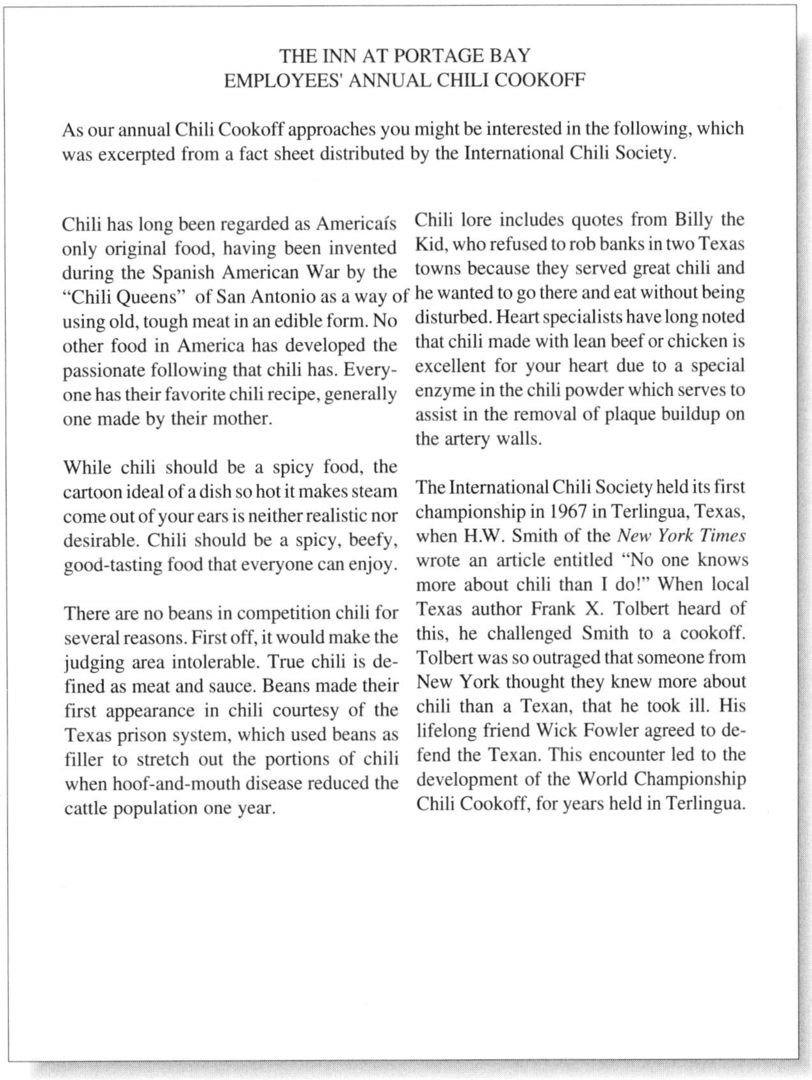

THE INN AT PORTAGE BAY
EMPLOYEES' ANNUAL CHILI COOKOFF

As our annual Chili Cookoff approaches you might be interested in the following, which was excerpted from a fact sheet distributed by the International Chili Society.

Chili has long been regarded as Americaís only original food, having been invented during the Spanish American War by the "Chili Queens" of San Antonio as a way of using old, tough meat in an edible form. No other food in America has developed the passionate following that chili has. Everyone has their favorite chili recipe, generally one made by their mother.

While chili should be a spicy food, the cartoon ideal of a dish so hot it makes steam come out of your ears is neither realistic nor desirable. Chili should be a spicy, beefy, good-tasting food that everyone can enjoy.

There are no beans in competition chili for several reasons. First off, it would make the judging area intolerable. True chili is defined as meat and sauce. Beans made their first appearance in chili courtesy of the Texas prison system, which used beans as filler to stretch out the portions of chili when hoof-and-mouth disease reduced the cattle population one year.

Chili lore includes quotes from Billy the Kid, who refused to rob banks in two Texas towns because they served great chili and he wanted to go there and eat without being disturbed. Heart specialists have long noted that chili made with lean beef or chicken is excellent for your heart due to a special enzyme in the chili powder which serves to assist in the removal of plaque buildup on the artery walls.

The International Chili Society held its first championship in 1967 in Terlingua, Texas, when H.W. Smith of the *New York Times* wrote an article entitled "No one knows more about chili than I do!" When local Texas author Frank X. Tolbert heard of this, he challenged Smith to a cookoff. Tolbert was so outraged that someone from New York thought they knew more about chili than a Texan, that he took ill. His lifelong friend Wick Fowler agreed to defend the Texan. This encounter led to the development of the World Championship Chili Cookoff, for years held in Terlingua.

This process involves:

- shortening the text block in the left column
- dividing the text block in the left column into two text blocks
- moving the large text blocks down each column
- flowing the small text block across both columns
- moving the small text block down the page

3. Sites is a document created using PageMaker. Open this publication and edit it to duplicate Figure 4.53. When you are done, save the publication as Tourist Sites.

Figure 4.53
Edited Sites publication

## TOURIST SITES

### THE INN AT PORTAGE BAY

Following is a sample of the most popular seasonal attractions found in our area. There is a comprehensive brochure listing all of the parks, museums, tourist attractions, and tours available in our lobby.

The Suquamish Museum

The Suquamish Museum is dedicated to the study of the Puget Sound Salish Indians, who were the original inhabitants of this area. Chief Seattle, for whom the City of Seattle is named, was from the Suquamish Tribe. The Museum's exhibition, which has toured in Europe, depicts the lives of the Puget Sound Indians prior to and after White settlement through photographs, artifacts, and interviews with tribal elders. The Suquamish Museum is located in one of the most beautiful settings in the Northwest, on the shores of Agate Pass, six miles north of Winslow on Highway 305. The hours are Monday through Thursday 10am - 5pm and Friday through Sunday 10am - 8pm. The admission is $2.50 for adults; $2.00 for senior citizens; and $1.00 for children under 12. Special arrangements are available for group or educational tours.

Whale Watching

Each summer visitors are treated to an amazing spectacle as Orca whales migrate from the Gulf of California to the waters of Alaska. Their path takes them through the San Juan Islands and provides a rare opportunity to see these beautiful creatures from a respectful distance.

The Tulip Festival

Early in April thousands of visitors flock to the Skagit Valley to enjoy the miles and miles of tulips as they bloom into a dazzling array of colors. Hundreds of varieties of daffodils, tulips, and other spring flowers make this a photographer's and artist's paradise. The climate, soil, and rain combined with the care of the Dutch settlers make the bulb and cut flower industry one of the most important in the region, with sales estimated at over $14 million. After touring the valley, visitors can enjoy a salmon barbecue, patterned after the native Indian recipes, at the nearby town of La Conner. The Skagit Valley is located on Interstate 5 at Mt. Vernon. The drive takes about one hour and 20 minutes from The Inn at Portage Bay.

The Peace Arch

Located on the United States and Canadian border, this park is dedicated to the friendship of the two countries. The park was opened in 1921 and was built with contributions from the school children in Washington and British Columbia. The Arch monument, which divides the highway, is a symbolic portal for the citizens who visit each country. The beautifully landscaped park provides a serene setting from which to view nearby Birch Bay. The Peace Arch State Park is located on Interstate 5 at the Canadian border. This is a spectacular park and one site that you will not want to miss. The drive takes about 45 minutes from The Inn at Portage Bay.

This process involves:

- typing *THE INN AT PORTAGE BAY*
- increasing the type size
- rotating *THE INN AT PORTAGE BAY* text block
- moving the text block to the left side of the page
- skewing the heading *TOURIST SITES* by 30 degrees
- creating a drop cap for the first letter of the first paragraph

4. Figure 4.54 shows a special effect created using the skewing process. Create this effect in a publication and save it as Heading.

Figure 4.54
Creating a special effect

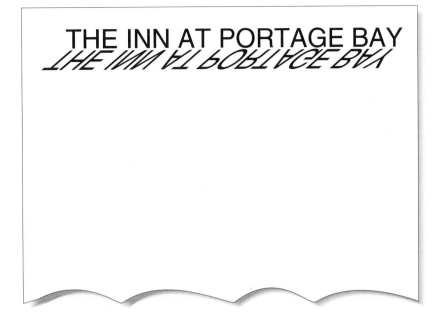

The process involves:

- starting a new publication
- typing the words *THE INN AT PORTAGE BAY*
- if necessary, changing the font to Arial
- changing the font size to 30
- copying the text block
- positioning one of the text blocks below the other
- flipping the bottom text block vertically
- skewing the text block 50 degrees
- aligning the text blocks as shown in Figure 4.54
- Experimenting by changing the:
  a. nonslanted text to bold
  b. space between characters (with the spacebar and the kerning nudge buttons)
  c. font and font size
  d. skewing degrees
  e. position of the text blocks

# CHAPTER 5

# Working with Graphics

Upon completion of this chapter you will be able to:

- Distinguish between the types of graphic images used in PageMaker
- Use the drawing tools
- Place graphics created in another program
- Modify graphic images
- Work with text and graphics
- Use the Group, Lock, and Mask features
- Position and modify frames with graphics
- Apply special effects to graphics

A desktop publishing program is distinguished from other types of software programs by its ability to merge text and graphic images and to use them for sophisticated design functions. Graphic images (or just graphics) include charts, pictures, drawings, and so on. In a document, graphics attract attention, enhance readability, and help illustrate a point. In this chapter you will learn how to work with graphics in PageMaker as well as how to merge text and graphics.

PageMaker treats each graphic image as an **object** (a distinct item, such as a text block, drawing, or picture) on the publication. **Graphic objects** are either independent or inline. An **independent graphic** is separate from the text block that surrounds it. Once you have placed an independent graphic, it stays in that position until you move it. An independent graphic can be placed apart from the text, or with the text flowing through it, wrapping around it, or jumping over it. An **inline graphic** is part of the text block that surrounds it. If the text moves, the graphic moves along with it. Using an inline graphic is the easiest way to embed an illustration in a specific paragraph of a publication and ensure that the illustration will remain in the same position within the paragraph, no matter how the publication is changed. Both independent and inline graphics have a boundary box with handles that you use to resize the graphic.

You determine whether a graphic object is independent or inline by the way you place or paste it. If you clicked an insertion point on the page using the text tool, the graphic is placed as an inline graphic. Otherwise, it is placed as an independent graphic.

## ADDING GRAPHICS TO A PUBLICATION

PageMaker provides three ways to add graphic objects to a publication. First, you can draw the graphic using any combination of the five PageMaker **drawing tools**, which create graphics in the shape of rectangles, squares, circles, ovals, polygons, and straight lines. However, none of these drawing tools allow you to make freehand drawings. Second, you can paste a graphic created in a different program or on another PageMaker publication from the Clipboard to the publication. Third, you can import (place) a graphics file created with a program specifically designed for producing graphics. Two common graphics programs are paint-type and draw-type programs.

A **paint-type (bitmap) graphic** represents the image as an array of dots, also called pixels. The paint programs used to create these graphics are flexible: they allow you to create freehand drawings, in much the same way as an artist would. Paint-type graphics can also be created by using a scanner to convert the printed images (such as artwork drawn on paper) or photographs into a graphics file, and then importing that file into PageMaker.

A **draw-type (vector) graphic** represents an image as a geometric shape. That is, each part of the graphic has a precise relationship to the other parts. For example, a pie chart is a draw-type graphic. Each slice or part of the pie is an exact percentage of the pie in relationship to all the other slices. Programs that create draw-type graphics include business (charts), engineering (computer-aided design), and illustration programs.

Graphics files created with graphics programs have an extension that identifies the type of file (paint, draw, and so on). For example, a .TIF file name extension identifies the file as a paint-type file in a **TIF** (**tagged image file**) format and a .PIC extension identifies the file as a draw-type file in a **PIC** (**picture**) format, created using a spreadsheet program. Figure 5.1 shows the icons that represent different graphics files as they are imported into PageMaker. You will learn more about the graphic file formats GIF and JPEG, used in developing documents for the World Wide Web, in Chapter 9.

**Figure 5.1**
Icons that represent different files as they are imported into PageMaker

| Icon | Used to Import |
|---|---|
| 🗂 | paint-type graphic |
| ▱ | draw-type graphic |
| ⊠ | tagged image file (TIF), GIF, JPEG, and Photo-CD format (GIF and JPEG are file formats that are commonly used for graphics displayed on the World Wide Web) |
| PS | image in Encapsulated PostScript (EPS) format, which is used with PostScript printers to produce a high-quality printed image |

## WORKING WITH IMPORTED GRAPHICS

In this section you will learn how to import a graphic object created using another program. Then you will learn how to move, resize, and crop the graphic. Last, you will learn how to work with text and graphics.

**Placing Graphics**

A drawing of Fort Worden, a historical building located near The Inn at Portage Bay, was scanned and saved in a TIF format with the name Fort. This paint-type graphic can be imported directly into PageMaker using the Place command in the File menu. Place this graphic on a new PageMaker publication.

1. Start the PageMaker program.

CTRL N
2. Select New from the File menu and click OK in the Document Setup dialog box.

3. If necessary, maximize the publication window, and move the Toolbox to the right side of the screen.

CTRL D
4. Select Place from the File menu.

The Place dialog box appears.

5. Locate the Fort file in the student files used with this book.

**6.** Click Fort.

Notice that the Place option in the lower-left corner of the Place dialog box indicates that this graphic will be placed as an independent graphic.

**7.** Click Open.

In a few moments the TIF icon appears.

**8.** Position the icon ⊠ at the 2-inch mark on both the vertical and horizontal rulers. See Figure 5.2.

**Figure 5.2**
Positioning the icon at the 2-inch marks on the vertical and horizontal rulers

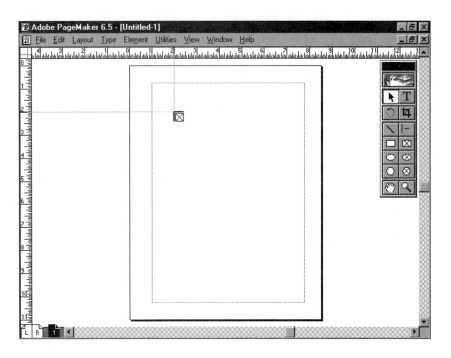

**9.** Click the mouse button to place the graphic object on the page. See Figure 5.3.

**Figure 5.3**
Selected graphic object

Handles

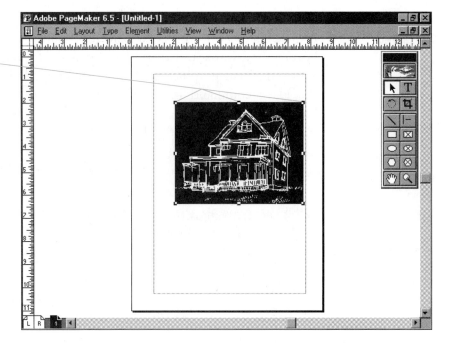

Notice that the object has handles, which indicates that it is selected. You can deselect the object by clicking a blank area in the publication window, and select it by clicking the object with the pointer or cropping tools. Practice deselecting and selecting the graphic.

**10.** Click a blank area to deselect the graphic.

**11.** Click the graphic to select it.

After a graphic object is selected, you can change its contrast as well as copy, move, delete, crop, and resize it.

Changing the Contrast and Lightness of Graphics

PageMaker allows you to change the appearance of a graphic by altering its lightness and contrast. This comes in handy when you want to improve the appearance of a graphic you need to use on a publication. Notice that the Fort graphic has a very dark background. To change this appearance, you use the Image Control dialog box. Before using the dialog box, make sure you select the graphic.

**1.** Point to Image in the Element menu.

**2.** Click Image Control.

Figure 5.4 shows the Image Control dialog box with the default settings.

Figure 5.4
Image Control dialog box
with default settings

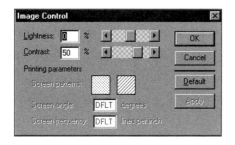

The options are:

- **Lightness,** which you change to lighten or darken the graphic image. The setting (in this case 0) is the percentage of light that appears in an image. The higher the percentage, the lighter the image.

- **Contrast,** which you adjust to change the lightness and darkness of the image in relation to its background. The higher the percentage, the greater the contrast.

- **Printing parameters,** which affect the printing of the publication and are set according to your printer's default settings. With PostScript printers you can specify a line screen for special effects; otherwise PageMaker automatically prints a dot screen.

- **Default button,** which returns all the settings in the dialog box to their defaults.

- **Apply button,** which you click to see how your new settings affect the image.

You will use this dialog box to change the lightness and contrast percentages. First, move the dialog box by clicking the title bar and dragging the box to the lower-right corner of the screen so you can see the graphic. When you drag the box, only the box's outline will move until you release the mouse button. (*Note*: Depending on the Windows setting for your computer, the entire dialog box might move.)

**3.** Point to the title bar.

**4.** Hold down the mouse button while you drag the outline of the dialog box to the lower-right corner of the screen. See Figure 5.5.

**Figure 5.5**
Moving the dialog box

Outline of dialog box

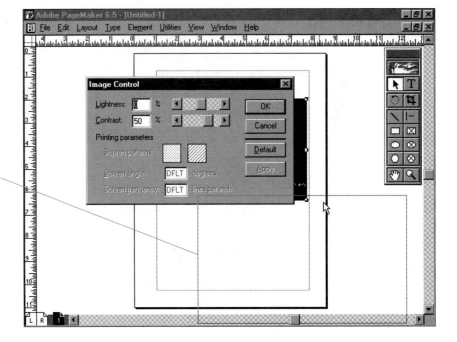

**5.** Release the mouse button.

Now change the Lightness setting to 50%. You can do this in two ways. You can either highlight the setting and type 50, or move the gray scroll box to the right until 50 appears in the Lightness box.

**6.** Point to the scroll box on the Lightness scroll bar.

**7.** Drag the box to the right until 50 appears.

**8.** Release the mouse button.

**9.** Click the Apply button to see the result of the change.

Notice that the higher percentage of lightness causes the image to appear lighter. Return to the default setting, and then change the contrast.

**10.** Click the Default button to return to the default settings.

**11.** Drag the Contrast scroll box to the left until the setting is −100.

**12.** Click the Apply button. See Figure 5.6.

Figure 5.6
Changing the contrast

Graphic with reduced
contrast

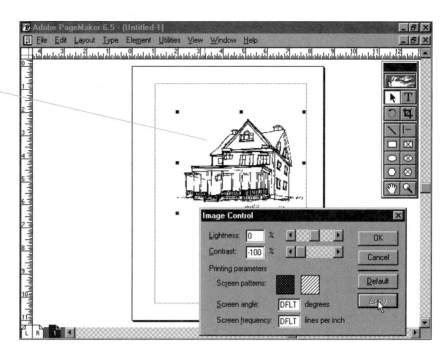

Notice that the negative number reduces the contrast between the image and the background. You will use this setting as you work with the graphic.

**13.** Click OK.

The dialog box closes and you're ready to resize the object.

## Resizing a Graphic

To change a graphic's size, you simply drag a handle toward the graphic to reduce its size and away to increase its size. When you change the size, the entire graphic stays in view. However, as shown in Figure 5.7, **resizing** the graphic might change its proportions. If you want to maintain the original proportions, hold down (SHIFT) as you resize the graphic.

Figure 5.7
Resizing the graphic

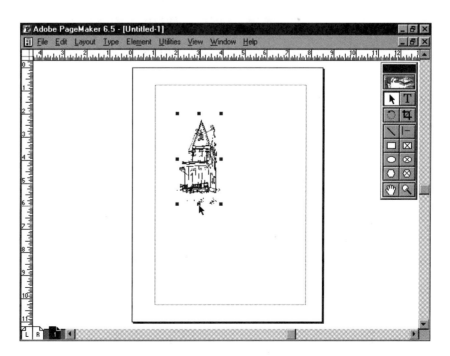

In the following steps you will re-create Figure 5.7. Although only one series of steps is needed to duplicate the figure, you will use two series of steps to practice reducing and enlarging the size of a graphic object. Start by reducing the size of the graphic object. (If you make a mistake when working with graphics, you can (in most cases) select the Undo command from the Edit menu to reverse the last action.

1. Point to the lower-right handle. See Figure 5.8.

**Figure 5.8**
Positioning the pointer

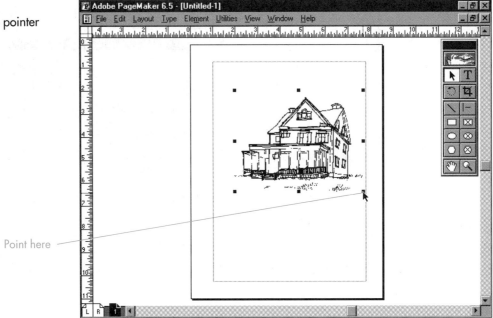

Point here

2. Hold down the mouse button until the double arrow and a boundary box appear.

3. Drag the handle toward the center of the graphic to the 4-inch mark on both the vertical and horizontal rulers. See Figure 5.9.

**Figure 5.9**
Dragging the handle toward the center of the graphic

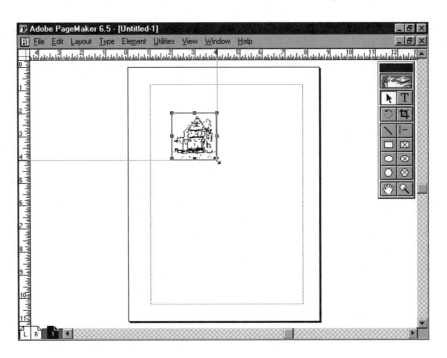

**4.** Release the mouse button.

Now enlarge the graphic object.

**5.** Point to the middle handle at the bottom of the graphic. See Figure 5.10.

**Figure 5.10**
Pointing to the middle handle at the bottom of the graphic

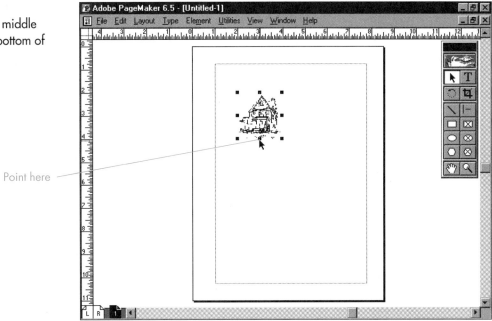

Point here

**6.** Hold down the mouse button until the double arrow ⬍ appears.

**7.** Drag the handle down to the 6-inch mark on the vertical ruler (refer to Figure 5.7).

**8.** Release the mouse button.

The object's size is increased, and its proportions changed. To restore the original proportions, hold down (SHIFT) while you hold down the mouse button.

**9.** Point to the middle handle at the bottom of the graphic.

**10.** Hold down (SHIFT).

**11.** Hold down the mouse button.

The original proportions of the graphic are restored.

**12.** Drag the handle up to the 4-inch mark on the vertical ruler. See Figure 5.11.

**Figure 5.11**
Dragging the handle to the 4-inch mark on the vertical ruler

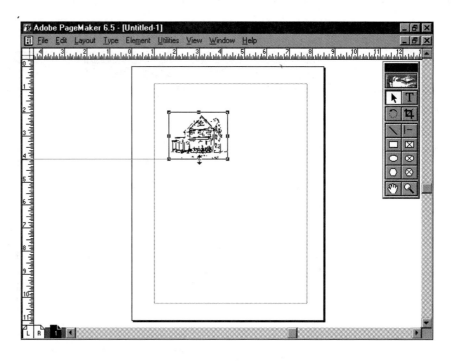

**13.** Release the mouse button.

**14.** Release SHIFT.

Once you resize a graphic, you might want to move, duplicate, or delete it.

---

**Moving, Copying, and Deleting Graphics**

You can use the pointer tool to move the graphic object anywhere on the document setup and the Pasteboard. Moving a graphic object does not change its proportions. The process is to point to the graphic (not to a handle), hold down the mouse button until the pointer changes to ▶, drag the graphic to the new location, and then release the mouse button.

**1.** Point to the middle of the graphic object.

**2.** Hold down the mouse button.

**3.** When the pointer changes to ▶, drag the graphic to the top of the page. See Figure 5.12.

Figure 5.12

Dragging the graphic to
the top of the page

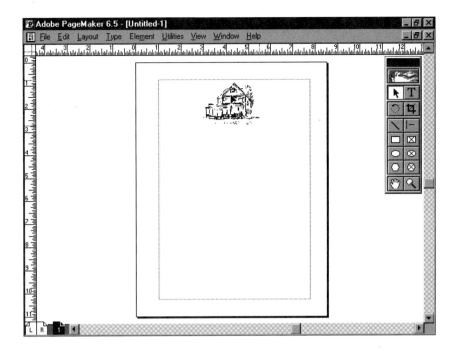

**4.** Release the mouse button.

To copy a graphic, you select the object and select the Copy command from the Edit menu. Then select the Paste option from the Edit menu. The graphic object is pasted to a position slightly offset from the original graphic. Make sure the graphic object is still selected (that is, the handles are visible), and then duplicate it.

**5.** Select Copy from the Edit menu.

**6.** Select Paste from the Edit menu.

The graphic is copied to a position slightly offset from the original. It might seem that there is only one graphic because these graphics overlap. To view both copies, you simply drag one off the other.

**7.** Point to the graphic.

**8.** Hold down the mouse button and drag the graphic to the 3-inch mark on the horizontal ruler and the 4-inch mark on the vertical ruler.

The copied graphic is now centered on the page and both graphics are visible, as shown in Figure 5.13 on the following page. However, only the graphic in the middle of the page displays boundary handles, indicating that it is selected.

Figure 5.13
Dragging the graphic to
the middle of the page

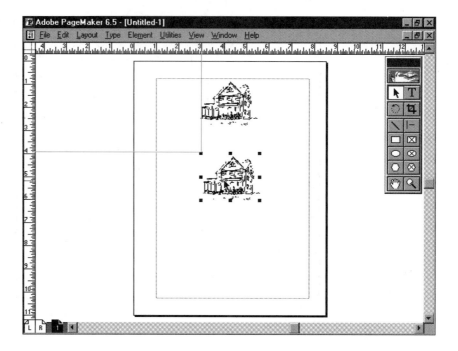

With the graphic object selected, you can delete it. Just select Clear from the Edit menu or press ⬭DELETE⬭. Delete the original graphic at the top of the page.

9. Click the graphic at the top of the page to select it.

10. Press ⬭DELETE⬭.

Your publication window should match Figure 5.14.

Figure 5.14
Result of deleting one of
the graphic objects

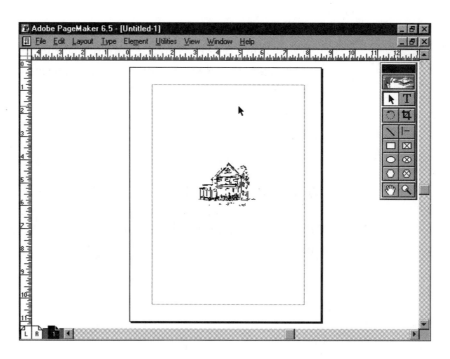

Next you'll change how much of the graphic appears onscreen.

PageMaker allows you to crop an imported graphic. **Cropping** means changing the amount of the image that is visible. To understand cropping, visualize a photograph you want to frame. You decide to try different frame sizes. Say you start out with a frame the same size as the photograph—the entire photo will be in view. As you reduce the frame size (crop), less and less of the photo will be in view. In other words, when you crop a graphic, you hide a portion of the graphic from view. You might crop a graphic to focus attention on a particular part of the image or to fit a graphic to a certain space within a publication.

To crop a graphic, you position the cropping tool on one of the handles of the selected graphic and drag the handle to the desired location. When you crop a graphic the part you trimmed off is not deleted; you can use the cropping tool to drag a graphic handle to redisplay the entire graphic.

1. Click the cropping tool ⊡ in the Toolbox to select it.

2. Position the cropping tool ⊠ on the graphic image.

3. Click the mouse button to select the graphic object and display its handles.

4. Position the cropping tool ⊠ on the lower-right handle. See Figure 5.15.

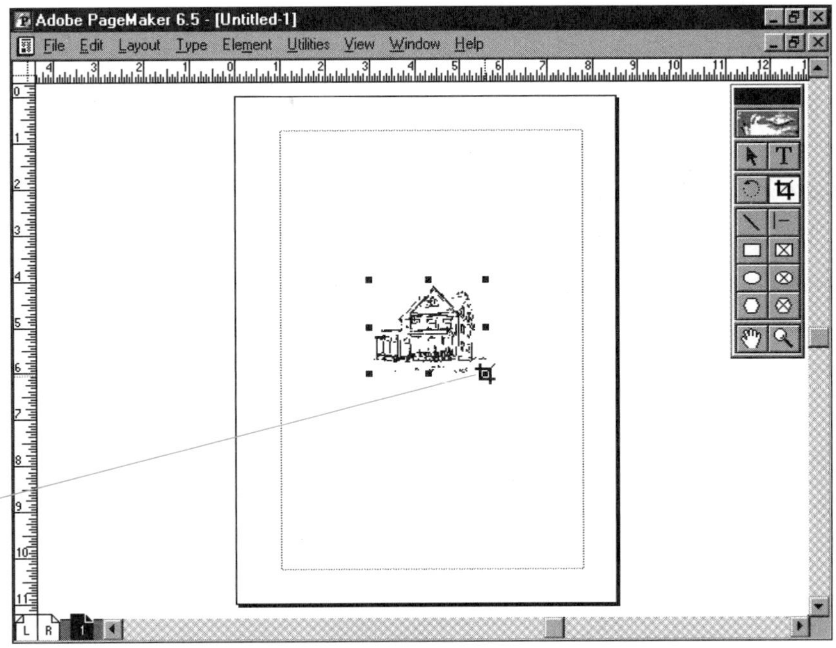

Figure 5.15
Positioning the cropping tool

Cropping tool on handle

**5.** Hold down the mouse button.

**6.** When the double arrow 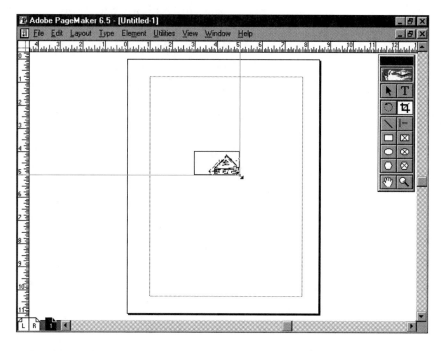 appears, drag the handle toward the center of the graphic object to the 5-inch marks on the horizontal and vertical rulers. See Figure 5.16.

**Figure 5.16**
Dragging the handle to the 5-inch mark on the horizontal ruler and the 5-inch mark on the vertical ruler

**7.** Release the mouse button.

Notice that only part of the graphic is now visible, but remember that the entire graphic is still intact. You have changed only the frame size. If you wanted to return to the original view, you could use the Undo command from the Edit menu or enlarge the frame by using the cropping tool to drag a handle away from the graphic rather than toward it.

In addition to changing the frame size, you can also move the graphic object within the frame and thus change the part of the graphic you view. You can reposition a graphic within its frame by positioning the cropping tool on the graphic (not on a handle), holding down the mouse button, and then moving the graphic in any direction.

**8.** Point to the middle of the graphic object.

**9.** Hold down the mouse button.

**10.** When the grabber hand icon appears, slowly move the graphic around the frame.

**11.** Return the graphic to the lower-right corner of the frame (refer to Figure 5.16). Release the mouse button.

Now return to the original view of the graphic by using the cropping tool to enlarge the frame.

**12.** Point to the lower-right handle.

**13.** Drag the handle to enlarge the frame to its original dimensions and deselect the graphic.

The graphic object should match the one shown in Figure 5.14. That is, the entire graphic should be visible and the graphic should be located near the center of the page. The cropping tool is useful as you work with graphics because it enables you to select and focus on the part of the graphic most relevant to your message.

## WORKING WITH TEXT AND GRAPHICS

Although graphic objects can stand alone on a publication page, they are most often accompanied by text. As mentioned earlier, a graphic object can be either part of the text (inline graphic) or separate from the text (independent graphic). Because an inline graphic becomes a fixed part of a text block, you have little flexibility in how you can manipulate inline graphics and text. An independent graphic, however, is separate from the text and you can integrate it with text in a variety of ways.

There are two basic ways to integrate text with an independent graphic. First, you can have the text **flow through** the graphic image—much like superimposing the text on top of the graphic, as shown in Figure 5.17 (left column of left page). Second, you can have the text **wrap around** the graphic. Every graphic object has a border with either a regular (rectangular) or irregular shape. This border determines how close the text will come to the graphic when you specify that text is to wrap around it. Three ways to wrap the text around a graphic shown in Figure 5.17. You can have the text flow all around the graphic (right column of left page); you have the text stop at the top of the graphic and continue to the next column (left column of right page); and you can have the text jump over the graphic (right column of right page).

**Figure 5.17**
Integrating text and graphics

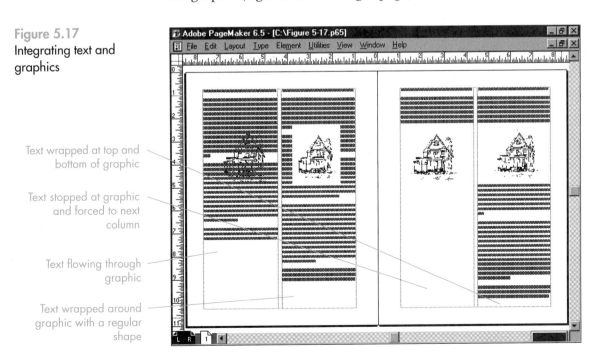

Text wrapped at top and bottom of graphic

Text stopped at graphic and forced to next column

Text flowing through graphic

Text wrapped around graphic with a regular shape

To specify the **text wrap**—the wrap and flow options—you use the Text Wrap dialog box, shown in Figure 5.18. The Text Wrap dialog box contains three wrap options and three text flow options. The first wrap option causes text to flow through the graphic. The second and third wrap options flow text around the graphic in a regular or irregular shape, respectively. Unless you change it, a graphic object will have a regular (rectangular) border around which text flows. If you specify that text is to wrap around the graphic, you must also specify the text flow, that is, stopping above, jumping over, or flowing completely around the graphic.

**Figure 5.18**
Text Wrap dialog box

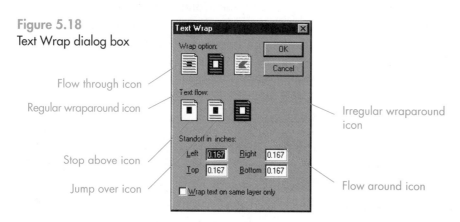

Flow through icon

Regular wraparound icon

Irregular wraparound icon

Stop above icon

Jump over icon

Flow around icon

You'll try some of these text wrap options.

**Flowing Text around a Graphic**

Worden—one of the student files used with this book—is a one-page, text-only document about Fort Worden that was created in Microsoft Word. You will place this document on the document setup and practice flowing text through and around the Fort graphic with which you've been working. The first step is to move the graphic object to the desired location on the document setup; you just completed this step in the previous section. The second step is to specify how you want the text to wrap around the graphic object. Complete the following steps to place the text and flow it around the graphic. (*Note:* This section and the comprehensive example later focus on text wrap and text flow techniques. The projects at the end of this chapter, where you will use these techniques, also address design considerations.)

1. Click the pointer tool ![pointer] in the Toolbox.

2. Click the graphic object to select it. See Figure 5.19.

Figure 5.19
Boundary box
surrounding the graphic
object

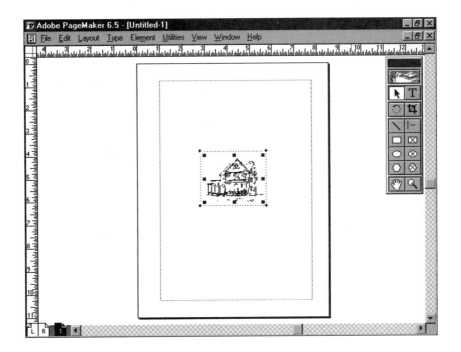

Figure 5.19 shows the boundary box surrounding the graphic object. When the text flows around the graphic, it stops outside this boundary. You'll see this after you place the text. First, you'll select flow and wrap options.

3. Select Text Wrap from the Element menu.

4. Click the regular wraparound icon under Wrap option (refer to Figure 5.18).

Notice that the flow around icon under Text flow is automatically selected and that the Standoff in inches boxes are filled in. **Standoff** is the distance from the graphic to the text. Increasing or decreasing this white space can alter the look of the page by making it appear lighter or darker. You will change the standoff after you experiment with different flow options.

5. Click OK.

6. Select Place from the File menu.

7. Select the Worden file and click Open.

**8.** Position the text icon 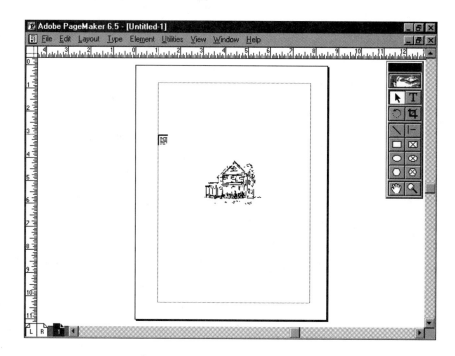 at the 3-inch mark on the vertical ruler. See Figure 5.20.

**Figure 5.20**
Positioning the text icon at the 3-inch mark on the vertical ruler

**9.** Click the mouse button to place the text wrapped around the graphic. See Figure 5.21.

**Figure 5.21**
Text wrapped around the graphic

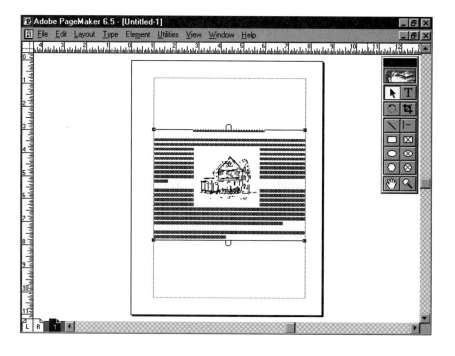

The document setup now contains two objects: a graphic and a text block. Each object can be independently modified, moved, and so on. Remember, to work with an object you must select it. Now, select the graphic object and change the text flow.

**10.** Click the graphic object to select it.

 **11.** Select Text Wrap from the Element menu.

**12.** Click the jump over icon in the Text flow options.

**13.** Click OK.

The text jumps over the graphic.

## Flowing Text through a Graphic

As mentioned earlier, flowing text through a graphic superimposes the text on a graphic. To flow text through a graphic object, make sure the graphic is selected, and then choose the flow through icon from the Text Wrap dialog box.

 **1.** Select Text Wrap from the Element menu.

**2.** Click the flow through icon under Wrap option.

**3.** Click OK.

The text flows through the graphic. Although the text and graphic are difficult to see in this case, the flow through option can be used effectively in some instances. For example, this option would be appropriate if you wanted to use a graphic as a background for text. Before continuing, change the text flow back to wraparound.

**4.** Select Text Wrap from the Element menu.

**5.** Select the regular wraparound icon under Wrap option.

**6.** Select the flow around icon under Text flow.

**7.** Click OK.

The graphic and text return to their original placement, as was shown in Figure 5.21.

## Changing the Graphic Boundary

You can change the size of a **graphic boundary**—the white space that surrounds the graphic object—by changing the standoff settings in the Text Wrap dialog box or by dragging the boundary lines. You can also change the shape of the graphic boundary so it is no longer a rectangle.

Figure 5.22 shows text flowing around the graphic in an irregular (non-rectangular) shape.

**Figure 5.22**

Text flowing around the graphic in an irregular shape

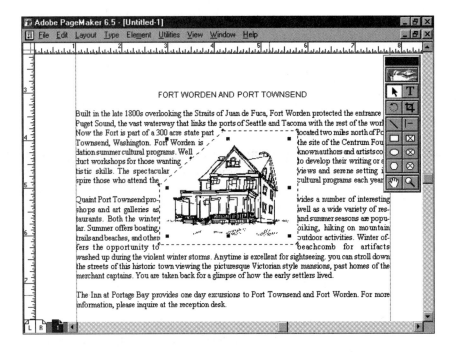

To change the boundary, you drag a diamond-shaped boundary handle in the appropriate direction. (Boundary handles are different from graphic handles.) As you drag a boundary handle, the adjacent handles act as anchors or hinges. Figure 5.22 was created by dragging the upper-left handle toward the middle of the graphic. You can also add boundary handles to shape the boundary box in any way you'd like. To add a handle, you simply click the boundary line. To remove a handle, you drag the handle until it covers another handle. In order to duplicate Figure 5.22 you need to add two handles to the figure. First, change the view to 75% Size so it is easier to work with the graphic handles.

1. Change the view to 75% Size.

2. Make sure the graphic is selected, and, if necessary, use the scroll bars to position the graphic in the middle of the screen.

3. Point to the center of the left boundary line, as shown in Figure 5.23.

Figure 5.23
Pointing at the boundary
line prior to adding a
handle

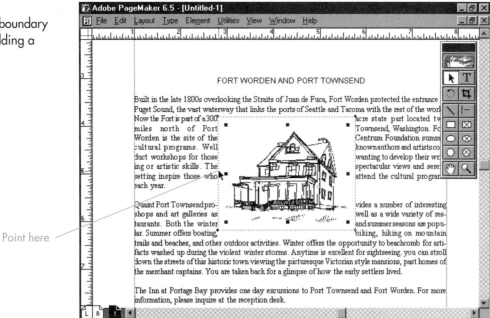

Point here

**4.** Click the mouse button to add a handle.

**5.** Point to the center of the top boundary line, as shown in Figure 5.24.

Figure 5.24
Pointing at the boundary
line and clicking to add
a handle

Point here

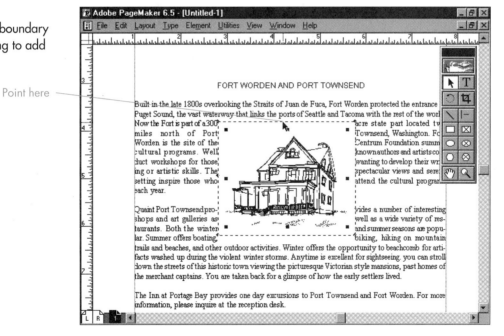

**6.** Click the mouse button to add a handle.

These two new handles will act as anchors as you drag the upper-left handle toward the center of the graphic to create the new boundary.

**7.** Point to the upper-left boundary handle.

**8.** Hold down the mouse button.

**9.** When the pointer changes to ⌖, drag the handle to the position shown in Figure 5.25.

**Figure 5.25**
Dragging the handle to create a new boundary

Drag

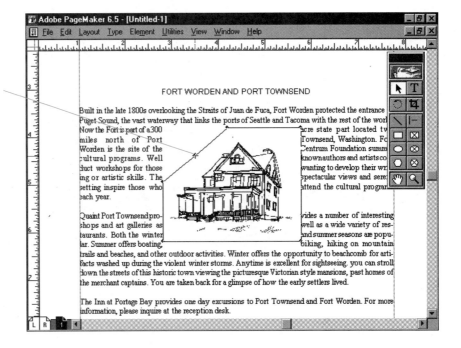

**10.** Release the mouse button.

The text flows around the graphic object according to the new boundary. Now save and close the publication.

CTRL 0

**11.** Change the view to Fit in Window.

SHIFT CTRL S

**12.** Select Save As from the File menu.

**13.** Select the appropriate drive and folder.

**14.** Type *Fort Worden* as the file name and click Save.

CTRL W

**15.** Select Close from the File menu.

This completes the section on working with text and graphics. If your study time is up, use the File menu to exit PageMaker.

## CREATING GRAPHICS WITH THE DRAWING TOOLS

In this section you will learn how to use the PageMaker drawing tools to create graphic objects. The drawing tools enable you to create rectangles, squares, ovals, circles, polygons, and straight lines at any angle. You can use each tool alone to create a simple shape; you can also use the tools in combination to create complex graphics with different fills and strokes to enhance a PageMaker publication.

Below is a brief description of each drawing tool.

- The **line tool** 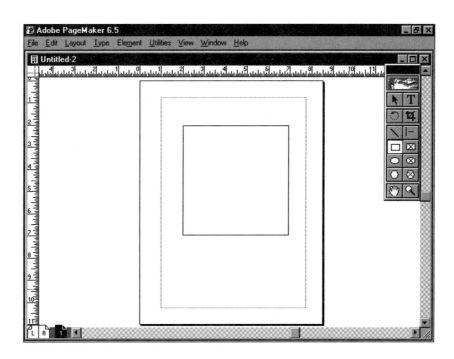 draws straight lines at any angle. (Hold down ⬚SHIFT⬚ to draw lines at 45° angles.)

- The **constrained line tool** draws lines at 45° angles.

- The **rectangle tool** draws rectangles with square corners. (Hold down ⬚SHIFT⬚ to draw squares. Select Rounded Corners from the Element menu to round the corners.)

- The **ellipse tool** draws ovals. (Hold down ⬚SHIFT⬚ to draw circles.)

- The **polygon tool** draws polygons.

You will practice using the rectangle, ellipse, constrained line, and line drawing tools to create various graphic objects. The process is to select the desired tool from the Toolbox and drag the crossbar to draw the graphic. Then you will modify, move, and delete the objects.

<table>
<tr><td>

**Drawing Rectangles and Squares**

**Figure 5.26**
Graphic object created using the rectangle drawing tool

</td><td>

Figure 5.26 shows a graphic object created using the rectangle drawing tool.

</td></tr>
</table>

You'll duplicate this figure by completing the following steps.

1. Start a new publication.

2. Click the rectangle tool 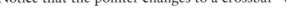 in the Toolbox.

3. Move the pointer to the document setup.

Notice that the pointer changes to a crossbar + .

**4.** Position the crossbar ✛ at the 2-inch marks on the vertical and horizontal rulers. See Figure 5.27.

**Figure 5.27**
Positioning the crossbar at the 2-inch vertical and horizontal marks

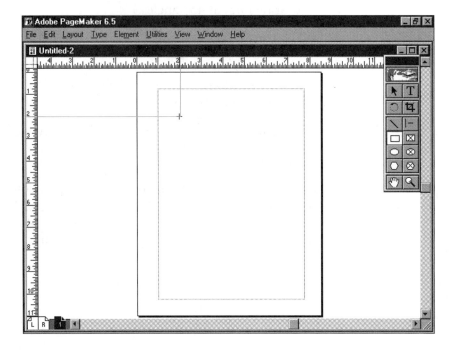

**5.** Hold down the mouse button and slowly drag the crossbar diagonally.

**6.** Position the crossbar at the 7-inch marks on the vertical and horizontal rulers. See Figure 5.28.

**Figure 5.28**
Diagonally dragging the crossbar to create the graphic

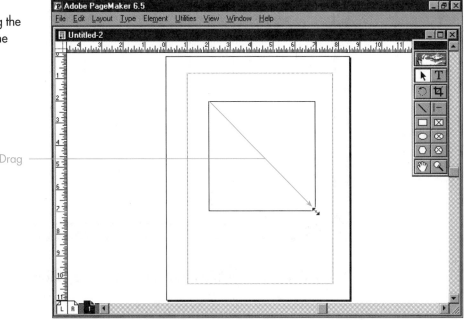

**7.** Release the mouse button.

The drawn graphic object, a square, can be selected, deselected, resized, moved, enhanced (by changing the lines used for the border and the shading within the graphic), or deleted. Notice the handles on the graphic, which indicate that it is selected. You can deselect the graphic by clicking a blank area.

8. Move the crossbar + to a blank area on the publication.

9. Click the mouse button to deselect the graphic object.

To select the graphic, use the pointer tool.

10. Click the pointer tool ▦ in the Toolbox.

11. Point to any border of the graphic.

12. Click the mouse button to select the graphic object.

Now practice resizing and moving the graphic. To resize a graphic, point to any handle and drag the handle to the desired location.

13. Point to the lower-right handle.

14. Hold down the mouse button and drag the handle toward the middle of the graphic.

15. Release the mouse button when the handle is at the 5-inch marks on the vertical and horizontal rulers.

16. Point to the middle handle at the bottom of the graphic.

17. Drag the handle down to the 7-inch mark on the vertical ruler.

18. Release the mouse button.

Notice that the graphic is now a rectangle. PageMaker allows you to reshape a rectangle into a square by holding down (SHIFT) while you drag a handle.

19. Point to the middle handle at the bottom of the graphic.

20. Hold down (SHIFT).

21. Hold down the mouse button.

The rectangle changes to a square. If you drag the handle, the square shape is retained.

22. Drag the handle up 1 inch.

23. Release the mouse button.

24. Release (SHIFT).

To move a drawn graphic, you point to any border (but not to a handle), wait for the pointer to change to ▶, and drag the graphic to the desired location.

25. Point to any border of the graphic.

26. Hold down the mouse button until the pointer changes to ▶.

**27.** Drag the graphic to the bottom of the page.

**28.** Release the mouse button.

**29.** On your own, drag the graphic to the middle of the screen.

Two graphic modifications you can make are to change the stroke of the border line and the fill within the border. For rectangular graphic objects, you can also change the shape of the corners. Figure 5.29 shows the graphic object with the corners rounded, the border thicker, and the inside shaded. (Whenever you change the corners, borders, or shading, you must first select the desired graphic object.)

Figure 5.29
Modifications to the
graphic object

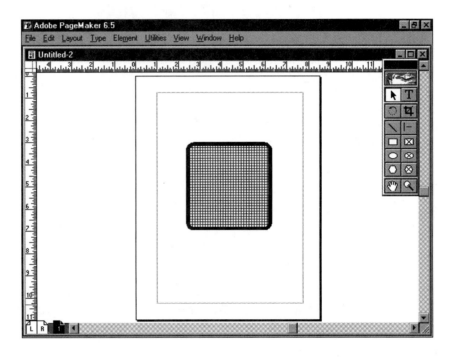

Do the following with the graphic object selected:

**1.** Select Rounded Corners from the Element menu.

Figure 5.30 shows the Rounded Corners dialog box with six choices. The square-corner option is highlighted.

Figure 5.30
Rounded Corners dialog
box

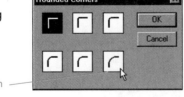

Select this option

**2.** Click the lower-right option.

**3.** Click OK.

**4.** Click a blank area to deselect the graphic.

The graphic now has rounded corners. Next, change the border stroke and the fill.

**5.** Click the graphic to select it.

**6.** Point to Stroke in the Element menu.

**7.** Click 12pt.

**8.** Point to Fill in the Element menu.

**9.** Click the last option.

CTRL U **10.** Select Fill and Stroke from the Element menu.

**11.** Click the down arrow in the Color box in the Fill section of the dialog box.

**12.** Click Blue.

**13.** Click OK.

The fill changes to blue. Your graphic should resemble the one shown in Figure 5.29. You can use the Fill and Stroke dialog box to change the fill, line, and color of a graphic. Before continuing, delete this graphic.

**14.** Press DELETE.

Next, you'll use the ellipse drawing tool.

## Drawing Ovals and Circles

The process for drawing ovals and circles is the same as for drawing rectangles and squares. You select the ellipse tool, position the crossbar on the publication page, and drag the crossbar to create the desired graphic. If you hold down SHIFT while you drag the crossbar, the graphic will take the shape of a circle. After creating the graphic, you can modify, move, resize, or delete it. Figure 5.31 shows a graphic object created using the ellipse drawing tool.

Figure 5.31
Graphic object created
using the ellipse tool

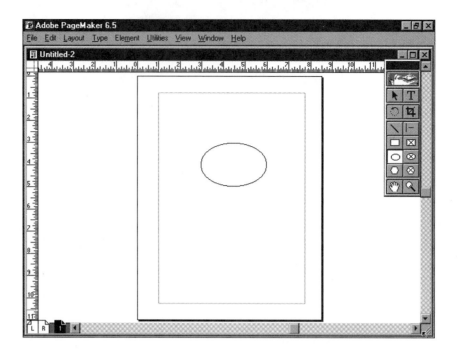

Complete the steps to draw a graphic similar to Figure 5.31.

1. Click the ellipse tool ⬭ in the Toolbox.

2. Position the crossbar + at the 3-inch marks on the vertical and horizontal rulers.

3. Drag the crossbar + to the 5-inch mark on the vertical ruler and the 6-inch mark on the horizontal ruler to recreate the graphic in Figure 5.31.

4. Release the mouse button.

Notice that there are eight handles with which to resize the graphic. Use the lower-middle handle to resize the graphic, to the size shown in Figure 5.32.

Figure 5.32
Resizing the graphic

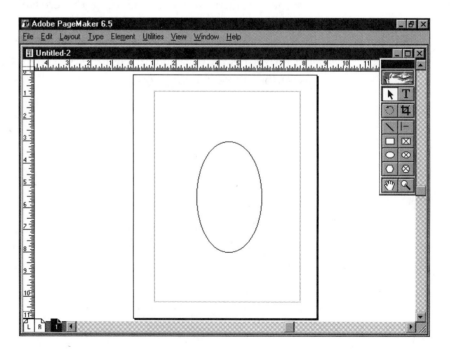

5. Click the pointer tool 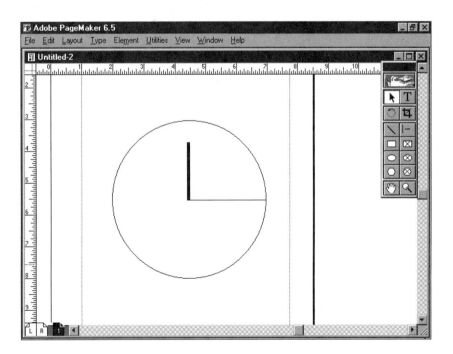 in the Toolbox.

6. Click the border of the graphic to display the handles.

7. Point to the lower-middle handle.

8. Drag the handle to the 8-inch mark on the vertical ruler to approximate Figure 5.32.

9. Release the mouse button.

Now use (SHIFT) to change the oval to a circle.

10. Point to the lower-middle handle.

11. Hold down (SHIFT) and the mouse button.

12. After the oval changes to a circle, release the mouse button.

13. Release (SHIFT).

As you can see, switching between ovals and circles is simple in PageMaker.

## Drawing Lines

PageMaker provides two line-drawing tools: line and constrained line. Both enable you to draw straight lines. The difference between them is that the constrained line tool draws lines only at 45° and 90° angles as measured from the crossbar's arm. The line tool can work like the constrained line tool if you hold down (SHIFT) as you drag one end of the line.

Practice using the constrained line tool by drawing lines inside the circle you just created. Figure 5.33 shows the circle with two lines, one wider than the other.

**Figure 5.33**
Circle with two lines, one wider than the other

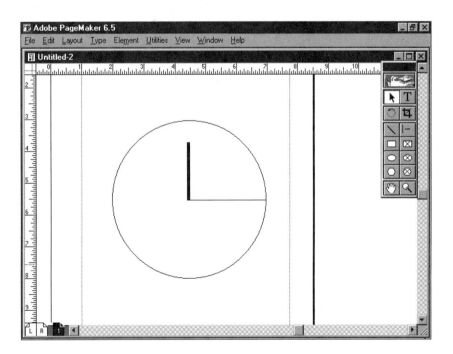

Complete the following steps to duplicate this figure.

1. Click the constrained line tool |− in the Toolbox.

2. Position the crossbar + in the middle of the circle.

3. Hold down the mouse button and drag the crossbar + across the page to the edge of the circle. See Figure 5.34.

**Figure 5.34**
Dragging the crossbar across the page to the edge of the circle

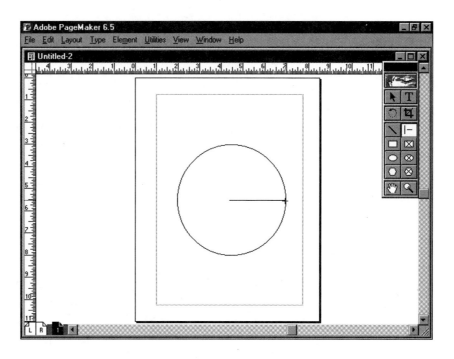

4. Release the mouse button.

The line is a separate graphic object which you can select, deselect, modify, resize, move, and delete. To change the line, you will rotate one end of it around the circle as though it were the second hand on a clock.

5. Click the pointer tool ▶ in the Toolbox.

6. Click the line to select it and display the handles.

7. Point to the handle at the right end of the line. See Figure 5.35.

Figure 5.35
Pointing to the handle at
the right end of the line

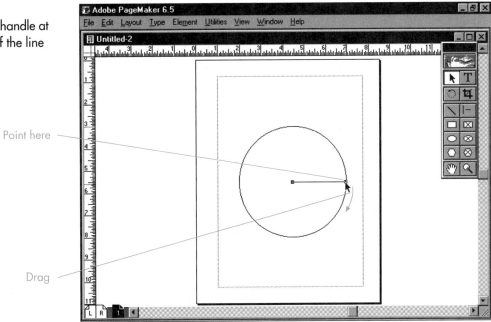

Point here

Drag

8. Hold down the mouse button and drag the handle around the circle.

9. When the line returns to its starting point, release the mouse button.

Now draw the other line and change its width. To make it easier to draw the line more precisely, change the view to 50% Size.

  10. Change the view to 50% Size.

11. Use the scroll bars to center the circle on the screen.

12. Click the constrained line tool |− in the Toolbox.

13. Point to the middle of the graphic.

14. Hold down the mouse button and drag the crossbar + upward to the point shown in Figure 5.33.

15. Release the mouse button.

16. Point to Stroke in the Element menu.

17. Click 8pt.

18. Click a blank area to deselect the graphic.

Before continuing, clear the document setup.

CTRL A  19. Choose Select All from the Edit menu.

DELETE  20. Select Clear from the Edit menu.

21. Close the publication without saving it.

This completes the section on using the drawing tools. If your practice time is up, use the File menu to exit PageMaker.

In this section you will learn how to use several special graphics and text features, such as working with multiple graphic objects, using different lines and fills, creating drop shadows, reversing lines, and reversing type. Figure 5.36 shows three text and graphic combinations. Each variation is a heading made up of graphic objects created using the drawing tools and the text *HISTORIC FORT WORDEN* placed on top of the graphic objects.

**Figure 5.36**
Three text and graphic combinations

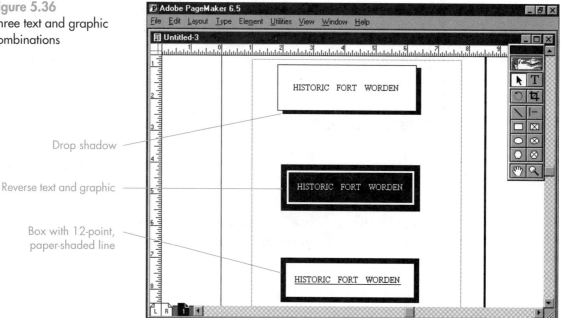

Drop shadow

Reverse text and graphic

Box with 12-point, paper-shaded line

The first heading has a **drop shadow**. Drop shadows are used to give the graphic an illusion of depth. You create them by drawing two identical boxes, one with a **solid shade** for the background and the other with a **paper shade** for the foreground. The paper-shaded graphic is placed over and slightly above and left of the solid box. The process is to select the Solid option from the Element Fill menu and draw the first box. Then copy the box so you have two identical shapes. Finally, change the fill of the second box to Paper and superimpose it over the first box. The paper fill is the same shade as the publication. Therefore when you choose this fill, only the border is visible. Complete the following steps to duplicate the first heading.

1. Start a new publication.

2. Point to the Fill option in the Element menu and click Solid.

3. Click the rectangle tool ▢ in the Toolbox.

4. Position the crossbar **+** at the 1-inch mark on the vertical ruler and the 2-inch mark on the horizontal ruler.

5. Drag the crossbar **+** to the 2½-inch mark on the vertical ruler and the 6½-inch mark on the horizontal ruler.

**6.** Release the mouse button.

Now copy the graphic.

**7.** Click the pointer tool 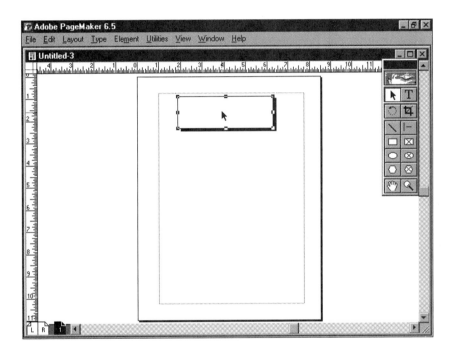 in the Toolbox.

**8.** Select the graphic, and on your own, copy and paste it.

The graphic is copied to a position slightly offset from the original. Now change the fill of the copied graphic to Paper and reposition it.

**9.** Point to Fill in the Element menu and click Paper.

**10.** Point to the middle of the paper graphic.

**11.** Hold down the mouse button.

**12.** When the pointer changes to ▶, drag the box up and to the left to position it on top of the solid graphic. See Figure 5.37.

Figure 5.37
Dragging the box to position it on top of the solid graphic

**13.** Release the mouse button.

**14.** Click a blank area to deselect the graphic.

You now have two graphic objects on the page, one **stacked** on top of the other. You can stack several objects and change the order of the stack. That is, in this case, you can place the solid-shaded graphic on top of the paper-shaded graphic. When you stack graphics and text objects, you need to know how to select each object and how to change the order of the stack. To select one object, click it with the pointer tool. You can also hold down (CTRL) while you continue to click additional objects. As you click, each object in the stack is selected in turn. To select two or more adjacent objects at one time, hold down (SHIFT) while you click the first and last objects. This procedure is useful for selecting more than one graphic to move. For example, to move the heading box you created, you need to select both graphic objects. Practice selecting and moving the heading.

**15.** Click the solid-shaded graphic to select it.

**16.** Hold down (SHIFT) while you click the paper-shaded graphic.

**17.** Release (SHIFT).

**18.** Point to the middle of the graphic.

**19.** Hold down the mouse button until the pointer changes to ▶.

**20.** Drag the graphic objects down the page.

**21.** Drag the graphic objects back to their previous location.

**22.** Click a blank area to deselect the graphic objects.

Now use the Element menu to change the order of the stacked objects. The Arrange command in the Element menu contains four options to change this order. **Bring to Front** moves the selected object in front of all other objects and **Send to Back** moves the selected object behind all other objects. **Bring Forward** moves the object one position toward the top of the stack and **Send Backward** moves the object one position toward the bottom of the stack. Because the paper-shaded graphic is on top, you will select it and send it to the back.

**23.** Click the paper-shaded graphic to select it.

**24.** Point to Arrange in the Element menu.

(SHIFT)(CTRL)( [ )    **25.** Click Send to Back.

The paper-shaded graphic moves behind the solid-shaded graphic. Now return the objects to their original stacking order. With the paper-shaded graphic still selected:

**26.** Point to Arrange in the Element menu.

(SHIFT)(CTRL)( ] )    **27.** Click Bring to Front.

These commands are very helpful when you have several layers stacked whose order you want to rearrange.

---

**Placing Text on a Graphic**

Next you will place the title *HISTORIC FORT WORDEN* on the drop shadow graphic you just created. Use the text tool to type this title on the Pasteboard. Then copy the text block to the heading. Start by using the Character Specifications dialog box to select a large type size.

(CTRL)( T )    **1.** Select Character from the Type menu.

**2.** Change the point size to 18 and click OK.

**3.** Click the text tool **T** in the Toolbox.

**4.** Position the I-beam as shown in Figure 5.38.

Figure 5.38
Positioning the I-beam

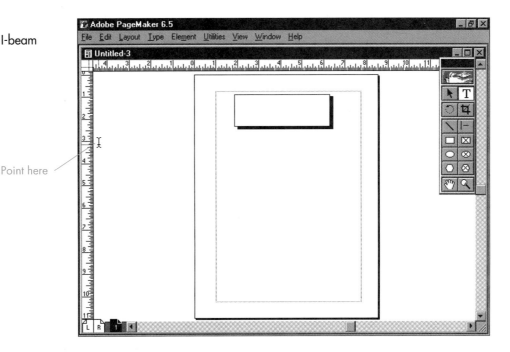

Point here

5. Click the mouse button to set an insertion point.

CTRL 1

6. Change the view to Actual Size.

7. Type *HISTORIC    FORT    WORDEN* (type four spaces between each word).

CTRL 0

8. Change the view to Fit in Window.

Now, using the pointer tool, drag the text onto the graphic.

9. Click the pointer tool  in the Toolbox and drag the text to the center of the graphic.

10. Click a blank area.

Now view the text in Actual Size.

11. Position the pointer on the text.

12. Click the right mouse button.

13. Click Actual Size.

CTRL 0

14. After viewing the heading, right-click and click Fit in Window.

This completes the first heading, which is text in a drop shadow box. The second heading you'll create combines two graphic objects and the text title. The solid-shaded graphic from the first heading is used as a background. The graphic on top of it is a thin-line rectangle, created using the rectangle drawing tool and selecting Reverse from the Stroke command in the Element menu. **Reverse** changes the stroke from solid to paper. The text is also reversed, so that it appears as a paper image on the solid background. You do this by selecting Reverse from the Type style command in the Type menu. Start by copying the solid-shaded graphic from the first heading and drawing the interior rectangle as a reverse line. Then copy the text title and reverse the text type.

1. Click the solid-shaded graphic to select it.

2. On your own, copy and paste the graphic.

Move the copy of the graphic to just below the first heading, as shown in Figure 5.36.

3. Drag the graphic to just below the first heading.

4. Click a blank area to deselect the graphic.

5. Point to Stroke in the Element menu and click 4pt.

6. Point to Stroke in the Element menu and click Reverse.

7. Click the rectangle tool 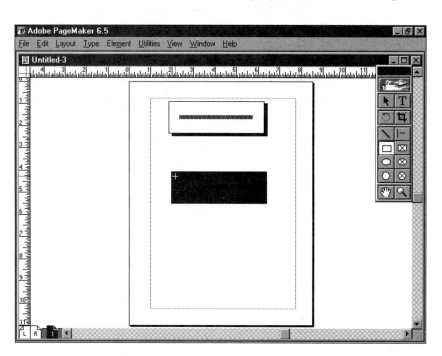 in the Toolbox.

8. Position the crossbar + within the graphic, as shown in Figure 5.39.

**Figure 5.39**

Positioning the crossbar within the graphic

9. Drag the crossbar + to draw the rectangle.

10. Release the mouse button.

Now copy the title from the first heading.

11. Click the pointer tool in the Toolbox.

12. On your own, copy and paste the text in the first heading.

The title is copied to the publication. Now move the title to the second heading box and reverse the text.

**13.** Drag the title to the heading box.

**14.** Click the text tool ⊡ in the Toolbox.

**15.** Point to the text with the I-beam. See Figure 5.40.

**Figure 5.40**
Positioning the I-beam

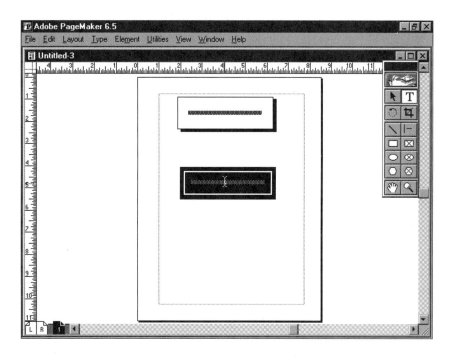

**16.** Triple-click to select the text.

**17.** Point to Type Style in the Type menu and click Reverse.

SHIFT CTRL V

**18.** On your own, deselect the text.

**19.** Click the pointer tool ⊡ in the Toolbox.

**20.** Point to Stroke in the Element menu and, if necessary, click Reverse to deselect the option.

Take a moment to view this new heading.

CTRL 1

**21.** Right-click the middle of the heading and click Actual Size.

CTRL 0

**22.** Right-click and click Fit in Window.

This completes the second heading. The third heading is composed of a box drawn with a 12-point, paper-shaded line, and the title with a 2-point underline. To complete this heading:

**1.** Point to Stroke in the Element menu and click 12pt.

**2.** Point to Fill in the Element menu and click Paper.

**3.** Click the rectangle tool ⊡ in the Toolbox.

**4.** Draw the box as was shown in Figure 5.36.

Now copy the text from the first heading.

5. Click the pointer tool in the Toolbox.
6. On your own, copy the text from the first heading.
7. Drag the text into the bottom heading box.
8. Deselect the text.

Now draw the underline. First, change the view to Actual Size.

CTRL 1

9. Right-click the middle of the heading and click Actual Size.
10. Point to Stroke in the Element menu and click 2pt.
11. Click the constrained line tool in the Toolbox.
12. Drag the crossbar + underneath the text to draw the underline.

CTRL 0

13. Right-click and click Fit in Window.

CTRL 5

14. Change the view to 50% Size.
15. Use the scroll bars to view all of the headings.

CTRL 0

16. Change the view to Fit in Window.

In this section, you tried only a few of the Stroke and Fill options, including Reverse and different lines and shades. You can use other features to enhance the appearance of documents and create special effects when working with graphic objects. (*Note:* Some printers will not print reverse text.)

## GROUPING AND LOCKING OBJECTS

In this section you will learn about grouping objects and locking them in place. **Grouping** combines two or more objects into one object, while **locking** anchors an object's position on a publication. Both grouping and locking are useful when you are working with several objects on the screen and you want to maintain a certain relationship among the objects and prevent accidentally moving or deleting objects. Earlier you selected the first heading by clicking the solid graphic and holding down SHIFT while you clicked the paper-shaded graphic. Then you moved these two objects as one. However, the grouping of these two objects was temporary. Clicking the mouse button would ungroup (separate) them. To make the grouping more permanent, you can select two or more objects and use the Group command in the Element menu. The objects remain grouped until you select the Ungroup command from the Element menu. This grouping feature allows you to keep various objects together as you edit a document. Practice this feature by grouping all of the headings.

1. Click the pointer tool 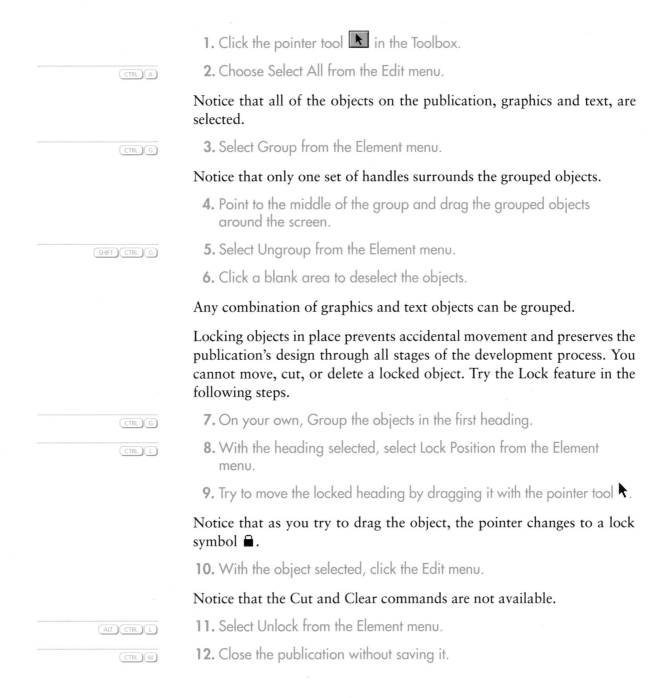 in the Toolbox.

CTRL A
2. Choose Select All from the Edit menu.

Notice that all of the objects on the publication, graphics and text, are selected.

CTRL G
3. Select Group from the Element menu.

Notice that only one set of handles surrounds the grouped objects.

4. Point to the middle of the group and drag the grouped objects around the screen.

SHIFT CTRL G
5. Select Ungroup from the Element menu.

6. Click a blank area to deselect the objects.

Any combination of graphics and text objects can be grouped.

Locking objects in place prevents accidental movement and preserves the publication's design through all stages of the development process. You cannot move, cut, or delete a locked object. Try the Lock feature in the following steps.

CTRL G
7. On your own, Group the objects in the first heading.

CTRL L
8. With the heading selected, select Lock Position from the Element menu.

9. Try to move the locked heading by dragging it with the pointer tool.

Notice that as you try to drag the object, the pointer changes to a lock symbol.

10. With the object selected, click the Edit menu.

Notice that the Cut and Clear commands are not available.

ALT CTRL L
11. Select Unlock from the Element menu.

CTRL W
12. Close the publication without saving it.

## WORKING WITH FRAMES AND GRAPHICS

In Chapter 4 you learned how to work with frames and text. Recall that a frame is a placeholder and aids in the layout of publications. The frame object can be in the shape of a rectangle, oval, or polygon. The process for creating a frame is to use the frame tools in the Toolbox to draw the frame and then place a graphic within the frame.

For a graphic that is larger than the frame, you can specify that the graphic be **clipped** to fit the frame. For a graphic that is smaller than the frame, you can specify that the graphic be **scaled** (or enlarged) to fit the frame. Or, you can have the frame resized to fit the graphic. In addition, you can specify the alignment of the graphic within the frame. Figure 5.41 shows a document with an ellipse frame.

Figure 5.41
An ellipse frame

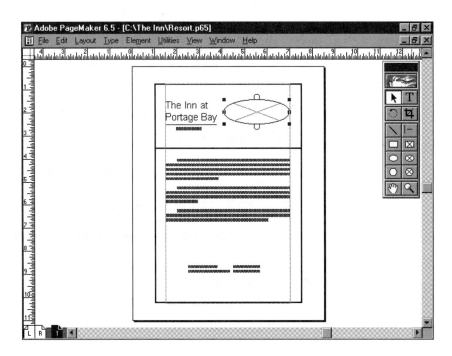

You will open a document from the student files used with this book, create the frame, and place a graphic in it.

**1.** Open the Resort publication and maximize the window.

**2.** Click the ellipse frame tool  in the Toolbox and draw the frame shown in Figure 5.41.

**3.** With the frame selected, select Place from the File menu.

**4.** Select Cottage and click Open.

The Cottage graphic is inserted into the selected frame.

**5.** Change the view to Actual Size and display the graphic.

You can change the location of the frame by dragging it with the pointer tool. You can also resize the frame.

**6.** Click the pointer tool  in the Toolbox.

**7.** Drag the frame around the document and then return it to the original location.

**8.** Resize the frame by dragging the lower-right corner handle down 1 inch.

CTRL O

CTRL D

CTRL 1

Now you can change the stroke size of the frame's border.

**9.** Point to Stroke in the Element menu and click Hairline.

Using frames provides flexibility in specifying the location and shape of a graphic.

**10.** On your own, delete the frame.

CTRL W

**11.** Close the publication without saving it.

The previous publication also can be created using a mask. A **mask**, similar to a frame, enables you to specify the shape of a displayed graphic. One advantage of using a mask is that you can experiment with which part of the graphic to display. To create a mask, you place a graphic on the publication. Then you draw an object with one of the PageMaker drawing tools and place the object over the graphic. Finally, you select both the object and the graphic and choose Mask from the Element menu. Complete the following to create a mask.

CTRL O

**1.** Open the Resort publication.

CTRL D

**2.** Place the Cottage graphic as shown in Figure 5.42.

**Figure 5.42**
Placing the graphic

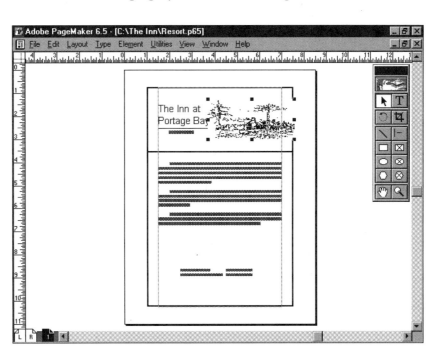

**3.** Click the ellipse tool 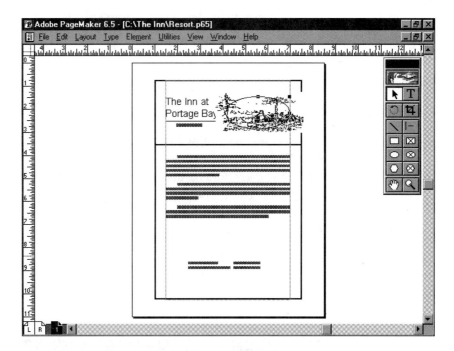 in the Toolbox and draw the object shown in Figure 5.43.

**Figure 5.43**
Drawing an ellipse object

**4.** Hold down (SHIFT) and click the pointer tool in the Toolbox.

**5.** Hold down (SHIFT) and click the edge of the graphic to select it.

**6.** Release (SHIFT) and the mouse button.

Both the graphic and the oval object should be selected.

(CTRL) (6)

**7.** Select Mask from the Element menu.

(CTRL) (1)

**8.** Change the view to Actual Size and display the graphic.

**9.** Click a blank area to deselect both objects.

The mask allows only a part of the graphic to be displayed. You can move the graphic to display a different part of it.

**10.** Click inside the mask to select the graphic.

**11.** Point inside the mask and drag the graphic around. See Figure 5.44.

Figure 5.44
Dragging the graphic
around within the mask

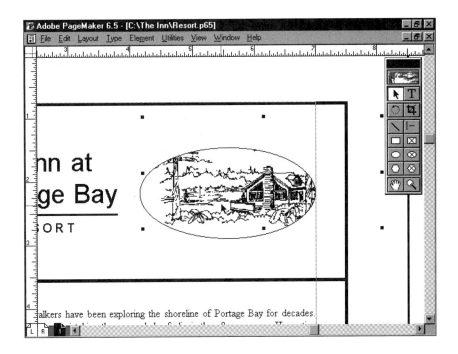

CTRL W  **12.** Close the publication without saving it.

Besides masking, PageMaker enables you to create other effects with graphics.

## TRANSFORMING A GRAPHIC

In Chapter 4 you learned how to create special effects by rotating, reflecting, and skewing text. These effects can also be applied to graphic objects, as shown in Figure 5.45.

Figure 5.45
Graphic transformed by
rotating, reflecting, and
skewing

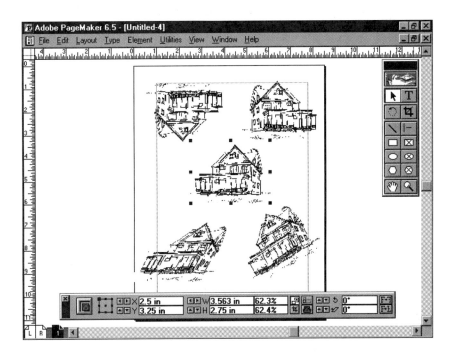

Complete the following to create the effects shown in Figure 5.45.

CTRL N and CTRL D

1. Start a new publication and place the Fort graphic.

2. Resize the graphic to approximately half of its original size.

3. Change the contrast of the graphic to match Figure 5.46.

Figure 5.46
Changing the graphic

Horizontal-reflecting button

Rotation box

Apply button

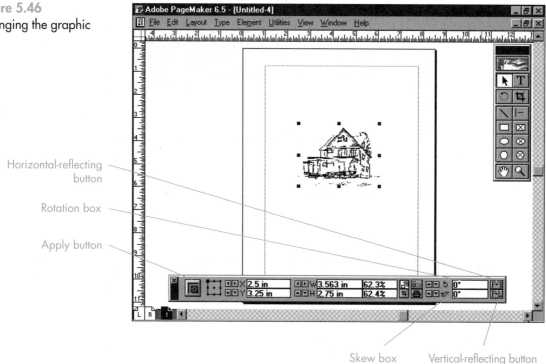

Skew box          Vertical-reflecting button

CTRL '

4. Display the Control palette and move it to the bottom of the screen.

Your screen should resemble Figure 5.46. Now use the Control palette to change the appearance of the graphic.

5. Click the horizontal-reflecting button �earrow (refer to Figure 5.46).

6. Click the horizontal-reflecting button again.

7. Click the vertical-reflecting button .

8. Click the vertical-reflecting button again.

9. Change the rotation to 30 degrees.

10. Click the apply button .

11. Change the rotation to 45, 90, and 180 degrees, clicking the apply button each time.

12. Change the rotation to 0 degrees and click the apply button .

13. Change the skew to 30 degrees and click the apply button .

14. Change the skew to −30 degrees and click the apply button .

**15.** Change the rotation and the skew to 40 degrees and click the apply button ▣.

**16.** Change the rotation and skew to 0 degrees and click the apply button ▣.

CTRL ` **17.** Close the Control palette.

CTRL W **18.** Close the publication without saving it.

As you can see, there is quite a variety of special effects you can use both individually and in combinations to create a distinct look for your publication.

## SUMMARY

You have learned one of the most important and powerful features of PageMaker—how to work with graphics. You know how to import graphics developed with another program and how to use the PageMaker drawing tools to create graphics and enhance publications. You have also learned how to resize, crop, move, and delete graphics as well as how to integrate graphics and text. In addition, you know how to use frames and masks.

## QUESTIONS

1. Distinguish between independent and inline graphics.

2. Describe the three ways to add graphics to a publication.

3. Distinguish between a paint-type and a draw-type graphic.

4. What are the steps for importing a graphic?

5. How do you resize a graphic?

6. Explain what is meant by cropping a graphic.

7. List and briefly explain the use of each PageMaker drawing tool.

8. List and briefly explain the three ways to wrap text around a graphic.

9. What is the process for changing a graphic boundary?

10. What is meant by *standoff?*

11. What combination of keystrokes is used to (a) individually select graphic objects that are stacked, (b) have more than one graphic object selected at a time, and (c) select all graphic objects on a page?

12. Explain how the Stroke and Fill commands can be used to enhance a graphic object.

13. Explain the difference between a mask and a frame.

14. True or False? The Control palette can be used to apply special effects such as rotating, reflecting, and skewing graphics.

1. To practice the skills you have learned in Chapter 5, you will create the publication shown in Figure 5.47, a flyer used to promote the Portage Bay Golf Club.

**Figure 5.47**
Project 5.1—Promotional flyer

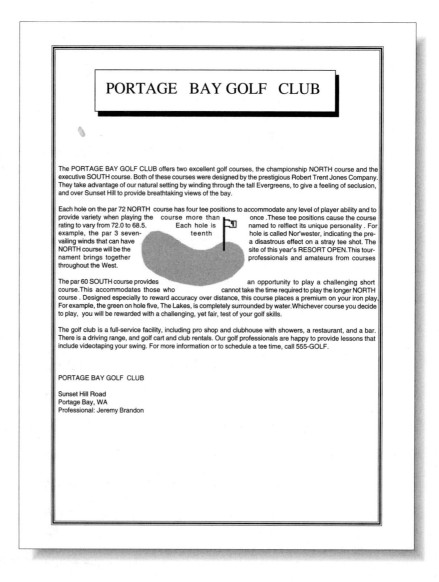

You will use two student files: Bay Golf is a text file created in Microsoft Word, and Ninth Green is a TIF file containing a graphic. You will start a new publication, place these two files, and edit the publication to duplicate Figure 5.47. Depending on the font you use and the placement of the graphic on the page, your finished publication might not match the figure exactly. The steps are:

- Start a new publication.

- Place the Ninth Green graphic in the middle of the page.

- Crop the graphic so that the border just frames it.

- Select the regular wraparound option from the Text Wrap dialog box.

- Place the Bay Golf text file.

- Use the pointer tool to select all the text.

- Move the text down the page to allow room for a heading.

- Change the boundary lines of the graphic to create the irregular shape. (*Hint:* Change the view to Actual Size.) You will need to set anchors and move the boundary line at several points. Again, it is not necessary to duplicate the figure exactly.

- Change the type to a larger size, such as 24 point.

- On the Pasteboard, type the heading *PORTAGE BAY GOLF CLUB* with three spaces between each word.

- On another area of the Pasteboard, draw a drop-shadow box large enough to surround the heading.

- Place the heading over the box.

- Move the heading and box to the top of the page. (*Hint:* Use SHIFT and the pointer tool to select all three components of the heading.)

- Draw a triple-line border slightly larger than the margin guides

- Save the publication as Golf Club.

- Print the publication.

2.    Figure 5.48 shows a document that The Inn at Portage Bay provides to its guests.

**Figure 5.48**
Project 5.2—Historical
Registry Publication

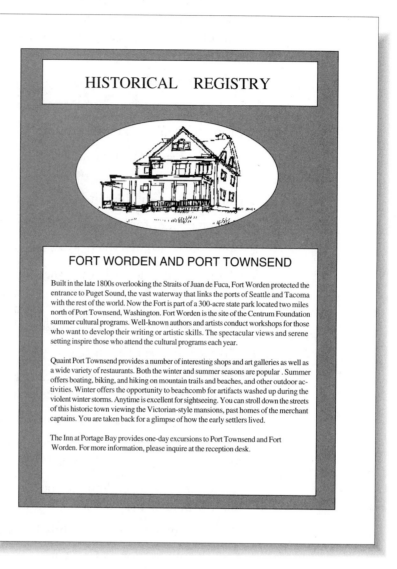

HISTORICAL    REGISTRY

FORT WORDEN AND PORT TOWNSEND

Built in the late 1800s overlooking the Straits of Juan de Fuca, Fort Worden protected the entrance to Puget Sound, the vast waterway that links the ports of Seattle and Tacoma with the rest of the world. Now the Fort is part of a 300-acre state park located two miles north of Port Townsend, Washington. Fort Worden is the site of The Centrum Foundation summer cultural programs. Well-known authors and artists conduct workshops for those who want to develop their writing or artistic skills. The spectacular views and serene setting inspire those who attend the cultural programs each year.

Quaint Port Townsend provides a number of interesting shops and art galleries as well as a wide variety of restaurants. Both the winter and summer seasons are popular . Summer offers boating, biking, and hiking on mountain trails and beaches, and other outdoor activities. Winter offers the opportunity to beachcomb for artifacts washed up during the violent winter storms. Anytime is excellent for sightseeing. You can stroll down the streets of this historic town viewing the Victorian-style mansions, past homes of the merchant captains. You are taken back for a glimpse of how the early settlers lived.

The Inn at Portage Bay provides one-day excursions to Port Townsend and Fort Worden. For more information, please inquire at the reception desk.

The Fit in Window view of the publication is shown in Figure 5.49.

Figure 5.49
Fit in Window view of
the document

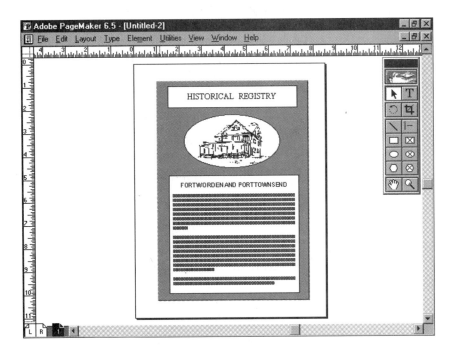

This publication contains the following objects:

- a solid-fill rectangle used as a background
- a paper-fill heading with the words HISTORICAL    REGISTRY
- an oval frame with a graphic
- a rectangular frame with text

Figure 5.50 shows the document setup with the background and the
two frames.

Figure 5.50
Document setup with the
background and two
frames

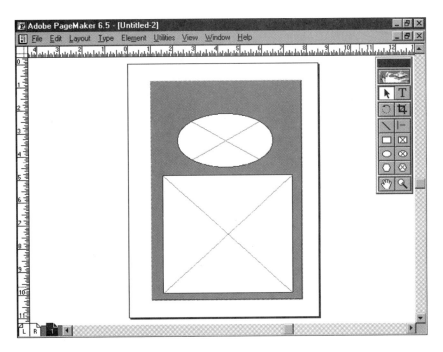

- Start a new publication.
- Draw a solid rectangle that is the same size as the margin guides.
- Change the Tint to 40%.(*Hint*: Use the Fill and Stroke dialog box.)
- Deselect the solid rectangle and change the fill to paper.
- Draw the two frames.
- Place the graphic named Old Fort into the oval frame . (*Hint*: Select the frame first.)
- Center the graphic in the frame. (*Hint*: Use the Frame Options dialog box, which you can open by selecting Frame in the Element menu.)
- Place the text document named Historic Fort into the rectangular frame.
- Center the text within the frame.
- Create the heading with the text *HISTORICAL   REGISTRY*.
- Save the publication with the name Historical Fort.
- Print the publication.

3.  Use the Help menu to search for and display the Help window called Manipulating an object using the Control palette. Read the information and then exit the Help function.

# CHAPTER 6

# Using Master Pages, Templates, and Style Sheets

**Upon completion of this chapter you will be able to:**

- **Explain how master pages differ from publication pages**
- **Work with double-sided and facing pages**
- **Create a publication from a template**
- **Replace text in a story**
- **Format text with styles**

This chapter focuses on how to use master pages, templates, and style sheets. The first part of the chapter introduces you to master pages, templates, and style sheets by directing you to create a new publication with master pages. In the second part, you will produce a newsletter for The Inn at Portage Bay using a newsletter template file that was previously designed and saved. In the third part, you will use a template script that comes with PageMaker to create a newsletter. In Chapter 7 you will learn how to create master pages, a template, and a style sheet.

PageMaker has two kinds of pages: publication pages and master pages. **Publication pages** are the pages that make up your document; you have worked on and created many publication pages in the previous chapters. **Master pages**, like an outline, plan what the publication pages will look like—in other words, they specify the format of a particular publication. With master pages you set up the general format for a publication's pages one time and then reuse the format for all the pages on the publication. This saves you time and helps to ensure a consistent look within a publication.

Anything you place on master pages appears on the publication pages. In addition to the elements from the master pages, publication pages contain text and graphics that are unique to these pages. Master pages can include such things as:

- a nonprinting layout grid, such as margin guides, column guides, and horizontal and vertical ruler guides

- text and graphics that appear on every page, such as a company logo, page number, name of publication, issue, and date

- placeholder or dummy text and graphics that show how the publication will look when completed

You can set up one master page for every page on the publication. You can set up left and right master pages to correspond to the left and right publication pages. Or you can set up multiple master pages and apply a specific master page to a specific publication page as needed.

To understand the relationship between master pages and publication pages, visualize your document as two layers of transparent paper—one layer of master page and one layer of publication page. You start with the master page layer, which contains the common elements that will appear in the document. Then on top of the master page you place the publication page, which contains the articles and graphics unique to that page. When you print the page, the elements from both the master page and the publication page layers are captured on one piece of paper.

Because you have two transparent layers, when you are on one layer, you cannot change elements of the other layer. In other words, you cannot modify or delete elements that are part of the master page layer while you are on the publication page layer even though those elements are visible. You must switch to the master page to edit the elements it contains.

## Exploring Master Pages

To better understand how master pages correspond to publication pages, you will create a new publication and change various master page settings. Pay attention to what happens as you change the settings and click between various pages.

1. Start the PageMaker program.

CTRL N

2. Select New from the File menu.

3. Enter the following values in the Document Setup dialog box, as shown in Figure 6.1:

   Double-sided: selected

   Facing pages: selected

   Number of pages: 4

   Inside (margin in inches): 3

**Figure 6.1**
Document Setup
dialog box

Type 4

Type 3

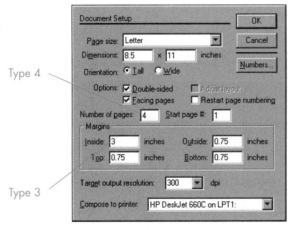

4. When your Document Setup dialog box matches Figure 6.1, click OK.

Your document setup should look like Figure 6.2. With an inside margin of 3 inches it will be easy for you to see the difference between inside and outside margins. Notice the page icons in the lower-left corner of your publication window. Publication page icons contain consecutive numbers, in this case *1* through *4*, which represent the four publication pages you specified in the Document Setup dialog box. Master page icons contain *L* and *R*, which represent the left and right master pages.

When you first see the publication window, the page 1 icon is highlighted, and one sheet of paper, corresponding to page 1, appears on your screen. Look carefully at the page in the publication window. Recall that the inside margin is 3 inches and the outside margin is 0.75 inch. Note that the inside margin for page 1 is on the left and the outside margin is on the right.

Figure 6.2
Publication window
with page 1,
a right-hand page

Move the Toolbox out of
the way as you work

3-inch inside margin

0.75-inch outside margin

Publication page icons

Master page icons

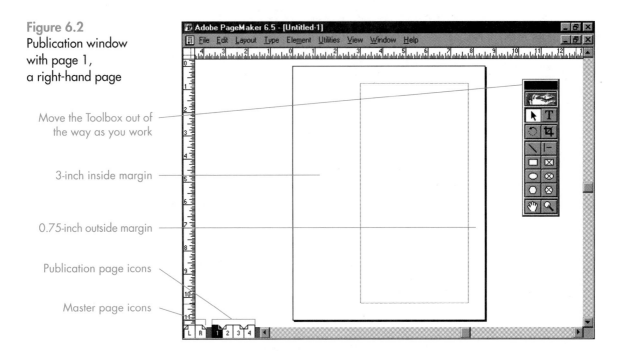

**5.** Click the page 2 icon.

Look at the publication page icons in the lower-left corner of the screen. The page 2 and 3 icons are highlighted. Pages 2 and 3 appear in the publication window together because you selected Facing pages in the Document Setup dialog box (refer to Figure 6.1). The **Facing pages** option allows you to simultaneously design two pages, a left and a right, and to see an open publication just as your readers will.

Next, notice the margins in the pages—3 inches and 0.75 inch. For a left-hand page, the inside margin is on the right; for a right-hand page, it is on the left. To clarify this arrangement, take a blank piece of notebook paper. Fold it in half as if it were going to be a birthday card. Draw a box in the area on each surface that will contain text, using 3 inches and 0.75 inch for the margins. Number the surfaces front-to-back from *1* to *4*. On each of the four surfaces, write *left* or *right*, beginning with *right* on page 1.

Thus, page 1 is a right-hand page, page 2 a left-hand page, and so on. The master page corresponding to page 1 carries the R icon. In fact, every odd-numbered page is a right-hand page and every even-numbered page is a left-hand page. Look at your publication window and notice how the L master page icon corresponds to the even-numbered page icons, and the R master page icon corresponds to the odd-numbered icons.

So when creating a master page for page 1, start with the R master page, not the L master page. It might seem backward because logic would seem to dictate that left should come first, but remember the card you created earlier. The first "page" of the card was a right page. Now that you understand how left and right master pages correspond to publication pages, click each page icon and look at the publication window.

**6.** Click the L master page icon. You'll see both the left and right master pages. See Figure 6.3.

Figure 6.3
Master pages displayed
as facing pages

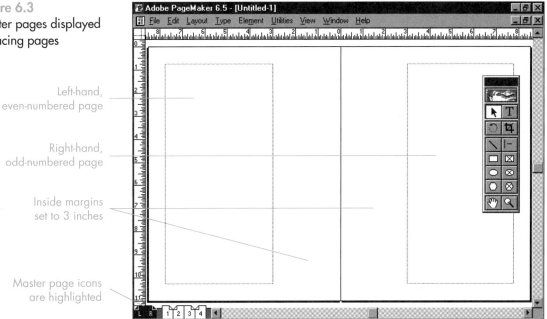

Left-hand,
even-numbered page

Right-hand,
odd-numbered page

Inside margins
set to 3 inches

Master page icons
are highlighted

**7.** Click the page 1 icon.

**8.** Click the page 2 icon. You see pages 2 and 3.

**9.** Click the page 4 icon.

As you've just seen, in a four-page document, pages 2 and 3 are facing pages; pages 1 and 4 do not have a facing page. That is why you see only one page when you click the icons for pages 1 and 4.

## Setting Columns on Master Pages

In this section, you will set two columns for the left master page and three columns for the right master page. This will help you see how left and right master pages correspond to publication pages.

**1.** Click the L master page icon.

Both master pages appear, ready for you to work on them.

**2.** Select Column Guides from the Layout menu.

**3.** Click Set left and right pages separately to select that option.

Left and Right boxes are available for setting a different number of columns on the left and right master pages. Figure 6.4 shows the Column Guides dialog box after you set columns for each master page.

Figure 6.4
Column Guides
dialog box

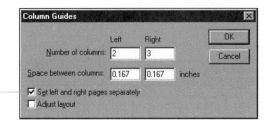

Click to select this option

4. Type 2 in the Left Number of columns box.

5. Press (TAB) twice.

6. Type 3 in the Right Number of columns box.

7. When your dialog box matches the one in Figure 6.4, click OK.

Your screen, similar to Figure 6.5, shows two columns on the left master page and three columns on the right. The inside and outside margins remain 3 inches and 0.75 inches respectively, from when you set up the publication.

Figure 6.5
Master pages
with columns

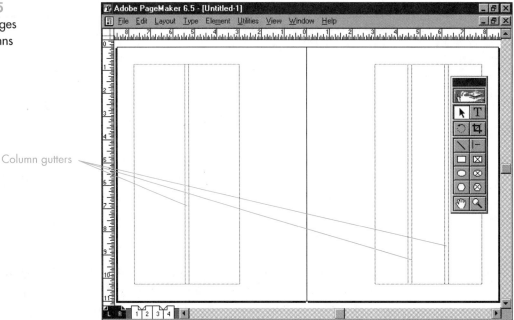

Column gutters

Click the publication page icons in the lower-left corner of the screen and look at the page layout.

8. Click the page 1 icon.

9. Click the page 2 icon.

Again, look at the two-page spread for pages 2 and 3 and note the differences between the pages.

10. Click the page 4 icon.

## Double-Sided and Facing Pages

The **Double-sided** option in the Document Setup dialog box enables you to create a publication whose pages will be printed back-to-back. In other words, page 1 is printed on one side of a sheet of paper and page 2 is printed on the other side of the same sheet. You can set the inside margins separately from the outside margins to allow room for binding (as with a book) or punching holes (as with pages for a three-ring binder). As you noticed earlier, the left and right pages in an odd- and even-page layout are mirror images of each other. When Double-sided is not selected, the publication is single-sided.

The Facing pages option allows you to view left and right pages at the same time on the Pasteboard. You see the publication as your reader will and can more easily create a pleasing spread. Facing pages is available only when Double-sided is selected.

Turn off Facing pages by doing the following.

1. Select Document Setup from the File menu.

2. Click the Facing pages check box to deselect it.

3. Click OK.

The master pages are still divided into left and right pages, but you can see only one page at a time onscreen. Look at each page and note the number of columns (two or three), which corresponds to the left or right master page. Also note that the inside and outside margins still correspond to the master pages.

4. Click the L master page icon.

5. Click the R master page icon.

6. Click the page 1 icon.

7. Click the page 2 icon.

8. Click the page 3 icon.

9. Click the page 4 icon.

Now look at the same document with single-sided pages. To change from double-sided to single-sided pages:

10. Select Document Setup from the File menu.

11. Click the Double-sided check box to deselect it.

Notice that the words *Inside* and *Outside* within the Margin in inches area changed to *Left* and *Right*. Because this publication is now single-sided, left and right margins make more sense than inside and outside margins.

12. Click OK.

Look at the master page and publication page icons in the lower-left corner of the publication window, as shown in Figure 6.6. All the page icons are now right-sided pages because just one kind of page occurs.

Figure 6.6
Publication set to single-sided, not double-sided, pages

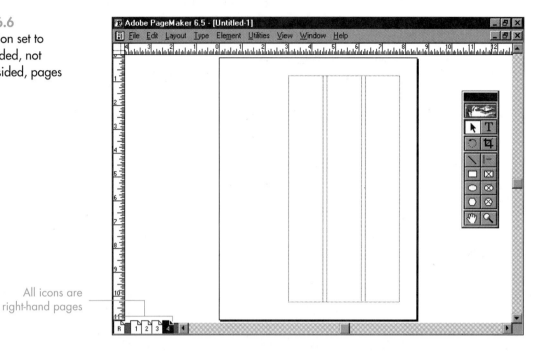

All icons are right-hand pages

**13.** On your own, click each master page and publication page icon.

Notice that every page looks the same: when Double-sided pages are deselected, only one kind of page occurs—a right page. Also, look at the page icons themselves. Notice that the upper-right corner of each page is folded down, indicating that it's a right page.

Now clear the Pasteboard of this publication.

CTRL W

**14.** Select Close from the File menu.

**15.** Click No when PageMaker asks if you want to save the publication.

Now that you've explored master pages—learned why page 1 of a publication corresponds to a right, not left, master page; experimented with setting columns on master pages; switched between double-sided and single-sided pages; and viewed the difference between facing and non-facing pages—it's time to explore templates.

## EXPLORING TEMPLATES

PageMaker creates two kinds of files that can be saved: publications and templates. Publications, which you've already worked with, are saved with the **.P65** file name extension; templates are saved with the **.T65** file name extension. The Save Publication dialog box contains a Save as type option, where you specify Publication, the default, or Template.

## Understanding Templates

A **template** is the outline of how an entire publication will look. It contains master pages, a Styles palette, and the publication's layout grid (you'll learn about grids in Chapter 7). A template is created once, saved, and used over and over to produce publications with a similar look but different content. With a template you can have a standard layout for your company's product brochures, for example. In the template you can specify the size of the brochure, include a company logo and name, insert placeholder text, and set up styles that define the character and paragraph attributes that will be used. Then you could produce different versions of the brochure for all the products based on the template. This way, you save time and ensure a consistent style, or look, for the brochures, enabling you to direct your energies to the content. The greatest advantages of templates are that they save time and provide design consistency.

To create a template, you begin as you would with any publication. You start a new publication, specify the number and size of pages, set up columns, make ruler guides, and type such information as headings that would appear whenever the template is used. Then you save the template by selecting Template from the Save as type option in the Save Publication dialog box. A template contains everything except the text and graphics specific to any particular issue of the newsletter, annual report, product brochure, or whatever publication the template is set up for.

To create a publication from a template, just open the template file. PageMaker automatically opens an unnamed copy of the template, so when you add the content to the publication and save it, you do not overwrite the template. Instead, the publication is saved as a publication file.

## Exploring the Template for The Inn's Newsletter

First you will open a template that came with the student files used with this book and explore its style sheet.

1. Select Open from the File menu.

2. Click Newsletter Template in the list of student files used with this book. Notice that PageMaker automatically selects Copy from the Open as options.

3. Click Open.

Figure 6.7 shows the newsletter template for the Inn on the Pasteboard. Notice the word *Untitled* in the title bar. One advantage of making a copy of a template as you open it is that when you save the publication, you will be prompted for a name. Thus, there is less danger of altering your original template with changes or text. A second advantage to using Copy is that any changes are made faster. When you select Original, every time you make a change, you have to wait for the computer to access the original file. This takes considerable time and noticeably slows down operations.

**Figure 6.7**
Page 1 of the
newsletter template

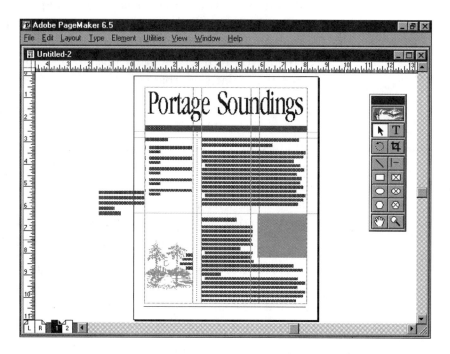

Look at the master and publication page icons in the lower-left corner of Figure 6.7. The page 1 icon is highlighted, which means you are looking at the template for the first publication page. Also notice that the newsletter text in this view appears as Greeked text. If you enlarged the view, you would see that the text is a series of repeated nonsense words. Most PageMaker templates use this text placeholder, called *Lorem ipsum* after the first two words in the file, to show how a completed publication would look with text. This allows the designer to concentrate on the layout, focusing on how the text will look in the publication without being distracted by the actual words. Also note that the graphics placeholders are tinted boxes.

## Selecting Palettes

There are many palettes that you can select from the Window menu and display on the Pasteboard, as shown in Figure 6.8. The **Styles palette** provides access to user-defined and default styles, which are collections of character and paragraph formatting attributes, including typeface, type size, leading, and alignment. For example, you can define one style for a headline and another for a caption. The **Master Pages palette** provides access to existing master pages and gives you control of the various page designs on the publication.

**Figure 6.8**
Window menu showing
the available palettes

Palettes

You will use the Styles and Master Pages palettes in the newsletter.

CTRL B

**1.** Select Show Styles from the Window menu.

SHIFT CTRL 8

**2.** If it is not already visible in the Styles palette, select Show Master Pages from the Window menu. See Figure 6.9.

**Figure 6.9**
Styles and Master Pages
palettes displayed
on Pasteboard

Your palettes might
contain additional
tabs or might be
combined differently

Nonprinting list of fonts
used in this publication

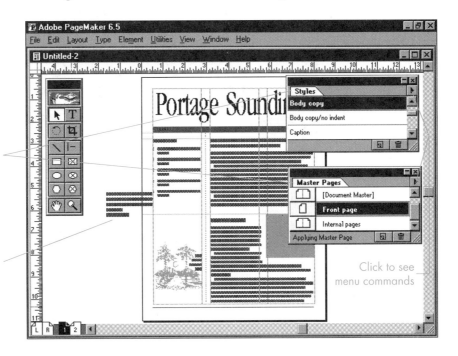

Your palettes might also show additional tabs for Colors and Layers. When you select a show palette command, the number of palettes that appear depends on how the last user organized palettes on this computer. Manipulating palettes on the Pasteboard is relatively easy. If you see extra palettes, do the following to remove them.

**3.** Click the tab of an extra palette to select it.

**4.** Drag the tab out of the palette to separate it from the existing palette.

**5.** Click the close button ☒ in the upper-right corner of the new palette to remove it from view.

**6.** Repeat steps 1-3 to remove any palette other than Styles and Master Pages palettes from view.

Each palette contains a menu of commands, which are available from a drop-down menu. You'll look at the commands available in each palette drop-down menu.

**7.** Click the triangle near the upper-right corner of each palette.

**8.** Click elsewhere onscreen to hide the menu.

While you're working, you might want to temporarily move the palettes out of view.

**9.** Press (TAB) to hide the palettes.

**10.** Press (TAB) to restore the palettes.

Palettes take up considerable space or "real estate" on the Pasteboard. To reduce the amount of space they need, you can combine the separate palettes into one palette, as shown in Figure 6.10, by dragging one palette onto the other.

**Figure 6.10**
**Combined Styles and Master Pages palette**

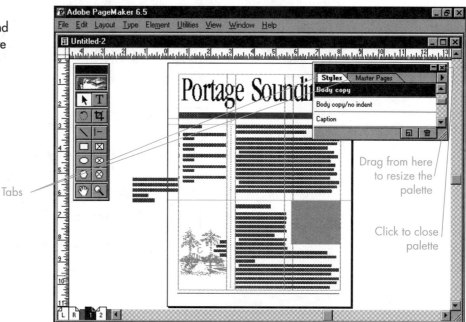

If your two palettes are not already combined:

**11.** Point to the Master Pages tab.

**12.** Drag the tab onto the Styles palette.

The Master Pages tab moves into the Styles palette and the empty palette disappears. You can resize a palette by pointing to the lower-right corner of the palette, and dragging the corner in any direction until the palette is the desired size. Click the tab you want to work with in a combined palette. You'll work more with palettes throughout the rest of the chapter.

In this section you will explore the styles in the Styles palette to gain a better understanding of how they work. As you look at the various styles, be careful not to make changes. But if you do inadvertently, revert to the previously saved version of the template. Look at the Headline style.

1. If necessary, click the Styles tab to select it. A selected tab is white.

2. Expand the palette so you can see more styles in the list, if necessary, by dragging down from the bottom of the palette or from the lower-right corner of the palette. You can also use the scroll bar in the Styles palette to scroll the styles.

3. Hold down CTRL while you click Headline in the Styles palette.

Because you pressed CTRL, the Style Options dialog box appears, as shown in Figure 6.11. The Headline style is completely defined here. You can examine or change the typeface, indentation, tab stops, and hyphenation control by clicking the appropriate button.

Figure 6.11
Headline style in the Style
Options dialog box

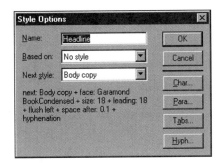

Explore the Headline style.

4. Click the Char button.

Note that the Character Specifications dialog box appears. Look at the font, size, and leading options for this style. Any changes you make within the dialog box will alter the Headline style.

5. Click Cancel.

Although you could also click OK, clicking Cancel is faster because it returns you immediately to the previous screen; OK updates the style sheet whether or not you have made changes.

6. On your own, click the Para, Tabs, and Hyph buttons to examine the corresponding dialog boxes. When you have finished in each box, click Cancel.

Look at each style listed in the Styles palette. Remember to hold down CTRL while you click the style name to open the Style Options dialog box.

## Determining Text Style

The styles in the Styles palette were used to create the master pages for the Portage Soundings newsletter. When you click an insertion point in the text, that text's style name is highlighted in the Styles palette.

1. Click the master pages icon to select it.
2. Click the text tool T in the Toolbox.
3. Click the I-beam within the masthead *Portage Soundings*.

The Styles palette should have *Newsletter masthead title* selected because you have positioned the I-beam within text that uses that style. As you can see, it is not critical for you to know the font used for a text section; you can always use PageMaker to determine its style.

For each of the following, notice what is selected in the Styles palette. If the palette is too narrow to display an entire style name, the name is abbreviated in the middle with ellipses.

4. Click the page 1 icon.
5. Change the view so you can see the story below *Soundings*, the top story in the two right-most columns.
6. Click the I-beam within the headline.
7. Click the I-beam within the first paragraph.
8. Click the I-beam within other paragraphs.
9. Move the view to the left column and click the I-beam within the text below *In This Issue*.

What you have been discovering is that when the I-beam is positioned within text, the Styles palette highlights the style of that text.

## Comparing Text on Master Pages to Text on Numbered Pages

To further understand how master pages relate to numbered publication pages, move the view to the newsletter masthead and repeat the exploration. As you position the I-beam within the text on the numbered pages, observe what happens to the Styles palette.

1. Click the I-beam within *Portage Soundings* on page 1.
2. Click the master page icons and find *Portage Soundings*.
3. Click an insertion point.
4. On your own, return to page 1.

What happened when you clicked an insertion point in the newsletter masthead with the page 1 icon selected? Did the Headline style in the Styles palette become highlighted? The answer is no. Why not? Because the text was created on the master pages. As stated earlier, text created on the master pages cannot be accessed or changed from a publication page, although it will print on the publication pages.

Now that you have explored master pages, templates, and styles, you will create a newsletter using a template created for this book. You will place some text, type other text, and place three graphics files. Figure 6.12 shows the finished newsletter you will create.

**Figure 6.12**
Completed newsletter
(page 1)

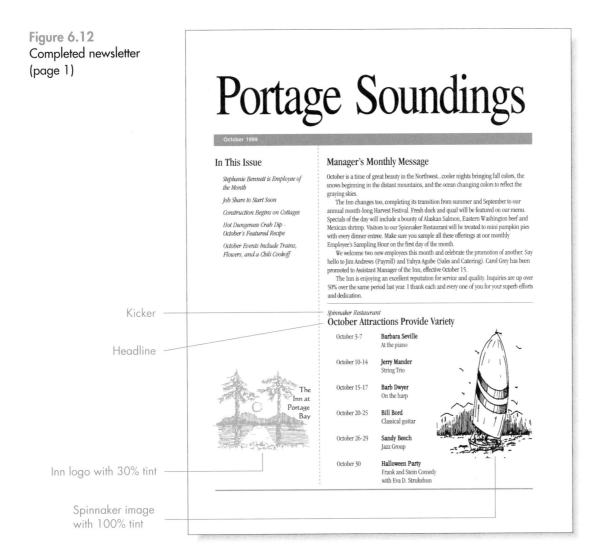

Kicker

Headline

Inn logo with 30% tint

Spinnaker image
with 100% tint

Figure 6.12
continued
Completed newsletter
(page 2)

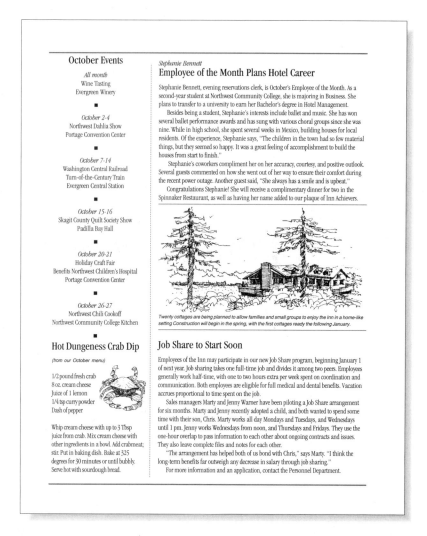

The Inn at Portage Bay produces a monthly two-page newsletter, *Portage Soundings*, for its employees. One purpose of the newsletter is to keep employees informed of factors that affect them, such as employment policies. A second purpose is to inform employees of local events, both at The Inn and in nearby communities, so employees can share this information with Inn guests. Finally, the newsletter highlights Inn achievements, such as when the Inn won an award for the Spinnaker Restaurant cuisine, and it also highlights employees and their achievements.

As you work on the newsletter, save it often. As a practice, *always* save before printing, especially if you are working on a network.

## Placing the Text Files in the Newsletter

The October issue of *Portage Soundings* has six articles and three TIF files. Five articles were written in Microsoft Word, and you will type the sixth one. Figure 6.13 lists all the text and graphics that will be used in the newsletter, their file names, and where they should appear.

Figure 6.13
Articles and graphics
to be placed in
*Portage Soundings*
newsletter.

| Article | Stored as | Placement |
|---|---|---|
| Manager's Monthly Message | October Message | Page 1 top |
| October Attractions Provide Variety | October Attractions | Page 1 bottom |
| Spinnaker graphic | Spinnaker | Page 1 bottom |
| Employee of the Month Plans Hotel Career | October Employee | Page 2 top right |
| Cottages graphic | Cottages | Page 2 middle right |
| Job Share to Start Soon | October Job Share | Page 2 lower right |
| Hot Dungeness Crab Dip | October Recipe | Page 2 lower left |
| Crab graphic | Crab | Page 2 lower left |

You will place each article after selecting a style from the Styles palette. In some cases, you will need to make minor adjustments to the headline or text alignment. Before continuing, check that:

- You have the student files listed in Figure 6.13 available.

- The view is 50% Size or 75% Size and you can see the space at the top of the second column where the Manager's Monthly Message article will be placed. (Refer to Figure 6.12.)

## Placing the Manager's Monthly Message

The Manager's Monthly Message is a short article that the manager writes as a way to communicate with The Inn's employees. It was written using Microsoft Word. The original article in Word is not formatted, as shown in Figure 6.14. Notice it has no paragraph indentation.

Figure 6.14
Manager's Monthly Message in Word format

Manager's Monthly Message
October is a time of great beauty in the Northwest...cooler nights bringing fall colors, the snows beginning in the distant mountains, and the ocean changing colors to reflect the graying skies.
The Inn changes too, completing its transition from summer and September to our annual month-long Harvest Festival. Fresh duck and quail will be featured on our menu. Specials of the day will include a bounty of Alaskan Salmon, Eastern Washington beef and Mexican shrimp. Visitors to our Spinnaker Restaurant will be treated to mini pumpkin pies with every dinner entree. Make sure you sample all these offerings at our monthly Employee's Sampling Hour on the first day of the month.
We welcome two new employees this month and celebrate the promotion of another. Say hello to Jim Andrews (Payroll) and Yahya Agube (Sales and Catering). Carol Grey has been promoted to Assistant Manager of the Inn, effective October 15.
The Inn is enjoying an excellent reputation for service and quality. Inquiries are up over 50% over the same period last year. I thank each and every one of you for your superb efforts and dedication.

When you import a file into PageMaker from a word processing program, the text goes through a filter. A **filter** allows PageMaker to interpret special codes saved with a document into PageMaker codes, such as Tab and Enter and the codes for bold and underline. Because each word processing program has its own codes, PageMaker comes with filters for the most widely used word processors. PageMaker does not have a filter for every word processing program sold, nor does it have a filter for versions of word processing programs that were released after the PageMaker version you are using was released.

Any file you import into PageMaker and place must go through a filter. PageMaker has filters for text, spreadsheet, database, and graphics programs. PageMaker has both import and export filters. The person who installed PageMaker on your computer either installed all the filters or selected only some to install. Because each filter requires space on the hard drive, it is not practical to install filters you won't use. You'll look at the list of filters installed on your computer in question 12 at the end of this chapter.

When you import text, font selection and size, paragraph indentation, and other choices are applied to the text file based on the style selected in the Styles palette. If no style is selected, the text will be placed using the publication's default style, which varies depending on how it was set by the previous user. You can see this style when you open a new publication and look at the default styles in the Styles palette.

To place the Manager's Monthly Message article:

1. Verify that the page 1 icon is highlighted.

2. Click the pointer tool in the Toolbox.

3. Click Body copy in the Styles palette.

4. Click the text block below the newsletter masthead to select it.

This step tells Pagemaker to place the imported text in the Body copy style.

5. Select Place from the File menu.

6. Click October Message from the student files.

7. Verify the following settings in the Place dialog box. See Figure 6.15:

| | |
|---|---|
| Replacing entire story: | selected |
| Show filter preferences: | not selected |
| Retain format: | not selected |
| Convert quotes: | selected |
| Read tags: | not selected |

Figure 6.15
Place dialog box

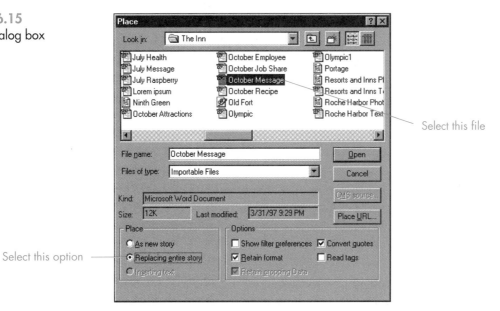

Select this file

Select this option

Many of the options you just selected are new choices and require some explanation. **As new story** places the file separate from existing stories on a publication. **Replacing entire story** deletes the selected text block and replaces it with the file you are placing. **Show filter preferences** allows you to specify additional options associated with certain filters. For example, when importing a GIF image, you can specify a range of image resolutions from 72 to 600 dpi. **Retain format** tells PageMaker to import the document's character and paragraph formatting and the style sheet along with the document. Some word processors (such as Microsoft Word) have their own style sheets. **Convert quotes** causes PageMaker to translate ordinary quotation marks (") into typeset quotation marks (" "). This also converts double hyphens to em dashes. You'll look up the definition of an em dash in a question at the end of the chapter. **Read tags** tells PageMaker to look for style names inside brackets within the imported text. PageMaker will apply the style to that paragraph. For example,

<Headline> President Declares Tax Cut

will cause PageMaker to import that paragraph with the Headline style as defined in the Styles palette. Recall that paragraph ends when there is a hard return, that is, when ⏎ ENTER was pressed.

The options in the Place dialog box are context specific to text and will change to other options when you select a graphics file to place.

**8.** When your screen matches Figure 6.15, click Open.

The text, defined as Body copy in the Styles palette, replaces the selected text block, which was only a placeholder. PageMaker changed the paragraph indentation in the source file (the original Word file) to reflect specifications in Body copy.

Now you need to change some of the text so that it appears the way you want it. Specifically, the title style will be changed to Headline and the first paragraph will be changed to Body copy/no indent. To change the style of the text:

**9.** Click the text tool $\boxed{T}$ in the Toolbox.

**10.** Click an insertion point anywhere in the words *Manager's Monthly Message* (or select the three words).

**11.** Click Headline in the Styles palette; you might need to scroll the Styles list. *Manager's Monthly Message* changes to 18-pt type.

**12.** Click an insertion point in the first paragraph.

**13.** Click Body copy/no indent. The first paragraph changes style.

As you were selecting styles in the Styles palette, you might have noticed the inclusion of a new style, Normal, with a disk icon next to it. This is a Word style that was imported with the text file. Because you selected Body copy prior to placing October Message, the imported text used that style and Normal, with its character specifications, was added to the Styles palette. If you click Normal when you have an insertion point in a paragraph, the font will change to Times New Roman and the other character specifications of the Normal style imported from Word.

This article is a bit shorter than the space planned in the template. You will move the blue separating line under the article. If you can't see the blue line, move the ruler guide. For this newsletter, you will move the line a bit closer to the end of the article.

**14.** Click the pointer tool $\boxed{\nwarrow}$ in the Toolbox.

**15.** Click the blue separating line.

**16.** Move the line so that it fits evenly and attractively between the bottom of the article and the line. See Figure 6.16.

**Figure 6.16**
**Repositioning the line**

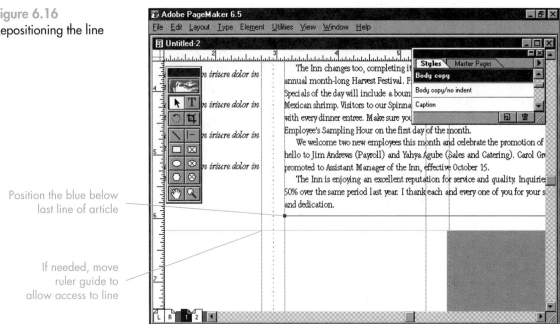

Position the blue below last line of article

If needed, move ruler guide to allow access to line

Note that positioning the line requires an element of personal judgment. With the first article in place, you're ready to import the second article.

All the *Lorem ipsum* text in this section disappeared when you placed the Manager's Monthly Message article, so you'll be placing the October Attractions article as a new story. After you place this article, you will change the style of two headlines, *Spinnaker Restaurant* and *October Attractions Provide Variety.*

*Spinnaker Restaurant* uses italic type; *October Attractions Provide Variety* uses normal type. The headline is *October Attractions Provide Variety;* whereas the name of the restaurant is called either a kicker or an eyebrow. A **kicker** or **eyebrow** appears above the headline in a different type style. Its purpose is to attract attention, provide information, and draw readers to the article. Often it is in smaller type, say a 12-point eyebrow over an 18-point headline. Look back at the finished newsletter in Figure 6.12 to see how an eyebrow appears over a headline.

To place the October Attractions article:

1. Click Attractions list in the Styles palette.

2. Select Place from the File menu.

CTRL D

3. Click October Attractions.

4. In the Place dialog box, make the following selections:

| | |
|---|---|
| As new story: | selected |
| Show filter preferences: | not selected |
| Retain format: | not selected |
| Convert quotes: | selected |
| Read tags: | not selected |

5. Click Open.

**6.** Click the text icon 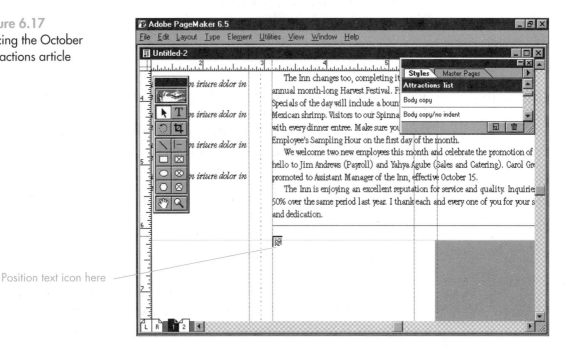 below the blue separating line to place the story. See Figure 6.17.

Figure 6.17
Placing the October
Attractions article

Position text icon here

**7.** On your own, expand the text block until you can see the three lines for the October 30 entry, as shown in Figure 6.18.

Figure 6.18
Expanding the text block

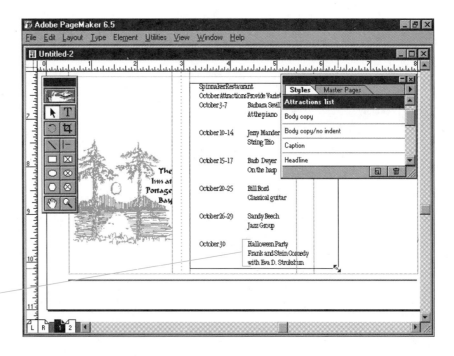

Extend the text block
so you can see
these three lines

With the article placed in the newsletter, you can change the style of *Spinnaker Restaurant* for the kicker.

**8.** Click the text tool T in the Toolbox.

**9.** Click an insertion point within the words *Spinnaker Restaurant*.

**10.** Click Kicker in the Styles palette.

Now, you'll change *October Attractions Provide Variety* to the Headline style.

**11.** Click an insertion point within *October Attractions Provide Variety*.

**12.** Click Headline.

**13.** If the headline doesn't fit on one line, move the graphics place holder and/or expand the text block to accommodate it. See Figure 6.19.

**Figure 6.19**
**Fitting the headline on one line**

Extend the text block so the headline fits on one line

Move the graphics placeholder if needed

Move the palette out of the way if necessary

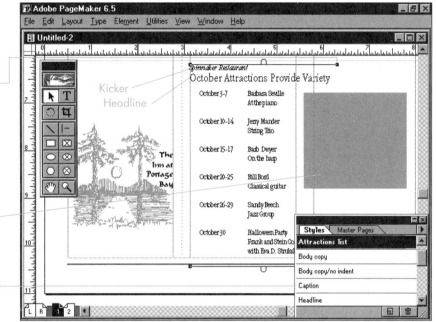

Next, you want to change the names of the performers to bold. Remember that you can use the menu command or the shortcut keys.

**14.** With the text tool  selected, use the I-beam to highlight the text you want to bold.

(SHIFT)(CTRL)(B)

**15.** Point to Type Style from the Type menu and click Bold.

**16.** On your own, bold the performers' names. When you are done, your screen should look like Figure 6.20.

Figure 6.20
October Attractions
with bolded
performers' names

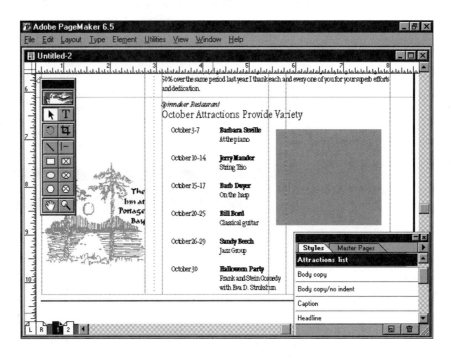

**Replacing a Graphics Placeholder**

To the right of the attractions list you just added, the template has a graphics placeholder, which suggests placement for a graphics file. The placeholder has 30% tint, giving it a gray appearance. This was done to help the desktop publisher visualize the layout prior to placing any graphics. A **tint** is a screened shade of an ink. The tint used here is an object-level tint and you can specify a percentage of base color, in this case black, to apply to an object, in this case a rectangle. If you place the Spinnaker file (or any other image) into a graphics placeholder with 30% tint, you will see a "faded" drawing similar to the Inn logo in the lower-left corner of the newsletter (refer to Figure 6.20). For some graphics files, this produces a nice effect. For the Spinnaker file, however, it is better to place it with 100% tint.

Before you experiment with both the 30% and 100% tint, this would be a good time to save the newsletter.

**1.** Select Save from the File menu.

**2.** Type *October Newsletter* for the file name. Note that the Publication file type is already selected for you.

**3.** Click Save.

Now you will place the Spinnaker Restaurant's symbol, a sailboat with full spinnaker, and change the tint.

**4.** Click the pointer tool in the Toolbox.

5. Click the graphics placeholder (the 30% tint rectangle).

CTRL U
6. Select Fill and Stroke from the Element menu.

7. Change Tint to 100% in the Fill portion. See Figure 6.21.

Figure 6.21
Fill and Stroke dialog box

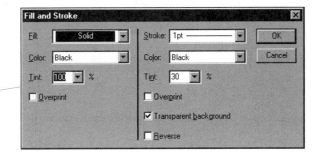

Fill Tint set to 100%

8. Click OK.

CTRL D
9. Select Place from the File menu.

10. Click Spinnaker.

11. In the Place dialog box, select Replacing entire graphic.

12. Click Open.

13. Click outside the graphic to deselect it.

CTRL S
14. On your own, save the newsletter.

15. On your own, experiment with different tints for the graphic. When you are done, return the tint to 100%.

Before proceeding, make sure everything you have placed so far looks correct. Move around the publication's second column and compare your page to the completed newsletter in Figure 6.12. If you need to redo a part, select the element and delete it. Then redo the appropriate set of steps. When you are satisfied that your newsletter looks correct, proceed to the next section.

**Listing the Newsletter Articles**

Your next task for page 1 is to list the newsletter articles below the *In This Issue* headline. You will replace the dummy text with the actual list.

This part of the completed newsletter looks like Figure 6.22.

**Figure 6.22**
After typing list of articles, reducing text block width, and typing the month and year

New date

New text to type

Revised width of text block

1. Click the grabber hand tool in the Toolbox and move the view until you can see the top of column 1 on page 1.

2. Click the text tool in the Toolbox.

3. Drag the I-beam over the placeholder text.

4. Type the text shown in Figure 6.22.

5. Use the pointer tool to reduce the width of the text block for improved line breaks. When you're done, your screen will look like Figure 6.22.

**Adding the Month and Year to the Masthead**

Your final task for page 1 is to type the month and year near the top of the publication, as shown in Figure 6.22. To type the month and year:

1. On your own, use the grabber hand tool to change the view to the left part of the masthead.

2. Click the text tool in the Toolbox.

3. Use the I-beam to select Month/Year.

4. Type *October* and the current year.

Page 1 is complete! Now you will use some of the skills you've learned to place three articles and two graphics on page 2.

Figure 6.23 shows the final layout of page 2 with all the specifications. The Employee of the Month article has a feature you haven't yet used, Style tags, which will make it easier to format the imported file. You will type the October Events list, keeping the format the same as the template. The Hot Dungeness Crab Dip recipe will be placed in a frame, rather than in a text block. This will give you experience with frames and show you an alternate way to position text.

**Figure 6.23**
Page 2 of the newsletter

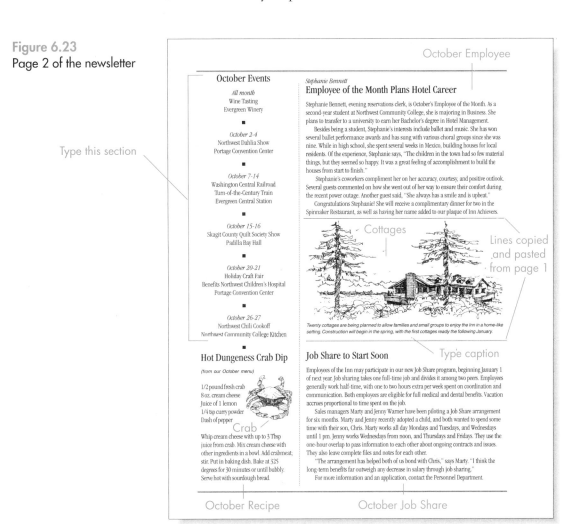

Completing page 2 requires you to use several options in addition to those you used on page 1. As you continue you might want to test your understanding by reading the specifications and trying the steps on your own. For other parts, you will want to follow the steps closely. To reproduce page 2, use either the specifications shown in Figure 6.23, the following steps, or a combination of the two.

The Employee of the Month article, shown in Figure 6.24, was written in Word. Style tags at the beginning of each paragraph name the style that PageMaker should apply when importing the text. The style tags match names in the Styles palette. Recall that a paragraph ends when [↵ ENTER] was pressed.

**Figure 6.24**
**October Employee article with style tags**

Style tags

<Kicker>Stephanie Bennett
<Headline>Employee of the Month Plans Hotel Career
<Body copy/no indent>Stephanie Bennett, evening reservations clerk, is October's Employee of the Month. As a second-year student at Northwest Community College, she is majoring in Business. She plans to transfer to a university to earn her Bachelor's degree in Hotel Management.
<Body copy>Besides being a student, Stephanie's interests include ballet and music. She has won several ballet performance awards and has sung with various choral groups since she was nine. While in high school, she spent several weeks in Mexico, building houses for local residents. Of the experience, Stephanie says, "The children in the town had so few material things, but they seemed so happy. It was a great feeling of accomplishment to build the houses from start to finish."
<Body copy> Stephanie's coworkers compliment her on her accuracy, courtesy, and positive outlook. Several guests commented on how she went out of her way to ensure their comfort during the recent power outage. Another guest said, "She always has a smile and is upbeat."
<Body copy>Congratulations Stephanie! She will receive a complimentary dinner for two in the Spinnaker Restaurant, as well as having her name added to our plaque of Inn Achievers.

As you place the article, watch how PageMaker automatically applies the appropriate styles.

1. Click the page 2 icon.

2. Change the view to display the upper-right corner of the publication page.

3. Use the pointer tool [▶] to select the text block.

4. Select Place from the File menu.

5. Click October Employee.

6. In the Place dialog box, make the following selections:

| | |
|---|---|
| Replacing entire story: | selected |
| Retain format: | not selected |
| Show filter preferences: | not selected |
| Read tags: | selected |
| Convert quotes: | selected |

7. Click Open.

8. If necessary, adjust the placement of the text block upward so the article fits above the graphics placeholder.

[CTRL] [D]

Note that all the manual style adjustment was done automatically because the imported file included style tags. As you can see, using style tags makes formatting an article very simple.

Placing the October Job Share Article

The October Job Share article goes at the bottom of the right column. First you will place the article. Then you will change the headline style to Headline.

Move your page view to the bottom of column 2 and select Body copy from the Styles palette. Again notice that the placeholder text disappeared after you placed the first article on this page. This occurred because the *Lorem ipsum* text was threaded between the two sections.

You will fill the bottom portion of the newsletter with text and reduce the size of the graphics placeholder as needed to make the text fit within the allotted space. Adjusting the graphic size is a trick that provides flexibility in the length of the articles you can place in a template.

Place this article on your own. The specifications you will need to complete this task are:

| | | |
|---|---|---|
| File name: | October Job Share | |
| Text style: | Body copy/no indent | Paragraph 1 |
| | Body copy | Other paragraphs |
| Headline style: | Headline | |
| Place dialog box options: | | |
| As new story: | selected | |
| Show filter preferences: | not selected | |
| Retain format: | not selected | |
| Convert quotes: | selected | |
| Read tags: | not selected | |

When you have correctly placed this article, proceed to the next section.

October Events is a listing of local activities in and around the Inn. This feature goes in the upper-left corner of page 2. You will first change your view so you can see this part of the newsletter. Then you will select the placeholder title and type it. You will select each part of the dummy text and replace it with the correct entry. Then you will change the dates to italics.

**1.** Change your view to the top of the first column on page 2. See Figure 6.25.

**Figure 6.25**
October Events section before replacing dummy text

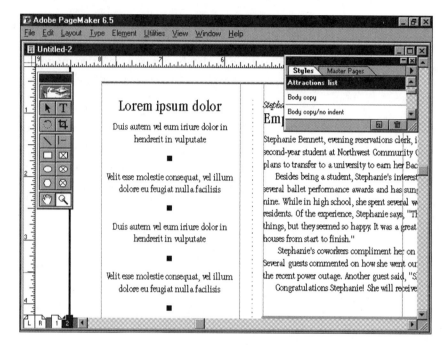

**2.** Click the text tool **T** in the Toolbox.

**3.** Use the I-beam to select the headline *Lorem ipsum dolor.*

**4.** Type *October Events.*

**5.** Select the next section of text, and type the correct text. See Figure 6.26.

Figure 6.26
October Events list
to type

**October Events**

*All month*
Wine Tasting
Evergreen Winery

◼

*October 2-4*
Northwest Dahlia Show
Portage Convention Center

◼

*October 7-14*
Washington Central Railroad
Turn-of-the-Century Train
Evergreen Central Station

◼

*October 15-16*
Skagit County Quilt Society Show
Padilla Bay Hall

◼

*October 20-21*
Holiday Craft Fair
Benefits Northwest Children's Hospital
Portage Convention Center

◼

*October 26-27*
Northwest Chili Cookoff
Northwest Community College Kitchen

**6.** Select the first line of text and change it to italics.

**7.** Repeat steps 5 through 6 for each listing in the October Events.

Next you'll complete the text in column 1.

## Placing the Hot Dungeness Crab Dip Recipe

The Hot Dungeness Crab Dip article goes in the lower-left corner in the frame. First you will place the recipe. Then you will change the headline style to Headline and the subheading to Caption. Next you will adjust the placement of the recipe so that its last line is flush (or even) with the last line of the article in the second column. Finally, you will place the TIF file called Crab. The specifications you will need to complete this task are:

| | |
|---|---|
| Text style: | Body copy/no indent |
| Headline style: | Headline |
| Subheading style: | Caption |
| Article: | October Recipe |
| Place dialog box options: | |
| Within frame: | selected |
| Everything else: | not selected |

Place the recipe and make changes to the headline and subheading. Adjust the recipe so that it lines up with the end of the Job Share article.

1. Click the pointer tool 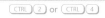 in the Toolbox.

2. Adjust the view so you can see the last line in both columns.

3. Pull a horizontal ruler guide to below the last line of one of the articles for a reference point.

4. Change the view to 200% or 400%.

5. Adjust either text block as needed by dragging it until the ends of the articles in the two columns are aligned. See Figure 6.27.

Figure 6.27
Aligning the ends of two articles using a ruler guide (200% Size view)

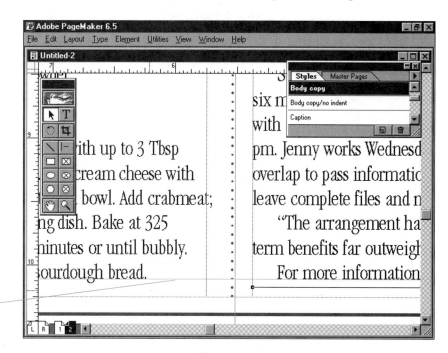

Horizontal ruler guide

Now you will place the crab graphic next to the ingredients in the recipe to fill in the excess white space.

6. Adjust the view so you can see the recipe's ingredients.

7. Click the pointer tool 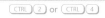 to deselect the adjusted article.

CTRL D

8. Select Place from the File menu.

9. Click Crab.

10. Select As independent graphic.

11. Click Open.

12. Position the graphic icon ⊠ at the upper-left corner of where you want to place the crab; click and drag the icon to the lower-right corner of where you want to place it. See Figure 6.28.

Figure 6.28
Crab graphic placed

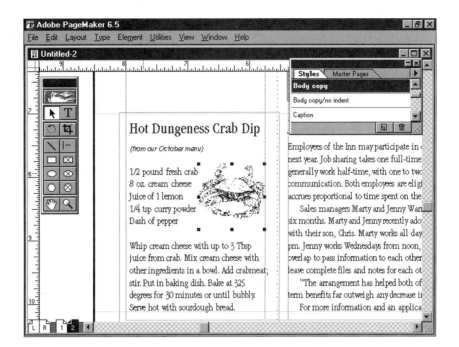

## Placing the Cottages Graphics File

You have just a few more tasks to finish creating this newsletter. Next you will place the Cottages graphic. You will size the graphic to fit the existing space, which is a trick you can use to accommodate articles of different lengths. Then you will type the caption. To place the file:

1. Click the pointer tool  to deselect the crab.

2. Adjust your view so you can see the graphics placeholder.

3. Click the graphics placeholder and delete it by pressing ◄─ BACKSPACE .

CTRL  D

4. Select Place from the File menu.

5. Click Cottages.

6. Select As independent graphic.

7. Click Open.

Notice that the mouse pointer has changed to a graphic image icon .

**8.** Position the graphic image icon ⊠ as shown in Figure 6.29.

**Figure 6.29**
Placing the
Cottages graphic

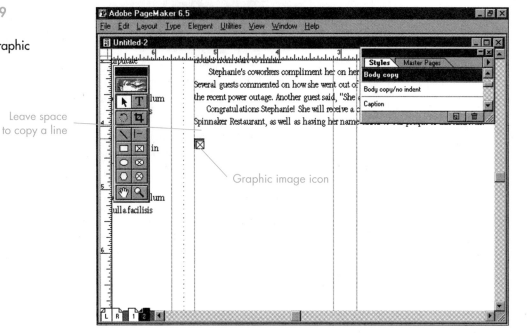

Leave space
to copy a line

Graphic image icon

**9.** Drag the icon diagonally from the upper-left corner to the lower-right corner, leaving enough space to type a two-line caption below the figure. See Figure 6.30.

**Figure 6.30**
Drag icon to indicate
graphic size
and placement

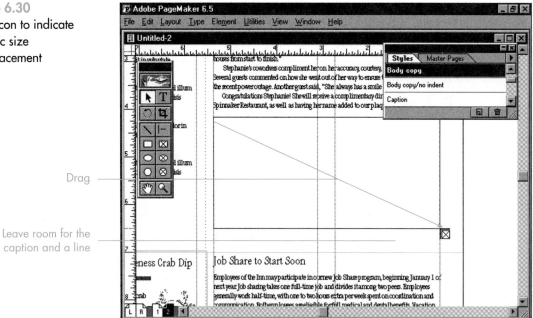

Drag

Leave room for the
caption and a line

**10.** Release the mouse button.

11. On your own, type the following caption below the graphic, using the Caption style:

*Twenty cottages are being planned to allow families and small groups to enjoy the Inn in a home-like setting. Construction will begin in the spring, with the first cottages ready the following January.*

If you don't like how the graphic is placed or sized, either delete the graphic and place it again or resize it using the techniques you learned in Chapter 5.

The last thing you will do is to copy the blue separating line from the first page and paste it twice on page 2 to frame the Cottages graphic.

12. Click the page 1 icon.

13. Click the pointer tool  in the Toolbox.

14. Click the blue line between the Manager's Monthly Message and October Attractions articles.

 15. Select Copy from the Edit menu.

16. Click the page 2 icon.

17. Adjust the view so you can see the Cottages graphic.

 18. Select Paste from the Edit menu.

19. Drag the line to a location above the graphic.

CTRL V 20. Select Paste from the Edit menu.

21. Drag the line to a location below the caption.

Your newsletter should look like Figure 6.12. Before printing the newsletter, you should save it, using Save As to make the file smaller.

SHIFT CTRL S 22. Select Save As from the File menu, and save the newsletter using the same file name.

Finally, you will print the newsletter.

CTRL P

**23.** Select Print from the File menu.

**24.** If you do *not* have a color printer, click Color, and select Print colors in black. See Figure 6.31.

**Figure 6.31**
Turning off color
before printing

Select this option to print
in black and white

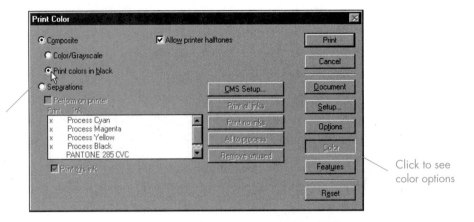

Click to see
color options

**25.** Click Print.

CTRL W

**26.** Select Close from the File menu to close the finished newsletter file.

In Project 1 at the end of this chapter you will create a July issue for *Portage Soundings*.

## WORKING WITH PAGEMAKER TEMPLATES

PageMaker contains 23 templates with sample business cards, brochures, calendars, a FAX cover sheet, an invitation, an invoice, newsletters, a resume, and a press release. You can use the templates as they are, or as starting points from which you customize and create your own template. The template you used for the October newsletter was adapted from the PageMaker Newsletter 1 template.

The templates that come with PageMaker are actually scripts. A **script** contains a series of commands to automate repetitive PageMaker tasks, such as setting up pages. When you open a PageMaker template script, the script runs its series of commands and you can watch the template being assembled. When you open a PageMaker template file, as you did for the October newsletter, the file opens like any PageMaker publication.

In this part of the chapter you will open a PageMaker newsletter template by running a script, explore the assembled template, and place an article with style tags. You will need to combine several text blocks before you place the article in order to accommodate the length of the article. Figure 6.32 shows the printed PageMaker template.

Figure 6.32
PageMaker Newsletter 2
template

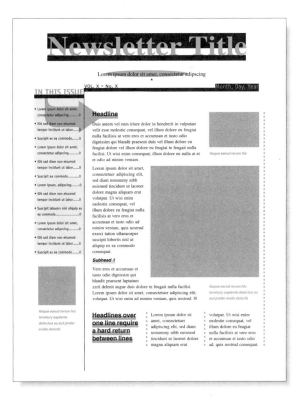

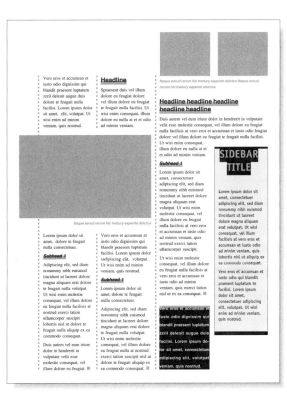

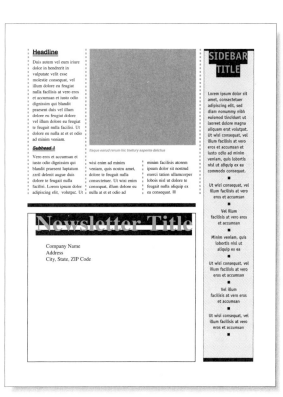

Figure 6.33 shows how the newsletter will look after you complete this section.

**Figure 6.33**
*Port Dorsey Times* after changes

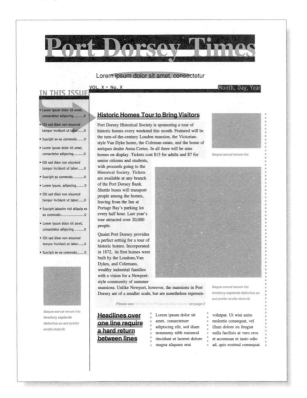

The template shown in Figure 6.32 is a four-page template named Newsletter 2. You'll run a script to set up the Newsletter 2 template.

1. Point to Plug-in Palettes in the Window menu and click Show Scripts.

2. Click the arrow next to the Template folder to display its contents.

3. Double-click Newsletter 2.

Watch as the script builds the newsletter. Be careful not to click the mouse button while the newsletter is being created, or you might cause an error that will close PageMaker. Depending on the speed of your computer, building the newsletter can take up to several minutes.

Exploring the
Newsletter Template

Explore the template by adjusting the view so you can see more detail on the pages. Click each page icon and look at the pages. In the steps that follow, you will look at the following:

- the text placeholders
- the number of text blocks
- the text styles

First, look closely at the text placeholders.

1. Adjust the view so you can read the text.

Notice the words in text placeholder. Recall from earlier in the chapter that PageMaker uses a file called *Lorem ipsum*, named after the first two words in the file, for all text placeholders. This dummy text is meant to show you how a publication will look with text.

Next, look at the stories on the page and determine how many text blocks there are.

2. Using the pointer tool [pointer icon], point to and click the story on page 1 under *Headline*.

Notice that there is no plus sign (+) in the bottom windowshade loop, which means the text block ends there. The lead article is longer than this text block, so you will thread it to page 3.

You can find additional information about the text by looking at Word Counter in the Utilities Plug-ins.

3. Point to Plug-ins in the Utilities menu and click Word Counter.

The characters, words, sentences, paragraphs, text blocks, and stories are totaled for the entire template. After looking at the information:

4. Click Close.

When composing newsletters you need to fit articles or stories to the space. The information available in Word Counter helps you do this.

Finally, you will explore the text styles in the template. Make sure the Styles palette appears on the screen. If it does not, select Show Styles from the Window menu. Using the text tool, click different parts of page 1 and look at which style in the Styles palette becomes highlighted. Click within:

- Newsletter Title

- Lorem ipsum below the newsletter title

- Headline

- Text below *IN THIS ISSUE*

- Caption below the graphics placeholder

- Subhead 1 in the second column

You should have seen each style highlighted in the Styles palette as you moved around the page.

## Creating the Newsletter Using a PageMaker Template

The Inn at Portage Bay is near Port Dorsey, a resort town of historic homes. The Inn sponsors a tour of the historic homes to raise money for the Historical Society and generate tourist traffic for the area. The Inn's desktop publishing staff produces a newsletter describing the homes on the tour.

To practice with a second template, and to use a PageMaker template, you will place one file and change the newsletter title in two places. In the projects at the end of the chapter, you will place other files and create articles to complete this four-page newsletter.

Before you begin, save the template as a publication file. Then close the Scripts palette to make more space on the Pasteboard.

CTRL S

1. Select Save from the File menu.

2. Type *Port Dorsey Times* as the file name, make sure Publication is selected as the file type, and then click Save.

3. Click the close button ☒ in the upper-right corner of the Scripts palette.

Now you can change the newsletter title.

4. Use the text tool T to highlight *Newsletter Title*.

5. Type *Port Dorsey Times*.

The newsletter title is too long for the masthead space. PageMaker has a command that you can use to reduce the width of the title.

6. Highlight the new title.

SHIFT CTRL X

7. Point to Horizontal Scale in the Type menu and click Normal.

**8.** Click outside the box.

**9.** Click the page 4 icon.

**10.** On your own, change *Newsletter Title* to *Port Dorsey Times.*

**11.** On your own, use Horizontal Scale to make the masthead fit on one page, using the highest percentage that will work. *Hint:* Don't forget to try values other than the defaults in the menu by selecting Other and typing different numbers.

---

**Placing the Text**

The text you will place on page 1 is a file named Historic Homes. It was created in Microsoft Word and has style tags. Figure 6.34 shows the file. Notice that the text block on page 1 of the template ends on the first page.

**Figure 6.34**
Historic Homes article with style tags

Style tags

<Headline>Historic Homes Tour to Bring Visitors
<Body copy>Port Dorsey Historical Society is sponsoring a tour of historic homes every weekend this month. Featured will be the turn-of-the-century Loudon mansion, the Victorian-style Van Dyke home, the Coleman estate, and the home of antiques dealer Anna Cortes. In all there will be nine homes on display. Tickets cost $15 for adults and $7 for senior citizens and students, with proceeds going to the Historical Society. Tickets are available at any branch of the Port Dorsey Bank. Shuttle buses will transport people among the homes, leaving from the Inn at Portage Bay's parking lot every half hour. Last year's tour attracted over 20,000 people.
Quaint Port Dorsey provides a perfect setting for a tour of historic homes. Incorporated in 1872, its first homes were built by the Loudons, Van Dykes, and Colemans, wealthy industrial families with a vision for a Newport-style community of summer mansions. Unlike Newport, however, the mansions in Port Dorsey are of a smaller scale, but are nonetheless representative of fine period architecture and furnishings. Later inhabitants built homes consistent with the architecture of the first homes. The area became famous for its fine antiques stores. Recently the business area has seen the addition of many fine restaurants and small shops with unique merchandise. Port Dorsey is a destination for weekend shoppers, but during the month of the Historical Homes Tour, visitors come from all over the country for the event.
<Subhead>Loudon Mansion
<Body copy>The Loudon mansion was built in 1898 and has twelve rooms, including a formal living room, parlor, dining room, library, kitchen, breakfast room, four bedrooms, and maid's quarters. Still owned by the Loudon family, it contains many original furnishings, including sofas, the dining room table, and oriental rugs. On two sides of the house is a wrap-around porch, or verandah as it is referred to by the Loudons, that overlooks the water and has expansive views of the San Juan Islands.
The current occupants are master gardeners, so this year, the Homes Tour will include the English country garden which was featured recently in Country Gardens magazine. Afternoon tea with an assortment of cakes is available in the garden for a small fee. Proceeds from the tea service will benefit the Port Dorsey Garden Society.
<Subhead>Van Dyke Home
<Body copy>The Victorian-style Van Dyke home was built in 1889, and has the steeply pitched roof, verge board trim, pointed Gothic windows, and board-and-batten siding characteristic of Victorian homes. Elaborate trim work, both inside and out, and a hexagonal cupola are other characteristics that make this a favorite on the tour. Inside, rich colors and tones of wood, wallpaper, and rugs are examples of the Victorian decor. Especially noteworthy is the central staircase, with hand-crafted banister. Many finely carved walnut pieces of furniture have been collected during the owners' travels and enhance the period feel.
<Subhead>Coleman Estate
<Body copy>The Coleman estate was built in 1920 and is now used for wedding receptions and special events. The fireplace in the drawing room has an elaborately carved wood mantel. Wainscoting, six-panel doors, and finely carved woodwork show off the fine craftsmanship of the time. Windowseats in the library alcove and the children's bedrooms are filled with soft cushions and pillows. There is a four-poster bed and Queen Anne highboy in the master bedroom. A grand piano is the centerpiece of the living room. During the tour, various pianists will be playing between noon and four each day.
<Body copy>Hours are 10 a.m. until 6 p.m. on all days.

The Historic Homes article will need that space as well as the space in two additional text blocks on pages 2 and 3, as shown in Figure 6.35.

**Figure 6.35**
Additional space needed
by Historic Homes file

Second text block

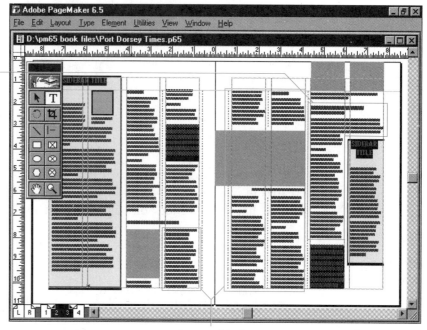

First text block

Rather than placing the article in the first text block and manually cutting and pasting the rest of the article into the two other text blocks, you will thread the three text blocks into one before placing the file. This will give you practice in combining text blocks as well as make placing the file very easy. Recall from Chapter 4 that the process of combining text blocks is to select the text in the second text block, cut it, click an insertion point at the end of the first text block, and paste the cut material.

You will add two text blocks from pages 2 and 3 to the text block on page 1. The first text block starts on page 2 below *Headline headline headline* and ends at the bottom of page 3, column 2. The second text block is the remainder of page 3, except for the boxed items. Refer to Figure 6.35 to see the two text blocks.

Combine these two text blocks with the text block on page 1 on your own or follow the steps here.

1. With the text tool **T** selected, use the I-beam to highlight the text block that starts on page 2. See Figure 6.36.

**Figure 6.36**
First text block selected

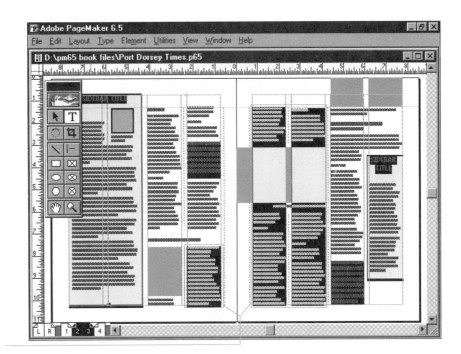

Selected text

CTRL X

**2.** Select Cut from the Edit menu.

**3.** Click the page 1 icon.

**4.** Click an insertion point at the end of the article. See Figure 6.37.

**Figure 6.37**
Click an insertion
point at the end
of the lead article

Click insertion point here

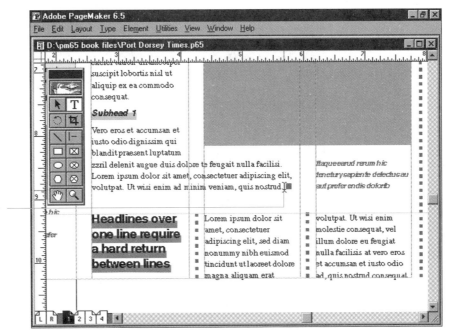

**5.** Select Paste from the Edit menu. The pasted text appears on top of other text and will look confusing, as shown in Figure 6.38.

**Figure 6.38**
**Text block after pasting text**

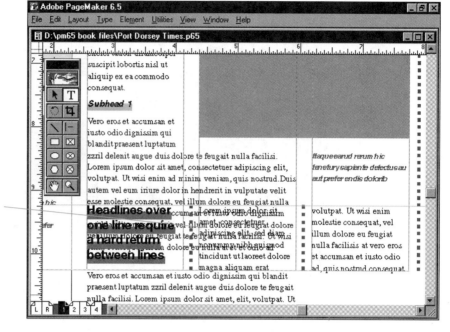

Pasted text overlaps other text

**6.** Use the pointer tool ▣ to select the text block.

**7.** Drag the windowshade loop up, as shown in Figure 6.39.

**Figure 6.39**
**Shortened text block**

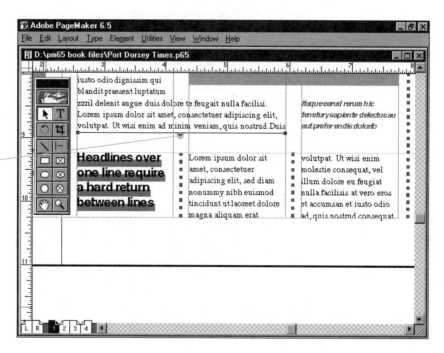

Drag Windowshade up to here

**8.** Click the red triangle in the loop. The pointer changes to the text icon ▤

**9.** Click the page 2 icon.

**10.** Click the text icon ▤ to the beginning of the empty space under *Headline headline headline.*

11. Click the red triangle at the bottom of the text block on page 2.

12. Place the text below the blue ruler guide in the first column on page 3.

13. Click the red triangle in the windowshade loop at the bottom of the first column on page 3.

14. On your own, place the text under the blue ruler guide in the second column on page 3.

15. Click outside the text block.

Repeat this process to thread the page 3, column 3 text block to the page 3, column 2 text block. After threading the last text block to the other two, expand the block to span columns 3 and 4, as shown in the second text block in Figure 6.35.

Now you're ready to place the Historic Homes file.

16. Click the page 1 icon.

17. With the pointer tool  selected, click the text block.

18. Select Autoflow from the Layout menu.

19. Select Place from the File menu.

20. Click Historic Homes.

21. Set the following options:

Replacing entire story:     selected

Read tags:     selected

22. Click Open.

On your own, explore pages 1–3 to see how Autoflow has made placing an article that spans several pages quite simple.

Publications use **jump lines**—"continued on page $x$" or "continued from page $y$"—to help the reader find the next or previous part of an article. The Historic Homes article spans three pages, as was shown in Figure 6.33, and will need some jump lines to keep the reader from becoming lost.

CTRL D

Find the jump lines in Figure 6.33. They are:

| Page | Jump Line |
|------|-----------|
| 1 | *Please see* Homes Tour Features Nine Homes *on page 2* |
| 2 | *continued from page 1* |
|  | *Please see* Homes *on page 3* |
| 3 | *continued from page 2* |

Pages 2 and 3 have headings above jump lines. They are:

| Page | Heading |
|------|---------|
| 2 | Homes Tour Features Nine Homes |
| 3 | Homes |

Start by typing the Headings.

1. Adjust your view so you are looking at *Headline headline headline* at the bottom of page 2.

2. Click the text tool **T** in the Toolbox, and select *Headline headline headline.*

3. Type *Homes Tour Features Nine Homes.*

4. Select the words you just typed.

5. Press (SHIFT)(CTRL)(1) to change the style to italics.

6. Adjust your view so you can see the top of the article on page 3.

7. Select Headline in the Styles palette.

8. With the text tool **T** selected, click an insertion point where the word *Homes* will be typed (refer to Figure 6.33).

9. Type *Homes.*

10. Repeat steps 4 and 5 to change the style to italics.

Now you're ready to type the jump lines. These use the Caption style, changed from left-justified to right-justified. You'll create the first jump line at the bottom of page 1 and then complete the other three on your own.

11. Adjust your view so you can see where the jump line will be placed.

12. Adjust the text block so you have space to type the jump line.

13. Select Caption from the Styles palette.

14. With the text tool **T** selected, click an insertion point.

15. Type *Please see Homes Tour Features Nine Homes on page 2.*

16. Adjust the text block so it spans two columns.

Your text is in bold italic. You want to take the bold off *Homes Tour Features Nine Homes* but leave it on the remainder of the text.

17. Select the words *Homes Tour Features Nine Homes.*

18. Press SHIFT CTRL B to turn bold off on the selected words.

19. Press SHIFT CTRL R to change to right justification.

Steps 18 and 19 used the shortcut keys to make the changes because it was easier than using the menus.

20. On your own, type the other jump lines. Adjust the text blocks as necessary.

As with most desktop publishing, you need to do several things to "clean up" the article. These are all things you have done previously, so here is a list of tasks to complete rather than a detailed list of steps:

1. Change the horizontal scale of the headline *Historic Homes Tour to Bring Visitors* to 95%.

2. Adjust the article so there are no widows or orphans.

3. Copy a small blue box that marks the end of an article and paste it to the end of the *Historic Homes* article.

In the projects at the end of the chapter, you will be asked to continue modifying this newsletter. But for now, save it using Save As to reduce the file size. If you want to print it, follow the directions for printing to either a color or a black and white printer.

## SUMMARY

You have created two newsletters using templates. One template was adapted by the authors from a PageMaker template. The other is a PageMaker script and can be found with the Plug-in Palettes command in the Window menu. Templates are valuable design tools and time savers. They allow you to quickly produce quality documents.

In this chapter you learned about templates, master pages, the Styles palette, placing text and graphics, and using placeholders. You replaced text, placed text in frames, and typed text. You applied styles from the Styles palette to format text. In the next chapter you will create a template for The Inn's Annual Report.

## QUESTIONS

1. What is a master page? What kinds of items appear on master pages?

2. State the advantages of using master pages.

3. What is the advantage of working with facing pages?

4. Is page 1 of a publication a left or right master page? Explain your answer.

5. Does page 1 of a publication have a facing page? Explain your answer.

6. For each of the following, state whether you would put it on a master page or a publication page.

    a. column guides

    b. page number

    c. grid

    d. table of contents for a newsletter

    e. masthead

    f. company logo

7. What is a template? What is included in it?

8. State the advantages of working with templates.

9. What are the advantages of working with a copy of a template or publication rather than the original?

10. What are the file name extensions for templates, publications, and picture files? Give a specific example of what could be found in each kind of file.

11. Compare and contrast templates and master pages.

12. Look at the list of filters installed on your computer. To do this, hold down CTRL while you select About PageMaker from the Help menu. Scroll down to find the filters section. Look at the Installed import filters and then close the dialog box.

13. What are the advantages and disadvantages of using style tags in a word processing file?

14. Using Help, make a list of the information you can learn about a text block.

15. Using Help, list the two ways to display master pages.

16. Using Help, determine what happens when you place a graphics file larger than 256K. (*Hint:* Look under a subtitle of Template.)

17. Using Help, explain how you hide some master page elements on a publication page.

18. Using Help, find the glossary of typographic terms and specifically, define an em dash.

1. Use Newsletter Template from the student files used with this book to create a July issue for the *Portage Soundings* newsletter. Refer to Figure 6.40 for article names and placement. Make sure you start with the template and not your saved October Newsletter. All the Word files have style tags.

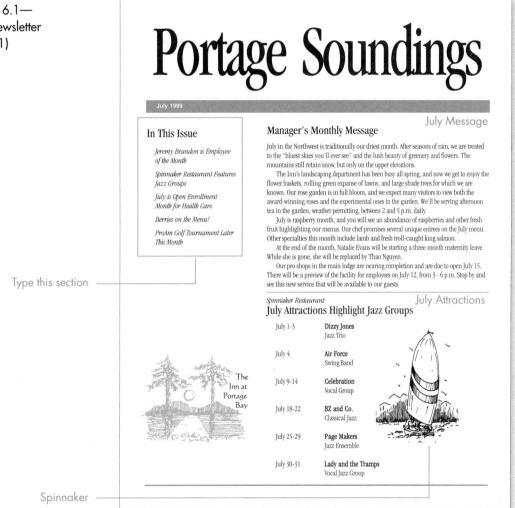

Type this section ⎯

Spinnaker ⎯

Figure 6.40
continued

Project 6.1—July
Newsletter (page 2)

You type
this section

## July Events

*Weekends in July*
Port Dorsey Historic Homes Tour

■

*Saturdays*
Shakespeare in the Park
Freedom Park

■

*July 4*
Fireworks
Freedom Park

■

*July 14-16*
Raspberry Festival
Various locations

■

*July 20-22*
ProAm Golf Tournament
Inn at Portage Bay

■

*July 29*
Air Show
Whidbey Naval Air Station

■

### It's the Berries!!!  July Raspberry

Our July menu will include these raspberry delights. Make sure you sample each during our Employee Sampling Hour on the first day of the month.

Raspberry ice cream
Cantaloupe and raspberry salad
Raspberry pie
Haddock with raspberry puree sauce
Raspberry bombe
Raspberry pudding
Raspberry cranberry muffins
Cold raspberry soup
Raspberry and peach trifle
Raspberry and blue cheese salad
Chocolate and raspberry decadence

*Jeremy Brandon*                                    July Employee

## Employee of the Month Loves Golf, All Sports

Jeremy Brandon, our golf pro, is July's Employee of the Month.

Jeremy was born in Olympia, Washington, and has lived in the Northwest all his life. He is a graduate of Arizona State University, where he had a dual major in Engineering and English. Attending on a golf scholarship, he won several NCAA titles and was ranked 23rd nationally for collegiate golfers. He plays tennis and has participated in the Seattle-to-Portland bicycle trip, as well as numerous treks around the San Juans on his bike.

Jeremy started playing golf with his parents when he was about 7. "I could barely hit the side of a barn at 50 feet when I first started," he said recently. But after many lessons, and watching golfers as a caddie for what seemed like forever, Jeremy began placing in tournaments. First there were local ones, where he admits, with characteristic understatement, "My play was a bit uneven." In high school, by his sophomore year, he started to place in every competition he entered. "At that point, things began to click and I had a good senior year." Good indeed, as Jeremy captured the individual state title and led his team to be Conference Champs.

Jeremy has been the golf pro at the Inn since it opened. His responsibilities include lessons, and he has organized the Golf mini vacations that have brought groups of visitors to our resort.

Congratulations Jeremy! He will receive a complimentary dinner for two in the Spinnaker Restaurant, as well as having his name added to our plaque of Inn Achievers.

Golf

*The Inn at Portage Bay ProAm Golf Tournament will take place July 20-22. Last year, 8,000 people came to watch the many pros and amateurs play on our course.*

### Health Care Changes  July Health

July is open enrollment month. If you wish to change your health care coverage, this is the time to do it. You may change your health care provider, the amount of your deductible, and make other decisions about your coverage. Barbara Van Dyke in Payroll has information packets and forms, and is able to answer your questions about coverage plans.

Non-smokers may reduce the cost of their health care by signing and returning the Non-Smoker Statement that accompanied your June paycheck. If you and your spouse have not used tobacco products in the past twelve months, sign the form and return it to Payroll. The deadline is July 15.

2. Use Fax Cover Sheet from the student files used with this book to create Figure 6.41. Replace the logo box with Portage TIF and type the name and address for the Inn.

Figure 6.41
Project 6.2—Fax
Cover Sheet

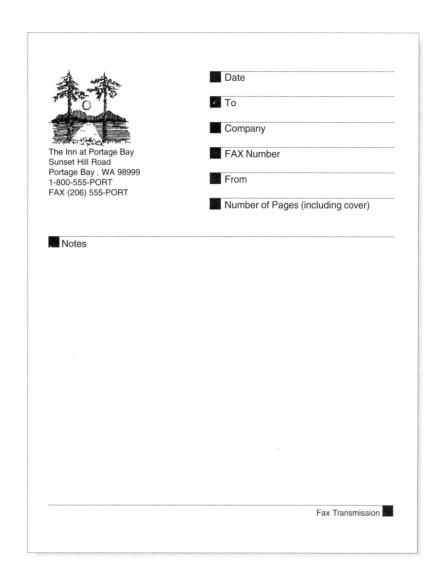

The Inn at Portage Bay
Sunset Hill Road
Portage Bay , WA 98999
1-800-555-PORT
FAX (206) 555-PORT

◼ Date

✓ To

◼ Company

◼ FAX Number

◼ From

◼ Number of Pages (including cover)

◼ Notes

Fax Transmission ◼

3. Run the appropriate Pagemaker script to build the template from which you will create the Press Release shown in Figure 6.42 and the Invoice shown in Figure 6.43. Replace the logo box with Portage TIF and type the correct address and phone number for the Inn.

Figure 6.42
Project 6.3—Press Release

**For more information, please contact:**

Name
The Inn at Portage Bay
Sunset Hill Road
Portage Bay, WA 98999
(800) 555-PORT

*For Immediate Release*

**Heading 1**

City, State (Month, Day,Year)—Duis autem vel eum iriure dolor in hendrerit in vulputate velit esse molestie consequat, vel illum dolore eu feugiat nulla facilisis at vero eros et accumsan et iusto odio dignissim qui blandit praesent luptatum zzril delnit augue duis dolore te feugait nulla facilisi.

Vel eum iriure dolor in hendrerit in vulputate velit esse molestie consequat, vel illum dolore eu feugiat nulla facilisis at vero eros et accumsan et iusto odio dignissim qui blandit praesent luptatum zzril delnit augue duis dolore te feugait nulla facilisi.

Autem vel eum iriure dolor in hendrerit in vulputate velit esse molestie consequat, vel illum dolore eu feugiat nulla facilisis at vero eros et accumsan et iusto odio dignissim qui blandit praesent luptatum zzril delnit augue duis dolore te feugait nulla facilisi. Vel illum dolore eu feugiat nulla facilisis at vero eros et accumsan et iusto odio dignissim qui blandit praesent luptatum zzril delnit augue duis dolore te feugait nulla facilisi.

**Heading 2**
Duis autem vel eum iriure dolor in hendrerit in vulputate velit esse molestie consequat, vel illum dolore eu feugiat nulla facilisis at vero eros et accumsan et iusto odio dignissim qui blandit praesent luptatum zzril delnit augue duis dolore te feugait nulla facilisi.

Vel eum iriure dolor in hendrerit in vulputate velit esse molestie consequat, vel illum dolore eu feugiat nulla facilisis at vero eros et accumsan et iusto odio dignissim qui blandit praesent luptatum zzril delnit augue duis dolore te feugait nulla facilisi.

Autem vel eum iriure dolor in hendrerit in vulputate velit esse molestie consequat, vel illum dolore eu feugiat nulla facilisis at vero eros et accumsan et iusto odio dignissim qui blandit.

(more)

Figure 6.43
Project 6.3—Invoice

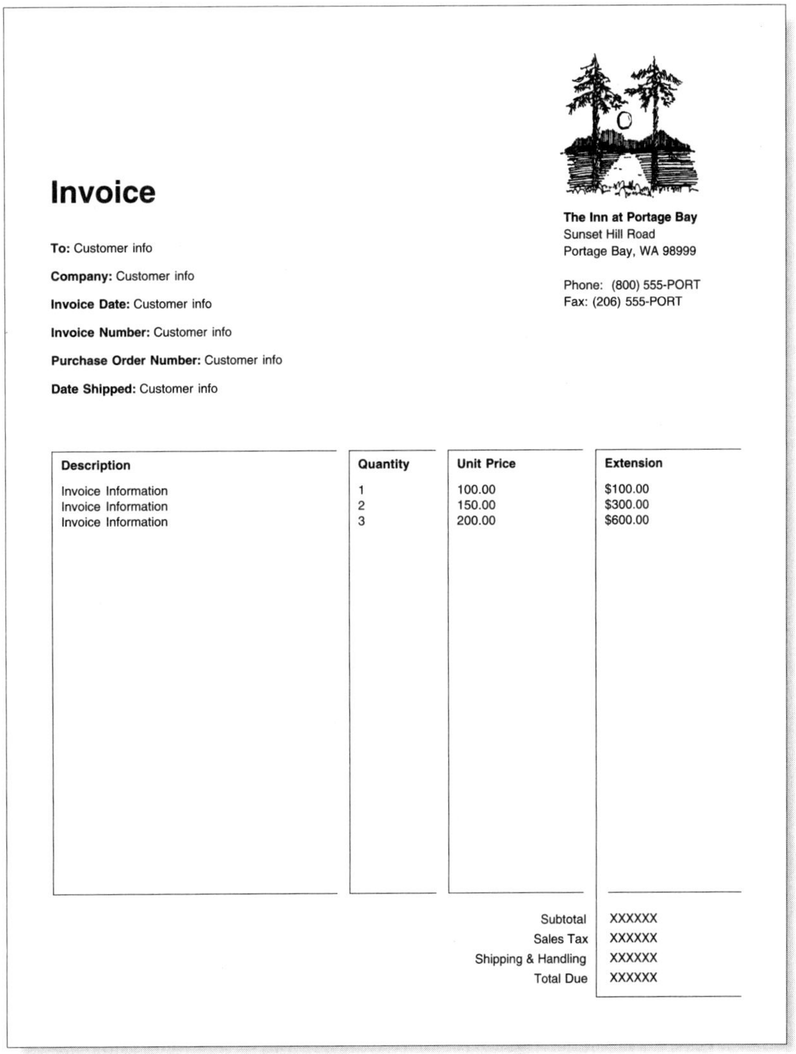

# Invoice

**The Inn at Portage Bay**
Sunset Hill Road
Portage Bay, WA 98999

Phone: (800) 555-PORT
Fax: (206) 555-PORT

**To:** Customer info

**Company:** Customer info

**Invoice Date:** Customer info

**Invoice Number:** Customer info

**Purchase Order Number:** Customer info

**Date Shipped:** Customer info

| Description | Quantity | Unit Price | Extension |
|---|---|---|---|
| Invoice Information | 1 | 100.00 | $100.00 |
| Invoice Information | 2 | 150.00 | $300.00 |
| Invoice Information | 3 | 200.00 | $600.00 |

| | |
|---|---|
| Subtotal | XXXXXX |
| Sales Tax | XXXXXX |
| Shipping & Handling | XXXXXX |
| Total Due | XXXXXX |

4. Using the *Port Dorsey Times* newsletter you started in this chapter, add articles to it as shown in Figure 6.44.

Figure 6.44
continued
Project 6.4—*Port Dorsey Times*, (page 1)

Type Table of
Contents

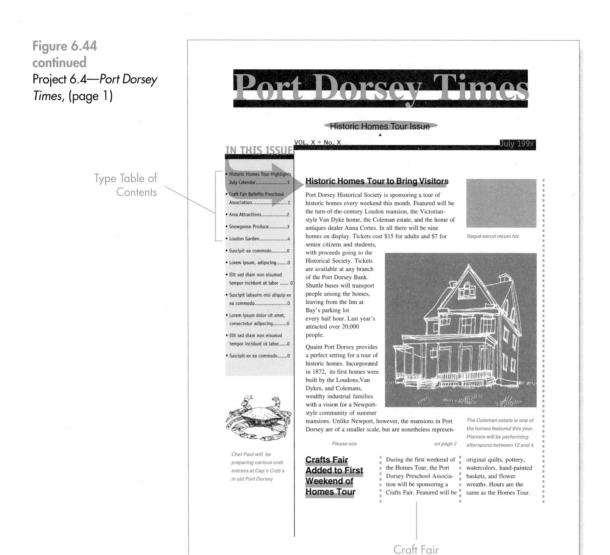

# Port Dorsey Times

Historic Homes Tour Issue

VOL. X • No. X                                        July 199x

**IN THIS ISSUE**

## Historic Homes Tour to Bring Visitors

Port Dorsey Historical Society is sponsoring a tour of historic homes every weekend this month. Featured will be the turn-of-the-century Loudon mansion, the Victorian-style Van Dyke home, the Coleman estate, and the home of antiques dealer Anna Cortes. In all there will be nine homes on display. Tickets cost $15 for adults and $7 for senior citizens and students, with proceeds going to the Historical Society. Tickets are available at any branch of the Port Dorsey Bank. Shuttle buses will transport people among the homes, leaving from the Inn at Bay's parking lot every half hour. Last year's attracted over 20,000 people.

Quaint Port Dorsey provides a perfect setting for a tour of historic homes. Incorporated in 1872, its first homes were built by the Loudons, Van Dykes, and Colemans, wealthy industrial families with a vision for a Newport-style community of summer mansions. Unlike Newport, however, the mansions in Port Dorsey are of a smaller scale, but are nonetheless represen-

*Please see                         on page 2*

*Itaque earud rerum hic*

*The Coleman estate is one of the homes featured this year. Pianists will be performing afternoons between 12 and 4.*

*Chef Paul will be preparing various crab entrees at Cap'n Crab's in old Port Dorsey*

### Crafts Fair Added to First Weekend of Homes Tour

During the first weekend of the Homes Tour, the Port Dorsey Preschool Association will be sponsoring a Crafts Fair. Featured will be original quilts, pottery, watercolors, hand-painted baskets, and flower wreaths. Hours are the same as the Homes Tour.

Craft Fair

Figure 6.44
continued
Project 6.4—*Port Dorsey Times,* (page 2)

Area Attractions

Tulips

*The Skagit Tulip Festival brings thousands of visitors annually*

## AREA ATTRACTIONS

Following is a sample of the most popular seasonal attractions found in our area. Tours of the first two attractions can be arranged at the information booth during the Homes Tour in Port Dorsey.

*The Tulip Festival attracts world-wide visitors*

The Skagit Valley Tulip Festival is held early in April. Thousands of visitors flock to the Skagit Valley to enjoy the miles and miles of tulips as they bloom into a dazzling array of colors. Hundreds of varieties of daffodils, tulips, and other spring flowers make this a photographer's and artist's paradise. The climate, soil, and rain combined with the care of the Dutch settlers make the bulb and cut-flower industry one of the most important in the region, with sales estimated at over $14 million. After touring the valley, visitors can enjoy a salmon barbecue, patterned after the native Indian recipes, at the nearby town of La Conner. The Skagit Valley is located on Interstate 5 at Mt. Vernon. The drive takes about one hour and 20 minutes from The Inn at Portage Bay.

The Suquamish Museum is dedicated to the study of the Puget Sound Salish Indians, who were the original inhabitants of this area. Chief Seattle, for whom the City of Seattle is named, was from the Suquamish Tribe. The museum's exhibition, which has toured in Europe, depicts the lives of the Puget Sound Indians prior to and after white settlement through photographs, artifacts, and interviews with tribal elders. The Suquamish Museum is located in one of the most beautiful settings in the Northwest, on the shores of Agate Pass, six miles north of Winslow on Highway 305. The hours are Monday through Thursday 10am - 5pm and Friday through Sunday 10am - 8pm. Admission is $6 for adults and $4 for children under 12 and senior citizens.

Located on the United States and Canadian border, Peace Arch State Park is dedicated to the friendship of the two countries. The park was opened in 1921 and was built with contributions from the schoolchildren in Washington and British Columbia. The Arch monument, which divides the highway, is a symbolic portal for the citizens who visit each country. The beautifully landscaped park provides a serene setting from which to view nearby Birch Bay. The Peace Arch State Park is located on Interstate 5 at the Canadian border. The drive takes about 45 minutes from The Inn at Portage Bay.

### Headline

Duis autem vel eum iriure dolor in hendrerit in vulputate velit esse molestie consequat, vel illum dolore eu feugiat nulla facilisis at vero eros et accumsan et iusto odio dignissim qui blandit praesent duis vel illum dolore eu feugiat dolore vel illum dolore eu feugiat te feugait nulla facilisi. Ut wisi enim consequat, illum dolore eu nulla at et et odio ad minim veniam.

#### *Subhead 1*

Vero eros et accumsan et iusto odio dignissim qui blandit praesent luptatum zzril delenit augue duis facilisi. Lorem ipsum dolor sit amet, consectetuer praesent luptatum zzril delenit augue duis adipis cing elit. Ut wisi enim ad minim veniam, luptatum zzril quis.

Lorem ipsum dolor sit amet, dolore te feugait nulla consectetuer.

#### *Subhead 1*

Adipiscing elit, sed diam nonummy nibh euismod tincidunt ut laoreet dolore

Lorem ipsum dolor sit amet, eaut nobis consectetuer adipiscing elit, volutpat. Ut wisi enim minim veniam, quis nostrud tempor cum nobis

magna aliquam erat dolore te feugait nulla volutpat. Ut wisi enim molestie facilisis at nostrud luptatum zzril consequat, vel illum dolore eu feugiat nulla facilisis facilisis at nostrud at nost rud exerci tation ullam corper suscipit lobortis nisl ut dolore te feugait nulla aliquip ex ea commodo consequat. ■

### *Homes Tour Features Nine Homes*

*continued from page 1*

*Itaque earud rerum hic tnetury sapente delctus*

tative of fine period architecture and furnishings. Later inhabitants built homes consistent with the architecture of the first homes. The area became famous for its fine antiques stores. Recently the business area has seen the addition of many fine restaurants and small shops with unique merchandise.

*Please see          on page 3*

Figure 6.44
continued

Project 6.4—*Port Dorsey
Times*, (page 3)

*Itaque earud rerum hic tnetury sapente delctus Itaque earud rerum hic tnetury sapente delctus*

### Homes

*continued from page 2*

Port Dorsey is a destination for weekend shoppers, but during the month of the Historical Homes Tour, visitors come from all over the country for the event.

master gardeners, so this year, the Homes Tour will include the English country garden which was featured recently in Country Gardens magazine. Afternoon tea with an assortment of cakes is available in the garden for

Especially noteworthy is the central staircase, with hand-crafted banister. Many finely carved walnut pieces of furniture have been collected during the owners' travels and enhance the period feel.

### Coleman Estate

The Coleman estate was built in 1920 and is now used for wedding receptions and special events. The fireplace in the drawing room has an elaborately carved wood mantel. Wainscoting, six-panel doors, and finely carved woodwork show off the fine craftsmanship of the time. Windowseats in the library alcove and the children's bedrooms are filled with soft cushions and pillows. There is a four-poster bed and Queen Anne highboy in the master bedroom. A grand piano is the centerpiece of the living room. During the tour, various pianists will be playing between noon and four each day.

Hours are 10 a.m. until 6 p.m. on all days. ■

Snowgoose Produce

*Itaque earud rerum hic tnetury sapente delctus*

### Loudon Mansion

The Loudon mansion was

built in 1898 and has twelve rooms, including a formal living room, parlor, dining room, library, kitchen, breakfast room, four bedrooms, and maid's quarters. Still owned by the Loudon family, it contains many original furnishings, including sofas, the dining room table, and oriental rugs. On two sides of the house is a wrap-around porch, or verandah as it is referred to by the Loudons, that overlooks the water and has expansive views of the San Juan Islands.

The current occupants are

a small fee. Proceeds from the tea service will benefit the Port Dorsey Garden Society.

### Van Dyke Home

The Victorian-style Van Dyke home was built in 1889, and has the steeply pitched roof, verge board trim, pointed Gothic windows, and board-and-batten siding characteristic of Victorian homes. Elaborate trim work, both inside and out, and a hexagonal cupola are other characteristics that make this a favorite on the tour. Inside, rich colors and tones of wood, wallpaper, and rugs are examples of the Victorian decor.

## SNOWGOOSE PRODUCE

Between Port Dorsey and the interstate is a wonderful way station for drivers. Snowgoose Produce is a roadside stand with a variety of fresh vegetables and fruits, seafood, and flowers. In addition, there are baskets from Kenya and handmade outdoor furniture from Maine. Probably the biggest attraction is the home-made ice cream generously scooped into waffle cones. Flavors include Latte chip yogurt, San Juan blackberry souffle, and raspberry chocolate torte. On a summer day, over 2,000 ice cream cones will be served.

To find Snowgoose Produce, pick up an area map at any house on the Homes Tour.

Vero eros et accumsan et iusto odio dignissim qui blandit praesent luptatum zzril delenit augue duis facilisi. Lorem ipsum dolor sit amet, consectetuer adipiscing elit, volutpat. veniam, quis nostrud.

Figure 6.44
continued
Project 6.4—*Port Dorsey
Times*, (page 4)

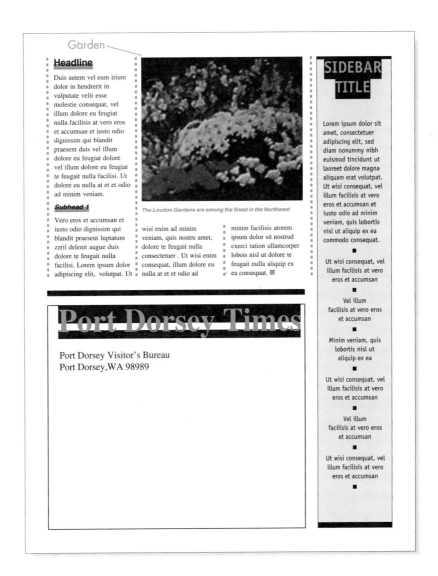

5. Using the *Port Dorsey Times* newsletter, replace all remaining text and graphics placeholders with text and graphics of your choosing to complete the newsletter.

6. Use page 1 of the PageMaker Brochure 1 to create Figure 6.45 on the next page.

   ■ Complete the brochure using your own text.

   ■ Add graphics that came with this book or add your own.

**Figure 6.45**
Project 6.6—Brochure

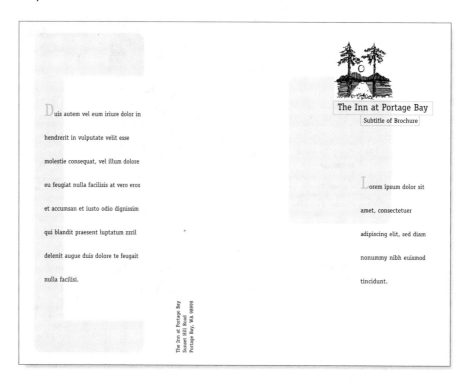

Duis autem vel eum iriure dolor in

hendrerit in vulputate velit esse

molestie consequat, vel illum dolore

eu feugiat nulla facilisis at vero eros

et accumsan et iusto odio dignissim

qui blandit praesent luptatum zzril

delenit augue duis dolore te feugait

nulla facilisi.

The Inn at Portage Bay

Subtitle of Brochure

Lorem ipsum dolor sit

amet, consectetuer

adipiscing elit, sed diam

nonummy nibh euismod

tincidunt.

The Inn at Portage Bay
Sunset Hill Road
Portage Bay, WA 98999

7. This project directs you to use the Add cont'd line in the Plug-ins. Do the following:

  ■ Run the PageMaker Newsletter 2 script.

  ■ Thread the text blocks from pages 2 and 3 together, as you did in the chapter.

  ■ Using the pointer tool, select the text block at the end of page 2.

  ■ Point to Plug-ins in the Utilities menu and click Add cont'd line. Specify bottom of text block for continuation line.

  ■ Select the jump line and change the style to Caption. Then select the text block at the top of page 3 and use the same steps to create a jump line at the top.

8. This project shows you the difference between placing text with Retain format selected and not selected. (If you need help, refer to the text near Figure 6.15.) Do the following:

  ■ Open Newsletter template from the student files.

  ■ Select the text where the Manager's Monthly Message will appear.

  ■ Place October Message twice: first with Retain format selected, and second with it not selected.

  Describe the differences in the appearance of the placed file for the two options of Retain format.

# CHAPTER 7

# Creating Master Pages, Grids, Style Sheets, and Templates

Upon completion of this chapter you will be able to:

- Create multiple master pages for a template
- Define *grid system* and use Grid Manager to create a grid
- Explain the purpose of a style sheet and modify the Styles palette
- Create a template
- Describe the differences between master pages and templates
- Insert automatic page numbers

In Chapter 6 you created a newsletter using a template created by the authors of this book. The template contained the layout, or underlying structure, for the newsletter. In this chapter you will learn how to create that underlying structure for PageMaker documents while working with master pages, grids, and style sheets. You will also be introduced to some design concepts and learn how to use PageMaker to execute design decisions. In the next chapter you will learn some of the guidelines for page design and experiment with design concepts.

**Figure 7.1**
Thumbnails of
pages 1-3 of the Annual
Report template

There are four components to the structure of documents: master pages, grids, style sheets, and templates. You will use each of these components to create an Annual Report for the Inn at Portage Bay. A portion of the template you will complete in this chapter is shown in Figure 7.1.

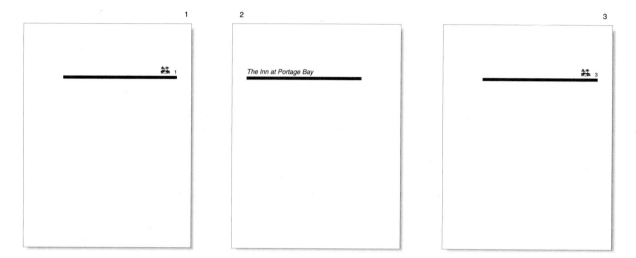

Figure 7.1 uses thumbnails to show page layout. **Thumbnails** are miniature versions of the pages of a publication, and are available from the Print Document dialog box. Once you specify the number of thumbnails to print on a page, the size of the thumbnails is determined. You'll learn more about thumbnails in a question at the end of the chapter.

To produce any desktop-published document, you need several skills. These include knowing how to use the software, identifying the publication's objective, designing the layout, and finally, creating the publication's copy.

Using desktop publishing software, such as PageMaker, shortens the time between the initial concept and the final production of a document. Sometimes the software user is the only person involved in all the steps—from the first design to the delivery of camera-ready copy. Although one person might possess all the skills needed to produce a quality document in PageMaker, knowing how to create a document in PageMaker does not necessarily ensure a well-designed brochure, newsletter, or Annual Report. Desktop publishing allows users to create well-designed documents, as well as poorly designed ones, much faster than was possible before. Thus it is important to plan a document before placing text and graphics on the page. This step will lead to (but not guarantee) a better design.

**Working with Master Pages**

Recall from Chapter 6 that master pages contain basic design elements, including margin guides, ruler guides, and column guides, and can contain text or art that will appear on every page, as well as page numbers.

Using master pages allows you to specify the format for a publication's pages one time and then reuse the format throughout the publication. Master pages save time when you are setting up a publication, and ensure a consistent look within a document.

Remember that objects placed on master pages appear on publication pages, but you cannot change them unless you switch to the master pages. You can add, change, and delete objects on master pages just as you do on publication pages.

Each publication contains either a default master page, or if the publication includes facing pages, a default master page spread, called the **Document Master**. Elements placed on the Document Master appear on all publication pages until you remove those elements. An R master page icon in the lower-left corner of the publication window indicates a Document Master page; L and R master page icons indicate a Document Master page spread.

You can name additional master pages either by duplicating the Document Master, as you'll do here, or by using the drop-down menu on the Master Pages palette. You can create a different master page for every publication page, or use a certain master page layout for specific pages in a publication.

For The Inn's Annual Report, you will open a new publication with 12 pages. Then you will duplicate the default Document Master to create three named master pages, which are summarized in Figure 7.2. By duplicating the Document Master for the other master pages, you ensure that any elements you place on the Document Master will also be placed on the named master pages. These elements will be a line and the words *The Inn at Portage Bay* for left master pages and a line, logo, and page number for right master pages. Finally, you will define a layout grid for each master page and apply it to several other pages.

**Figure 7.2**
**Master pages summary**

| Master page name | Rows | Columns |
|---|---|---|
| Document Master | 3 | 3 |
| 1 column | 3 | 1 |
| 2 column | 3 | 2 |
| 3 column | 3 | 3 |

In order to define the three named master pages, you need to place the Master Pages palette on the Pasteboard. You'll also want to use the Styles palette in this chapter, so you'll place it on the Pasteboard now. Recall that you can combine or separate palettes by dragging the appropriate tab from one palette to another. You should create a palette that contains only Master Pages and Styles tabs to reduce the amount of space they take on the Pasteboard.

1. Start PageMaker.

SHIFT CTRL 8

2. Select Show Master Pages from the Window menu.

CTRL B

3. Select Show Styles from the Window menu.

4. If necessary, combine the palettes into one and click the Master Pages tab. See Figure 7.3.

**Figure 7.3**
Styles and Master Pages palettes combined

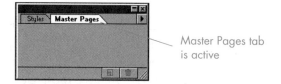

Master Pages tab is active

Notice that the Master Pages palette is empty; there are no master pages defined because there is no open publication. Next open a new publication with 12 pages.

CTRL N

5. Select New from the File menu.

6. In the Document Setup dialog box, type *12* for the number of pages.

7. Click OK.

Look at the Master Pages palette and notice that it now contains two entries: [None] and [Document Master]. If you want to add more publication pages to the document without having the elements on the Document Master show, apply the None master page.

**Creating Multiple Master Pages**

You will create three different master pages, named *1 column*, *2 column*, and *3 column*, by duplicating the Document Master.

1. Click the pointer tool  in the Toolbox, and drag the Document Master to the master page button  on the Master Pages palette. See Figure 7.4. The Duplicate Master Page dialog box appears.

**Figure 7.4**
Duplicating Document Master

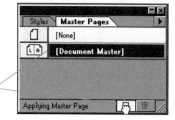

Click and drag to master page button

2. In the Name of new Master box, type *1 column*. See Figure 7.5.

Figure 7.5
Duplicate Master Page
dialog box

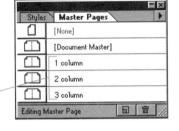

Type 1 column

Click Duplicate

**3.** Click Duplicate.

**4.** On your own, create two additional master pages and name them *2 column* and *3 column*. When you are done, your Master Pages palette should look like Figure 7.6.

Figure 7.6
Master Pages palette after creating the named master pages

Named Master pages

Now that you have named the master pages needed to create the template, you're ready to specify the layout grids for each.

**Working with Grids**

Creating a publication is like building a house in many ways; most importantly, both require planning. You expect an architect to plan the overall house design before construction begins. The same is true for a publication—you should expect to plan the basic page design before production begins. To continue the analogy, both houses and pages require underlying structures on which a product is built, and both require design and planning to succeed. In the case of a publication, a grid provides the structure on which to build pages. A **grid** is a set of nonprinting horizontal and vertical lines that divide the page into rectangles, which you use to place headlines, text, graphs, and pictures.

Using a grid system has many advantages. A grid gives the publication a unified appearance and shows the proportions you used to design a page. A grid system imposes organization on an untrained designer and helps the designer place page elements consistently and accurately. It makes the publication look planned and coordinated, especially when a team of people is working on the same project. All team members can keep the established grid in mind as they compose text and graphics for the project. Readers get used to the grid you present for a specific publication and come to expect a certain "look and feel," such as for different issues of a newsletter. For all these reasons, it is wise to start with a grid.

Figure 7.7 shows examples of standard grid systems. All the grids shown are divided into two, three, or four columns, which divide the page vertically. In the last example, horizontal lines create a series of rectangular guides to complete the grid system.

**Figure 7.7**
Examples of grid systems

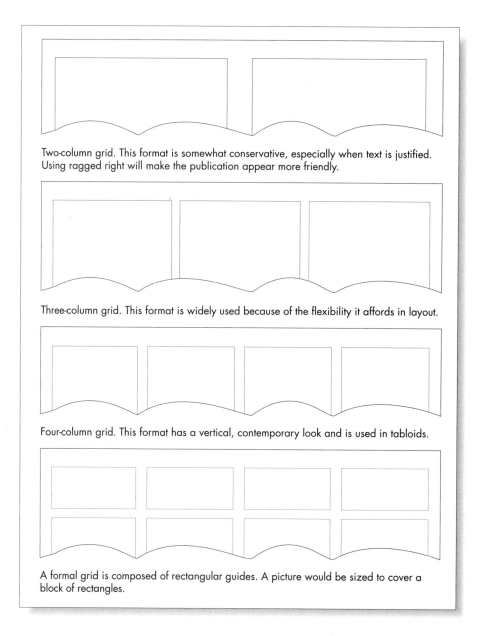

Two-column grid. This format is somewhat conservative, especially when text is justified. Using ragged right will make the publication appear more friendly.

Three-column grid. This format is widely used because of the flexibility it affords in layout.

Four-column grid. This format has a vertical, contemporary look and is used in tabloids.

A formal grid is composed of rectangular guides. A picture would be sized to cover a block of rectangles.

After the grid system is set up, you or the designer would make additional decisions about the inclusion and design of headers and footers, page numbers, and text and graphic elements. The established grid provides a guide for placing these elements on the page.

Page layout does not always mean staying strictly inside the grid. For example, in a four-column grid, a graph or picture might be placed across three columns, as shown in Figure 7.8. Designers rarely place an element across half columns. Using half columns, such as one and a half columns of a four-column grid, can imply that the underlying grid structure actually contains more columns; in which a four-column grid might actually be an eight-column grid.

**Figure 7.8**
Variation on grid photo spans three columns

Courtesy of Sheila Hoffman, Newsletters and More

A second variation on the grid system is to define columns of unequal width, although there should still be an underlying grid of equal columns. For example, in a grid system with two columns in proportions of one-third and two-thirds of the page, the underlying grid is three columns. The narrow, one-third column can be filled with text or used as a scholar's margin, as is done in this book.

Figure 7.9 illustrates columns of unequal width.

**Figure 7.9**
Columns of uneven width

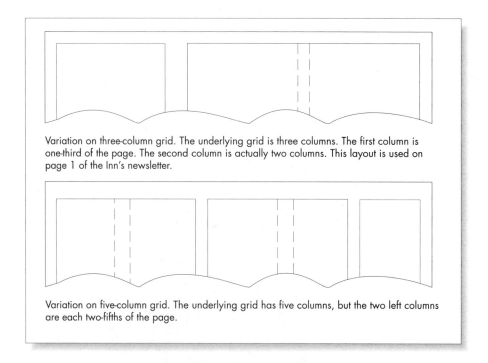

Variation on three-column grid. The underlying grid is three columns. The first column is one-third of the page. The second column is actually two columns. This layout is used on page 1 of the Inn's newsletter.

Variation on five-column grid. The underlying grid has five columns, but the two left columns are each two-fifths of the page.

A **scholar's margin** is a column of predominantly white space that is on either the outside edge or the left side of a page. Its purpose is to add visual interest to the page, allow for emphasis of key items, and draw the reader into the text. The scholar's margin might contain section headings, boxed items that enhance body text, or pull quotes. A **pull quote** is text from the body copy repeated somewhere else for emphasis. A pull quote can appear in the scholar's margin near the quote in context. Pull quotes can also appear within the body text in larger print.

A third grid variation is to leave blank one or more sections across the top of the page, as shown in Figure 7.10. This allows the space for chapter or section headings, lead-in quotes, or other items that enhance a reader's interest. The idea is similar to that of the scholar's margin, but the blank space is at the top of the page rather than in the margin.

A grid is critical to good page design and layout, but it should be an organizational tool rather than a design prison.

Figure 7.10
Variation on grid layout

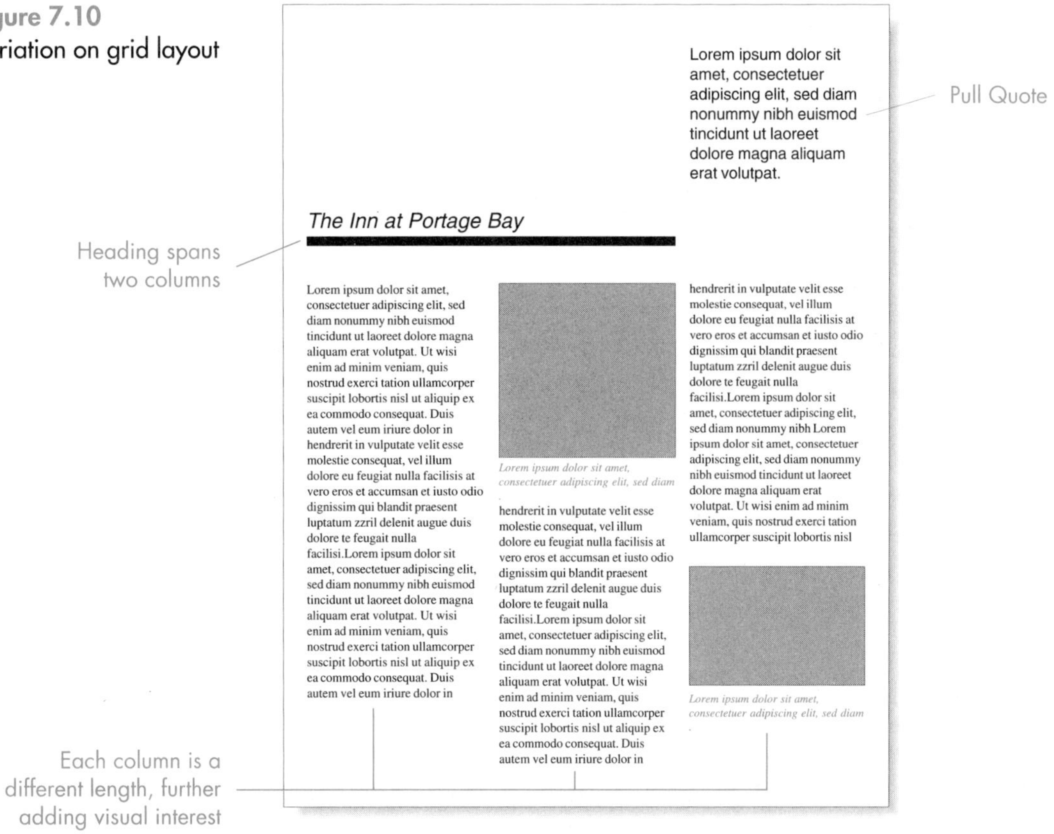

Pull Quote

Lorem ipsum dolor sit amet, consectetuer adipiscing elit, sed diam nonummy nibh euismod tincidunt ut laoreet dolore magna aliquam erat volutpat.

Heading spans
two columns

*The Inn at Portage Bay*

Lorem ipsum dolor sit amet, consectetuer adipiscing elit, sed diam nonummy nibh euismod tincidunt ut laoreet dolore magna aliquam erat volutpat. Ut wisi enim ad minim veniam, quis nostrud exerci tation ullamcorper suscipit lobortis nisl ut aliquip ex ea commodo consequat. Duis autem vel eum iriure dolor in hendrerit in vulputate velit esse molestie consequat, vel illum dolore eu feugiat nulla facilisis at vero eros et accumsan et iusto odio dignissim qui blandit praesent luptatum zzril delenit augue duis dolore te feugait nulla facilisi.Lorem ipsum dolor sit amet, consectetuer adipiscing elit, sed diam nonummy nibh euismod tincidunt ut laoreet dolore magna aliquam erat volutpat. Ut wisi enim ad minim veniam, quis nostrud exerci tation ullamcorper suscipit lobortis nisl ut aliquip ex ea commodo consequat. Duis autem vel eum iriure dolor in

*Lorem ipsum dolor sit amet, consectetuer adipiscing elit, sed diam*

hendrerit in vulputate velit esse molestie consequat, vel illum dolore eu feugiat nulla facilisis at vero eros et accumsan et iusto odio dignissim qui blandit praesent luptatum zzril delenit augue duis dolore te feugait nulla facilisi.Lorem ipsum dolor sit amet, consectetuer adipiscing elit, sed diam nonummy nibh euismod tincidunt ut laoreet dolore magna aliquam erat volutpat. Ut wisi enim ad minim veniam, quis nostrud exerci tation ullamcorper suscipit lobortis nisl ut aliquip ex ea commodo consequat. Duis autem vel eum iriure dolor in

hendrerit in vulputate velit esse molestie consequat, vel illum dolore eu feugiat nulla facilisis at vero eros et accumsan et iusto odio dignissim qui blandit praesent luptatum zzril delenit augue duis dolore te feugait nulla facilisi.Lorem ipsum dolor sit amet, consectetuer adipiscing elit, sed diam nonummy nibh Lorem ipsum dolor sit amet, consectetuer adipiscing elit, sed diam nonummy nibh euismod tincidunt ut laoreet dolore magna aliquam erat volutpat. Ut wisi enim ad minim veniam, quis nostrud exerci tation ullamcorper suscipit lobortis nisl

*Lorem ipsum dolor sit amet, consectetuer adipiscing elit, sed diam*

Each column is a
different length, further
adding visual interest

---

## Creating a Grid

PageMaker comes with a Plug-in utility called **Grid Manager** that simplifies the task of creating a grid. The Grid Manager enables you to:

- specify columns and the gutter space between them, which divides a page vertically

- specify horizontal rules, which proportionally divide a page into rows

- mirror a page, which copies a left-page grid and flips it to a right-page grid or vice versa

- clone a page, which copies the grid from one page to another

- apply a grid to master pages and specific publication pages

You have set up three master pages—named *1 column*, *2 column*, and *3 column*—in addition to the Document Master, which PageMaker creates for every publication. You will define the grid for each master page and then apply each master page to publication pages as determined by the Annual Report writer. Figure 7.11 lists which master pages to apply to publication pages.

**Figure 7.11**
Applying master pages to publication pages

| Master page name | Apply to pages |
| --- | --- |
| *1 column* | 1, 4–6, 9 |
| *2 column* | 2, 7, 8, 11 |
| *3 column* | 3, 10, 12 |

Start by defining the grid for the Document Master and applying it.

1. Point to Plug-ins in the Utilities menu.

2. Click Grid Manager. The Grid Manager dialog box appears, as shown in Figure 7.12.

**Figure 7.12**
Grid Manager dialog box

Apply area

Define grid area

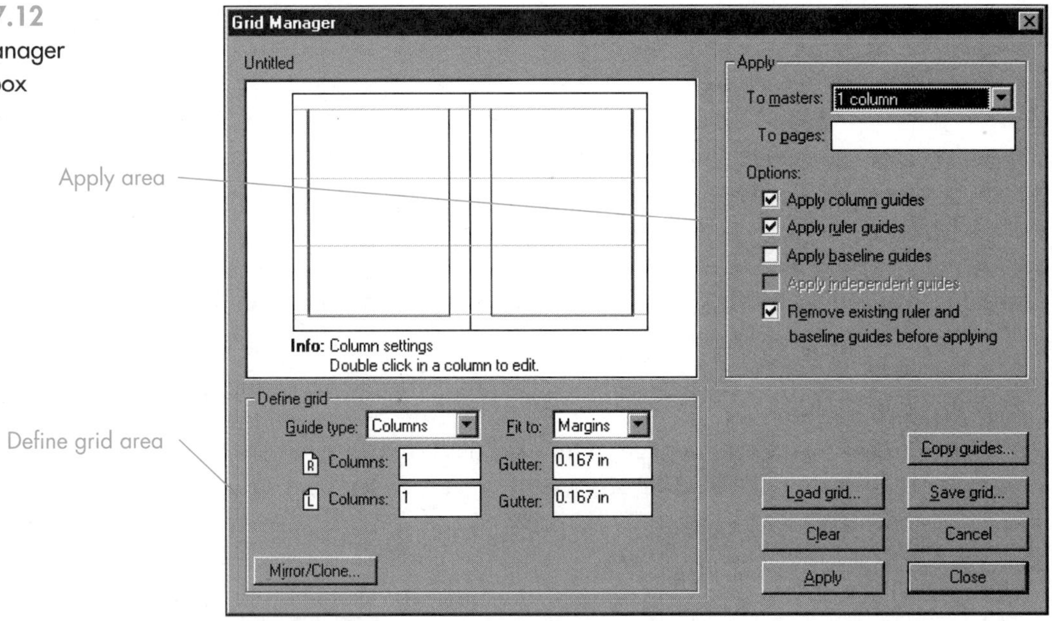

You will use the Apply and Define grid areas in the chapter, and explore the other options in a question at the end of the chapter.

3. Click the down arrow next to the To masters box in the Apply section.

4. Select Document Master from the list.

5. In the Define grid section, set Guide type to Columns and then type *3* in the R Columns box and *3* in the L Columns box.

6. Click the down arrow next to the Guide type box.

7. Select Rulers.

8. In the Rows box, type *3* if necessary. R and L Columns should be set to 0. See Figure 7.13.

**Figure 7.13**
Document Master grid selections

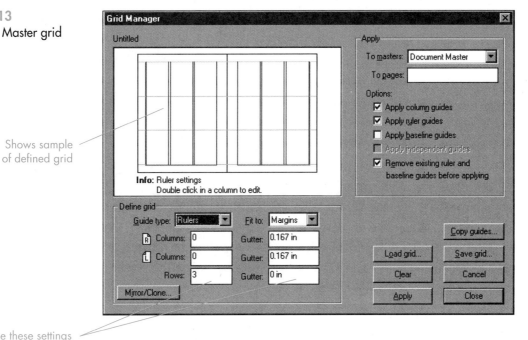

Shows sample of defined grid

Use these settings

9. When your screen matches Figure 7.13, click Apply in the lower-right corner of the dialog box.

You have defined Document Master with a 3-by-3 grid. Next you will define the *1 column* master page as a 3-rows-by-1-column grid.

10. Click the down arrow next to the Apply To masters box.

11. Select 1 column from the list.

12. Click an insertion point in the To pages box.

13. Type *1, 4-6, 9* for the page numbers you want to apply this master page to.

14. Select Columns from the Guide type box, and type *1* in the R Columns box and *1* in the L Columns box.

15. Select Rulers from the Guide type box.

**16.** Type *3* in the Rows box. R and L Columns should be set to 0. See Figure 7.14.

**Figure 7.14**
1 column master page grid selections

Notice how pages reflect your choices

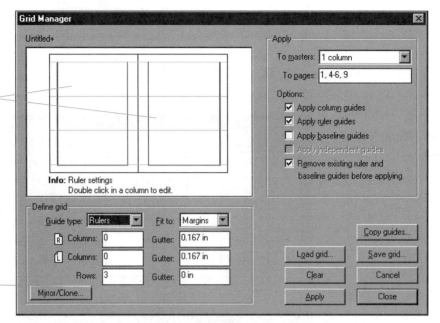

Click Apply to apply your selections to the specific pages

Notice how the preview of the master pages changes to reflect your choices.

**17.** When your screen matches Figure 7.14, click Apply in the lower-right corner of the dialog box.

You have defined the *1 column* master page with one column and three rows. Although the rows are separated by ruler guides, the columns are separated by column guides. The reason you are using column guides instead of ruler guides for the columns is so that when you place text on the pages, the text block will conform to the column boundaries. Ruler guides do not define the width of text blocks. This becomes important when you have two or more columns on a page.

**18.** On your own, define the *2 column* and *3 column* master pages, as specified in Figure 7.15. Make sure you click Apply for each master page.

**Figure 7.15**

Defining the 2 column and 3 column master pages in Grid Manager

| Apply to masters | Apply to pages | Columns |
|---|---|---|
| *2 column* | 2, 7, 8, 11 | 2 |
| *3 column* | 3, 10, 12 | 3 |

**19.** When you are done, click Close.

To verify that you correctly applied *1 column*, *2 column*, and *3 column* master pages to the correct publication pages, click through the page icons and verify your view with the list in Figure 7.11. If your publication does not match, open Grid Manager again and redo any parts that don't match.

## Working with Style Sheets

As graphic designers create various styles for a publication, they collect the list of styles in a **style sheet**. In PageMaker, a style sheet is called the Styles palette.

Each **style** is a set of instructions for formatting text and includes a font and size; a choice of normal, bold, or italic; and paragraph characteristics, such as indentation and margins. Headline, Caption, and Body copy are some of the standard styles used in PageMaker publications. For example, you might use Times New Roman 30 bold for a headline, Times New Roman 14 italic for a subheading, and Times New Roman 10 for body text. Each of the three styles can have different indentation, as well as different left and right margins. In PageMaker terms, all the styles for one publication make up a Styles palette. A graphic designer would call this a style sheet.

To select the Styles palette (which you placed on the Pasteboard earlier), click the Styles tab. You can see the six default PageMaker styles: Body text, Caption, Hanging indent, Headline, Subhead 1, and Subhead 2. Using the Define Styles dialog box in the Type menu, you can add, modify, or delete styles. In this way, each style can be customized for any publication.

## CREATING THE STYLES PALETTE FOR THE INN'S ANNUAL REPORT

In this section, you will modify four styles, delete two styles, and create two styles for The Inn's Annual Report. This will give you the opportunity to work with adding, changing, and deleting styles.

The Inn's Annual Report will use six different styles: Body text, Caption, Headline, Subhead 1, Page number, and Pull quote. The first four are part of the default Styles palette and will require modification. You will create Page number and Pull quote, both based on Subhead 1. Finally, you will delete Subhead 2 and Hanging indent, two default styles.

The styles for this project will use the Times New Roman and Arial typefaces. The styles and their specifications are summarized in Figure 7.16.

**Figure 7.16**
**Style sheet for Annual Report**

| Style name | Specifications |
| --- | --- |
| Body text | next: Same style + face: Times New Roman + size: 11 + leading: auto + flush left + space after: 0.3 + hyphenation |
| Caption | next: Same style + face: Times New Roman + italic + size: 10 + leading: auto + color: Blue + flush left |
| Headline | next: Same style + face: Arial + bold + size: 30 + leading: auto + flush left + incl TOC |
| Page number | Subhead 1 + next: Same style – italic + size: 14 + flush right |
| Pull quote | Subhead 1 + next: Same style – italic + size: 14 |
| Subhead 1 | Headline + next: Body text – bold + italic + size: 18 |

Prior to creating and manipulating styles, explore the default styles.

1. Click the Styles tab on the palette.

2. Press ⎡CTRL⎤ while you click the style name you want to explore.

The Style Options dialog box appears. Compare the specifications for the style you're exploring to those for Body text in Figure 7.16. Note that you can modify a single style at a time from the Style Options dialog box, but you'll use Define Styles from the Type menu so that you can access all the styles, rather than only one.

3. When you are done looking at the Style Options dialog box, click Cancel to close it.

4. Explore the other styles by repeating steps 2 and 3. For at least one style, click the Char (Options), Para (Rules, Spacing), Tabs, and Hyph (Add) buttons as well as the sub-functions listed in parentheses.

Now that you have a sense of what the default styles look like, you're ready to modify them.

## Modifying Styles

You will make all the changes to the styles so your specifications will match Figure 7.16. First you will change four styles, then you will add two styles, and finally you will delete two styles.

CTRL 3

**1.** Select Define Styles from the Type menu.

You will see the Define Styles dialog box. Now you can change the Body text style.

**2.** Click Body text.

**3.** Click Edit. The Style Options dialog box appears, as shown in Figure 7.17.

**Figure 7.17**
Style Options dialog box for Body text

You will make three changes to the Body text style: size will change from 12 to 11 points; first indent will change from 0.333 to 0; and space after will change from 0 to 0.3. The first modification is part of Character Specifications and the other two are part of Paragraph Specifications.

**4.** Click Char.

**5.** Change Size to 11 points. See Figure 7.18.

**Figure 7.18**
Character Specifications dialog box for Body text

Type or select 11 points

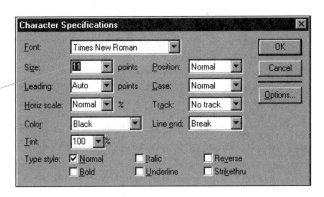

**6.** Click OK to record the change.

**7.** Click Para.

**8.** Change First indent to 0 inches.

**9.** Change Paragraph space After to 0.3 inches. See Figure 7.19.

**Figure 7.19**
Paragraph Specifications
dialog box for Body text

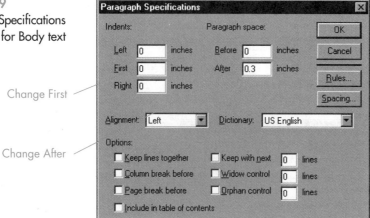

Change First

Change After

**10.** Click OK.

**11.** In the Style Options dialog box on your screen, compare the Body text specifications to those in Figure 7.16. Make sure they match, and then click OK.

Some of the specifications may be new to you. **Flush left** means the text will be aligned to the left margin. **First indent** refers to how far the first line in a paragraph will be indented. **Space after** indicates how much space will appear below the last line of a paragraph. **Next style** specifies the name of the style that should be applied to the text following a **hard return** (the end of a paragraph that occurs when you press ⏎ ENTER). The specifications also show the selection of hyphenation.

**12.** On your own, change the specifications for Caption, Headline, and Subhead 1.

To do this, click the style name, compare the specifications on the screen to those in Figure 7.16, and make the appropriate changes in the Character Specifications and Paragraph Specifications dialog boxes. Make sure you click OK after you make changes. Continue until the specifications for each style in your Style Options dialog box match those shown in Figure 7.16.

When you have made changes to Caption, Headline, and Subhead 1, continue to the next section, leaving the Define Styles dialog box on your screen.

## Adding a New Style

The Annual Report designers want to use pull quotes, which you recall are short quotes selected to stimulate interest in an article and transform people who would scan an article into people who will read an article. This design element will require a style to be added. Because the style will be used for pull quotes, its name will be "Pull quote." Its style will be based on Subhead 1, with a font specification of Arial 14 Normal.

Because you are going to base Pull quote on Subhead 1, start by selecting Subhead 1.

1. Click Subhead 1 in the Define Styles dialog box.

2. Click New.

3. In the Name box, type *Pull quote* (do *not* press ⏎ ENTER ).

4. Look at Based on. If it is not Subhead 1, type *S* in the Based on box. This selects a style that starts with the letter *S,* either Subhead 1 or Subhead 2. Make sure Subhead 1 is selected.

5. Click Char.

6. Verify that Arial is selected.

7. Change Size to 14.

8. For Type style, click Normal. See Figure 7.20.

**Figure 7.20**
Character Specifications dialog box for Pull quote

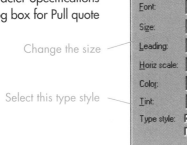

Change the size

Select this type style

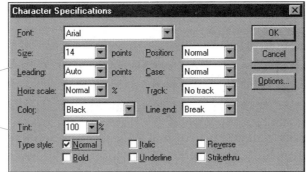

9. When the Character Specifications dialog box looks like Figure 7.20, click OK.

This returns you to the Style Options dialog box. Compare the specifications to Figure 7.16. If they don't match, make the appropriate changes.

10. Click OK to return to the Define Styles dialog box.

11. On your own, add a second style, named *Page number*, to the Styles palette.

Your Define Styles dialog boxes for each style should match the specifications in Figure 7.16.

**Deleting a Style**

The last task for modifying the Styles palette is to delete the Hanging indent and Subhead 2 styles using the Remove button. First select the style you want to delete, and then click Remove to delete it. If you don't do these steps in this order, you will remove whichever style is selected. You should still be in the Define Styles dialog box.

**1.** Select Hanging indent. See Figure 7.21.

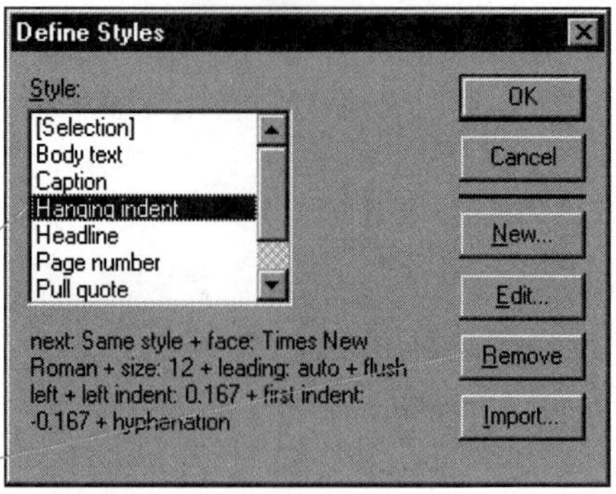

**Figure 7.21**
Define Styles dialog box
before removing
Hanging indent

Click style first

Click Remove second

**Define Styles**

Style:

[Selection]
Body text
Caption
Hanging indent
Headline
Page number
Pull quote

OK

Cancel

New...

Edit...

Remove

Import...

next: Same style + face: Times New
Roman + size: 12 + leading: auto + flush
left + left indent: 0.167 + first indent:
-0.167 + hyphenation

**2.** Click Remove.

**3.** Select Subhead 2.

**4.** Click Remove.

**5.** Click OK.

The Styles palette should now contain six named styles: Body text, Caption, Headline, Page number, Pull quote, and Subhead 1. In addition, you will see a style named No style.

**6.** Click OK to close the Define Styles dialog box.

You have set up your first style sheet by defining the styles for The Inn's Annual Report. In the next section, you'll use some of the styles.

## WORKING WITH TEMPLATES

As you learned earlier, a template is the framework for a publication. It contains master pages, a grid, and a Styles palette. Templates are files that can be used repeatedly to speed up the creation of publications and ensure consistency between publications. Templates, if carefully designed with duplicated Styles palettes and the same grid, add continuity to the whole family of publications put out by a business.

Template files are stored with a .T65 file name extension. Every time you open a template, PageMaker automatically selects the Copy option. This means you open an untitled copy of the template on which you would typically place text, graphs, and pictures. Then you save the document as a publication, with a .P65 (publication) extension. Sometimes, you'll want to open a template, make changes, and save it with the same name. In that case, you would click Original in the Open publication dialog box.

As you saw in Chapter 6, PageMaker comes with a variety of templates to help you in publication layout. There are templates for creating a business card, brochures, calendars, a manual, newsletters, an invoice, an envelope, and a fax cover sheet—to name but a few. You can use or modify these templates as well as create your own.

**Comparing Master
Pages and Templates**

Some of the same phrases can be used to describe both master pages and templates. Both describe the publication's underlying structure. Both give the publication consistency and allow layout to be done faster. In some cases, no difference exists between a particular set of master pages and a template for a publication. But these terms cannot be used interchangeably. Master pages are merely one aspect of templates, but templates can also contain individual page layouts and style sheets.

For the Inn's Annual Report, you will add some design elements on the Document Master pages and an automatic page number for the right-hand pages. When you are done, your Document Master pages will look like Figure 7.22.

**Figure 7.22
Left and right Document
Master pages**

In the projects at the end of this chapter, you will also place some dummy text and graphics on a few pages.

1. Click the L or R master page icons to display the Document Master pages.

2. Click the constrained line tool |– in the Toolbox.

3. Point to Stroke in the Element menu.

4. Click 8pt.

5. Draw the line over the two left columns, as shown in Figure 7.23.

**Figure 7.23
Drawing a line on the left
Document Master page**

Use the grid to help
position the line

Publication page icons

Document Master
page icons

The Inn at Portage Bay

Adobe PageMaker 6.5 - [Untitled-1]
File  Edit  Layout  Type  Element  Utilities  View  Window  Help

Styles    Master Pages
Body text
Caption
Headline
Page number
Pull quote

L R  1  2  3  4  5  6  7  8  9  10  11  12

**6.** Select Copy from the Edit menu.

CTRL C

**7.** Select Paste from the Edit menu.

CTRL V

**8.** Move the pasted line to the right Document Master, as shown in Figure 7.24.

**Figure 7.24**
Copying the line to the right Document Master page

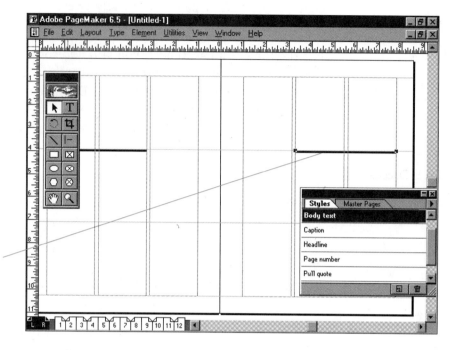

Drag line to right page

**9.** Adjust your view so you can see the right Document Master.

**10.** Click off the line to deselect it.

**11.** Adjust your view so you can see the area above the right side of the line you just moved.

**12.** Click the text tool **T** in the Toolbox.

**13.** Click Page number in the Styles palette.

**14.** Click an insertion point above the line.

**15.** Press CTRL ALT P

This places a page number marker on the page. As you look at all the right pages, they will have the appropriate page number in that location. **RM** means "right master." Had you put the page number marker on a left page, you would see **LM**, for left master. If necessary, drag the page number marker closer to the line.

**16.** Click the rectangle drawing tool ▭ in the Toolbox.

**17.** Point to Stroke in the Element menu.

**18.** Click Hairline.

**19.** Draw a rectangle to the left of the page number marker. Use Figure 7.25 as a guide.

Figure 7.25
Placement of graphic on
right master page

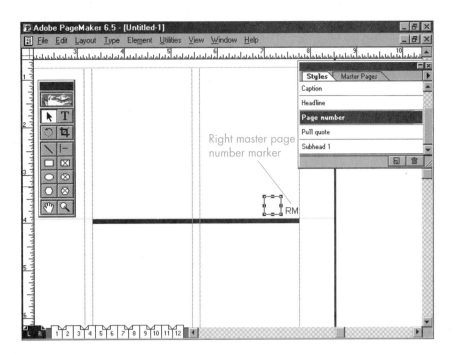

Right master page
number marker

CTRL  D

**20.** With the rectangle still selected, choose Place from the File menu.

**21.** Click Portage.

**22.** In the Place section, select Replacing entire graphic.

**23.** Click Open.

**24.** Click outside the graphic to deselect it. Adjust the graphic or page number marker, if necessary. See Figure 7.26.

Figure 7.26
Right Document Master
page after placing
Portage graphic

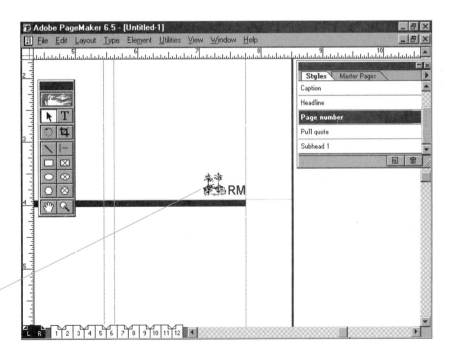

Portage graphic
placed next to page
number marker

Adjust your view so you can see above the line on the left Document Master. You will select Subhead 1 and type *The Inn at Portage Bay*.

**25.** Click Subhead 1 in the Styles palette.

**26.** Click the text tool $\boxed{T}$ in the Toolbox.

**27.** Click an insertion point above the line.

**28.** Type *The Inn at Portage Bay.*

**29.** Adjust the text block to a width of two columns so the words fit on one line.

**30.** Move the text block so the descenders of g and y are a good distance from the line.

You have completed the placement of elements on the Document Master page spread. Click the page icons to see how the Document Master has been applied to all the pages. Adjust the view to see the page numbers on the right pages.

## Saving and Printing a Template

With the grid system in place, the Styles palette updated for the Annual Report, and the page number markers on the Document Master pages, you're ready to save the template. Then you'll print the first two pages.

**1.** Select Save from the File menu.

**2.** In the File name box, type *Annual Report Template.*

**3.** Click the down arrow next to the Save as type box.

**4.** Select Template.

**5.** Click Save.

**6.** Print pages 1 and 2 of the template for your portfolio.

You'll continue working on the template in the projects at the end of the chapter.

## SUMMARY

You have created multiple master pages; used Grid Manager to define a grid; added, changed, and deleted styles in the Styles palette; added page number markers; saved your work as a template; and printed two pages of the template. By defining a grid, you put a framework on the publication. By defining styles, you outlined the character and paragraph specifications for the publication. These PageMaker features allow you to execute design decisions and put a publication plan into a file. Other people in an organization can then use your design decisions to create a publication more easily.

1. Name the four components to the structure of documents.

2. Open Annual Report Template, which you created in this chapter. Click the 4–5 page spread. Click an insertion point in the words *The Inn at Portage Bay*. What happened? Why?

3. What is the difference between the Document Master and a named master page?

4. Describe how to combine palettes on the Pasteboard.

5. Define *grid* and explain its purpose.

6. Define *style sheet* and explain its purpose.

7. What are the two ways to change styles? Which do you prefer? Why?

8. What keys do you press to produce a page number marker?

9. Using Help, answer the following questions:

   a. What is the difference between mirroring and cloning a grid?

   b. In Grid Manager, what is the effect of selecting the option Apply baseline guides?

   c. How do you change the master on one page of a two-page spread?

   d. What is the maximum number of thumbnails you can print on a page?

## PROJECTS

1. Choose a magazine or newsletter. Determine its grid. Guess at the different styles in its Styles palette. Critique the design. Do you like it? Why or why not?

2. Look at Figure 7.27. Identify the different styles used. Develop a style sheet for the publication naming each style and guessing at the character specifications.

**Figure 7.27**
Project 7.2—Identifying styles

*Lorem ipsum dolor sit amet*

Lorem ipsum dolor sit amet, consectetuer adipiscing elit, sed diam nonummy nibh euismod tincidunt ut laoreet dolore magna aliquam erat volutpat. Ut wisi enim ad minim veniam, quis nostrud exerci tation ullamcorper suscipit lobortis nisl ut aliquip ex ea commodo consequat. Duis autem vel eum iriure dolor in hendrerit in vulputate velit esse molestie consequat, vel illum dolore eu feugiat nulla facilisis at vero eros et accumsan et iusto odio dignissim qui blandit praesent luptatum zzril delenit augue duis dolore te feugait nulla facilisi.

Lorem ipsum dolor sit amet, consectetuer adipiscing elit, sed diam nonummy nibh euismod tincidunt ut laoreet dolore magna aliquam erat volutpat. Ut wisi enim ad minim veniam, quis nostrud exerci tation ullamcorper suscipit lobortis nisl ut aliquip ex ea commodo consequat.

*Lorem ipsum*

*Lorem ipsum dolor sit amet, consectetuer adipiscing elit, sed diam nonummy nibh euismod tincidunt ut laoreet dolore magna aliquam erat volutpat.*

Lorem ipsum dolor sit amet, consectetuer adipiscing elit, sed diam nonummy nibh euismod tincidunt ut laoreet dolore magna aliquam erat volutpat. Ut wisi enim ad minim veniam, quis nostrud exerci tation ullamcorper suscipit lobortis nisl ut aliquip ex ea commodo consequat. Duis autem vel eum iriure dolor in hendrerit in vulputate velit esse molestie consequat.

Vel illum dolore eu feugiat nulla facilisis at vero eros et accumsan et iusto odio dignissim qui blandit praesent luptatum zzril delenit augue duis dolore te feugait nulla facilisi.

Lorem ipsum dolor sit amet, consectetuer adipiscing elit, sed diam nonummy nibh euismod tincidunt ut laoreet dolore magna aliquam erat volutpat. Ut wisi enim ad minim veniam, quis nostrud exerci tation ullamcorper suscipit lobortis nisl ut aliquip ex ea commodo consequat. Duis autem vel eum iriure dolor in hendrerit in vulputate velit esse molestie consequat, vel illum dolore eu feugiat nulla facilisis at vero eros et accumsan et iusto odio dignissim qui blandit praesent luptatum zzril delenit augue duis dolore te feugait nulla facilisi.

Lorem ipsum dolor sit amet, consectetuer adipiscing elit, sed diam nonummy nibh euismod tincidunt ut laoreet dolore magna aliquam erat volutpat. Ut wisi enim ad minim veniam, quis nostrud exerci tation ullamcorper suscipit lobortis nisl ut aliquip ex ea commodo consequat. Duis autem vel eum iriure dolor in hendrerit in vulputate velit esse molestie consequat, vel illum dolore eu feugiat nulla facilisis at vero eros et accumsan et iusto odio dignissim qui blandit praesent luptatum zzril delenit augue duis dolore te feugait nulla facilisi.

Quip facilisi

3. Go to page 10 in The Inn's Annual Report template and put *Lorem ipsum* text placeholders and a graphics placeholder on the page, using Figure 7.28 as a guide. Paste the *Lorem ipsum* text several times and thread the text together into one text block.

Figure 7.28
Project 7.3—Adding dummy text and graphics placeholders

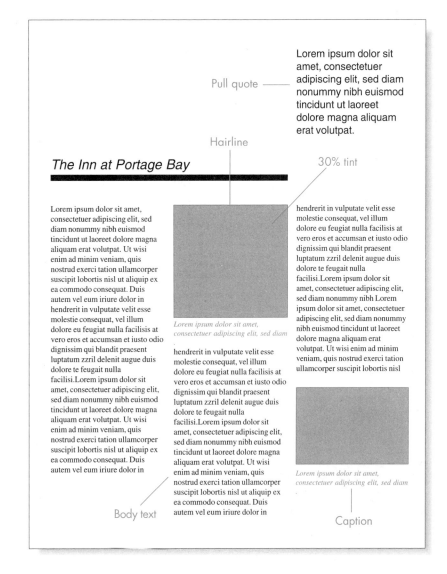

Pull quote

Lorem ipsum dolor sit amet, consectetuer adipiscing elit, sed diam nonummy nibh euismod tincidunt ut laoreet dolore magna aliquam erat volutpat.

Hairline

*The Inn at Portage Bay*

30% tint

Lorem ipsum dolor sit amet, consectetuer adipiscing elit, sed diam nonummy nibh euismod tincidunt ut laoreet dolore magna aliquam erat volutpat. Ut wisi enim ad minim veniam, quis nostrud exerci tation ullamcorper suscipit lobortis nisl ut aliquip ex ea commodo consequat. Duis autem vel eum iriure dolor in hendrerit in vulputate velit esse molestie consequat, vel illum dolore eu feugiat nulla facilisis at vero eros et accumsan et iusto odio dignissim qui blandit praesent luptatum zzril delenit augue duis dolore te feugait nulla facilisi.Lorem ipsum dolor sit amet, consectetuer adipiscing elit, sed diam nonummy nibh euismod tincidunt ut laoreet dolore magna aliquam erat volutpat. Ut wisi enim ad minim veniam, quis nostrud exerci tation ullamcorper suscipit lobortis nisl ut aliquip ex ea commodo consequat. Duis autem vel eum iriure dolor in

*Lorem ipsum dolor sit amet, consectetuer adipiscing elit, sed diam*

hendrerit in vulputate velit esse molestie consequat, vel illum dolore eu feugiat nulla facilisis at vero eros et accumsan et iusto odio dignissim qui blandit praesent luptatum zzril delenit augue duis dolore te feugait nulla facilisi.Lorem ipsum dolor sit amet, consectetuer adipiscing elit, sed diam nonummy nibh euismod tincidunt ut laoreet dolore magna aliquam erat volutpat. Ut wisi enim ad minim veniam, quis nostrud exerci tation ullamcorper suscipit lobortis nisl ut aliquip ex ea commodo consequat. Duis autem vel eum iriure dolor in

Body text

hendrerit in vulputate velit esse molestie consequat, vel illum dolore eu feugiat nulla facilisis at vero eros et accumsan et iusto odio dignissim qui blandit praesent luptatum zzril delenit augue duis dolore te feugait nulla facilisi.Lorem ipsum dolor sit amet, consectetuer adipiscing elit, sed diam nonummy nibh Lorem ipsum dolor sit amet, consectetuer adipiscing elit, sed diam nonummy nibh euismod tincidunt ut laoreet dolore magna aliquam erat volutpat. Ut wisi enim ad minim veniam, quis nostrud exerci tation ullamcorper suscipit lobortis nisl

*Lorem ipsum dolor sit amet, consectetuer adipiscing elit, sed diam*

Caption

4. Create the template for a menu for the Inn's Spinnaker Restaurant. Use Figure 7.29 as a guide. Include three separate master pages and a Styles palette. The graphic is Spinnaker.tif.

**Figure 7.29**
Project 7.4—Menu template

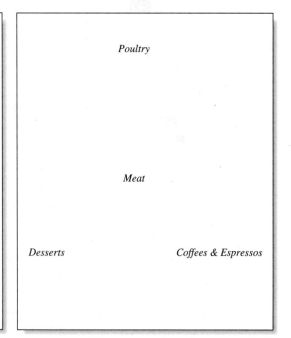

5. Create a template of your own menu design for The Inn's Spinnaker Restaurant. Before designing the menu, study various menus. Include two separate master pages, a grid, and a Styles palette.

6. The Inn produces a Daily Activities Schedule for its conference rooms. Create a template for the rooms. Copy and paste the lines and filled boxes so they are all the same size. Use Figure 7.30, which contains the Portage.tif graphic as a guide.

**Figure 7.30**
Project 7.6—Daily Activities Schedule template

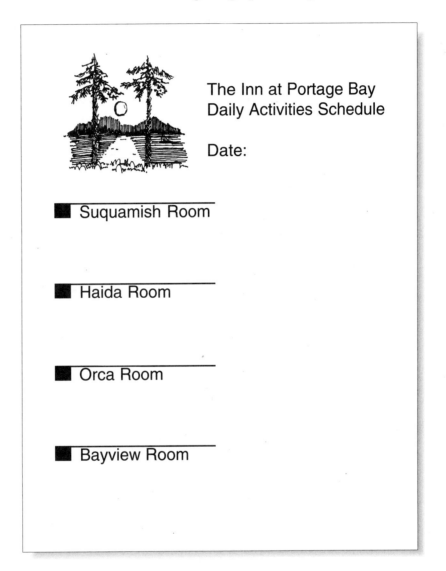

7. The Spinnaker Restaurant has different daily specials. Create a template for the Daily Specials. Use the word *Date* as a placeholder. Use tabs and leaders next to each category. See Figure 7.31.

**Figure 7.31**
Project 7.7—Daily
Specials template

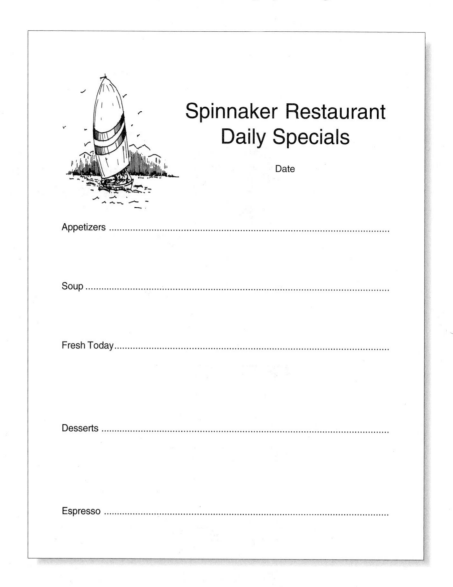

8. Create a template for a business card. Include one master page and a Styles palette. Use Figure 7.32 as a guide.

**Figure 7.32**
Project 7.8—Business
card template

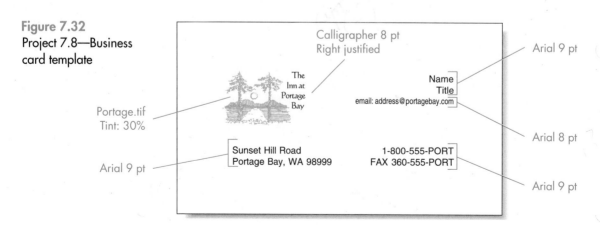

# CHAPTER 8

# Design Concepts

Upon completion of this chapter you will be able to:

- Recognize components that enhance or detract from page layout

- Differentiate between serif, sans serif, decorative, and dingbat fonts

- Describe the impact of font choice on a publication's readability

- Describe several different drop cap treatments

- Design headlines that will draw readers to an article

- Know when to use bold and italic for emphasis

- Consider and resolve hyphenation issues

- Understand how color elements affect design

- Explain the importance of the terms *optical center* and *eye dwell* to design

- Understand the principles of graphic placement

Desktop publishing is more than learning keystrokes to operate PageMaker or a comparable software package. Desktop publishing integrates graphic design with the productivity of a computer to give the user two previously unavailable advantages: speed in producing camera ready material and the ability to experiment with publication page layout.

PageMaker has many operational rules. Design, on the other hand, has few rules. There are no formulas or steps you can follow to produce a good design. However, there are general principles that guide design considerations. In addition, research from the advertising industry can set you on the path to creating professional-looking designs. But sometimes you'll deliberately go against the established guidelines and accepted practices to achieve a certain look or emphasis.

Thus, a willingness to experiment is critical to the design process. PageMaker enables you to experiment with different fonts and layouts with relative ease. Commercially available packages of fonts and clip art increase the design choices available to you. Scanners enable you to import photographs and other original artwork into your design. Draw programs make it easy for an artist to quickly create artwork. With so many possibilities, it is easy to understand why the words *right* and *wrong* do not apply to design. Instead, designs are described as only *poor, good,* and *better.*

A caution: One short chapter cannot completely teach you design. Indeed, entire courses of study are devoted to design concepts and practices. This chapter will introduce and describe some design guidelines, show you both good and bad design examples, allow you to critique layouts, increase your awareness of design, and give you the opportunity to try a few specific techniques.

You might not agree with every guideline presented here. In fact, any two designers will have different opinions about the ideas put forth in this chapter. In other words, design is perceived differently by each person. Also, what works in one publication with one audience does not necessarily work in a different setting. That's why few design rules exist, but guidelines and examples abound. And remember, sometimes going against the guidelines can yield positive results.

This chapter is organized into four sections. First, a short discussion of general considerations will create a context in which basic design decisions can be made. Second is a discussion about choosing typefaces and related issues. Third, a short overview of color and its use in publications. Finally, concepts of page layout and design are presented. Finally, some comments about applying these ideas and integrating them with restraint complete the chapter.

## GENERAL DESIGN CONSIDERATIONS

When designing any publication, you should first identify its objectives and intended audience. To determine the objectives, ask questions such as: What is the purpose of this catalog, brochure, or newsletter? Is the purpose to inform, sell, or increase name familiarity? What, if any, change of behavior do you expect after a person sees the publication? Do you want or expect a response? Will the person have more technical or financial information after reading the piece? Is the objective to increase the public's positive feelings about the company? What image should the publication project: formal, friendly, or other?

Audience is another consideration. Who will receive the advertisement, flyer, or prospectus? What is the age and education level of the audience? How familiar is the audience with the source of the publication?

Answering these questions helps you to make some design decisions. For example, do the objectives and audience require high-quality, average-quality, or low-quality production? Keep in mind that what works well for one audience might fall flat with a different group. Design is driven by a publication's purpose and objectives as well as by knowing and understanding the target audience.

## CHOOSING TYPEFACES AND RELATED ISSUES

Typefaces, or fonts, intended for bodies of text are categorized as serif and sans serif. A **serif** is a line or curve extending from the end of a letter, such as on the typeface for this text. The French word *sans* means without, so a **sans serif** typeface is one without extensions at the end of the letter, such as that for the headings on this page. A third category of fonts is **decorative fonts**, very stylized letter forms that work well in limited quantities on a page. A fourth category is **dingbats**, which are small pictures that are "typed" and can be used as bullets, pasted together to make borders, or enlarged to use like clip art. Examples of these different typefaces are shown in Figure 8.1.

**Figure 8.1**
Serif, sans serif, and decorative fonts

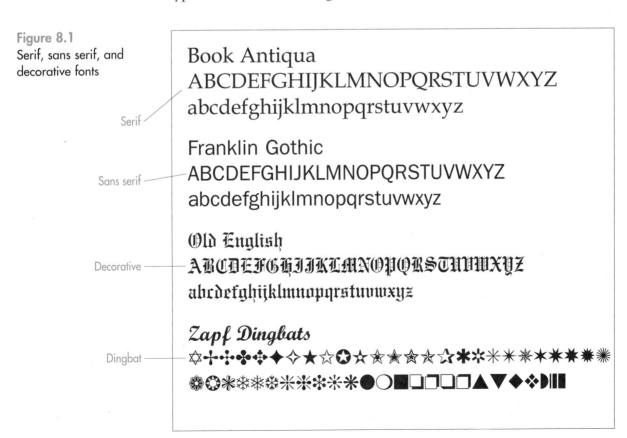

Serif

Sans serif

Decorative

Dingbat

PageMaker and Windows 95 combined come with more than 100 fonts that you can use in PageMaker. Several companies, including Adobe, Bitstream, and Microsoft, sell font packages that you can use with PageMaker to increase the options available. Some packages are compatible only with Windows-based PCs whereas others are compatible only with Macintosh. In the past few years, many typographers have designed scores of new fonts, which you can often view and purchase on the Web.

Every font has a name, such as Helvetica, Times Roman, or Futura. Some font names are company specific. Two typefaces might resemble one another when placed side by side on a page but will have minor design distinctions and different names because the fonts were developed by different designers and published by different companies. Companies that publish fonts are called **type foundries**.

The origins of fonts are as varied as their appearance.

- **Garamond** was developed by Claude Garamond in his French foundry and was probably first used around 1545. By the end of the sixteenth century, Garamond had become the standard European typeface. This classic, old-style face is still used today.

- **Times Roman** was designed by Stanley Morison in 1931 for the *Times* of London newspaper. Many foundries have produced variations of this font and have called them similar names, such as Times, Times New Roman, and Tms Rmn.

- German type designer Paul Renner created **Futura** in 1928. Futura is an example of the Bauhaus principle of functionalism, in which form follows function. It is a sans serif font with letter forms that have only their bare essentials.

- Sumner Stone designed three integrated type families for Adobe: **Stone Informal, Stone Sans,** and **Stone Serif**. Stone Informal was developed specifically for desktop publishing and laser printer technology. When used in the same publication, the three Stone typefaces work together to provide an integrated look.

Figure 8.2 shows the six fonts mentioned here.

Figure 8.2
Six fonts

Garamond
ABCDEFGHIJKLMNOPQRSTUVWXYZ
abcdefghijklmnopqrstuvwxyz

Times Roman
ABCDEFGHIJKLMNOPQRSTUVWXYZ
abcdefghijklmnopqrstuvwxyz

Futura
ABCDEFGHIJKLMNOPQRSTUVWXYZ
abcdefghijklmnopqrstuvwxyz

Stone Informal
ABCDEFGHIJKLMNOPQRSTUVWXYZ
abcdefghijklmnopqrstuvwxyz

Stone Sans
ABCDEFGHIJKLMNOPQRSTUVWXYZ
abcdefghijklmnopqrstuvwxyz

Stone Serif
ABCDEFGHIJKLMNOPQRSTUVWXYZ
abcdefghijklmnopqrstuvwxyz

Bitstream created the first typeface specifically developed for digital electronic typesetting—called Charter. Its serifs are square and easily digitized, and the font looks good on both low-resolution laser printers and high-resolution typesetters. It is similar to the Adobe Times Roman font. Compare the appearance of the serif fonts shown in Figure 8.3. In particular, compare the uppercase and lowercase Gs in each typeface.

Figure 8.3
Various serif fonts

Baskerville
ABCDEFGHIJKLMNOPQRSTUVWXYZ
abcdefghijklmnopqrstuvwxyz

Bookman
ABCDEFGHIJKLMNOPQRSTUVWXYZ
abcdefghijklmnopqrstuvwxyz

**Claredon**
**ABCDEFGHIJKLMNOPQRSTUVWXYZ**
**abcdefghijklmnopqrstuvwxyz**

Garamond
ABCDEFGHIJKLMNOPQRSTUVWXYZ
abcdefghijklmnopqrstuvwxyz

Goudy
ABCDEFGHIJKLMNOPQRSTUVWXYZ
abcdefghijklmnopqrstuvwxyz

Lubalin Graph
ABCDEFGHIJKLMNOPQRSTUVWXYZ
abcdefghijklmnopqrstuvwxyz

Palatino
ABCDEFGHIJKLMNOPQRSTUVWXYZ
abcdefghijklmnopqrstuvwxyz

Souvenir
ABCDEFGHIJKLMNOPQRSTUVWXYZ
abcdefghijklmnopqrstuvwxyz

Tiffany
ABCDEFGHIJKLMNOPQRSTUVWXYZ
abcdefghijklmnopqrstuvwxyz

Sans serif text is clean, simple, and projects rationality and objectivity (although not always readability). An example is Helvetica, named after the Latin word for Switzerland, designed by Max Miedinger, a Swiss, in 1957. Compare the different sans serif fonts in Figure 8.4. Again, compare the letter forms of each font; In particular look at the *G's* and *y's*.

Figure 8.4
Various sans serif fonts

Bauhaus
ABCDEFGHIJKLMNOPQRSTUVWXYZ
abcdefghijklmnopqrstuvwxyz

Eras
ABCDEFGHIJKLMNOPQRSTUVWXYZ
abcdefghijklmnopqrstuvwxyz

Eurostile
ABCDEFGHIJKLMNOPQRSTUVWXYZ
abcdefghijklmnopqrstuvwxyz

Franklin Gothic
ABCDEFGHIJKLMNOPQRSTUVWXYZ
abcdefghijklmnopqrstuvwxyz

Helvetica
ABCDEFGHIJKLMNOPQRSTUVWXYZ
abcdefghijklmnopqrstuvwxyz

Helvetica Condensed
ABCDEFGHIJKLMNOPQRSTUVWXYZ
abcdefghijklmnopqrstuvwxyz

Letter Gothic
ABCDEFGHIJKLMNOPQRSTUVWXYZ
abcdefghijklmnopqrstuvwxyz

Optima
ABCDEFGHIJKLMNOPQRSTUVWXYZ
abcdefghijklmnopqrstuvwxyz

Univers 55
ABCDEFGHIJKLMNOPQRSTUVWXYZ
abcdefghijklmnopqrstuvwxyz

All the fonts in Figures 8.3 and 8.4 are the same point size. Notice, however, that two fonts of equal point size require different amounts of space on the page. Also notice how some letter forms have thick and thin strokes, such as Tiffany, while others are uniform in their strokes, such as Helvetica. Both these elements—the space needed for each letter and the amount of stroke variation—contribute to the "color" of the type's appearance on the page.

Serifs create a line at the top and bottom of a text line and guide the eye in the same way that railroad tracks guide a train. Sans serif text does not have that line, and the eye has difficulty reading, wanting instead to leave the text line and wander through the body of the text.

For body text, a serif font is preferred for readability. Research has shown that comprehension of text blocks with serifs is 75 percent to 80 percent whereas comprehension of text blocks set in a sans serif typeface is 20 percent to 30 percent. Serif text is described as old-fashioned, friendly, and easy to read. Sans serif text is described as clean, sleek, modern, and more difficult to read in large quantities. Figure 8.5 shows the same paragraphs set in serif and sans serif fonts to illustrate this point. Notice in the sans serif text how each stroke of every letter has the same width. Contrast this with serif text, where each letter has thick and thin parts. This contributes to a serif font's readability.

**Figure 8.5**
Compare readability of serif and sans serif fonts

| Serif type | Sans serif type |
| --- | --- |
| Fourscore and seven years ago our fathers brought forth on this continent a new nation, conceived in Liberty, and dedicated to the proposition that all men are created equal. | Fourscore and seven years ago our fathers brought forth on this continent a new nation, conceived in Liberty, and dedicated to the proposition that all men are created equal. |
| Now we are engaged in a great civil war, testing whether that nation, or any nation so conceived and so dedicated, can long endure. We are met on a great battlefield of that war. We have come to dedicate a portion of that field, as a final resting-place for those who here gave their lives that that nation might live. It is altogether fitting and proper that we should do this. | Now we are engaged in a great civil war, testing whether that nation, or any nation so conceived and so dedicated, can long endure. We are met on a great battlefield of that war. We have come to dedicate a portion of that field, as a final resting-place for those who here gave their lives that that nation might live. It is altogether fitting and proper that we should do this. |

A sans serif font is usually used for headlines to provide contrast against a serif font, which is most often used for text. Figure 8.6 shows a sans serif headline with serif text. Sans serif fonts are also appropriate for publications that contain very little text, such as announcements and advertisements.

Figure 8.6
Serif text with
sans serif headline

# Lincoln Dedicates Sacred Battlefield

Fourscore and seven years ago our fathers brought forth on this continent a new nation, conceived in Liberty, and dedicated to the proposition that all men are created equal.

Now we are engaged in a great civil war, testing whether that nation, or any nation so conceived and so dedicated, can long endure. We are met on a great battlefield of that war. We have come to dedicate a portion of that field, as a final resting-place for those who here gave their lives that that nation might live. It is altogether fitting and proper that we should do this.

In the past few years, font publishers have created a variety of decorative fonts. These fonts are best used when the words are part of the art in a publication, or for an invitation or announcement. Although you wouldn't want to read pages of text in decorative fonts, they add interest and are a nice contrast to serif and sans serif fonts when used for emphasis. Figure 8.7 shows several examples of decorative fonts, and Figure 8.8 is an invitation that uses two decorative fonts appropriately.

Figure 8.7
Decorative fonts

BALLOON
ABCDEFGHIJKLMNOPQRSTUVWXYZ

Brush Script
ABCDEFGHIJKLMNOPQRSTUVWXYZ
abcdefghijklmnopqrstuvwxyz

Freeform
ABCDEFGHIJKLMNOPQRSTUVWXYZ
abcdefghijklmnopqrstuvwxyz

Snell
ABCDEFGHIJKLMNOPQRSTUVWXYZ
abcdefghijklmnopqrstuvwxyz

Cloister Open Face
ABCDEFGHIJKLMNOPQRSTUVWXYZ
abcdefghijklmnopqrstuvwxyz

**Figure 8.8**
Using decorative fonts

You are invited To Suzy Wilcox's 7Th

# BiRTHDAY PARTY

Eraser Dust 30 point

Suzy's House
529 Kecker STreeT
MonTocs, New York        Lefty Casual 14 point
May 4 1:00-4:30
Please respond To Suzy's Mom by April 31
847-7349

Dingbat fonts also help to add visual interest to a publication. Holidays, Wingdings, Woodtype Ornaments 1, and ZapfDingbats are examples of dingbat fonts. Figure 8.9 shows an example of dingbats in a publication.

**Figure 8.9**
Example of Zapf
Dingbats used as bullets

## Features include:

❖ Waterfront location

❖ 224 deluxe guest rooms

❖ Fireplaces, suites

❖ Meeting rooms

❖ Indoor tennis, pool, jacuzzi, fitness center

❖ Championship golf course

❖ Award-winning restaurant

Although there are no rules for what size type you should use in a publication, there are guidelines to help you choose the appropriate size depending on the application. Figure 8.10 suggests some general guidelines for font size.

Figure 8.10
General guidelines
for font sizes

| Element | Point Size |
| --- | --- |
| Headlines | 48 maximum, 14 minimum |
| Subheads | half of headline size; 20 minimum recommended |
| Body copy | 8 to 13; 10 is a good choice |

In general, use larger headlines for important messages and smaller headlines for less important messages. Medium-sized headlines range from 24 to 36 points. A headline set in 24-point type should not have a subhead because half of 24 is 12 points, less than the suggested minimum of 14 points for a subhead.

Body copy point sizes traditionally range between 6 and 13 points, with 8 to 12 points most common. Research has shown that 10-point type is the most readable to general audiences. Children and young adults do better with 11-point type. It can be difficult to get enough text within the area of eye focus with 12-point type. Type that is 14 points and larger is used for text other than text blocks, such as for flyers, and is called **display type**. Figure 8.11 shows examples of fonts set for these purposes.

Figure 8.11
Different point sizes
in different fonts

**Folio Bold 36**

Century Oldstyle 36

**Eurostile Bold 24**

**Garamond Bold 24**

Univers 18

Univers Extended 18

Univers Condensed 18

Sabon 12  **Futura Bold 12**

Sabon 10  **Futura Bold 10**

*Important headlines should be set in 24- to 36-point type*

*Body copy is best in the 10- to 12-point range*

A current trend is to set an oversized initial capital letter, called a **drop cap**, to begin the first paragraph of an article or section of text. Guidelines for drop caps include using a type size three to four times the size of the body copy. In other words, if the body copy is set in 10 points, the initial cap should be set in 30 to 40 points. The initial cap can be linked with three, four, or more lines of body text. Some magazines use drop caps that are eight lines in height, which projects an avant garde design. Paragraphs with oversized initial caps draw 15 percent more readers than paragraphs without drop caps.

PageMaker makes creating drop caps easy. The Drop cap Plug-in in the Utilities menu will size and place an oversized cap. In the Drop cap dialog box, you specify the size of the drop cap you want in terms of number of lines.

Use a readable font, such as Arial, for the oversized cap. Another idea is to use a very ornate font, such as Augsburger Initials or Old English Text. Use it once, or perhaps twice, per page in a diagonal line to unify the page and facing pages. A capital letter can also hang in the margin or be boxed for added emphasis. Be careful that oversized caps on the same page do not spell anything. Figure 8.12 shows many of these concepts.

**Figure 8.12**
Using oversized caps

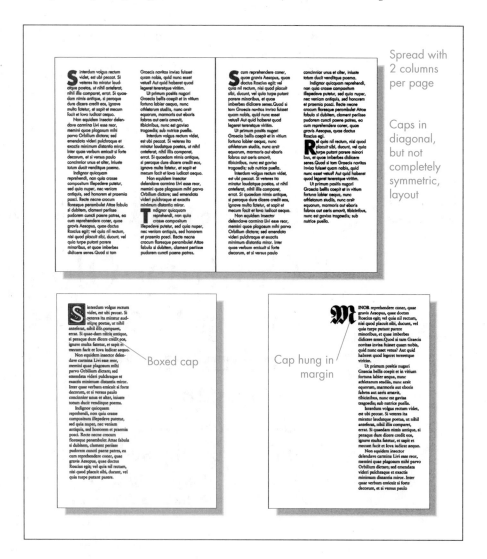

Figure 8.13 shows six different drop cap treatments you can create in PageMaker. Example 1 used the Drop cap Plug-in from the Utilities menu to create a 3-line drop cap. In example 2, notice how the text follows the shape of the letter A; you'll duplicate this drop cap in a project at the end of the chapter. For example 3, the drop cap was created for 6 lines and then the font for the cap was changed to Helvetica. In example 4, the drop cap was cut from the text, and the top three lines of the text block were reduced in width to accommodate the large A; the bottom 4 lines are a separate text block. Example 5 shows a drop cap created from the Plug-in Utilities and changed to Old English Text. In example 6, an 84-point Helvetica A was created on the Pasteboard, and the horizontal scale was reduced to 70%. Then the text block of the top line was reduced in width and the letter was pasted to align with the baseline of the top line.

**Figure 8.13**
Different drop
cap treatments

Augue duis dolore te feugait nulla facilisi. Lorem ipsum dolor sit amet, consectetuer adipiscing elit,sed diam nonummy nibh euismod tincidunt ut laoreet dolore magna aliquam erat volutpat. Ut wisi enim ad minim veniam, quis nostrud exerci tation ullamcorper suscipit lobortis nisl ut aliquip ex ea commodo consequat. Duis autem vel eum iriure dolor in hendrerit in vulputate velit esse molestie consequat,vel illum dolore eu feugiat nulla facilisis.

Example 1

Augue duis dolore te feugait nulla facilisi. Lorem ipsum dolor sit amet, consectetuer adipiscing elit, sed diam nonummy nibh euismod tincidunt ut laoreet dolore magna aliquam erat volutpat. Ut wisi enim ad minim veniam, quis nostrud exerci tation ullamcorper suscipit lobortis nisl ut aliquip ex ea commodo consequat. Duis autem vel eum iriure dolor in hendrerit in vulputate velit esse molestie.

Example 2

Augue duis dolore te feugait nulla facilisi. Lorem ipsum dolor sit amet, consectetuer adipiscing elit, sed diam nonummy nibh euismod tincidunt ut laoreet dolore magna aliquam erat volutpat. Ut wisi enim ad minim veniam, quis nostrud exerci tation ullamcorper suscipit lobortis nisl ut aliquip ex ea commodo consequat. Duis autem vel eum iriure dolor in hendrerit in vulputate velit esse molestie consequat, vel illum dolore eu feugiat nulla facilisis at vero eros et accumsan et iusto odio dignissim qui blandit praesent luptatum zzril delenit augue duis dolore te feugait nulla facilisi.

Example 3

Augue duis dolore te feugait nulla facilisi. Lorem ipsum dolor sit amet, consectetuer adipiscing elit, sed diam nonummy nibh euismod tincidunt ut laoreet dolore magna aliquam erat volutpat. Ut wisi enim ad minim veniam, quis nostrud exerci tation ullamcorper suscipit lobortis nisl ut aliquip.

Example 4

Augue duis dolore te feugait nulla facilisi. Lorem ipsum dolor sit amet, consectetuer adipiscing elit, sed diam nonummy nibh euismod tincidunt ut laoreet dolore magna aliquam erat volutpat. Ut wisi enim ad minim veniam, quis nostrud exerci tation ullamcorper suscipit lobortis nisl ut aliquip ex ea commodo consequat. Duis autem vel eum iriure dolor in hendrerit in vulputate velit esse molestie.

Example 5

Augue duis dolore te feugait nulla facilisi. Lorem ipsum dolor sit amet, consectetuer adipiscing elit, sed diam nonummy nibh euismod tincidunt ut laoreet dolore magna aliquam erat volutpat. Ut wisi enim ad minim veniam, quis nostrud exerci tation ullamcorper suscipit lobortis nisl ut aliquip ex ea commodo consequat. Duis autem vel eum iriure dolor in hendrerit in vulputate velit esse molestie consequat, vel illum dolore eu feugiat nulla facilisis at vero eros et accumsan et iusto odio dignissim qui blandit praesent luptatum zzril delenit augue duis dolore te feugait nulla facilisi.

Example 6

## Spacing Between Lines, Words, Letters, and Paragraphs

Leading, the vertical spacing between lines of type, can be adjusted to improve the readability and appearance of a publication. Recall from Chapter 4 that "automatic" leading is 120 percent of the type size. For 10-point type, the default is 12-point leading. Although it is easier to use automatic leading, some designers prefer to select a specific leading to produce the look they want. Reduced leading can help a headline appear as a cohesive unit. Increasing leading in body copy lightens up the appearance and makes the text block less gray. Figure 8.14 illustrates some of these concepts.

**Figure 8.14**
Headline layouts with different leading values

Century Schoolbook, 30pt type with Auto Leading (120% of 30 is 36)

Lincoln Dedicates
Sacred Battlefield

Century Schoolbook, 30pt type with 33.5pt leading

Lincoln Dedicates
Sacred Battlefield

Century Schoolbook, 30pt type with 30.5pt leading

Lincoln Dedicates
Sacred Battlefield

Letter spacing is controlled by kerning. As explained in Chapter 4, PageMaker has an automatic pair-kerning function. Desktop publishers can override the results through manual kerning. When two or more characters are united and appear as one, it is called a **ligature**. Examples of ligatures are fi, fl, and œ. The Matthew Carter/Cherie Cone version of Galliard includes ligatures as part of its base font set, adding a sense of style to typeset publications.

Force justify spaces a word across a column. When you expand the space between the letters, the word or words become a design element. In Figure 8.15, *The Inn at Portage Bay* was force justified across a text block to produce an interesting visual effect. Other techniques were used to produce this figure, and they are explained in a project at the end of the chapter.

Figure 8.15
Using words as
a design element

# THE INN AT
# PORTAGE BAY

Extra space between paragraphs adds lightness to a publication's appearance and diminishes the gray. Figure 8.16 contrasts two columns with different paragraph spacing.

Figure 8.16
Two columns with different paragraph spacing

Lorem ipsum dolor sit amet, consectetuer adipiscing elit, sed diam nonummy nibh euismod tincidunt ut laoreet dolore magna aliquam erat volutpat. Ut wisi enim ad minim veniam, quis nostrud exerci tation ullamcorper suscipit lobortis nisl ut aliquip ex ea commodo consequat.

Duis autem vel eum iriure dolor in hendrerit in vulputate velit esse molestie consequat, vel illum dolore eu feugiat nulla facilisis at vero eros et accumsan et iusto odio dignissim qui blandit praesent luptatum zzril delenit augue duis dolore te feugait nulla facilisi.

Ut wisi enim ad minim veniam, quis nostrud exerci tation ullamcorper suscipit lobortis nisl ut aliquip ex ea commodo consequat. Duis autem vel eum iriure dolor in hendrerit in vulputate velit esse molestie consequat, vel illum dolore eu feugiat nulla facilisis at vero eros et accumsan et iusto odio dignissim qui blandit praesent luptatum zzril delenit augue duis dolore te feugait nulla facilisi.

Lorem ipsum dolor sit amet, consectetuer adipiscing elit, sed diam nonummy nibh euismod tincidunt ut laoreet dolore magna aliquam erat volutpat. Ut wisi enim ad minim veniam, quis nostrud exerci tation ullamcorper suscipit lobortis nisl ut aliquip ex ea commodo consequat.

Duis autem vel eum iriure dolor in hendrerit in vulputate velit esse molestie consequat, vel illum dolore eu feugiat nulla facilisis at vero eros et accumsan et iusto odio dignissim qui blandit praesent luptatum zzril delenit augue duis dolore te feugait nulla facilisi.

Ut wisi enim ad minim veniam, quis nostrud exerci tation ullamcorper suscipit lobortis nisl ut aliquip ex ea commodo consequat. Duis autem vel eum iriure dolor in hendrerit in vulputate velit esse molestie consequat, vel illum dolore eu feugiat nulla facilisis at vero eros et accumsan et iusto odio dignissim qui blandit praesent luptatum zzril delenit augue duis dolore te feugait nulla facilisi.

## Headline Creation

The purpose of a headline is to "grab" readers, to get them to read the article. Two factors contribute to how successfully a headline grabs readers. First is the content of the headline and the general interest of the story to the readers. Second is the font and type size.

As mentioned previously, headlines provide contrast to body text when a font different from the body text and neighboring headlines is used. Recall that 14- to 48-point type is recommended for headlines, while subheads should be set half that size. Subheads should be a minimum of 20 point, and thus are mostly used with headlines of 40 point or more.

Some publications, such as *The New York Times*, set headlines as titles, with the first letters of most words capitalized. Other publications set headlines in the form of a sentence and capitalize accordingly. Headlines can be one to three lines, but two lines is optimal. Avoid separating a headline from its body copy with a line or bar.

Another technique that works well to increase readership is to use an eyebrow, or kicker, above a headline. Recall from Chapters 6 and 7 that an eyebrow is a few words in smaller type above the headline that arouse interest. Eyebrows, headlines, and subheads for one article should be set in the same typeface, but with size and style variations. For example, a headline may be Helvetica 40 bold with a subhead in Helvetica 20 italic. Figure 8.17 shows some headline layouts.

**Figure 8.17**
Headline layouts

An eyebrow, or kicker, above the headline can bring readers into the text. Eyebrow is 14pt italic; headline is 24pt normal

Headlines and subheads should be in different type sizes. Headline is 24pt, subhead is 14pt

*Consumer Prices Increase 4.8%*
## President Sets Budget Meeting; Congress Divided on Tax Relief

## President Sets Budget Meeting
Congress Divided on Tax Relief

Considerations for headlines include deciding on left, right, or center alignment; appropriate leading for letter spacing and word spacing; and weight of typeface. Experiment with the options available and, through trial and error, critiques, and finally experience, you will eventually develop a feel for what works.

Always keep in mind that the key concern in all typeface decisions is communication. Which combination of typeface, size, leading, and layout of text block best communicates your intended message to the readers?

## Emphasis

Italic and bold type in small amounts adds emphasis, but body text set in all italic is difficult to read, as is text set completely in bold. Use italic for mild emphasis within text or for contrast in headlines. Use bold for stronger emphasis and for headlines that shout the message. Figure 8.18 compares effective and ineffective use of italic and bold type.

Figure 8.18 (part 1)
Using italic and bold type for emphasis

*Fourscore and seven years ago our fathers brought forth on this continent a new nation, conceived in Liberty, and dedicated to the proposition that all men are created equal.*

*Now we are engaged in a great civil war, testing whether that nation, or any nation so conceived and so dedicated, can long endure. We are met on a great battlefield of that war. We have come to dedicate a portion of that field, as a final resting-place for those who here gave their lives that that nation might live. It is altogether fitting and proper that we should do this.*

*But, in a larger sense, we cannot dedicate, we cannot consecrate, we cannot hallow this ground. The brave men, living and dead, who struggled here, have consecrated it far above our poor power to add or detract. The world will little note nor long remember what we say here, but it can never forget what they did here. It is for us, the living, rather, to be dedicated here to the unfinished work which they who fought here have thus far so nobly advanced.*

**Fourscore and seven years ago our fathers brought forth on this continent a new nation, conceived in Liberty, and dedicated to the proposition that all men are created equal.**

**Now we are engaged in a great civil war, testing whether that nation, or any nation so conceived and so dedicated, can long endure. We are met on a great battlefield of that war. We have come to dedicate a portion of that field, as a final resting-place for those who here gave their lives that that nation might live. It is altogether fitting and proper that we should do this.**

**But, in a larger sense, we cannot dedicate, we cannot consecrate, we cannot hallow this ground. The brave men, living and dead, who struggled here, have consecrated it far above our poor power to add or detract. The world will little note nor long remember what we say here, but it can never forget what they did here. It is for us, the living, rather, to be dedicated here to the unfinished work which they who fought here have thus far so nobly advanced.**

Too much italic or bold is difficult to read

Figure 8.18 (part 2)

Fourscore and seven years ago our fathers brought forth on this continent a new nation, conceived in Liberty, and dedicated to the proposition that *all* men are created equal.

Now we are engaged in a great civil war, testing whether that nation, or *any* nation so conceived and so dedicated, can long endure. We are met on a great battlefield of that war. We have come to dedicate a portion of that field, as a final resting-place for those who here gave their lives that that nation might live. It is altogether fitting and proper that we should do this.

But, in a larger sense, we *cannot* dedicate, we *cannot* consecrate, we *cannot* hallow this ground. The brave men, living and dead, who struggled here, have consecrated it *far* above our poor power to add or detract. The world will little note nor long remember what we say here, but it can never forget what they did here. It is for us, the living, rather, to be dedicated here to the unfinished work which they who fought here have thus far so nobly advanced.

Fourscore and seven years ago our fathers brought forth on this continent a new nation, conceived in Liberty, and dedicated to the proposition that **all** men are created equal.

Now we are engaged in a great civil war, testing whether that nation, or **any** nation so conceived and so dedicated, can long endure. We are met on a great battlefield of that war. We have come to dedicate a portion of that field, as a final resting-place for those who here gave their lives that that nation might live. It is altogether fitting and proper that we should do this.

But, in a larger sense, we **cannot** dedicate, we **cannot** consecrate, we **cannot** hallow this ground. The brave men, living and dead, who struggled here, have consecrated it far above our poor power to add or detract. The world will little note nor long remember what we say here, but it can never forget what they did here. It is for us, the living, rather, to be dedicated here to the unfinished work which they who fought here have thus far so nobly advanced.

Italic gives mild emphasis

Bold gives stronger emphasis

You should avoid underlining text for emphasis because a reader's eyes have difficulty distinguishing between the words and the underline. Also, descenders are obscured by the line, which further inhibits readability.

All uppercase letters (or all caps) is an effect some people overuse in text, producing a telegram-like appearance. All cap text is difficult to read because all the letters have a similar shape and size. The ascenders and descenders in lowercase text help differentiate letters, increase comprehension, and add visual interest.

All caps or underlining for emphasis is a holdover from the days of the typewriter. Then, capital letters and underlining were our only emphasis options. Now, however, we can easily use bold and italic, among other design variables, to add emphasis. Figure 8.19 shows how difficult a lot of underlining or all caps can be to read. Figure 8.20 illustrates how using a mixture of caps and lowercase letters contributes to reading comprehension.

Figure 8.19
Overuse of underlining and all caps

Fourscore and seven years ago our fathers brought forth on this continent a new nation, conceived in Liberty, and dedicated to the proposition that all men are created equal.

Now we are engaged in a great civil war, testing whether that nation, or any nation so conceived and so dedicated, can long endure. We are met on a great battlefield of that war. We have come to dedicate a portion of that field, as a final resting-place for those who here gave their lives that that nation might live. It is altogether fitting and proper that we should do this.

But, in a larger sense, we cannot dedicate, we cannot consecrate, we cannot hallow this ground. The brave men, living and dead, who struggled here, have consecrated it far above our poor power to add or detract. The world will little note nor long remember what we say here, but it can never forget what they did here. It is for us, the living, rather, to be dedicated here to the unfinished work which they who fought here have thus far so nobly advanced.

FOURSCORE AND SEVEN YEARS AGO OUR FATHERS BROUGHT FORTH ON THIS CONTINENT A NEW NATION, CONCEIVED IN LIBERTY, AND DEDICATED TO THE PROPOSITION THAT ALL MEN ARE CREATED EQUAL.

NOW WE ARE ENGAGED IN A GREAT CIVIL WAR, TESTING WHETHER THAT NATION, OR ANY NATION SO CONCEIVED AND SO DEDICATED, CAN LONG ENDURE. WE ARE MET ON A GREAT BATTLE-FIELD OF THAT WAR. WE HAVE COME TO DEDICATE A PORTION OF THAT FIELD, AS A FINAL RESTING-PLACE FOR THOSE WHO HERE GAVE THEIR LIVES THAT THAT NATION MIGHT LIVE. IT IS ALTO-GETHER FITTING AND PROPER THAT WE SHOULD DO THIS.

BUT, IN A LARGER SENSE, WE CANNOT DEDI-CATE, WE CANNOT CONSECRATE, WE CANNOT HALLOW THIS GROUND. THE BRAVE MEN, LIVING AND DEAD, WHO STRUGGLED HERE, HAVE CONSE-CRATED IT FAR ABOVE OUR POOR POWER TO ADD OR DETRACT. THE WORLD WILL LITTLE NOTE NOR LONG REMEMBER WHAT WE SAY HERE, BUT IT CAN NEVER FORGET WHAT THEY DID HERE. IT IS FOR US, THE LIVING, RATHER, TO BE DEDICATED HERE TO THE UNFINISHED WORK WHICH THEY WHO FOUGHT HERE HAVE THUS FAR SO NOBLY ADVANCED.

Body copy difficult to read

Figure 8.20
Word shapes

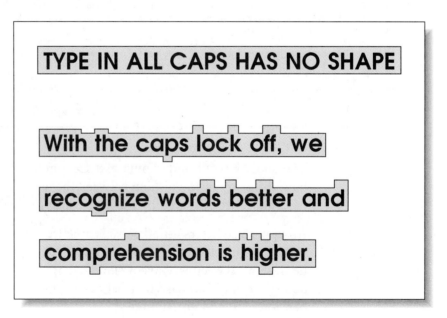

TYPE IN ALL CAPS HAS NO SHAPE

With the caps lock off, we

recognize words better and

comprehension is higher.

An effective variation of underlining is shown in Figure 8.21. The line under the words *Portage Bay* is broken and angled to add a graphic-like quality. To create the angle along the "broken" edges of the line, the polygon tool was used to draw one polygon that overlapped the descender of the letter *g* and one that overlapped the descender of the *y*. For each polygon, the Stroke was changed to None and the Fill to Paper. Thus, for each letter the three overlapping elements are the line, the letter, and the polygon. These were arranged so the letter appeared on top, the polygon next, and the line in the back. The polygon's angled sides made the angled cut on the line. Although PageMaker has limited drawing capabilities, they can be used to produce some graphic effects.

**Figure 8.21**
Broken underline

# The Inn at
# Portage Bay

## Justified and Nonjustified Text

When you justify text, the text lines up on both the right and the left margins. Nonjustified text with an uneven right margin is called **ragged right**; with an uneven left margin, ragged left.

Justified text lends a formal feel to a publication. When you specify justified text, PageMaker determines how many words can fit on a line, and then uses proportional spacing to evenly distribute the characters and word spaces on the line. You can override some spacing problems that arise with manual kerning, but it is not practical to use manual kerning throughout a long document.

Ragged-right text has a more casual appearance. Nonjustified text is appropriate for some newsletters, catalogs for particular products, and for companies that want to project a friendly, informal image. Figure 8.22 shows how the same paragraph looks different with ragged-right and right-justified text.

In some instances, you will want ragged-left text—for example, on a page with an irregular graphic. Or you can create a look where text in the lower-right quadrant of a page is "finished" on the outside column and "unfinished" on the inside. This can appear unsettling or disorganized, so use this technique carefully and deliberately for special emphasis. Figure 8.23 shows two pages of facing text where left and right justification work well.

Figure 8.22
Ragged-right and right-justified text

Fourscore and seven years ago our fathers brought forth on this continent a new nation, conceived in Liberty, and dedicated to the proposition that all men are created equal.

Now we are engaged in a great civil war, testing whether that nation, or any nation so conceived and so dedicated, can long endure. We are met on a great battlefield of that war. We have come to dedicate a portion of that field, as a final resting-place for those who here gave their lives that that nation might live. It is altogether fitting and proper that we should do this.

But, in a larger sense, we cannot dedicate, we cannot consecrate, we cannot hallow this ground. The brave men, living and dead, who struggled here, have consecrated it far above our poor power to add or detract. The world will little note nor long remember what we say here, but it can never forget what they did here. It is for us, the living, rather, to be dedicated here to the unfinished work which they who fought here have thus far so nobly advanced.

Fourscore and seven years ago our fathers brought forth on this continent a new nation, conceived in Liberty, and dedicated to the proposition that all men are created equal.

Now we are engaged in a great civil war, testing whether that nation, or any nation so conceived and so dedicated, can long endure. We are met on a great battlefield of that war. We have come to dedicate a portion of that field, as a final resting-place for those who here gave their lives that that nation might live. It is altogether fitting and proper that we should do this.

But, in a larger sense, we cannot dedicate, we cannot consecrate, we cannot hallow this ground. The brave men, living and dead, who struggled here, have consecrated it far above our poor power to add or detract. The world will little note nor long remember what we say here, but it can never forget what they did here. It is for us, the living, rather, to be dedicated here to the unfinished work which they who fought here have thus far so nobly advanced.

**Today's successful business competitors know how to shake a client's hand before they even meet.**

They know that reaching customers and clients these days takes more than an outstanding product or service. It takes aggressive marketing and public relations strategies rolled into an exceptional communications package that will distinguish your company or nonprofit from the competition.

DesignWorks helps small businesses and nonprofits define and achieve their growth and fundraising goals by creating innovative marketing and public relations campaigns that bring your product, service or issue directly to the audience you want to reach.

Whether you want to raise customer satisfaction, bottom-line sales, funds, public awareness, or just eyebrows, DesignWorks can help you plan and implement the winning strategy.

**Here's how we do it.**

- **message development**
  DesignWorks will help you identify market opportunities and create the right message to reach your target audience.

- **integrated public relations and marketing campaigns**
  Because direct marketing by itself rarely produces the results you want, DesignWorks will coordinate publicity and promotion activities to boost your visibility and name recognition and help you meet your marketing goals.

- **publications management**
  From quick-print flyers to 4-color annual reports, DesignWorks offers you superb copy development, graphic design and duplication services for your short-run or high-volume printing needs.

- **direct mail services**
  Direct mail pieces are only as effective as your mailing list. DesignWorks relies upon expert list brokers to ensure your mailing hits your target audience. We'll also ensure accurate package assembly and mailing preparation.

- **mailing lists**
  DesignWorks offers full mailing list maintenance services. We can merge/purge for you, develop prospect lists or teach you how to do it in-house.

- **tracking and evaluating results**
  How did we do? DesignWorks will help you analyze the results of your campaign and calculate the return on your investment.

P. O. Box 1672
Mercer Island, WA 98040

Tel.206.236.2553
Fax.206.230.8782

Courtesy of Lari Power, Island Graphic Services

You might run into a common problem with justified text. Depending on leading and kerning, justified text might contain patches of white space that appear as "rivers" or "lakes" when you view the publication from a distance, as shown in Figure 8.24. Experimenting with the leading and kerning can solve this problem and give the publication a more even look.

**Figure 8.24**
Effects of leading and tracking, or letter spacing, on justified text

But, in a larger sense, we cannot dedicate, we cannot consecrate, we cannot hallow this ground. The brave men, living and dead, who struggled here, have consecrated it far above our poor power to add or detract. The world will little note nor long remember what we say here, but it can never forget what they did here. It is for us, the living, rather, to be dedicated here to the unfinished work which they who fought here have thus far so nobly advanced. It is rather for us to be here dedicated to the great task remaining before us - that from these honored dead we take increased devotion to that cause for which they gave the last full measure of devotion - that we here highly resolve that these dead shall not have died in vain; that this nation, under God, shall have a new birth of freedom; and that government of the people, by the people, for the people, shall not perish from the earth.

Auto leading (120% of point size), no tracking

Extra leading (150% of point size), very loose tracking

But, in a larger sense, we cannot dedicate, we cannot consecrate, we cannot hallow this ground. The brave men, living and dead, who struggled here, have consecrated it far above our poor power to add or detract. The world will little note nor long remember what we say here, but it can never forget what they did here. It is for us, the living, rather, to be dedicated here to the unfinished work which they who fought here have thus far so nobly advanced. It is rather for us to be here dedicated to the great task remaining before us - that from these honored dead we take increased devotion to that cause for which they gave the last full measure of devotion - that we here highly resolve that these dead shall not have died in vain; that this nation, under God, shall have a new birth of freedom; and that government of the people, by the people, for the people, shall not perish from the earth.

## Hyphenation in Ragged-right Text

**Hyphenation** separates a word between two syllables, leaving the beginning of the word at the end of one line and moving the remainder to the beginning of the next line. In PageMaker, you can turn automatic hyphenation on or off in the Hyphenation dialog box from the Type menu. You can specify Manual only, Manual plus dictionary, or Manual plus algorithm. For a description of these options, look in Help under Hyphenation.

You also specify a hyphenation zone in the Hyphenation dialog box. The **hyphenation zone** is an acceptable area in a line of text for breaking the text, either with hyphenation or by shifting the word that doesn't fit to the next line. Hyphenation zones apply only to text that is not justified.

Changing the width of the hyphenation zone affects the visual appearance of a text block. In general, the smaller the hyphenation zone, the closer each line comes to the right margin. A small hyphenation zone creates more two- and three-letter word divisions because only a small amount of space is allocated for hyphenation. When the last word in the line doesn't fit, and the word starts to the left of the hyphenation zone, PageMaker tries to hyphenate it. If the word breaks conveniently at a syllable, the word will be hyphenated. A larger hyphenation zone creates a more ragged appearance with fewer small word divisions because most words are shorter than the width of the hyphenation zone, and will fit without hyphenation. Figure 8.25 shows the same text with two different hyphenation zones.

**Figure 8.25**
Hyphenation zones

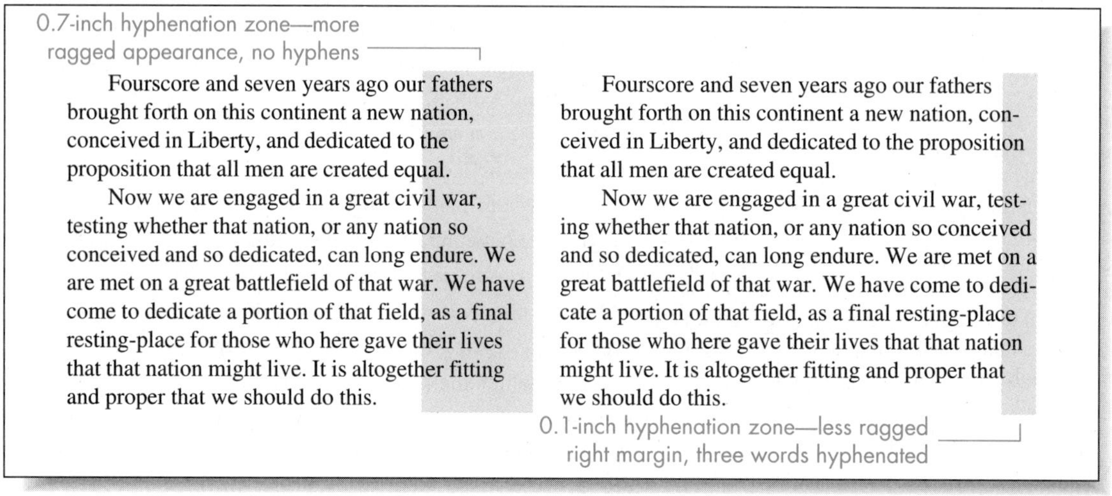

0.7-inch hyphenation zone—more ragged appearance, no hyphens

Fourscore and seven years ago our fathers brought forth on this continent a new nation, conceived in Liberty, and dedicated to the proposition that all men are created equal.

Now we are engaged in a great civil war, testing whether that nation, or any nation so conceived and so dedicated, can long endure. We are met on a great battlefield of that war. We have come to dedicate a portion of that field, as a final resting-place for those who here gave their lives that that nation might live. It is altogether fitting and proper that we should do this.

Fourscore and seven years ago our fathers brought forth on this continent a new nation, conceived in Liberty, and dedicated to the proposition that all men are created equal.

Now we are engaged in a great civil war, testing whether that nation, or any nation so conceived and so dedicated, can long endure. We are met on a great battlefield of that war. We have come to dedicate a portion of that field, as a final resting-place for those who here gave their lives that that nation might live. It is altogether fitting and proper that we should do this.

0.1-inch hyphenation zone—less ragged right margin, three words hyphenated

Hyphenation slows readers down because they must read a portion of the word, look to the next line for the remainder of the word, and then put the two pieces together. As a guideline, hyphenation should occur in no more than 3 percent of the lines in a publication, and no more than three consecutive hyphens should occur. You will learn about a way to limit the number of consecutive lines with hyphenated words in a question at the end of the chapter.

## COLOR IN A PUBLICATION

Our world is filled with vibrant colors, and you can use PageMaker to design color layouts. However, color is the most complex element of design. Understanding which colors to use, how to combine them, and the impact on readers requires considerable study. This section introduces you to some of the vocabulary and concepts, but focuses more on low-cost color considerations that provide variety.

Every color has three characteristics: hue, value, and saturation. **Hue** is the name of the color, such as red, green, or blue. **Value,** or screening, refers to the percentage of color a hue contains. PageMaker uses **tint** to describe color value, which are in percentages from 0 to 100. **Saturation** is the relative brilliance or intensity of a color. High-saturation colors include less black and are purer, such as royal blue. Low-saturation colors include more black and appear dark and dull.

When you define a color, you identify whether it is a spot color, a process color, or a tint of the spot or process color. **Spot colors** are premixed inks from standard color choices. **Process color** mixes the four **CMYK** colors—cyan, magenta, yellow, and black—to create a complex palette of thousands of colors. You can use a tint to vary either spot or process color and increase the number of colors available. By using a tint of a spot color, you create variety without greatly increasing cost.

You can give the illusion of color by using tints of black. Look at Figure 8.26, which was created by replacing nine boxes of different fill tints with the Portage graphic. This figure shows how tint can create an interesting effect. Tint can mimic color and add visual interest.

**Figure 8.26**
**Graphic with different tints**

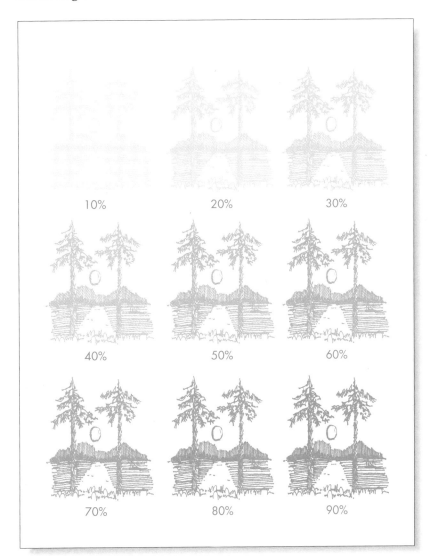

Type also projects a sense of color on a page. Letter forms have different weights and, when placed on the page as blocks of text, a light or dark appearance. Figure 8.27 shows twelve fonts with varying weights and color.

Figure 8.27
Fonts with varying weights and color

Fourscore and seven years ago our fathers brought forth on this continent a new nation, conceived in Liberty, and dedicated to the proposition that all men are created equal.
Garamond

Fourscore and seven years ago our fathers brought forth on this continent a new nation, conceived in Liberty, and dedicated to the proposition that all men are created equal.
Garamond Light Condensed

Fourscore and seven years ago our fathers brought forth on this continent a new nation, conceived in Liberty, and dedicated to the proposition that all men are created equal.
Garamond Book Condensed

Fourscore and seven years ago our fathers brought forth on this continent a new nation, conceived in Liberty, and dedicated to the proposition that all men are created equal.
Officina Sans

Fourscore and seven years ago our fathers brought forth on this continent a new nation, conceived in Liberty, and dedicated to the proposition that all men are created equal.
Officina Serif

Fourscore and seven years ago our fathers brought forth on this continent a new nation, conceived in Liberty, and dedicated to the proposition that all men are created equal.
Comic Sans MS

Fourscore and seven years ago our fathers brought forth on this continent a new nation, conceived in Liberty, and dedicated to the proposition that all men are created equal.
Palatino

Fourscore and seven years ago our fathers brought forth on this continent a new nation, conceived in Liberty, and dedicated to the proposition that all men are created equal.
Arial

**Fourscore and seven years ago our fathers brought forth on this continent a new nation, conceived in Liberty, and dedicated to the proposition that all men are created equal.**
**Korinna Heavy**

𝕱ourscore and seven years ago our fathers brought forth on this continent a new nation, conceived in Liberty, and dedicated to the proposition that all men are created equal.
Engravers Old English

**Fourscore and seven years ago our fathers brought forth on this continent a new nation, conceived in Liberty, and dedicated to the proposition that all men are created equal.**
**Britannic Bold**

**Fourscore and seven years ago our fathers brought forth on this continent a new nation, conceived in Liberty, and dedicated to the proposition that all men are created equal.**
**Impact**

## PAGE LAYOUT AND DESIGN

The purpose of the layout is to pull people into the publication and create readers out of people who would otherwise just scan pages. Creating an area of visual interest on every page helps to promote readership. A graphic or picture is one way to draw a reader's eye to the page.

Figure 8.28 shows how graphics can create visual interest on a page.

Figure 8.28
Using graphics to
increase visual interest

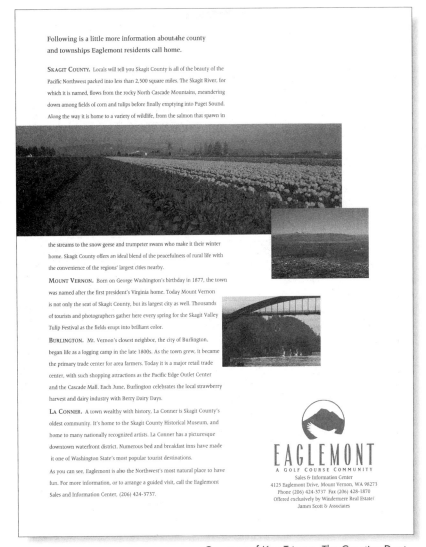

Courtesy of Ken Trimpe, The Creative Dept.

Another principle of page layout is to use white space to enhance readability. Wide margins, indentation, and drawings increase readability. Avoid the temptation to fill every part of the page with text. Too much type looks dense and heavy on the page and does not invite the reader into the publication. White space, used properly, makes documents easier to read.

Compare the different use of white space with the same text in Figure 8.29.

**Type filling entire page**

**Same text with white space better utilized**

TUITION

Island Sound is a small performing choir of approximately 55 members. Director's and accompanist's salaries, sheet music, notebooks, risers, costumes, props, rehearsal space, printing costs, and retreats are part of the budget. The Choir Board makes every attempt to maximize the return on your tuition.

Tuition for the year is set by the Board prior to auditions. Half is payable in September, with the remainder due in January. Tuition not paid by the due date is subject to a $10 late fee. Checks should be made payable to Island Sound and sent to the choir address. Special arrangements for tuition payment may be made by contacting the treasurer. A limited number of partial scholarships are available. Requests should be made in writing to the Choir Manager by the first Tuesday in September and January.

In order to perform, a choir member's tuition must be paid. Tuition is NOT refundable should a choir member decide to leave the choir for any reason.

TICKET SALES

Ticket sales are an important part of our budget income. In order to keep tuition at a reasonable cost, each family is responsible for a certain number of concert tickets. Some families sell their allocation while others choose to invite family and friends and give them tickets. However families choose to do it, we rely on ticket income to meet expenses.

TOUR

The Choir usually tours as a group in late June. Previous destinations have been Hawaii, Idaho, Portland, and Las Vegas. Plans are announced in the fall, and a schedule of payments is sent to members. A nonrefundable deposit secures a member's place on tour.

Once a member has submitted a deposit, the tour director makes reservations, calculates costs based on the number of participants, and commits funds to a variety of items. Occasionally, a member changes plans and withdraws from tour. All changes to tour by members must be made in writing to the Choir Manager. Persons who withdraw may be liable for expenses already committed by the tour director.

The tour is optional and no casting parts are determined by participation or non-participation in Tour.

---

*Island Sound Choir*

**Tuition**

Island Sound is a small performing choir of approximately 55 members. Director's and accompanist's salaries, sheet music, notebooks, risers, costumes, props, rehearsal space, printing costs, and retreats are part of the budget. The Choir Board makes every attempt to maximize the return on your tuition.

Tuition for the year is set by the Board prior to auditions. Half is payable in September, with the remainder due in January. Tuition not paid by the due date is subject to a $10 late fee. Checks should be made payable to Island Sound and sent to the choir address. Special arrangements for tuition payment may be made by contacting the treasurer. A limited number of partial scholarships are available. Requests should be made in writing to the Choir Manager by the first Tuesday in September and January.

In order to perform, a choir member's tuition must be paid. Tuition is NOT refundable should a choir member decide to leave the choir for any reason.

**Ticket Sales**

Ticket sales are an important part of our budget income. In order to keep tuition at a reasonable cost, each family is responsible for a certain number of concert tickets. Some families sell their allocation while others choose to invite family and friends and give them tickets. However families choose to do it, we rely on ticket income to meet expenses.

**Tour**

The Choir usually tours as a group in late June. Previous destinations have been Hawaii, Idaho, Portland, and Las Vegas. Plans are announced in the fall, and a schedule of payments is sent to members. A nonrefundable deposit secures a member's place on tour.

Once a member has submitted a deposit, the tour director makes reservations, calculates costs based on the number of participants, and commits funds to a variety of items. Occasionally, a member changes plans and withdraws from tour. All changes to tour by members must be made *in writing* to the Choir Manager. Persons who withdraw may be liable for expenses already committed by the tour director.

The tour is optional and no casting parts are determined by participation or non-participation in Tour.

---

Understanding five design principles will assist you in designing effective and attractive pages: optical center and eye flow, eye dwell, balance, optical weight, and graphic orientation and placement.

## Optical Center and Eye Flow

When first viewing a page, the eye focuses on the **optical center** of the page, which is slightly above and to the left of the physical center of the page. Then the eye traces a *z*-like pattern—called **eye flow**—from left to right and top to bottom on the page, as shown in Figure 8.30.

The **terminal area**, in the lower-right quadrant of the page, is where the eye flow ends and the reader leaves the page. To keep interest on the page, place a strong graphic in this area. It could be the company logo, a coupon, or a telephone number. When designing a page, you should ask: What is the last image you want the reader to have? Avoid placing a negative image or text block in the terminal area, such as a cigarette ad with the Surgeon General's warning in the terminal area of the page.

Look again at Figure 8.28. The photograph of tulips pulls you into the page above the optical center. The logo with contact information is in the terminal area.

## Eye Dwell

Research shows that the eye spends different amounts of time in different quadrants of the page. The top half of the page holds the eye for 60 percent of the time; the bottom half for 40 percent, as shown in Figure 8.31. You can improve **eye dwell** by placing a photo or another attention-grabber in a lower eye-dwell quadrant to focus attention in that area of the publication.

Look at Figure 8.28 again; the use of the logo in the lower-right corner increases the probability that the reader will spend more than the 15 percent of time usually allotted to that quadrant of the page.

**Figure 8.30**
Optical center, eye flow

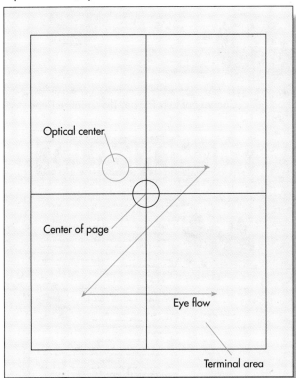

**Figure 8.31**
Eye dwell

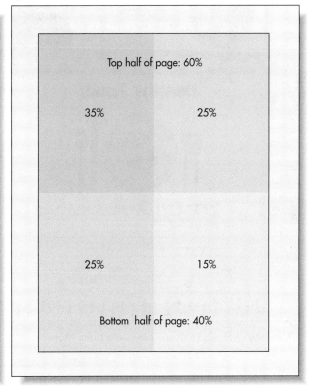

## Balance

There are two basic approaches to page layout: symmetric and asymmetric. In **symmetrical** layout, elements such as text and graphics are balanced across a horizontal, vertical, or diagonal line. The image is conservative, orderly, and formal.

Figure 8.32 shows examples of symmetrical layouts.

**Figure 8.32**
Examples of symmetrical layouts

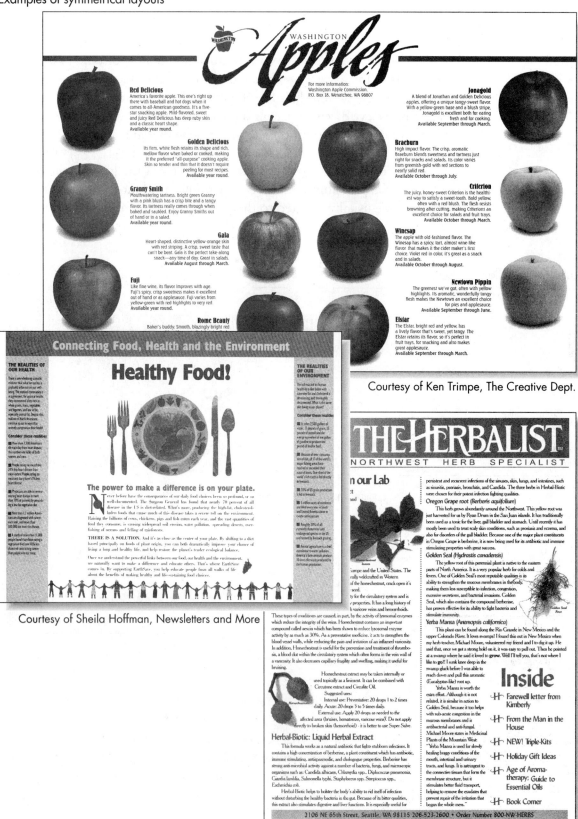

Courtesy of Ken Trimpe, The Creative Dept.

Courtesy of Sheila Hoffman, Newsletters and More

Courtesy of Sheila Hoffman, Newsletters and More

In **asymmetrical** layout, text and graphics are balanced with optical weight. Asymmetrical layouts are more energetic and dynamic. For this type of effect, designers use an odd number of visuals in page layout. Figure 8.33 shows an example of an asymmetrical layout.

Figure 8.33
Example of asymmetrical layout

Courtesy of Ken Trimpe, The Creative Dept.

**Optical Weight**

**Optical weight** is the ability of a graphic component to attract the reader's eye. Some guidelines for understanding optical weight are listed in Figure 8.34.

Figure 8.34
Guidelines for optical weight

| Higher Optical Weight | Lower Optical Weight |
| --- | --- |
| Large | Small |
| Dark | Light |
| Color | Black, white, gray |
| Irregular shape | Regular shape |

In other words, a small, dark shape can balance a larger, light shape. Figure 8.35 illustrates this principle.

Courtesy of Overlake Hospital Medical Center

## Graphic Orientation and Placement

When choosing a graphic, consider its orientation and placement. The graphic should bring the reader *into* the publication, rather than direct the reader's focus outward. Notice in Figure 8.36 how the chair and sculpture both face inward, toward the text.

**Figure 8.36**
Graphic orientation directs the reader's eye inward; word wrap increases visual interest

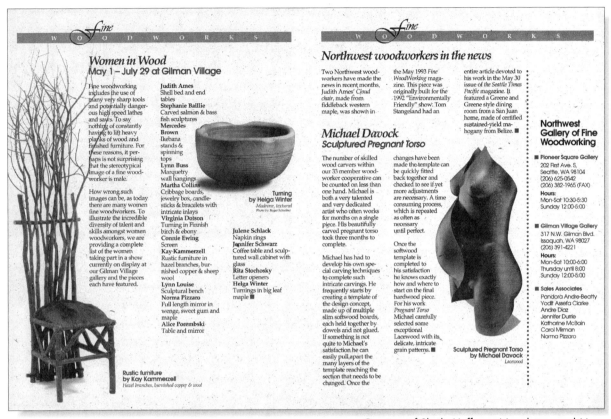

Courtesy of Sheila Hoffman, Newsletters and More

Another consideration is **word wrap,** or **runaround**. Allowing a graphic to "intrude" a column of text creates a less formal and more artistic feel to the publication. Look again at Figure 8.36, which illustrates how word wrap increases visual interest.

You can also go outside the layout grid to enhance interest and provide visual surprise. Pulling a picture or another visual into a wide margin or using a large drop cap are two ways to accomplish this, as shown in Figure 8.37. Also notice how the apple display is oriented toward the center of the page.

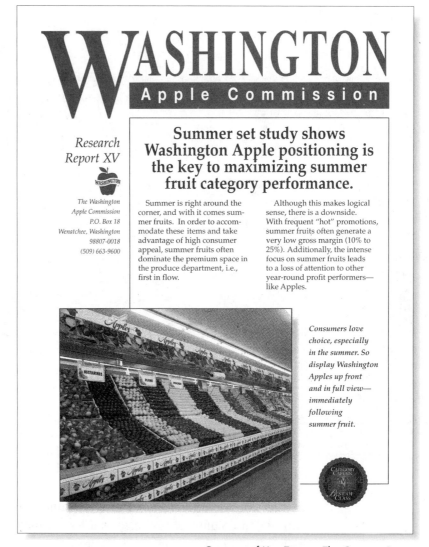

Courtesy of Ken Trimpe, The Creative Dept.

Another critical layout concern is keeping track of the overall design. When you have facing pages, you are constantly moving between the detail of a particular section and the overall look of the two-page spread. A layout that looks good on two individual pages can appear disorganized when the pages are placed side by side. Look at two facing pages and be aware of how they work, or do not work, together.

Content

*What* the publication says also contributes to its success. The words on a page are called **copy** and Figure 8.38 shows how the copy works together with the design to create an integrated publication. This brochure was commissioned by the Washington Dairy Products Commission to encourage schools to buy milk coolers because when milk sits nonrefrigerated, children won't buy it. Three of the headlines use a play on words to bring the readers (school officials) into the text. The screening of color from high tint to low tint in COOL IT! reinforces the theme of temperature by looking cool. Ken Trimpe, art director, and Jeanne Drury, copywriter, worked as a team to produce the COOL IT! brochure.

### Figure 8.38
Copy and design create an integrated publication

Courtesy of Ken Trimpe, The Creative Dept.

While designers have many opinions about design, they commonly agree that restraint is important. For example, including every font and type size available on one page is not advisable. Figure 8.39 shows a newsletter that was created without a thought for restraint in type.

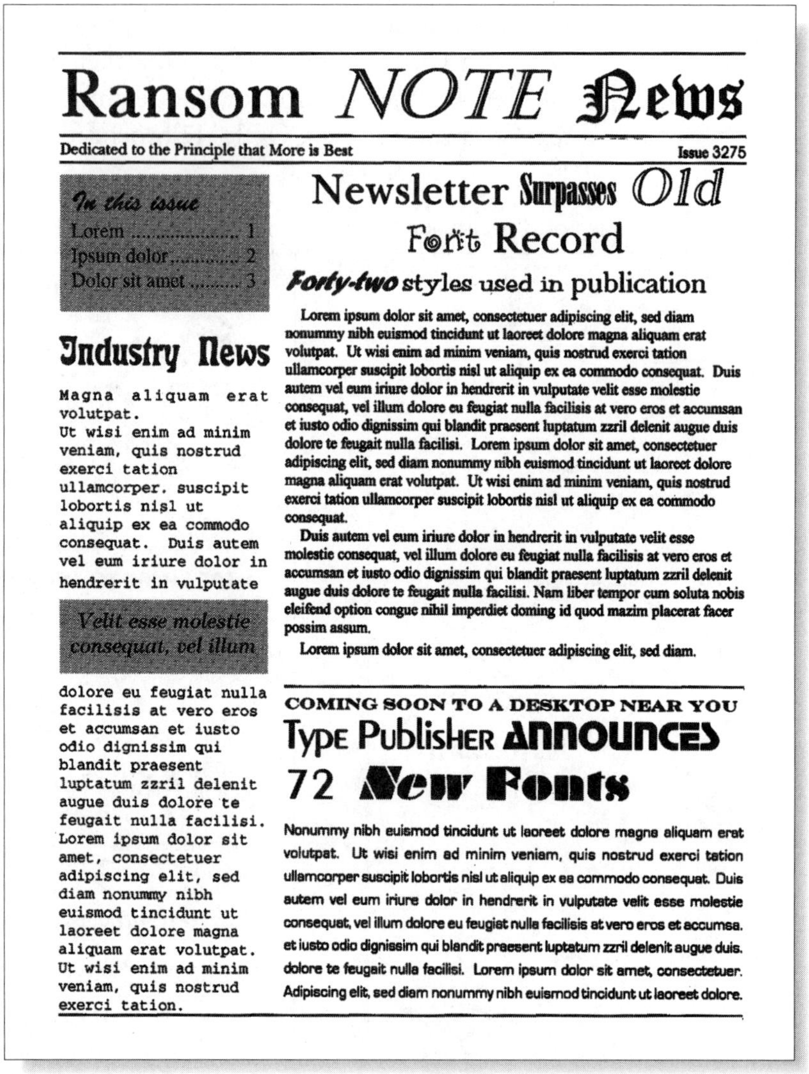

# Ransom NOTE News

Dedicated to the Principle that More is Best — Issue 3275

*In this issue*
Lorem .......... 1
Ipsum dolor .......... 2
Dolor sit amet .......... 3

## Industry News

Magna aliquam erat volutpat.
Ut wisi enim ad minim veniam, quis nostrud exerci tation ullamcorper. suscipit lobortis nisl ut aliquip ex ea commodo consequat. Duis autem vel eum iriure dolor in hendrerit in vulputate

*Velit esse molestie consequat, vel illum*

dolore eu feugiat nulla facilisis at vero eros et accumsan et iusto odio dignissim qui blandit praesent luptatum zzril delenit augue duis dolore te feugait nulla facilisi. Lorem ipsum dolor sit amet, consectetuer adipiscing elit, sed diam nonummy nibh euismod tincidunt ut laoreet dolore magna aliquam erat volutpat. Ut wisi enim ad minim veniam, quis nostrud exerci tation.

## Newsletter Surpasses Old Font Record

### Forty-two styles used in publication

Lorem ipsum dolor sit amet, consectetuer adipiscing elit, sed diam nonummy nibh euismod tincidunt ut laoreet dolore magna aliquam erat volutpat. Ut wisi enim ad minim veniam, quis nostrud exerci tation ullamcorper suscipit lobortis nisl ut aliquip ex ea commodo consequat. Duis autem vel eum iriure dolor in hendrerit in vulputate velit esse molestie consequat, vel illum dolore eu feugiat nulla facilisis at vero eros et accumsan et iusto odio dignissim qui blandit praesent luptatum zzril delenit augue duis dolore te feugait nulla facilisi. Lorem ipsum dolor sit amet, consectetuer adipiscing elit, sed diam nonummy nibh euismod tincidunt ut laoreet dolore magna aliquam erat volutpat. Ut wisi enim ad minim veniam, quis nostrud exerci tation ullamcorper suscipit lobortis nisl ut aliquip ex ea commodo consequat.

Duis autem vel eum iriure dolor in hendrerit in vulputate velit esse molestie consequat, vel illum dolore eu feugiat nulla facilisis at vero eros et accumsan et iusto odio dignissim qui blandit praesent luptatum zzril delenit augue duis dolore te feugait nulla facilisi. Nam liber tempor cum soluta nobis eleifend option congue nihil imperdiet doming id quod mazim placerat facer possim assum.

Lorem ipsum dolor sit amet, consectetuer adipiscing elit, sed diam.

COMING SOON TO A DESKTOP NEAR YOU

## Type Publisher Announces 72 New Fonts

Nonummy nibh euismod tincidunt ut laoreet dolore magna aliquam erat volutpat. Ut wisi enim ad minim veniam, quis nostrud exerci tation ullamcorper suscipit lobortis nisl ut aliquip ex ea commodo consequat. Duis autem vel eum iriure dolor in hendrerit in vulputate velit esse molestie consequat, vel illum dolore eu feugiat nulla facilisis at vero eros et accumsa. et iusto odio dignissim qui blandit praesent luptatum zzril delenit augue duis. dolore te feugait nulla facilisi. Lorem ipsum dolor sit amet, consectetuer. Adipiscing elit, sed diam nonummy nibh euismod tincidunt ut laoreet dolore.

**Figure 8.39**
A lack of restraint results in a cluttered, haphazard design

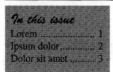

It is also not a good idea to use too many special effects on a single page, such as drop caps, nonjustified text, and pulling a picture into a margin. The sum of all the special effects can have an overwhelming and cluttered look, as if the designer had a checklist of special effects that had to appear on one page. Restraint is wise advice.

Desktop publishing is the first real creative step forward since the invention of movable type. Now you can speed up the design process and experiment with different fonts, layouts, and techniques with relative ease. Through mastering PageMaker, understanding basic design concepts, and experimenting, you will produce quality documents that effectively communicate your intended message.

Look again at Figure 8.37. Design techniques used here include an oversized cap, pull quote, photo outside grid, shadow behind the photo, use of right-justified text in the first column, reverse print, and ragged-right text. The design works because the designer pulled everything together into a well-integrated, cohesive layout. Look to designs you find pleasing for ideas you can incorporate into your own publications.

## QUESTIONS

1. Explain the importance of identifying audience and objectives to publication design. What design elements are influenced by your understanding of audience and objectives? Be specific.

2. What are the physical distinctions between serif and sans serif fonts? When would you use serif fonts? When would you use sans serif fonts?

3. What reactions do people have to serif and sans serif fonts? Do you agree with these characterizations? Explain.

4. Describe decorative and dingbat fonts. When would you use each?

5. What is the purpose of a headline? Give examples of headlines that show different design concepts.

6. When should italic and bold be used? When should they not? When should you use underlining and all caps?

7. Explain the difference between justified and nonjustified text. What design considerations influence decisions about when to use each?

8. Define *optical center* and *eye flow*. What is their importance to page layout?

9. Explain *eye dwell*. What is its impact on page design?

10. Give an example of how to use optical weight for balance.

11. Evaluate a magazine, advertisement, brochure, or catalog. Who is the audience? Is the appearance formal or friendly? Look at the fonts. How many are used? What design features are used? How effective is the page layout and overall appearance?

12. Using Help, list the steps to avoid hyphenating more than three consecutive lines.

13. Using Help, define and contrast the following Hyphenation features:

a. Manual only

b. Manual plus dictionary

c. Manual plus algorithm

## PROJECTS

1. Look at Figure 8.35. Identify the grid. Evaluate the design for font, justification, emphasis, optical center and eye flow, balance, optical weight, graphic placement, and white space. What is your overall response to the spread?

2. Look at Figure 8.40. Identify the grid. Evaluate the design for font, justification, emphasis, optical center and eye flow, balance, optical weight, graphic placement, and white space. What is your overall response to the spread?

**Figure 8.40**
Project 8.2—Identifying design elements

We catch a train for Baltimore and Camden Yard. What a beautiful ball park. I could actually enjoy baseball. Great tour by Nolan Roberts. Lots of history and . . . what a beautiful ball park!

*- Brown*

The Birds are at home to face those forces of evil, the Oakland A's. We have paid scalper prices to see the future of baseball - a stadium designed for *only* baseball. No dumb dome, no cylindrical monolith, no astro-turf. The game is a sellout, as are all the games at Oriole Park. Hometown boys in black and orange have no trouble tonight. Charlie and I take our sons for a walk around the concourse. We go up a ramp near home plate. Through the tunnel I see the bright lights and green grass. I hold Jeffrey's hand and close my eyes. I reach out my other hand and find my father leading me to the Fenway Park third base grandstand 35 years ago. Seattle, if you build it, we will come.

*- Miller*

Bruce Williams

HARBORSIDE, BALTIMORE.
Bruce Williams

3. Figure 8.41 is from the same publication as Figure 8.40. Is the design consistent? Explain.

**Figure 8.41**
Project 8.3—Comparing design elements

Kim Munizza

The mountain top at Monticello is an experience that will stay with Sharon and I for a long time. The planning, the reading, the anticipation, and the drama of approach, will never do justice to the joy of finally, *the experience*. The world of Thomas Jefferson was one of considerable thoughtfulness, after education. His projects developed over time and were typically the result of experimentation designed to lead to superior solutions. It is so exciting to see the odd little projects which fill the house and show the genius of the man. My favorite is the seven day clock that requires the weights to go through the floor into the basement. I respect the person that will cut holes in their floor to accommodate an experiment. Bravo!

*- Brown*

This was a beautiful place to visit and certainly a "must see" when in the vicinity. But, I still found it hard to accept the fact that slaves maintained these grounds on a daily basis. T.J. was more concerned with the religious rights of the free white man than racial equality itself. So, in spite of its beauty, Monticello had a bitter-sweet flavor that would not disappear for me.

*- Bennett*

Monticello
8.25.93

Wolf Saar

Don Doman

4. Look at Figure 8.42. Identify the grid. Evaluate the design for font, justification, emphasis, optical center and eye flow, balance, optical weight, graphic placement, and white space. What is your overall response to the spread?

**Figure 8.42**
Project 8.4—Identifying design elements

Courtesy of Adobe Magazine

5. Look at Figure 8.43. Identify the grid. Evaluate the design for font, justification, emphasis, optical center and eye flow, balance, optical weight, graphic placement, and white space. What is your overall response to the spread?

**Figure 8.43**
Project 8.5—Identifying
design elements

# HOT SHEET

Featuring the hottest ads of the month nationwide.

VOLUME IV / ISSUE 2                                         March 1997

## Retailers Strike Gold in "Great Red Rush of '97"

### IN PRODUCE, TIMING IS EVERYTHING.

In produce, like most everything in life, you've got to be able to switch gears quickly when opportunities "crop" up unexpectedly.

Take this year's 98-million-box Washington Apple crop, for example. With 35 million boxes of crisp, smaller size Red Delicious apples in storage, smart retailers are doing some heavy advertising and displaying.

### WHAT'S THAT SOUND? OPPORTUNITY KNOCKING!

As you know, all Washington Reds are profitable, but according to Commission President Steve Lutz, Sizes 100 and smaller, both bagged and bulk, are "where the action is" this time around. All you have to do is think "Red Delicious," promote aggressively, and take advantage of the big promotional blitz that's now taking place.

Here's one of the many smart retailers that have jumped at the opportunity and have proven, once again, that "there's gold in them thar Reds."

### A 1,500 PERCENT SALES INCREASE AIN'T HALF BAD!

What can you say about a one-week Kroger promo that raked in a quarter-million in sales? How'd they do it!

According to Jeff Ryg, assistant produce merchandiser for the 82-store chain in Dallas, Texas, they featured 8-pound bags of Washington Reds at $3.99 each. And "bagged" incredible sales. "You'd have to sell a lot of potatoes, onions or bananas to get that kind of $4 ring at the till", he said. Ryg also said the promo was not only great for Kroger, but a great value for their customers, too. "They got premium Washington fruit for *less than 50 cents a lb."*

### NEITHER IS A MIND-BOGGLING 2,500 PERCENT INCREASE!

Kroger subsequently ran another front page feature for a buy-one-get-one-free promo of 3-pound bagged Reds and

Goldens which produced *"mind-boggling sales."*

Ryg said that before the sale was even over they had sold 12 times more bagged Goldens, and 13 times more bagged Reds, than normal and "couldn't keep the shelves stocked."

Best of all, Ryg reported no cannibalization of the bulk business whatsoever. "Sales of our Washington 88 size Reds were constant throughout both specials."

Courtesy of Ken Trimpe, The Creative Dept.

6. Look at the two newsletters in Figure 8.44. One is a remake of an older design. Comment on the design elements in the new masthead, as well as other elements of design in the new newsletter.

**Figure 8.44**

Project 8.6—Comparing design elements of newsletters

Before

After

Courtesy of Sheila Hoffman, Newsletters and More

7. Look at Figure 8.45, which is an identity packet for Wall Street Custom Clothiers that consists of a business card, notecard, envelope, and newsletter. Comment on the elements that are part of the overall design.

8. Create your own issue of Ransom Note News. Use as many poor design elements as you can. In the text of your newsletter, describe each feature and why the design is poor.

9. Make a directory of fonts from your machine, similar to the ones shown in Figures 8.3 and 8.4.

10. Using tints, place a graphic file to show the differences between the tints, similar to Figure 8.26. Start by placing nine boxes with different fills. Place the file, using the Replacing entire graphic option.

11. Using three columns, create a font sampler with varying weights and color, similar to Figure 8.27. Select fonts that progress from light to dark.

**Figure 8.45**
Project 8.7—Evaluating an identity packet

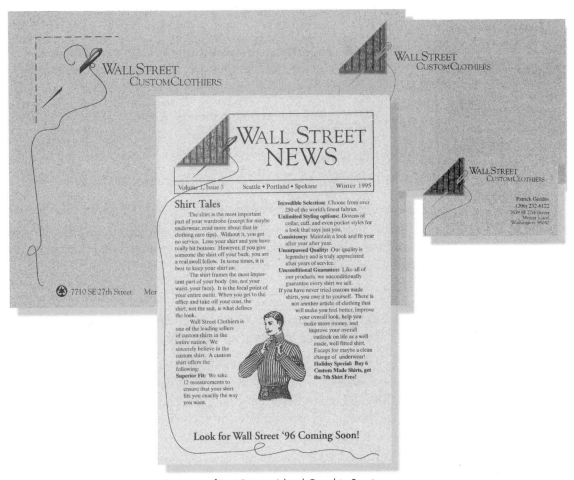

Courtesy of Lari Power, Island Graphic Services

12. Create Figure 8.15, using reverse type and force justify. Press the spacebar once between the letters and three times between the words. At the beginning and end of the top line, there is lowercase letter *p*, which have not been changed to reverse type and are not visible. Before you set the top line to reverse type, it will look like "pT H E   I N N   A Tp".

13. Create Figure 8.46, using a 30% tint for the text and 100% tint for the shadows. The numbers are in 48-point type and the *AM* and *PM* are in 36-point type. The "standing" numbers are 30% tint and the shadows are 100% tint. Experiment with different skewing values for the shadows.

**Figure 8.46**
Shadows

14. Create a drop cap similar to example 2 in Figure 8.13, where the text follows the shape of the letter form, by doing the following:

   a. Cut the initial letter from the text and paste it outside the text block.

   b. Enlarge the letter to the size you want, at least 4 to 6 times the body text point size. Reduce the size of the text block so the windowshade handles are as close as possible to the letter.

   c. In a separate text block, type a period in reverse type. Reduce the size of the text block.

   d. Move the period close to the letter's text block.

   e. Group the two text blocks to create a graphic element.

   f. Move the drop cap to the location with the rest of the text.

   g. In the Text Wrap dialog box, select the middle icon in the top row and the right icon in the bottom row. For standoff values, type 0 for all.

   h. Adjust the graphic boundary to the shape of the letter.

15. Find a publication that uses various elements of design. Write a paper describing the elements and their impact on the effectiveness of the piece.

16. Interview a graphic designer who uses a desktop publishing program. Ask the designer to describe some publications he or she has created and the design decisions made for each. Report back to the class.

# CHAPTER 9

# Designing Publications for the Web

Upon completion of this chapter you will be able to:

- **Describe the Internet and the World Wide Web**
- **Describe HTML documents and browsers**
- **Understand design considerations for developing Web page documents**
- **Create a PageMaker document with hyperlinking**
- **Export a PageMaker publication as an HTML document**

There are many parallels between the communications revolution spawned by the Internet and the publication revolution spawned by desktop publishing. Both occurred as a result of technological advances, both give enormous power to individuals, and both are fraught with potential problems. Desktop publishing resulted from the development of personal computers, page description software (such as PageMaker), and the laser printer. These items give individuals the opportunity to create high-quality publications from their desktops. Unfortunately, these items also enable individuals with few design skills to create extremely poor-quality documents. Similarly, the development of the Internet and software that can be used to easily create a document for display on the World Wide Web (WWW or Web) allows almost any individual or organization to become a worldwide publisher. The potential problem is poorly designed, unattractive documents that have little valuable content and are hard to navigate. Nevertheless, the Web has become a major medium for information, communications, and commerce. Therefore, individuals as well as organizations are seeking ways to publish documents online. With PageMaker, they have the flexibility to develop publications that can be distributed in print as well as displayed on the World Wide Web.

## WHAT ARE THE INTERNET AND THE WORLD WIDE WEB?

The **Internet** is a vast communications system that links computers around the world, as illustrated in Figure 9.1. With the Internet, students away at college can stay in touch with their friends and family around the country and world; business travelers can check messages and access client account information; kids can play interactive games; researchers can collaborate on projects; and people can shop from electronic catalogs. Perhaps the most compelling aspect of the Internet is the vast amount of information available to anyone with a computer, modem, software, and Internet access.

**Figure 9.1**
The Internet—linking computers around the world

The Internet has been in use for decades. It was originally developed by the U.S. government and educational research institutions as a way to link together different types of computers and allow government-sponsored research to be shared. Until the early 1990s, companies and individuals generally were not interested in the Internet. However, three events helped to cause a dramatic increase in the interest in and use of the Internet.

First was the development of a visual interface for the Internet—the **World Wide Web**—that a person using a **browser** program (such as Netscape Navigator or Microsoft Internet Explorer) can easily search for information. Second was the creation of **HyperText Markup Language** (HTML), the formatting standard in which Web pages are written. These HTML documents form the basis of the Web. Third was the commercialization of the Internet. Companies saw an opportunity not only to communicate with new and potential customers, but also to actually sell their products through the Internet. As a result, software developers like Adobe, who makes PageMaker, have enhanced their products to work with the Web.

## Formatting with HyperText Markup Language

Before you can begin to create Web pages, you need to understand how HyperText Markup Language works. HyperText Markup Language is used to format the appearance of a document and to create links (called **hyperlinking**) that allow the user to navigate through the document. Formatting, such as centering a heading or underlining a word, is done through the use of tags. Figure 9.2 shows two Web pages as they appear to the user in a browser and their corresponding source files, which show the HTML tags used to format the text for these pages.

### Figure 9.2
Two Web pages and the HTML tags used to format the text

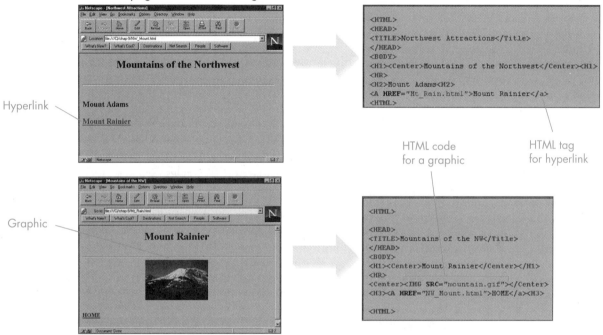

Hyperlink

Graphic

HTML code for a graphic

HTML tag for hyperlink

Each HTML tag appears within brackets and most tags are used in pairs. For example, the <Center> and </Center> pair causes whatever comes between them to be centered. The <B> and </B> tags cause whatever comes between them to be displayed in bold. The top example in Figure 9.2 includes the following tags for the heading Mountains of the Northwest:

- the HTML H1 style tag to determine the character attributes

- the <Center> </Center> tags to position the text on the page

When you create a hyperlink in HTML, you must identify the source object (such as a word or graphic) for the link and the destination for the link. In the top example in Figure 9.2, the words Mount Rainier are underlined and in another color, indicating that they are hyperlinked. The corresponding HTML file shows the code that creates the link to the other page. When the user clicks Mount Rainier, the bottom page is displayed. Similarly, the word HOME on the bottom page is linked to the top page. When the user clicks HOME, the top page reappears.

HTML also enables the developer to easily insert graphics into the document. The bottom page in Figure 9.2 shows a graphic and the corresponding code that specifies what graphic will be displayed. In this case, the name of the graphic is mountain.gif. You can view the code for a Web page from within a browser.

You can use a word processing program to create a simple HTML document by typing in the text and the appropriate formatting codes or by using an HTML editor to insert the codes automatically. You can also use PageMaker to export a publication to HTML; the codes are automatically added.

## Using the Web as a Source of Graphics

As you've seen in earlier chapters, well-placed illustrations enhance and add interest to a publication. The Web is an excellent source for locating and purchasing clip art and photographs. Virtually every company that sells stock illustrations has a Web site from which you can search its database for the material you want, pay for the items, and often **download** them (transfer them to your computer). Figure 9.3 shows the PhotoDisc Web site (http://www.photodisc.com). PhotoDisc has more than 50,000 digital images in categories such as People and Lifestyles; Science, Technology, and Medicine; Nature, Wildlife, and the Environment; and Business and Occupations. Their images, primarily photographs, are **royalty free** so that once you pay for an image you can display it on your Web page indefinitely without paying additional fees. Notice in Figure 9.3 that you can search and download images, order from the CD-ROM collection, and obtain a company catalog.

Figure 9.3
PhotoDisc Web site

One way to locate graphics is to search the Web with a search engine. However, narrowing the search so that you obtain manageable results can be a challenge. For example, searching for Northwest Resorts from the Excite search engine resulted in more than 1,200 references to Web pages that contained the words "Northwest Resorts."

Whenever you use the Web to obtain material, such as graphic images, take care to ensure that you do not violate the copyright laws. If you deal with well-known companies, such as PhotoDisc, who control the copyright to the materials they distribute, then you won't have to worry about unauthorized use of someone else's property.

## PLANNING A PUBLICATION TO EXPORT TO HTML

As with other types of publications, you should plan the general layout of the pages you intend to create and, in the case of Web pages, how they will be linked. An added challenge to your planning is the current limitations of HTML and Web browsers. These limitations affect the way you use type and graphics in a publication, and the way you lay out pages.

### Type Considerations for Web Pages

When designing a printed publication, you select a font for its appearance, readability, and spacing. With a Web page, the font and thus the line breaks and letter and word spacings are determined by the browser from which the document is viewed. As a result, the line endings and column lengths you see in a PageMaker publication are not preserved when you export the publication to HTML. The type attributes that are controlled by the browser and not preserved include:

- Font, type size, and leading
- Tracking and kerning
- Outline and Shadow styles
- Tabs and indents

The type attributes that are preserved include bold, italic, underline, reverse, and text color.

The easiest way to address the type limitations of HTML is by working with HTML styles, which are similar to PageMaker styles. Another way to control the text appearance is to work in an image-editing program, save the text as a bitmap file, and then place the file in your publication as a graphic. Because the text is displayed as a graphic, the text attributes (font, spacing, and so forth) are preserved when you export the publication to HTML.

### Graphics Considerations for Web Pages

Unlike PageMaker publications, which support graphics in TIF, BMP, and EPS file formats, HTML supports graphics only in GIF and JPEG file formats. When you export a publication that contains a graphic, PageMaker automatically converts the imported graphic to GIF or JPEG format (your choice). Both these file formats compress the graphic, reducing its file size. The smaller the file size, the less time it takes for the graphic image to be sent over the Internet and appear on the user's screen. GIF (Graphics Interchange Format) files are best for line drawings and JPEG (Joint Photographers Expert Group) files are best for photographs. Keep in mind that graphic objects drawn with PageMaker drawing tools (such as the line, rectangle, and ellipse tools) are not exported. However, horizontal lines drawn with the PageMaker line tool or constrained line tool appear as horizontal rules in an HTML document.

## Page Layout Considerations for Web Pages

By now, you should be familiar with the WYSIWYG (What You See Is What You Get) feature in PageMaker. Because of the limitations in HTML and flexibility in Web browsers, you cannot see a WYSIWYG display of an exported publication. When you export a PageMaker publication to HTML, you see only an approximation or general suggestion of the page layout. You should keep in mind the following layout considerations when exporting a PageMaker publication to HTML.

- Nonrectangular text wrap shapes are not supported. Therefore, you should use only the rectangular text wrap or avoid text wraps altogether.

- The content of a frame is exported but not the surrounding border of the frame. Any part of an object that extends beyond the frame's border is cropped when the publication is exported.

- Masked objects are unmasked when a publication is exported to HTML. You can crop an image before exporting in order to achieve a similar look.

- Overlapping objects are separated when exported to HTML and might cause unacceptable results.

- Transformed objects (skewed, rotated, flipped) revert to their original orientation when exported to HTML. You can use an image-editing program to transform objects and then place them in a publication as graphics files before you export the publication.

Figure 9.4 shows a PageMaker publication viewed in the publication window and in a browser. Notice the changes that occurred after the document was exported to HTML.

## Minimizing Conversion Problems

Because of the text, graphics, and page layout limitations, it is important to keep the page design simple. Another way to minimize conversion problems is to use HTML styles. As mentioned earlier, HTML styles, similar to PageMaker styles, enable you to quickly apply fonts, type sizes, type styles, alignment, and other formatting features to selected text. HTML styles are recognized by Web browsers and help ensure the desired layout.

Figure 9.4
Viewing same
publication in PageMaker
and in a Web browser

Original PageMaker
publication

# Employee News

**New Computers**

Great News! All employee computers will be replaced during the next three months. These will be multimedia ready systems with Pentium Pro processors, 32MB of RAM, 2GB hard drive, 8X CD-ROM drive, and speakers. We will replace the oldest computers first. You will be notified of the replacement schedule by Tech Services. They will need approximately two hours to install each new computer. This will include backing up and reinstalling all of your files. In addition to replacing your computer, the system software will be upgraded to Windows 95 and your applications software will be upgraded to Office 97, including Word, Excel, Access, and PowerPoint. Workshops will be scheduled to provide training in the new features of the software.

**Flower Show and Sale**

The Fifth Annual Flower Show and Sale will be held on Saturday , May 15ᵗʰ, from 9:00am until 5:00pm in the courtyard. Everyone is invite to participate by bringing up to five flower arrangements. Awards will be given for best arrangements in

the following categories: Grand Prize, Most Colorful, Most Artistic, and Most Unusual. Prizes will be gift certificates to the Green Thumb nursery. Pictures of the prize winners will be submitted to the local paper with information about the gardener. This year, for the first time, we are allowing you to sell your flower arrangements. Refreshments will be served, so join us for this wonderful event.

**Music in the Park**

This year we are proud to announce that our employees' group will be sponsoring one of the Music in the Park events. This series of concerts is held at 7:00pm on the first and third Wednesdays of every month throughout the summer. The concerts are held at the outdoor amphitheater at Luther Burbank park. We will be sponsoring a string quartet from Cascadia College. This is an opportunity for us to contribute to the community and gain recognition for our group. In addition, we will be able to sell refreshments to generate some revenue. If you would like to volunteer for this event, contact Judy at extension 2299.

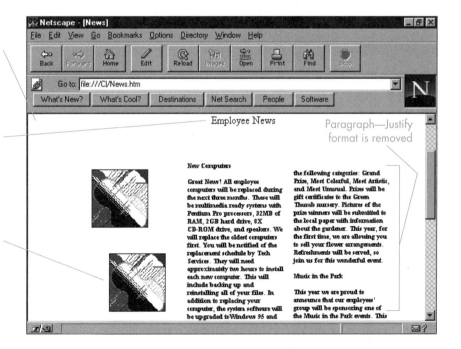

Same publication exported
to HTML and displayed in
Netscape browser

Heading—different font
and size

Drawn objects—
rectangle and fill
disappear

Paragraph—Justify
format is removed

Figure 9.5 lists the HTML styles available in PageMaker.

Figure 9.5
HTML styles available in
PageMaker

| HTML Style | How Text appears in Web Browser |
| --- | --- |
| H1 through H6 | Six levels of headings; H1 is the largest |
| Address | Sets short text apart from body text |
| Blockquote | Sets one or more paragraphs apart from body text |
| Body Text | Normal paragraphs |
| Definition List | List format; each paragraph is indented |
| Directory List | List Format; each paragraph is indented and a bullet is added before each paragraph |
| Menu List | Similiar to Ordered List but more compact |
| Ordered List | Use for a numbered list |
| Preformatted | Prevents text from being reformatted when changes are made to a browser's style definitions |
| Unordered List | Use for a bullet list; browser adds a bullet before each item |

Remember that the display of text formatted with a style depends on the browser's definition of that style. Thus, text tagged with a particular style might appear differently when viewed with different browsers.

## DEVELOPING A PUBLICATION TO EXPORT TO HTML

Before you begin to develop a publication to display on the Web, it is helpful to create a **storyboard,** which shows the general layout of each page and the intended links between pages. The storyboard provides an overall view of your design, helps ensure that you include all text, graphics, and links, and becomes a guide for creating the publication. Figure 9.6 shows a storyboard with the planned layout for a four-page PageMaker publication.

Figure 9.6
The Storyboard

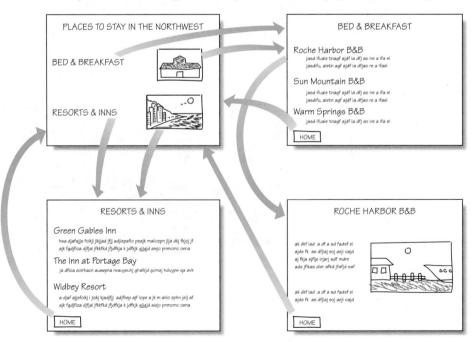

You will create the PageMaker publication shown in Figure 9.7, which is based on this sto.ryboard, and export it as an HTML document. Page 1 is considered the **Home Page** because it appears first when the document is opened in a browser. The other three pages contain a HOME button, which links each page back to this Home Page.

Figure 9.7
Completed PageMaker
publication

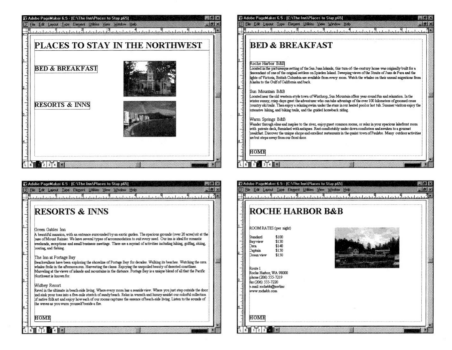

Refer to Figure 9.7 as you read the descriptions in Figure 9.8 of the objects on each page.

Figure 9.8
Object on each page

| | Object | Type | HTML Style | Link |
|---|---|---|---|---|
| Page 1 | PLACES TO STAY IN THE NORTHWEST | text | H1 | none |
| | horizontal line | drawn line | none | none |
| | BED & BREAKFAST | text | H2 | page 2 |
| | RESORTS & INNS | text | H2 | page 3 |
| | top photo | placed graphic | none | page 2 |
| | bottom photo | placed graphic | none | page 3 |
| Page 2 | BED & BREAKFAST | text | H1 | none |
| | body text | placed text | none | none |
| | Roche Harbor B&B | text | none | page 4 |
| | HOME button | text | H3 | page 1 |

Figure 9.8
Object on each page
(continued)

|  | Object | Type | HTML Style | Link |
|---|---|---|---|---|
| Page 3 | RESORTS & INNS | text | H1 | none |
|  | body text | placed text | none | none |
|  | HOME button | text | H3 | page 1 |
| Page 4 | ROCHE HARBOR B&B | text | H1 | none |
|  | photo | placed graphic | none | none |
|  | body text | placed text | none | none |
|  | HOME button | text | H3 | page 1 |

In general, the steps for developing this publication and converting it to an HTML document are:

- Type, draw, or place the objects with the appropriate styles on each page.

- Create the hyperlinks and test them.

- Add the HOME button to the master pages.

- Export the publication to HTML.

- View the HTML document using a Web browser.

Now that you know the components of the pages, you're ready to create them.

## Creating the Four Pages

The first page you will create is the Home Page (also called the welcome page) that appears when the HTML document is opened with a browser. You'll start with a new publication set to the dimensions appropriate for Web documents. In this case you will use the 500 x 335 Browser - small page size, which approximates the display area in a browser.

 CTRL N

1. Start the PageMaker program and select New from the File menu.

2. Select 500 x 335 Browser - small as the Page size.

3. Click OK.

4. If necessary, maximize the publication window.

With the document setup on the Pasteboard, you're almost ready to insert the objects into the page, starting with the main heading that will use the HTML H1 style. First, add the HTML styles to your Styles palette.

 CTRL B

5. Select Show Styles from the Window menu.

6. If necessary, click the Styles tab to select it.

7. Click the triangle button ▶ and select Add HTML Styles from the drop-down menu, as shown in Figure 9.9.

Figure 9.9
Adding HTML styles to
the Styles palette

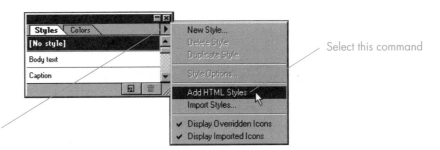

Click here

Select this command

The HTML styles are added to your Styles palette. This process might take a few minutes, depending on the speed of your computer.

**8.** Scroll the list of styles and click HTML H1.

**9.** Click the text tool T in the Toolbox and type the heading *PLACES TO STAY IN THE NORTHWEST* at the top of the page.

**10.** Save the publication as Places to Stay.

Refer back to the storyboard in Figure 9.6. Notice that the next object you need to add is the horizontal line. When the publication is exported to HTML and displayed in a browser, this line will appear as a horizontal rule line.

**11.** Use the constrained line tool |− to draw the horizontal line shown in Figure 9.10.

Figure 9.10
Drawing the horizontal
line

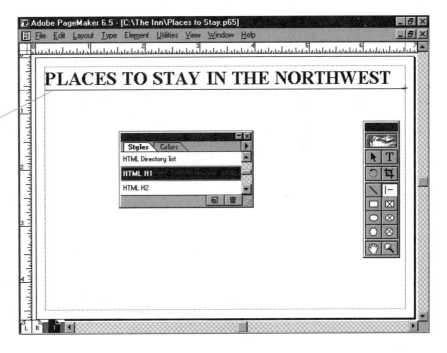

Draw this line

As you can see on the storyboard, the Home Page contains two subheadings. You'll enter the text for the subheadings next. Begin by changing the heading style.

**12.** Click HTML H2 in the Styles palette to change to that style.

**13.** Use the text tool T to type the subheading *BED & BREAKFAST*.

**14.** Use the pointer tool ▶ to select the subheading and then resize the text block, as shown in Figure 9.11.

**Figure 9.11**
Reducing the windowshade

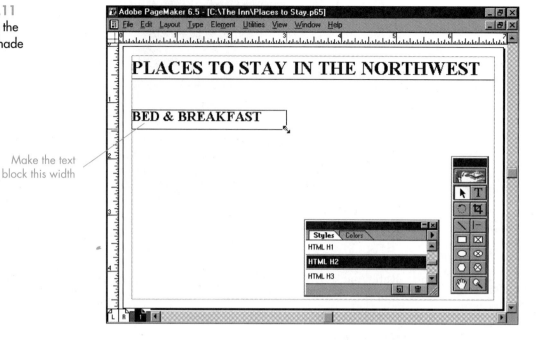

Make the text block this width

**15.** Type the second subheading, *RESORTS & INNS*, and resize the text block.

Continue by placing the two graphics. Although both pictures are saved in a TIF file format, PageMaker will automatically convert them to GIF or JPEG format (your choice) when you export the publication to HTML.

CTRL D

**16.** Select Place from the File menu.

**17.** Select the Bed and Breakfast Photo file and click Open.

**18.** Place the graphic as shown in Figure 9.12.

**Figure 9.12**
Bed and Breakfast photo

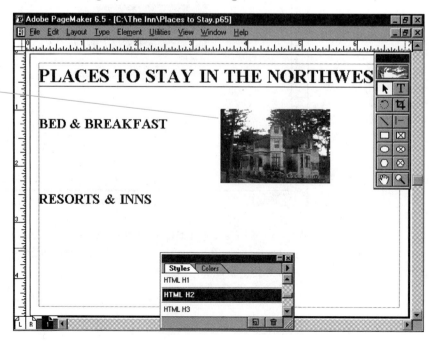

Place photo in this location

**19.** On your own, place the Resorts and Inns Photo file as shown in Figure 9.13.

**Figure 9.13**
**Resorts and Inns photo**

Place photo directly below first photo

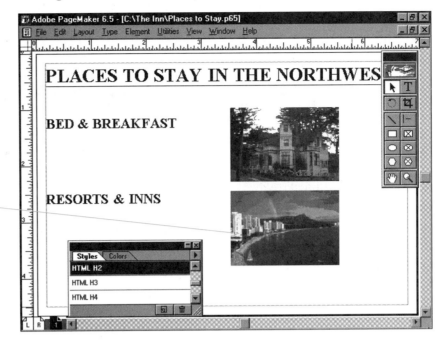

CTRL S

**20.** Save the publication.

**Now you will create the other three pages.**

**21.** Select Insert Pages from the Layout menu and insert three pages after the current page.

**22.** Verify that page 2 is displayed.

**23.** Type the heading *BED & BREAKFAST* using the HTML H1 style.

**24.** Place the text document named Bed and Breakfast Text as shown in Figure 9.14.

**Figure 9.14**
**Placing the Bed and Breakfast text**

Position text block here

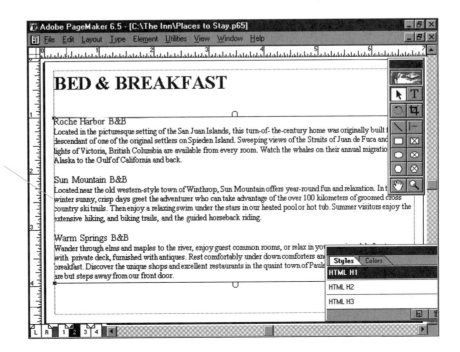

**25.** Display page 3.

**26.** Type the heading *RESORTS & INNS* with the HTML H1 style.

CTRL D

**27.** Place the text document named Resorts and Inns Text as shown in Figure 9.15.

**Figure 9.15**
Placing the Resorts and
Inns text

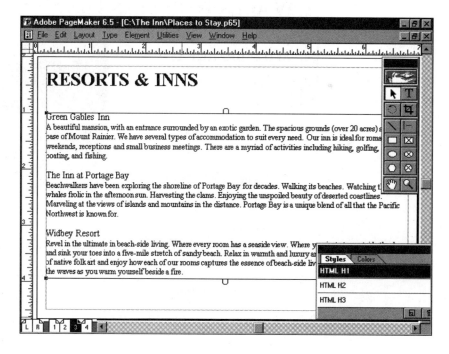

**28.** Display page 4.

**29.** On your own, create page 4. The heading is *ROCHE HARBOR B&B*, the text is a file named Roche Harbor Text, and the graphic is named Roche Harbor Photo. (*Note*: Resize the Roche Harbor Text text block after placing it.)

CTRL S

**30.** Save the publication.

Now that you have developed the pages, you can create the links between them.

## Creating the Hyperlinks

To create a link in PageMaker you set a **source** (an object such as text or a graphic that can be clicked to jump the viewer to another location) and a **destination** or **anchor** (the location you want appears when the source is clicked). Each source can jump to only one anchor, but any number of sources can jump to the same anchor. In this case, for example, you will link the BED & BREAKFAST text on page 1 (a source) with page 2 (the destination). You will also link the photo associated with BED & BREAKFAST on page 1 (another source) with page 2 (the same destination).

The general process to create a hyperlink is:

- Select the destination. This can be done by displaying the page and, if you want, selecting an object on the page.

- Display the Hyperlinks palette and create a new anchor.

- Select the source object.

- Use the Hyperlinks palette to specify the selected object as a new source.

You'll follow this process as you hyperlink the BED & BREAKFAST text on page 1 to page 2.

1. Display page 2.

2. Use the text tool T to highlight the B in BED & BREAKFAST. This will be the destination.

CTRL 9

3. Select Show Hyperlinks from the Window menu.

4. Click the triangle button ▶ on the Hyperlinks palette to display the menu. See Figure 9.16.

**Figure 9.16**
Displaying the hyperlink options

Selected text for anchor

Click to create anchor

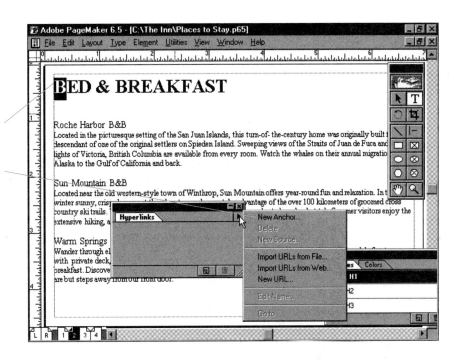

5. Click New Anchor.

6. Type *Page 2* as the name and click OK.

7. Display page 1.

**8.** Use the text tool [T] to select BED & BREAKFAST. See Figure 9.17. (*Note*: Always use the text tool to select all the letters that you want a user to be able to click to execute the link.)

**Figure 9.17**
Selecting BED &
BREAKFAST

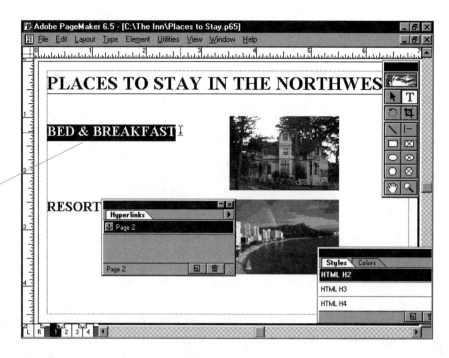

Selected text for source

**9.** Click the triangle button [▶] on the Hyperlinks palette to display the menu.

**10.** Click New Source.

**11.** Type *BED & BREAKFAST text page 1* for the name and click OK.

Look at the Hyperlinks palette in Figure 9.18. Notice that Page 2 is the destination (indicated by the anchor button [⚓]) and the BED & BREAKFAST text page 1 is the source (indicated by its indent). All the sources linked to a particular anchor are indented below the destination on the Hyperlinks palette. This will become more apparent as you create the rest of the hyperlinks. The rectangle after BED & BREAKFAST text page 1 indicates that the text is selected onscreen.

**Figure 9.18**
Hyperlinks palette

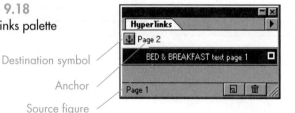

Destination symbol

Anchor

Source figure

Before continuing, take a moment to test the hyperlinks.

**12.** Click the grabber hand tool [✋] in the Toolbox.

Notice that a colored border appears around the words BED & BREAK-FAST. This border is automatically placed around an object to indicate that it is hyperlinked. For text, this kind of object is known as a **hotword(s)**.

**13.** Point to BED & BREAKFAST.

Notice how the pointer changes to ⟨ᵐ⟩. This symbol will appear whenever you point to a source object with the grabber hand tool ⟨ᵐ⟩ and indicates that the object is hyperlinked.

**14.** Click the words BED & BREAKFAST.

The view jumps to page 2. You might need to reposition the page on the screen. You can either use the grabber hand tool, which is selected, to drag the page into the center of the Pasteboard, or select Fit in Window from the View menu.

**15.** Display page 1.

Now create a second source (the graphic) for the Page 2 destination.

**16.** Use the pointer tool �\ to select the Bed & Breakfast graphic.

**17.** Click the anchor symbol ⚓ next to the words Page 2 on the Hyperlinks palette.

**18.** Type *Bed & Breakfast graphic page 1* as the name and click OK.

**19.** If necessary, scroll the Hyperlinks palette to display the Page 2 anchor.

Study the Hyperlinks palette and notice that there are now two sources for the Page 2 destination. Continue by specifying the hyperlinks for page 3.

**20.** Display page 3.

**21.** Use the text tool T to highlight the R in RESORTS.

**22.** Click the triangle button ▶ on the Hyperlinks palette and select New Anchor.

**23.** Type *Page 3* as the name and click OK.

**24.** Display page 1.

**25.** Use the text tool T to highlight RESORTS & INNS.

**26.** Click the anchor symbol ⚓ next to Page 3 on the Hyperlinks palette.

**27.** Type *RESORTS & INNS text page 1* as the name and click OK.

**28.** Use the pointer tool ▲ to select the Resorts and Inns graphic.

**29.** Click the anchor symbol ⚓ for Page 3 on the Hyperlinks palette.

**30.** Name the source *Resorts & Inns graphic page 1* and click OK.

**31.** On your own, test all of the hyperlinks.

CTRL S **32.** Save the publication.

The final hyperlinking you will do is to link the words Roche Harbor B&B on page 2 with page 4.

**33.** On your own, link Roche Harbor B&B on page 2 with page 4 as follows:

- Display page 4.

- Use the text tool ☐T☐ to select the destination.

- Add an anchor named *Page 4*.

- Select the desired text on page 2 and specify it as the source with the name *Roche Harbor B&B page 2*.

**34.** Test the hyperlink.

CTRL S

**35.** Save the publication.

Now that you've linked together the four pages, you'll create a HOME button to link each page back to the Home Page.

---

## Creating the HOME Button

As users click various hyperlinks and explore a multiple-page HTML document, they weave a path that might become difficult to retrace. Although they could backtrack using the commands available within their browser, this can become time-consuming if they have clicked a number of links. When you design an HTML document, it is important to include a way for users to return to the Home Page no matter where they are in the document. You should place a hyperlink back to the Home Page on each page to provide a way to navigate back. A simple way to do this is to place the hyperlinked word or graphic on the left and right master pages, as shown in Figure 9.19.

**Figure 9.19**
HOME button placed on the master page

Create the Home button at bottom of the master page

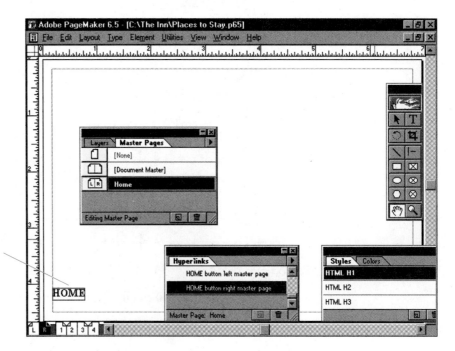

Complete the following to place the word HOME at the bottom of each master page and link it with page 1. Start by creating an anchor for page 1.

1. Display page 1.

2. Use the text tool 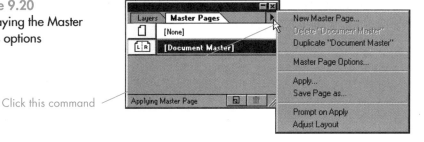 to highlight the letter P in PLACES.

3. Use the Hyperlinks palette to create a new anchor named *Home Page*.

SHIFT CTRL 8

4. Select Show Master Pages from the Window menu.

5. Click the triangle button to display the drop-down menu. See Figure 9.20. (*Note:* Your Master Pages palette might be combined with different palettes than shown.)

**Figure 9.20**
**Displaying the Master Pages options**

Click this command

6. Click New Master Page.

7. Name the new master page *Home* and click OK.

8. If necessary, click the R master page icon in the lower-left corner of the publication window.

9. Click the text tool  in the Toolbox.

10. Click the Styles tab and select HTML H3 from the Styles Palette.

11. Click an insertion point at the lower-left corner of the page, as shown in Figure 9.21.

**Figure 9.21**
**Clicking an insertion point**

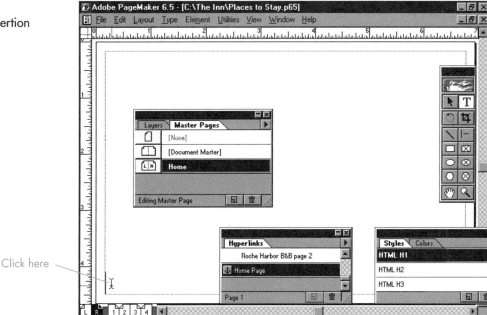

Click here

**12.** Type *HOME*.

**13.** Click the L master page icon in the lower-left corner of the publication window.

**14.** Verify that HTML H3 is selected in the Styles palette, click an insertion point in the lower-left corner of the page, and type *HOME*.

**15.** Click the triangle button on the Master Pages palette and click Apply.

Because you do not want the HOME button to appear on page 1 (the Home Page), you need to specify the range of pages to which you want to apply the *Home* master pages.

**16.** Change the Page range to 2-4 and click Apply.

Now hyperlink the HOME button on each master page to page 1.

**17.** Use the text tool $\boxed{T}$ to select the word HOME.

**18.** Click the anchor symbol $\boxed{\text{⚓}}$ for Home Page on the Hyperlinks palette and type *HOME Button left master page*.

**19.** Click OK.

**20.** Display the right master page.

**21.** Use the text tool $\boxed{T}$ to select the word HOME.

**22.** Click the anchor symbol $\boxed{\text{⚓}}$ on the Hyperlinks palette and type *HOME Button right master page*.

**23.** Click OK.

Now test the HOME button.

**24.** Display page 1.

**25.** Click the grabber hand tool $\boxed{\text{🖑}}$ in the Toolbox.

**26.** Click RESORTS to jump to page 3.

**27.** Click HOME to return to the Home Page.

**28.** On your own, test the HOME button on all the pages.

**29.** Save the publication.

With all the links in place, your publication is complete.

## EXPORTING A PUBLICATION TO HTML

Now you are ready to export the publication to HTML and test it in a browser. When you export the publication, all the styles, graphics, and other text and objects are tagged with the appropriate HTML codes. The process is to select Export from the File menu and choose HTML. The Export HTML dialog box shown in Figure 9.22 appears. This dialog box allows you to create a new HTML document.

**Figure 9.22**
Export HTML dialog box

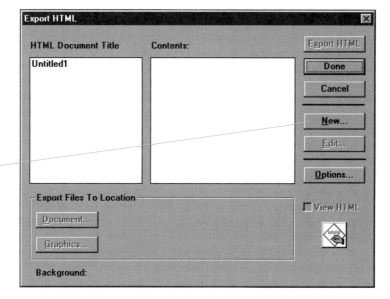

Click New to select publication pages to export to HTML

You'll export the completed publication to HTML now.

1. Point to Export in the File menu and click HTML.

2. Click New in the Export HTML dialog box.

The Export HTML: New Document dialog box shown in Figure 9.23 appears. You use this dialog box to specify a document title, which will be displayed in the title bar at the top of the browser window. You can also specify which pages or stories of a PageMaker publication you want to export as an HTML document.

**Figure 9.23**
Export HTML: New Document dialog box

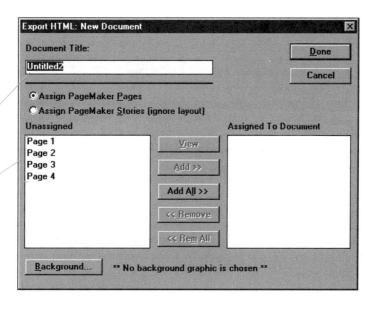

Type *Northwest Places to Stay*

Assign all these pages to the new document

3. Type *Northwest Places to Stay* in the Document Title box.

**4.** Click Add All to specify that all pages of the publication should be exported.

**5.** Click Done.

Next you will specify the location in which to store the HTML document. You can specify a separate location for the graphics contained in the document, but it is recommended that you store them in the same location.

**6.** Click Document as the Export Files To Location option.

**7.** Specify the location in which you want to store the document.

**8.** Name the document *Places to Stay in the NW* in the Document Save As dialog box.

**9.** Click OK to return to the Export HTML dialog box.

**10.** Click Export HTML.

A message box shows the progress of the export process.

---

**Displaying an HTML Document Using a Web Browser**

Now you are ready to view the HTML document from a Web browser. This way you can verify that the document will appear on the Web as you intended. You can do this without linking to the Internet, if you have a browser available on the computer you are using.

**1.** Start the Web browser.

**2.** Select the appropriate command to open the HTML file you just created. (*Note:* This procedure varies depending on the browser you are using.)

Figure 9.24 shows the HTML document opened in Netscape Navigator.

**Figure 9.24**
HTML document opened using the Netscape browser

Headings wrapped to two lines

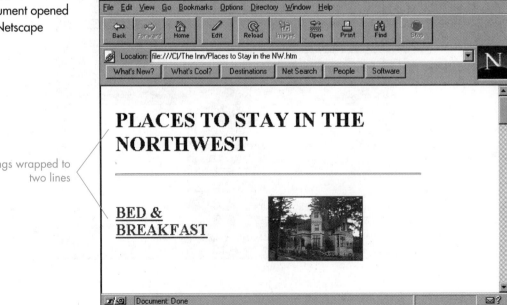

At times, the HTML document in the browser will appear somewhat different than in the PageMaker publication. For example, notice that in Netscape the headings have each wrapped to two lines. If you note differences that you don't like, you can return to the publication and adjust the text, graphics, or other objects to make the document appear more the way you planned. In this case, you could reduce the size of each heading to make them fit on a single line.

**3.** Scroll the page to view the bottom of page 1.

Notice that each page is separated by a rule line. These rule lines were automatically inserted between the publication pages when the publication was exported to HTML.

**4.** Take a few moments to test the links and view the document.

**5.** When you are finished, exit the browser.

If you have another browser available, use it to display the document. See if you can notice any differences in the document from browser to browser.

## USING ADOBE PDF FILES

Earlier, you learned about the design limitations of converting publications to HTML. PageMaker provides a way for you to develop a publication and display it with a Web browser without any changes appearing in the document. This is done using PDF (Portable Document Format) files, which retain the page layout, color, graphics, and type of the original document. Two programs are needed to create PDF files from PageMaker: **Acrobat Distiller** converts PostScript files to PDF and **Acrobat Reader** enables you to view and print the files.

The process of creating a PDF file for electronic distribution is the same as creating any PageMaker publication. After you develop the publication, you export it as a PDF file. If the PDF file will be viewed from a Web browser, the user must have Acrobat Reader installed on his or her computer. Acrobat Reader comes with PageMaker and can also be downloaded from the Adobe Web site.

## SUMMARY

In this chapter you explored parallels between the communications revolution and the publishing revolution. You learned about the Internet and the World Wide Web. You became familiar with HTML as a formatting standard for creating documents that are viewed on the Web using a browser. You studied the limitations in creating PageMaker publications that are exported to HTML and ways to address these limitations. Finally, you learned how to use PageMaker to create publications that include hyperlinks for the Web, and the process for exporting them to HTML.

1. What are the parallels between the communications revolution spawned by the Internet and the publications revolution spawned by desktop publishing?
2. True or False? HyperText Markup Language (HTML) is a set of styles developed by PageMaker.
3. A _____ allows you to view HTML-based documents on the World Wide Web.
4. What are the HTML tags you use to center a heading?
5. True or False? The Web is an excellent source for clip art and photographs.
6. What are three type attributes that are specified in PageMaker and are not preserved when a publication is exported to HTML?
7. True or False? An easy way to address the HTML limitations in the use of text is by using HTML styles.
8. True or False? Overlapping objects are separated when exported to HTML.
9. How many levels of HTML heading styles are there?
10. Creating hyperlinks using HTML requires identifying an object to be linked and the destination for the link. PageMaker calls the object to be linked the _____ and the destination the _____ .

1. Enhance the Places to Stay in the Northwest PageMaker publication by doing the following:
   - Choose one of the resorts or inns on page 3 and add a page for it. You should develop the text and obtain the photo for this page.
   - Link the name of the resort on page 3 to the new page.
   - Add a button to page 4 that links to page 2 and a button for page 5 that links to page 3.
   - Save the publication as Places2.
   - Export the publication to HTML with the name Places2 Online.
   - View the HTML document using a Web browser.
2. Create your own PageMaker publication and export it to HTML. Begin by creating a storyboard for the document, which should include:
   - At least four pages
   - At least two HTML heading styles
   - At least two styles other than heading styles (*Hint:* Experiment with using the list styles.)
   - At least 2 graphics
   - A rule line
   - A HOME button using a graphic
   
   Plan a storyboard as a guide to create the document. Save the publication with a name of your choice. Export the publication to HTML and view the document in a browser.
3. Open a publication that you have previously developed for print only. Export the publication as an HTML document. Use a Web browser to view the document.
   a. List the parts of the document that are not displayed as desired and explain why this may occur.
   b. Change the document so that when using a Web browser, the document appears more like the original publication.
4. Using Help, learn more about publishing on the Internet, and PDF and HTML files. (*Hint:* Look up "Internet: choosing between PDF and HTML documents" in the Help Topics index.)

# CHAPTER 10

# Working with Text in Story Editor

Upon completion of this chapter you will be able to:

- Describe the differences between layout and story views
- Enter new text in Story Editor
- Use the spelling checker
- Import a word processing file into story view
- Place an imported story from story view into layout view
- Use the Find and Change commands
- Use the Control palette in story view

In previous chapters you worked with text in layout view. You created new text for publications by typing paragraphs, and you worked with text blocks. PageMaker also has a built-in word processor, called **Story Editor,** that provides a faster, more powerful way to edit text. Story Editor enables you to check the spelling in a story and search for and replace text. It also reduces the amount of time you have to wait for text you type to appear onscreen.

In this chapter you will use Story Editor to create the publication shown in Figure 10.1. You will type the first paragraph and import three other paragraphs as two different stories. Then you will combine the two stories into one text block using the procedure you learned in Chapter 4. The process demonstrated in this chapter to create this four-paragraph publication is not the most straightforward method available; it would be more logical to deal with four paragraphs as one file. This approach was chosen to illustrate the features of Story Editor while lessening your typing time with a short publication. The techniques used for these paragraph-length stories also apply to longer publications.

**Figure 10.1**
Finished publication

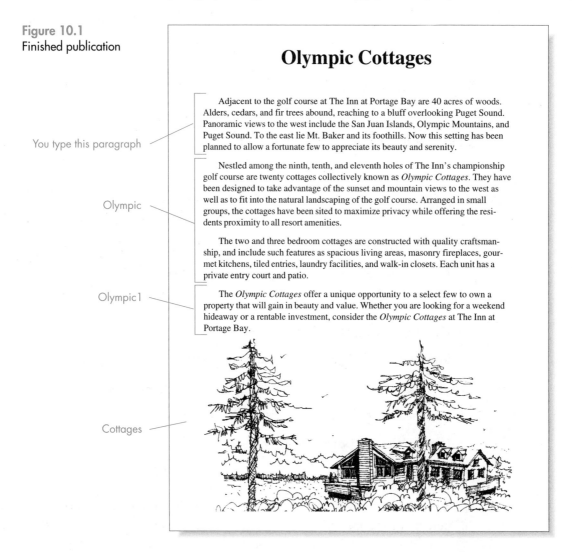

# Olympic Cottages

You type this paragraph

Adjacent to the golf course at The Inn at Portage Bay are 40 acres of woods. Alders, cedars, and fir trees abound, reaching to a bluff overlooking Puget Sound. Panoramic views to the west include the San Juan Islands, Olympic Mountains, and Puget Sound. To the east lie Mt. Baker and its foothills. Now this setting has been planned to allow a fortunate few to appreciate its beauty and serenity.

Olympic

Nestled among the ninth, tenth, and eleventh holes of The Inn's championship golf course are twenty cottages collectively known as *Olympic Cottages*. They have been designed to take advantage of the sunset and mountain views to the west as well as to fit into the natural landscaping of the golf course. Arranged in small groups, the cottages have been sited to maximize privacy while offering the residents proximity to all resort amenities.

The two and three bedroom cottages are constructed with quality craftsmanship, and include such features as spacious living areas, masonry fireplaces, gourmet kitchens, tiled entries, laundry facilities, and walk-in closets. Each unit has a private entry court and patio.

Olympic1

The *Olympic Cottages* offer a unique opportunity to a select few to own a property that will gain in beauty and value. Whether you are looking for a weekend hideaway or a rentable investment, consider the *Olympic Cottages* at The Inn at Portage Bay.

Cottages

## LAYOUT VIEW VERSUS STORY VIEW

When you first open a PageMaker publication, you are in **layout view**, where you can manipulate the way your publication will look, and you can work with text and graphics. You switch to **story view**, a text-only window that appears on top of layout view, by selecting Edit Story from the Edit menu. In story view, you can work only with text; text processing and screen redraw is faster because graphics are not available.

Figure 10.2 shows the same publication in layout and story views. In story view, notice that the Toolbox is inactive, or gray. This is because text processing is the only option available. Notice that the Styles palette remains active in both views. Also notice the title bar, which displays the first 20 or so characters of the story file name. The shortened name appears because a story is not a complete file, but rather part of a publication, which can be made up of one or more stories. Another difference between the two views is the menu bar. The Layout and Element menus are available only in layout view. The Story menu is available only in story view. As you'll see, certain commands can be accessed only in layout view while other commands can be accessed only in story view. Some commands are available in both views.

**Figure 10.2**
Publication in layout view

Layout view icon

Menus available only in layout view

Toolbox is active

Graphic can be viewed in layout

Publication in story view

Story view icon

Menu available only in story view

Sidebar with paragraph styles

Toolbox is gray and inactive

Graphic not available in story view

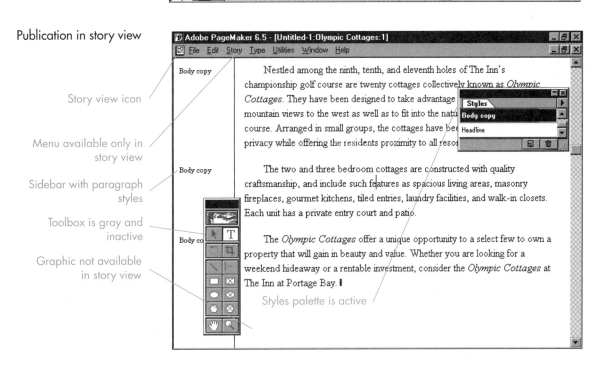

Now that you're familiar with some of the differences between layout view and story view, you'll open a new publication and switch to Story Editor.

1. Start the PageMaker program.

CTRL O
2. Select Open from the File menu.

3. Open Olympic Template and if necessary, maximize the publication window.

CTRL E
4. Select Edit Story from the Edit menu.

You have entered Story Editor; your screen should look like Figure 10.3. Take a few moments to look at the story view. First, look at the styles in the Styles palette.

**Figure 10.3**
Olympic Template in story view

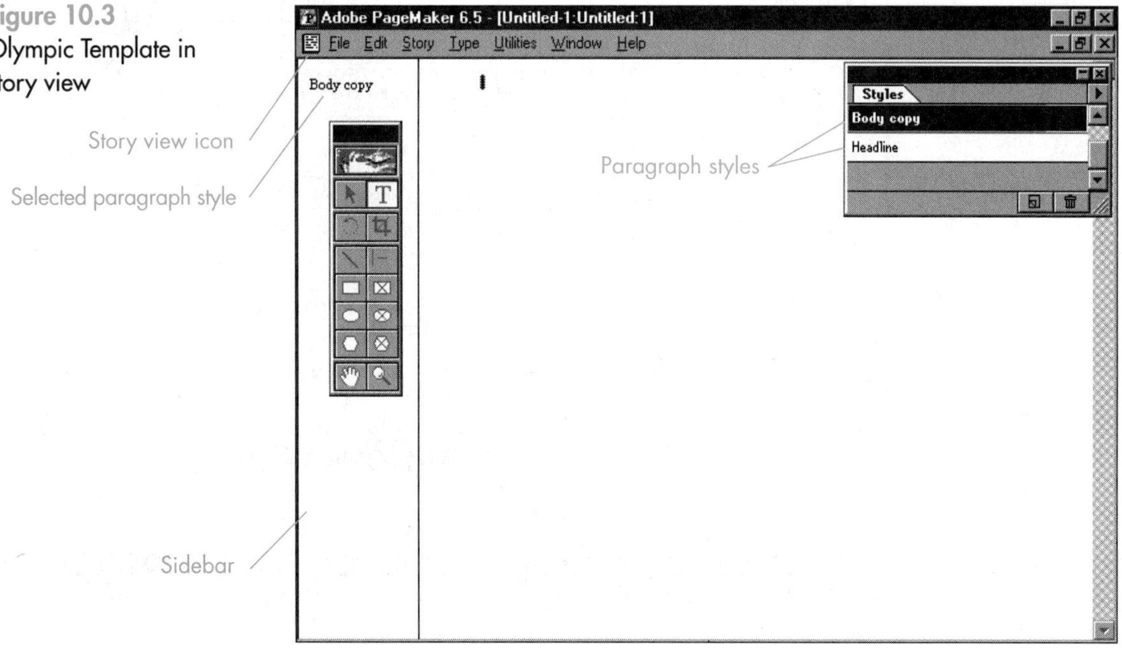

Story view icon

Selected paragraph style

Paragraph styles

Sidebar

5. Click Headline in the Styles palette. Notice how the paragraph style appears in the sidebar.

Recall that you can press CTRL while clicking the style name to open the Style Options dialog box. As you look at the style specifications, note that Body copy is Times New Roman 14 and Headline is Times New Roman 30 Bold.

6. On your own, look at the style specifications for the two styles in the Styles palette.

7. Click any tool in the Toolbox.

Nothing happens because the Toolbox is not active, as indicated by its gray color.

The menu bar in Story Editor is different from that in layout view. The menus for story view are shown in Figure 10.4.

Figure 10.4
Menus in story view

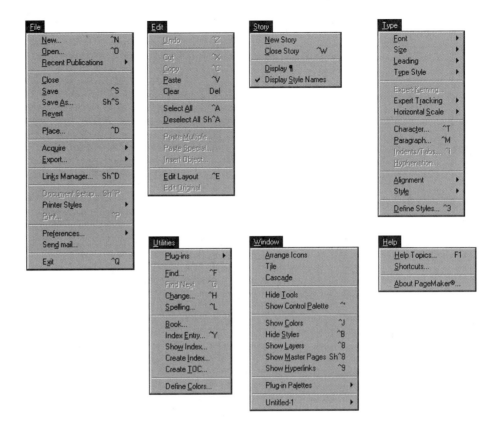

**8.** On your own, explore each menu in both story and layout views.

In order to compare the menus in each view, you'll need to toggle between story view and layout view. One method is to use the Edit menu, as you did earlier to switch to story view.

**9.** Select Edit Layout from the Edit menu.

CTRL E

**10.** Press CTRL E to return to story view.

You can also use the View icons to switch between the views.

**11.** Click the Story View icon 🗎 next to File in the menu bar.

CTRL F6

**12.** Click Next.

CTRL F6

**13.** Select Next from the Layout View icon 🗎.

On your own, use these methods to toggle between the two views. When you are done, return to story view.

## TYPING TEXT IN STORY EDITOR

The first thing you will do is type the title *Olympic Cottages* using the Headline style. In story view, the words will be left justified, but in layout view the text will be centered, as specified in the Headline style.

**1.** Click Headline in the Styles palette.

**2.** Type *Olympic Cottages*.

**3.** Press ( ↵ ENTER ).

Notice that the style for the new paragraph in the sidebar is Body copy. This is because Body copy was specified as Next style in the Headline style specifications.

Now you will type the first paragraph of the document. Make sure that you make the mistakes noted in the figure so you can use the spelling checker.

**4.** Type the paragraph shown in Figure 10.5.

**Figure 10.5**
**First paragraph**

Type with the three errors
highlighted in the text

Adjacent to the golf course at The Inn at Portage Bay is 40 acres of woods. alders, cedars, and fir trees abound, reaching to a bluff overlooking Puget Sound. Oanoramic views to the west include the San Juan Islands, Olympic Mountains, and Puget Sound. To the east lie Mt. Baker and its foothills. Now this setting has been planned to allow a fortinate few to appreciate its beauty and serenity.

Look at the Pasteboard. Notice that the headline and body copy appear to be the same size even though the headline is actually 30 points and the body copy is 14 points. This is because Story Editor shows all text as the same size, unlike layout view, which shows the text formatted according to the specified point size. On closer inspection, notice that the headline is in bold whereas the body copy is in normal type. In story view, some style specifications, such as bold and all caps, will be visible, while others, such as centering and different point sizes, will not be visible. In layout view, all specifications are visible. In other words, you see exactly what your printed page will look like in layout view because of the WYSIWYG feature, whereas what you see in story view is not what you get on your printed page.

## USING THE SPELLING CHECKER

As you typed the first paragraph of text for this publication, you intentionally made some spelling errors. Story Editor has a spelling checker that you can use to correct text you type or import into a story. You'll use the spelling checker to correct any mistakes in the paragraph you typed. *Note:* If you made more errors than those in the figure, read this entire section first to determine the best way to correct them.

( CTRL )( L )

**1.** Select Spelling from the Utilities menu.

The Spelling dialog box shown in Figure 10.6 appears. Notice that Current story is the default selection. Current story tells Story Editor to check the entire story so you don't have to move the cursor to the top of the document before you begin checking, as some word processors require.

Figure 10.6
Spelling dialog box

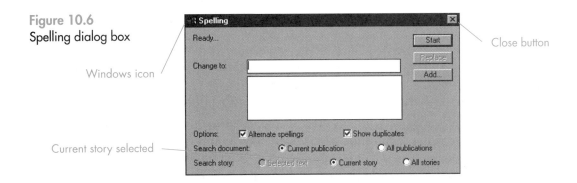

When the spelling checker finds a word that does not match any word in its 100,000-word dictionary, it will highlight the word and list alternatives. It also checks for proper capitalization and duplicated words (such as "the the").

**2.** Click Start.

The first possible error is the capitalization of the word *alder* at the beginning of the second sentence. You have three choices: ignore, replace, or add the word to the dictionary.

**3.** Click the capital A.

**4.** Click Replace to accept the capitalization change suggested by the spelling checker and find the next possible error.

Sometimes a word is misspelled but the suggested replacements list does not contain the correct spelling. This can happen when you type something like *oanoramic* for *panoramic*. In this case, you'll have to type a correction for the misspelled word. See Figure 10.7.

Figure 10.7
Typing a correction

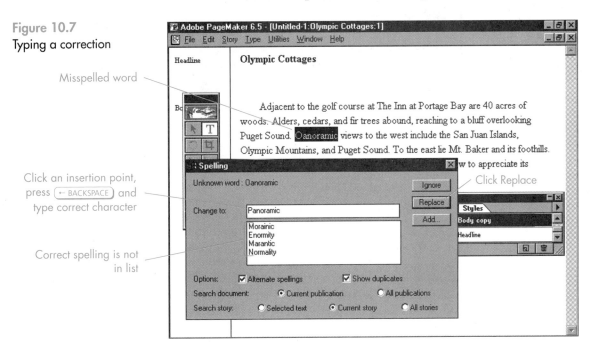

**5.** Click an insertion point in the Change to box.

**6.** Press (← BACKSPACE) to delete the incorrect characters.

**7.** Type the correct character.

**8.** Click Replace.

Sometimes the highlighted word is correct although it is not in the dictionary. You can either add it to the dictionary by clicking Add or leave the word as is and not add it to the dictionary by clicking Ignore. *Puget* is a correctly spelled word that is not in the dictionary. In this case, you do not want to add the word to the dictionary.

**9.** Click Ignore.

The next word the spelling checker highlights is *fortinate*, a misspelling of the word *fortunate*. You'll select a correct spelling from the list and then click Replace. An alternate method is to double-click the replacement word. Figure 10.8 shows both methods.

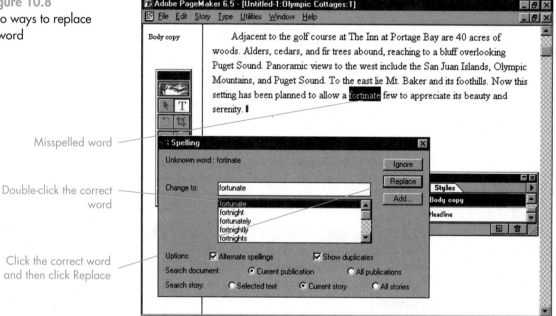

**10.** Move the pointer to the correctly spelled word in the list.

**11.** Click the replacement word.

**12.** Click Replace.

**13.** On your own, correct any other spelling errors in the story.

The Spelling dialog box will tell you when the spelling check is complete. When you are done checking the current story, you should remove the dialog box from the screen. There are two ways to do this.

**14.** Click the Windows 95 icon [icon] in the Spelling title bar and click Close, *or* click the close button [X] in the Spelling title bar.

You should be aware that the spelling checker finds misspellings in your publication, but it cannot tell if the wrong word was used (for example, *form* instead of *from*). Therefore, it is always a good idea to read the publication again, slowly, to find mistyped words the spelling checker does not identify.

## IMPORTING AND PLACING A STORY

The second and third paragraphs for the Olympic Cottages publication are stored in the student file called Olympic. This file was created in Word, and recall that PageMaker has a filter to recognize Word files. You'll import this text file and append it to the end of another story. Then you'll place this story in layout view.

**Importing a Story into Story Editor**

Make sure you are in Story Editor and your insertion point is at the beginning of the second paragraph.

1. If necessary, press ↵ ENTER at the end of the paragraph to create a second paragraph.

2. Select Place from the File menu to open the Import to Story Editor dialog box.

3. Click Olympic (do *not* double-click).

4. In the Place section, click Inserting text.

5. Make sure the Read tags option is selected.

6. Make sure the Retain format option is not selected.

7. Click Open.

The publication now contains three paragraphs. These three paragraphs are recognized as a single story because the typing and importing were done in one story window from within Story Editor. Recall that when you imported the Olympic file you clicked Inserting text. This added the imported text to the existing story rather than creating a new story. Thus, you now have one story. You'll import another paragraph as a second story.

The fourth and final paragraph is stored as the student file Olympic1. You will import it as a new story twice so that you can explore more of the features of Story Editor.

8. Select Place from the File menu to open the Import to Story Editor dialog box.

9. Click Olympic1.

10. Make sure As new story is selected.

11. Make sure Retain format is not selected.

**12.** Make sure Read tags is selected.

**13.** Click Open.

Notice that a new window appears, with a title bar The Olympic Cottage:1 and the new paragraph.

**14.** On your own, import the same story again.

Now you have an additional story called The Olympic Cottage:2 on top of your other windows. This shows how two stories are named when they both begin with the same sentence. Also, with three stories open you can experiment with moving among several stories.

**15.** If your screen does not match Figure 10.9, select Cascade from the Window menu.

**Figure 10.9**
**Story view after importing the fourth paragraph twice**

First three paragraphs in story view

Fourth paragraph in story view

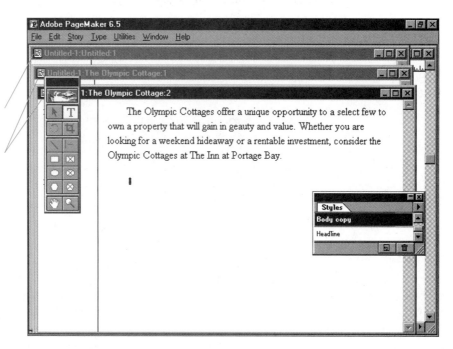

**16.** Point to Untitled-1 in the Window menu. See Figure 10.10.

Figure 10.10
Window menu in story
view

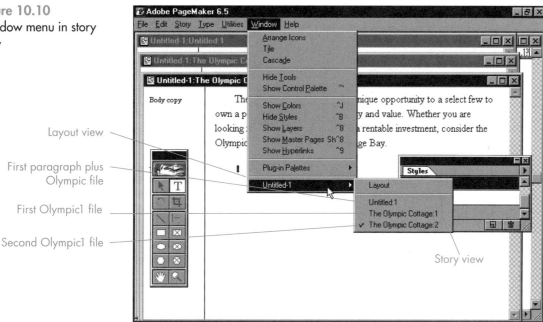

Layout view

First paragraph plus
Olympic file

First Olympic1 file

Second Olympic1 file

Story view

**17.** Click an unchecked title to move to it.

**18.** On your own, click the Window menu and select the other stories to move to them.

An alternate method to move to another story when several stories are in the window is to point to the story's title bar and click. The stories must be either cascaded or tiled on the Pasteboard. First Cascade the windows, and then try moving or selecting a story.

**19.** Select Cascade from the Window menu.

Now you can see all the open stories.

**20.** Move a window by dragging its title bar to a different location.

**21.** Select Cascade from the Window menu.

**22.** Select a layer by clicking its title bar.

Before continuing, you should close The Olympic Cottage:1, a duplicate story:

**23.** On your own, select The Olympic Cottage:1.

**24.** Select Close from the Story View icon 🖼 of The Olympic Cottage:1 window *or* click the close button ⊠ in the title bar.

PageMaker will display a warning message telling you that the story has not been placed, as shown in Figure 10.11. Because you don't need this duplicate story, you'll discard it.

Figure 10.11
PageMaker warning
message

**25.** Click Discard.

On your screen, you should have two stories: Untitled:1 and The Olympic Cottage:2.

Placing Stories in Layout View

The next step is to place the two stories from Story Editor into layout view. First you will place Untitled:1, and then you will place The Olympic Cottage:2.

Make sure Untitled:1 is on the screen and is active, as shown in Figure 10.12. Now you can place Untitled:1 in layout view.

Figure 10.12
Untitled:1 active in story view

Story is "active" because title bar is highlighted

Toolbox has been moved so you can see paragraph styles

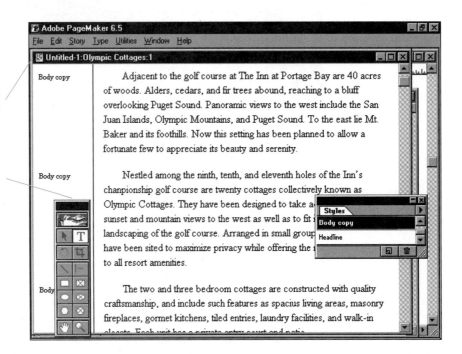

1. Select Edit Layout from the Edit menu.

2. Place the text icon  on the publication page near the upper-left corner and click.

3. Remove the windowshades by clicking outside the text block.

Now place The Olympic Cottage:2 as a second story; first select it, and then place it.

4. Point to Untitled-1 in the Window menu, and then click The Olympic Cottage:2.

Your view switches to Story Editor with The Olympic Cottage:2 selected.

5. Select Edit Layout from the Edit menu.

6. Place the text icon  below the existing text and click.

You have placed two stories. To verify that they are indeed two stories and not one, use the pointer tool from the Toolbox. Click one of the top three paragraphs. Notice that the windowshade defines these paragraphs as one text block. Click outside the windowshade. Click the last paragraph. Again, the windowshade appears around the text block. In layout view, you have two stories or text blocks.

Earlier in the chapter you used the spelling checker on the paragraph you typed. Because you can't assume that imported text is error-free, you should always run the spelling checker on any document you import. Recall that the spelling checker is in the Utilities menu.

**7.** Click the Utilities menu.

Notice that the Spelling option is unavailable in layout view. The spelling checker is available only in Story Editor. You need to return to story view to spell-check the entire document:

**8.** Select Edit Story from the Edit menu.

This moves you to Story Editor.

**9.** Select Spelling from the Utilities menu. The Spelling dialog box opens.

**10.** Click All stories in the Search story section.

**11.** Click Start, and correct any spelling errors you find.

**12.** When you're done, close the Spelling dialog box.

It's always a good idea to check imported text for spelling errors rather than to assume it is error-free.

It will be better to combine the two text blocks (or stories) into one for ease of handling. This process was first introduced in Chapter 4 and was repeated in Chapter 6. Recall that the technique involves first selecting and cutting one of the text blocks, clicking an insertion point in the other text block, and pasting the cut text into it. You must be in layout view to combine the text blocks.

**13.** On your own, switch to layout view.

**14.** Adjust the view so you can see the last paragraph at 75% Size. You should be able to see some of the third paragraph.

**15.** Select the text tool **T** in the Toolbox.

**16.** Move the I-beam to the beginning of the last paragraph. Click an insertion point and drag the I-beam over the paragraph to select it.

**17.** Delete the paragraph by selecting Cut from the Edit menu.

**18.** Move the I-beam to the end of the first text block. Click an insertion point.

**19.** Select Paste from the Edit menu.

**20.** Click the I-beam after the word *patio* (between the two joined text blocks).

**21.** Press $\boxed{\text{← ENTER}}$.

Now you have combined the two text blocks into one and still have four paragraphs. Verify that you have one text block.

**22.** Click the pointer tool  in the Toolbox.

$\boxed{\text{CTRL}}\boxed{0}$ **23.** Adjust the view to Fit in Window.

**24.** Click the Greeked text.

You should see the windowshades around the complete document.

## USING FIND AND CHANGE

Story Editor also has a feature that allows you to find specific text and change it to other text or another style, such as bold or italic. You will use the Find and Change commands in Story Editor to find every occurrence of *Olympic Cottages* in the body text and change the style to italic. The headline will remain bold and will not be changed to italic.

$\boxed{\text{CTRL}}\boxed{E}$ **1.** Select Edit Story from the Edit menu.

$\boxed{\text{CTRL}}\boxed{H}$ **2.** Select Change from the Utilities menu.

The Change dialog box appears.

**3.** Click Char attributes. See Figure 10.13.

**Figure 10.13**
**Change dialog box in story view**

Click to open Change Character Attributes dialog box

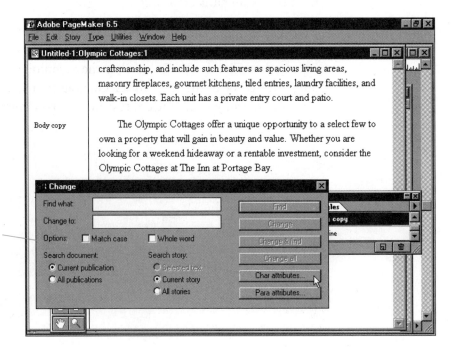

The Change Character Attributes dialog box appears. You'll set the text to find at 14 point, which matches the Body copy style.

**4.** In the Find what section, click the Size down arrow and select 14.

**5.** In the Find what section, select Normal as the Type style.

**6.** In the Change to section, select Italic as the Type style. See Figure 10.14.

**Figure 10.14**
**Change Character**
**Attributes dialog box**

Change the size to match
Body copy specifications

Select this attribute to find

Select this attribute to
change to

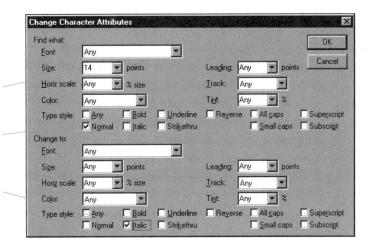

**7.** Click OK.

You return to the Change dialog box.

**8.** Click an insertion point in the Find what box.

**9.** Type *Olympic Cottages*. See Figure 10.15.

**Figure 10.15**
**Changing text from**
**normal to italic**

Type the text you want to
change

Click to change all
instances of *Olympic
Cottages* in 14 point to
italic

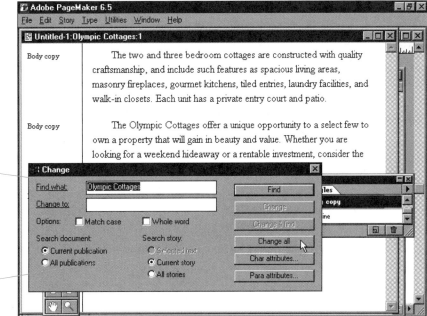

**10.** Click Change all.

All instances of *Olympic Cottages* in the Body copy style change to italic.

**11.** On your own, close the Change dialog box.

Look for the phrase *Olympic Cottages* in the story and notice that the words are in italic.

CTRL E **12.** On your own, switch to layout view.

Look at the text to verify that the style changes also appear in layout view.

**Other Word Processing Features**

Cursor-control keys are another feature of word processors. They allow you to move the insertion point quickly around the document, up and down a screen, and to the beginning or end of a line or sentence. Story Editor's cursor-control keys are summarized in Figure 10.16. These keys also work in layout view.

**Figure 10.16**
**Cursor-control keys**

| Key | Action |
|---|---|
| HOME | Go to beginning of line |
| END | Go to end of line |
| CTRL HOME | Go to beginning of sentence |
| CTRL END | Go to end of sentence |

CTRL E **1.** Switch to story view.

**2.** Click an insertion point anywhere in the story.

**3.** On your own, use the cursor-control keys to move around the document.

CTRL E **4.** On your own, use the cursor-control keys to move around the document in layout view.

The Control palette, which you used in layout view in earlier chapters, also works in story view.

CTRL E **5.** Return to story view.

 **6.** Select Show Control Palette from the Window menu.

Notice that the Control palette works in both the character and paragraph views.

**7.** Click an insertion point and select some words of text.

**8.** On your own, experiment with some of the Control palette options while in story view.

Remember, you won't be able to see all the style changes you make with the Control palette while you are in story view. When you are done, undo any changes you made, and return to layout view.

To complete the document, you will import a TIF file named Cottages and place it at the bottom of the publication page.

1. Click the pointer tool in the Toolbox.

2. Adjust your view so you can see the empty space at the end of the page.

CTRL D

3. Select Place from the File menu to open the Place dialog box.

4. Click Cottages.

5. Verify that As independent graphic is selected.

6. Click Open. If you get a message indicating how much space the graphic would occupy in your file, click Yes.

7. Drag the graphic icon diagonally below the text to fill the available space. Use the pointer tool to resize the graphic if needed.

8. Click the pointer tool to deselect the graphic.

CTRL S and CTRL P

9. Save and print your publication.

SHIFT CTRL S

10. Use Save As to save the publication as a smaller file.

You final publication will look like Figure 10.1.

## SUMMARY

Story Editor provides a faster, more powerful way to edit text than in layout view. Within Story Editor you can type text, check for spelling errors, and search for and replace text or styles. You can import text from other word processors in story view and format text using the Styles palette and the Control palette. Story Editor makes it easier for you to work with text.

## QUESTIONS

1. List the features of Story Editor.

2. What are the advantages of word processing in story view rather than in layout view?

3. What can't you do in story view?

4. What can't you do in layout view?

Using Help, answer the following questions.

5. Select Shortcuts from the Help menu and click Story. List the shortcut keys for the following:

   a. Edit Story/Edit Layout (toggle)

   b. Close current story window only

    c. Close all open stories in pub

    d. Cascade all open stories in all open pubs

    e. Tile all open stories in all open pubs

    f. Check spelling

    g. Change

    h. Find

    i. Find next

6. What is an Adobe Common User Interface (ACUI)? What are the changed shortcuts that are ACUIs? *Hint:* Click the Changed Shortcuts tab.

## PROJECTS

1. Using Story Editor, type the text shown in Figure 10.17. Complete the publication so that it looks like Figure 10.17.

**Figure 10.17**
Project 10.1—Typing a publication

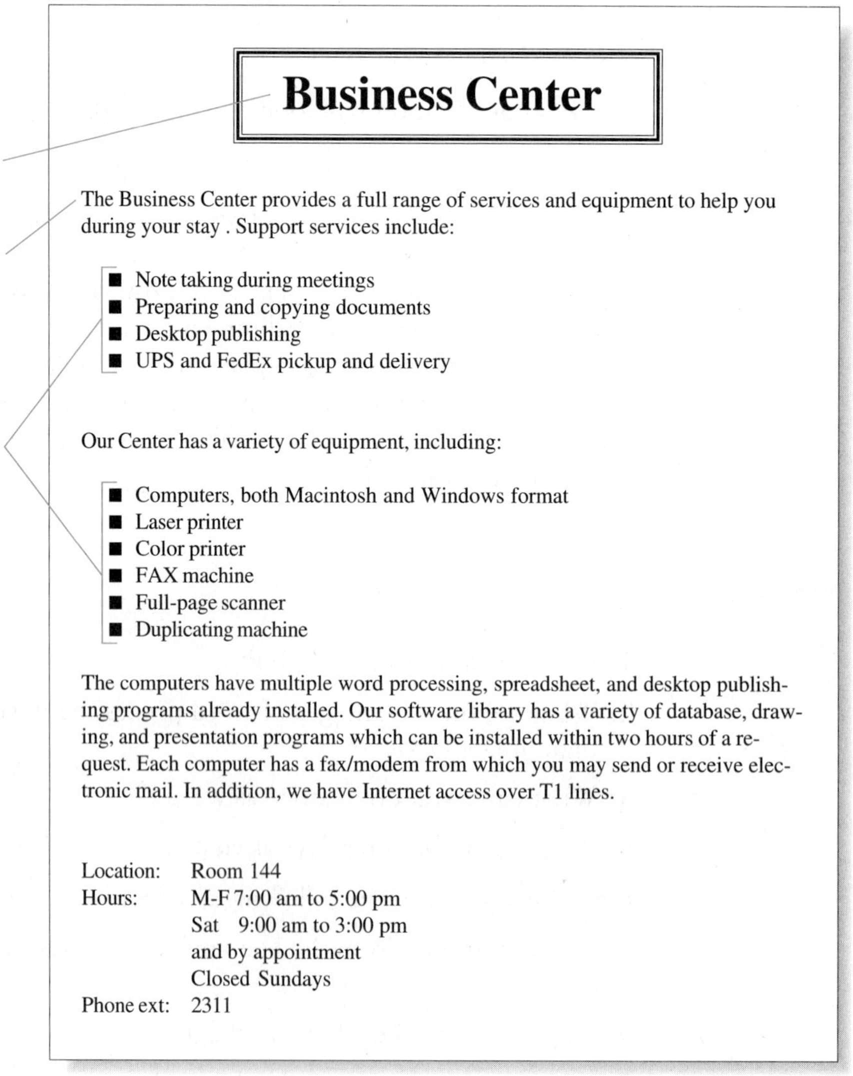

Times New Roman bold 30 pt

Times New Roman 14 pt

Use Bullets and Numbering

# Business Center

The Business Center provides a full range of services and equipment to help you during your stay . Support services include:

- Note taking during meetings
- Preparing and copying documents
- Desktop publishing
- UPS and FedEx pickup and delivery

Our Center has a variety of equipment, including:

- Computers, both Macintosh and Windows format
- Laser printer
- Color printer
- FAX machine
- Full-page scanner
- Duplicating machine

The computers have multiple word processing, spreadsheet, and desktop publishing programs already installed. Our software library has a variety of database, drawing, and presentation programs which can be installed within two hours of a request. Each computer has a fax/modem from which you may send or receive electronic mail. In addition, we have Internet access over T1 lines.

| | |
|---|---|
| Location: | Room 144 |
| Hours: | M-F 7:00 am to 5:00 pm |
| | Sat   9:00 am to 3:00 pm |
| | and by appointment |
| | Closed Sundays |
| Phone ext: | 2311 |

2. Using Story Editor, type the text shown Figure 10.18. Complete the publication so that it looks like Figure 10.18.

**Figure 10.18**
Project 10.2—Creating
a publication

Times New Roman bold
30 pt

Times New Roman 14 pt

Golf

# Portage Pro Shops

The Inn at Portage Bay has a set of Pro Shops designed to meet your needs for tennis, bicycling, swimming and golf. Our sales staff includes experts who participate in the sports and know the technical specifications of the equipment. They can advise you on sales and help you make your individual, family or group stay more enjoyable.

In the tennis department, the shop carries a selection of rackets, balls, and apparel. We can string your new racket or restring your old racket with your choice of string. You may make reservations for courts, lessons, and the ball machine in the shop. In addition, our staff can help you organize a tournament for your group.

In the bicycle department, we have bicycles available for rental. Enjoy the nearby scenic trails at your own pace with a box lunch from the Portage Pub and a complimentary map. Bicycles may be rented for a half-day or on a daily basis. Discounts are available for rentals of three or more days.

In the swimwear department, we carry a full selection of famous name swimwear for men, women, and children. Also available are goggles, beach towels, and sand toys.

Our golf department has golf balls, gloves and apparel available for purchase. You may rent clubs, arrange for lessons, and make reservations for tee times in the Pro Shop. We can help you organize a golf tournament for your group. Packages are available for golf club rental, lessons, and greens fee.

No matter what your needs, our professional staff can assist you. Hours are 10 - 5 weekdays and 11 - 5 weekends.

3. Use the brochure you worked on in Chapter 6 (Project 6.6, Figure 6.45), or open Brochure 1, a PageMaker template. Select blocks of text and change them in Story Editor so that the brochure matches Figure 10.19, on the next page. Place the photo named Beach and the graphic named Crab. Save and print the publication.

4. Open the publication you created in this chapter. Use the Find and Change commands to change all occurrences of the phrase *The Inn at Portage Bay* to bold. Save and print the publication. *Note:* Use Save As to reduce the size of the saved file.

5. Open the publication you created in this chapter. Use the Find and Change commands to change all occurrences of the phrase *The Inn at Portage Bay* to Arial. Save and print the publication. *Note:* Use Save As to reduce the size of the saved file.

Figure 10.19
Project 10.3—Creating a Brochure

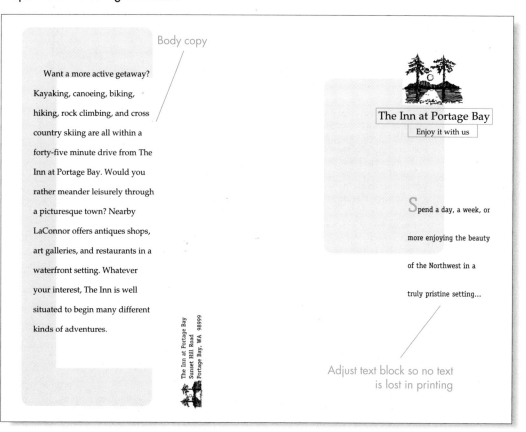

Body copy

Want a more active getaway? Kayaking, canoeing, biking, hiking, rock climbing, and cross country skiing are all within a forty-five minute drive from The Inn at Portage Bay. Would you rather meander leisurely through a picturesque town? Nearby LaConnor offers antiques shops, art galleries, and restaurants in a waterfront setting. Whatever your interest, The Inn is well situated to begin many different kinds of adventures.

The Inn at Portage Bay
Sunset Hill Road
Portage Bay, WA 98999

The Inn at Portage Bay
Enjoy it with us

Spend a day, a week, or more enjoying the beauty of the Northwest in a truly pristine setting...

Adjust text block so no text is lost in printing

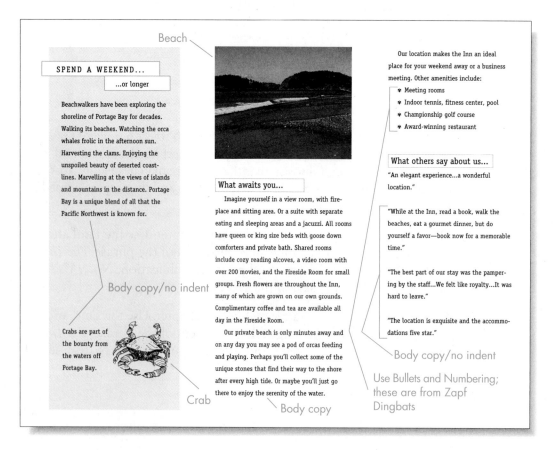

Beach

SPEND A WEEKEND...
...or longer

Beachwalkers have been exploring the shoreline of Portage Bay for decades. Walking its beaches. Watching the orca whales frolic in the afternoon sun. Harvesting the clams. Enjoying the unspoiled beauty of deserted coast-lines. Marvelling at the views of islands and mountains in the distance. Portage Bay is a unique blend of all that the Pacific Northwest is known for.

Body copy/no indent

Crabs are part of the bounty from the waters off Portage Bay.

Crab

What awaits you...

Imagine yourself in a view room, with fire-place and sitting area. Or a suite with separate eating and sleeping areas and a jacuzzi. All rooms have queen or king size beds with goose down comforters and private bath. Shared rooms include cozy reading alcoves, a video room with over 200 movies, and the Fireside Room for small groups. Fresh flowers are throughout the Inn, many of which are grown on our own grounds. Complimentary coffee and tea are available all day in the Fireside Room.

Our private beach is only minutes away and on any day you may see a pod of orcas feeding and playing. Perhaps you'll collect some of the unique stones that find their way to the shore after every high tide. Or maybe you'll just go there to enjoy the serenity of the water.

Body copy

Our location makes the Inn an ideal place for your weekend away or a business meeting. Other amenities include:

♣ Meeting rooms
♣ Indoor tennis, fitness center, pool
♣ Championship golf course
♣ Award-winning restaurant

What others say about us...
"An elegant experience...a wonderful location."

"While at the Inn, read a book, walk the beaches, eat a gourmet dinner, but do yourself a favor—book now for a memorable time."

"The best part of our stay was the pamper-ing by the staff...We felt like royalty...It was hard to leave."

"The location is exquisite and the accommo-dations five star."

Body copy/no indent

Use Bullets and Numbering; these are from Zapf Dingbats

# CHAPTER 11

# Assembling Publications into a Book

Upon completion of this chapter you will be able to:

- List the steps necessary to create a book
- Mark index entries
- Create cross-references in an index
- Open multiple publications at the same time
- Assemble a book list
- Compile an index for a book
- Develop a table of contents
- Print a book

PageMaker automates much of the work involved in producing the camera-ready copy for a book or other long publication. Simply stated (and for our purposes), a **book** is a series of related PageMaker publications that together create a long document. Once you've listed all the publications that are part of the book, creating an index and table of contents, and accurately numbering the pages requires just a few clicks of the mouse. PageMaker makes these usually tedious tasks easy.

The most important step in creating a successful book is careful planning, which will help make the process of assembling the book much simpler. First, you should determine the overall design and layout of the book and each publication to ensure consistency throughout the finished document. Then you can create a template and master pages for the book with design elements common to every page. Next, you should decide which styles, such as Headline or Subhead 1, will appear in the table of contents, and specify that those styles are defined to be included in the TOC (table of contents). With your planning complete, you're ready to create the book.

Creating a book is a multistep process. First, you must create the publications that will be part of the book. For each publication, open the book template, insert or remove pages as needed, create the publication, save it as a PageMaker publication, and then use the Index Entry command to identify which terms will appear in the index. Second, create empty publications for the table of contents and for the index. Third, assemble all the publications, including the table of contents and index publications, into a book list. Fourth, use the Create Index and Create TOC commands to compile a complete index and accurate table of contents. Finally, print the book.

As you can see, creating a book is more complex than merely creating a publication. But with careful planning, PageMaker will make the generation of an index and table of contents, the accurate numbering of pages, and printing the entire book easier and less time-consuming.

## THE EMPLOYEE BENEFITS BOOK

In this chapter you will create the Employee Benefits book shown in Figure 11.1. This book will contain four publications: a table of contents, a publication with three pages, a publication with two pages, and an index. You will start by exploring the Styles palettes and marking index entries for the two existing publications—Benefit 1 and Benefit 2. Next you will use the Benefit Template to create two empty publications: the index and the table of contents. Then you will assemble a book list in the index and copy the list into the rest of the publications, use PageMaker to generate the index and table of contents, and save these two publications. Finally, you will print the book.

Figure 11.1
Employee Benefits book

Create using the
PageMaker
Create TOC
command

Benefit 1.p65
3 pages

Benefit 2.p65
2 pages

Create using
the PageMaker
Create Index
command

The process and skills presented for this short book are the same as needed for longer books, whose publications might be produced by multiple people. For example, different authors might write chapters for the book, but they would all base their publications on the same template, which includes master pages and a Styles palette. An editor could revise the documents for style and consistency. Another person could take responsibility for indexing the complete publication; good indexing requires special skills. As you can see, assembling a long book would complete the same steps as a short book, but the project would be more complex.

## Exploring the Styles Palette for Benefit 1

The main text for the Employee Benefits book is stored in two publications: Benefit 1.p65 and Benefit 2.p65. Both publications were created from the Benefit Template and thus have the same style sheet. You will explore the style sheet for Benefit 1.

1. Start the PageMaker program and if necessary place the Styles palette on the Pasteboard.

2. Open Benefit 1.

Look at the Pasteboard and notice that the Styles palette contains three styles: Body text, Headline, and Subhead 1. Begin by exploring the Body text style.

3. Press (CTRL) and click Body text.

Figure 11.2 shows the Style Options dialog box. Look at the specifications for Body text. Notice that this style is not set up to be included in the table of contents.

**Figure 11.2**
Style Options dialog box
for Body text

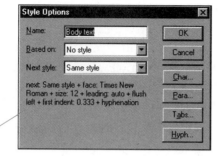

*incl TOC is not part of
the Body text style*

**4.** Click Para.

Figure 11.3 shows the Paragraph Specifications dialog box for Body text. Again, note that the Include in table of contents option is not selected.

**Figure 11.3**
Paragraph Specifications
dialog box for Body text

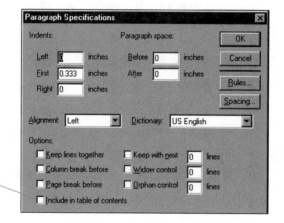

*Include in table of
contents is not selected*

**5.** Click Cancel to return to the Style Options dialog box.

**6.** Click Cancel to return to the publication window.

Now explore the Headline style.

**7.** Press CTRL and click Headline.

**8.** Click Para.

Note that the Include in table of contents option is not selected for this style.

**9.** Click Cancel to return to the Style Options dialog box.

**10.** Click Cancel to return to the publication window.

Finally, explore the Subhead 1 style.

**11.** Press CTRL and click Subhead 1.

**12.** Click Para.

Notice that the Include in table of contents option is selected in the Paragraph Specifications dialog box for Subhead 1.

**13.** On your own, return to the publication window.

Because the Include in table of contents option was selected only for Subhead 1, any text using the Subhead 1 style will be included in the table of contents when you click Create TOC from the Utilities menu, which you will do later in this chapter. The other two styles—Body text and Headline—will not be included in the table of contents. On your own, select the text tool and click different text elements to see which are in the Subhead 1 style.

## CREATING INDEX ENTRIES

PageMaker has a powerful indexing feature that simplifies the process of creating an index. You select the words you want included in the index, and PageMaker keeps track of the page references and compiles the index for you.

Although PageMaker will automate the clerical steps for creating an index, a person must select the proper references for a topic. Thus, the difficulty in creating an index in PageMaker is not in marking entries, but in selecting appropriate entries. Have you ever looked up a topic in an index but didn't find an entry because that topic was referenced by another word? Unfortunately, there are no computer tools available to completely automate indexing.

As with the book, good indexing requires planning. Perhaps a logical place to start is to look at some good and some bad indexes, and try to determine what works and what doesn't work. Then you can apply what you've learned to your own index. You should also allot time to review and evaluate the references you choose for the index. One helpful strategy is to highlight the words and phrases you plan to include in the index on a hard copy of a publication.

When you create your own index, expect to fill approximately 5 to 10 index pages per every 100 text pages. For each 5 pages of text, you should allow about 1 hour for indexing. Using these guidelines, a 100-page book would require 5 to 10 index pages and about 20 hours to complete the indexing process. The actual amount of time needed will vary depending on the complexity of the book and the skill of the indexer.

PageMaker allows you to create three levels of index entries with page references and has the power to cross-reference topics. For this project, you will index all the subheadings and several other words within the text as page references, using one level of entry, and add a cross-reference.

In a more complex book, your index topics may have second- and third-level subtopics related to the primary topic.

Figure 11.4 illustrates three different levels in an index.

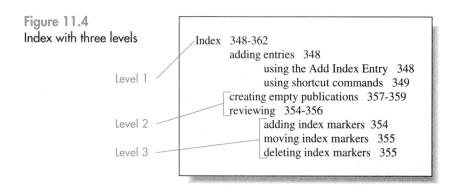

**Figure 11.4**
Index with three levels

Level 1

Level 2

Level 3

**Adding a Page Reference**

You'll begin by marking the words and phrases in the publication that will have page references in the index. Figure 11.5 shows the Benefit 1 publication with the planned page reference index entries highlighted.

**Figure 11.5**
Pages 2–4 of Employee Benefits book with index entries highlighted

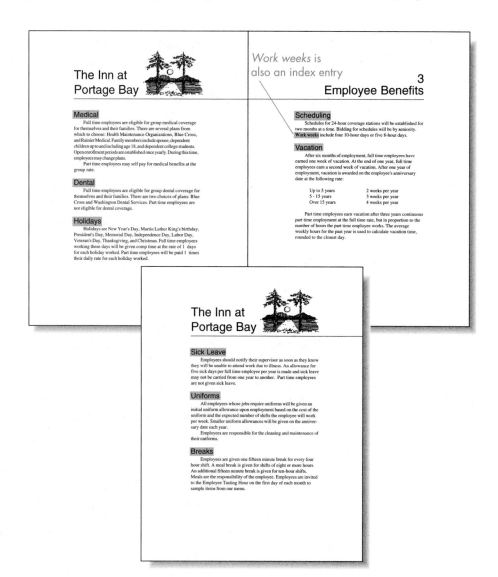

The first word to add an index entry for is *Medical*, the first heading in the document.

1. Click the page 2 icon, if necessary.

2. Adjust the view so you can see the area of text around *Medical*.

3. Click the text tool **T** in the Toolbox.

4. Double-click *Medical* to select it.

CTRL Y
5. Select Index Entry from the Utilities menu.

The Add Index Entry dialog box appears, as shown in Figure 11.6. You will use all the defaults, which indicate that the entry is a page reference for the topic Medical on the current page.

**Figure 11.6**
Add Index Entry dialog box

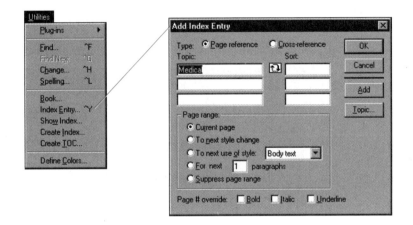

6. Click OK.

Now you'll add an index entry for *Dental*, using shortcut keys.

7. Select the subheading *Dental*.

8. Press CTRL Y.

9. Press ↵ ENTER to accept all the defaults and return to the publication window.

You'll continue to add other page reference index entries. Add an index entry for each highlighted word and phrase shown in Figure 11.5.

10. On your own, add index entries for *Holidays, Scheduling, Vacation, Sick Leave, Uniforms,* and *Breaks,* as well as the phrase *Work weeks.* Adjust the view as necessary.

You have marked a page reference index entry for all the headings—*Medical, Dental, Holidays, Scheduling, Vacation, Sick Leave, Uniforms,* and *Breaks*—as well as for the phrase *Work weeks.* Next, you will cross-reference the word *Illness* to *Sick Leave.*

Adding a
Cross-reference

Cross-referencing allows you to list one topic under multiple titles in the index. A **cross-reference** lists the different words a person might use to look up a topic in the index with a reference, or pointer, to the index entry that contains the page references. In our example, the Employee Benefits book calls one section Sick Leave. Because someone might look for this topic under *Illness*, you will create a cross-reference for *Illness* that lists "*See* Sick Leave." Because *Sick Leave* is the primary reference, that entry will have the page number. In a more complex book, there might be several logical ways in which a person would look up a topic in an index. A skilled indexer will include enough terms and cross-references to help the reader easily locate information without making the index so large it is unwieldy.

You'll add a cross-reference with the word *illness*.

1. Select *illness* from page 4 of the publication, as shown in Figure 11.7.

**Figure 11.7**
Selecting *illness* for cross-referencing

Word to cross-reference

Look on page 4

CTRL Y

2. Select Index Entry from the Utilities menu.

3. Replace the *i* in *illness* with a capital *I*.

4. Click Cross-reference under the title bar.

Five options for the wording of the cross-reference appear.

**5.** Click See, as shown in Figure 11.8.

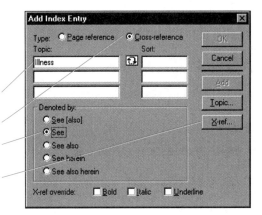

**6.** Click X-ref.

The Select Cross-Reference Topic dialog box appears, as shown in Figure 11.9.

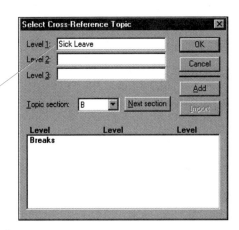

**7.** Type *Sick Leave* in the Level 1 box (refer to Figure 11.9).

**8.** Click OK to return to the Add Index Entry dialog box.

**9.** Click OK.

You return to the publication window. The cross-reference is complete.

You can also type a different index title for the entry rather than use the text you selected in the publication. For example, the phrase *maintenance of their uniforms* appears within the Uniforms section. Although you will select this text in the publication, you'll revise the topic so *Uniform maintenance* appears as the entry in the index.

**1.** Select *maintenance of their uniforms,* as shown in Figure 11.10.

**Figure 11.10**
*Selecting maintenance of their uniforms*

Select this phrase

Look on page 4

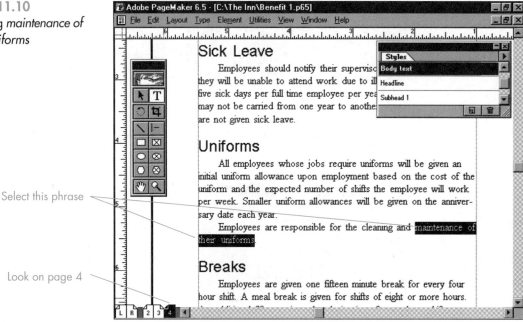

**2.** Select Index Entry from the Utilities menu.

CTRL Y

**3.** Type *Uniform maintenance* as the Topic. See Figure 11.11.

**Figure 11.11**
*Typing an index entry topic*

Type *Uniform maintenance* as new topic

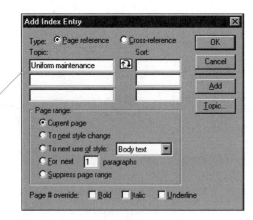

**4.** Click OK.

**5.** On your own, add an index entry for *comp time* on page 2 of the publication, but change the Topic to *Comp time.*

**6.** On your own, add an additional index entry for *Sick Leave* on page 4 of the publication, but change the Topic to *Leaves*.

With some words marked for the index, you can look at the entries.

## LOOKING AT THE INDEX

You have identified many index topics for the Benefit 1 publication. There are two ways you can review the index at this point. The first is from story view; the second is with the Show Index command.

**Story View**

Within story view you can see which text has been indexed by looking for the index markers ◨ in the text. You can add index markers with the Copy and Paste commands, move them with the Cut and Paste commands, and delete them with the Cut command. For now, you will look at the text you have been working with, but you will not make any changes.

**1.** Click an insertion point anywhere in the document.

CTRL E

**2.** Select Edit Story from the Edit menu.

**3.** If necessary, scroll until you see indexed text. Figure 11.12 shows three index entries in story view.

**Figure 11.12**
**Examining index entries in story view**

Toolbox and Styles palette have been removed so you can see the index entries

Index entries show with ◨

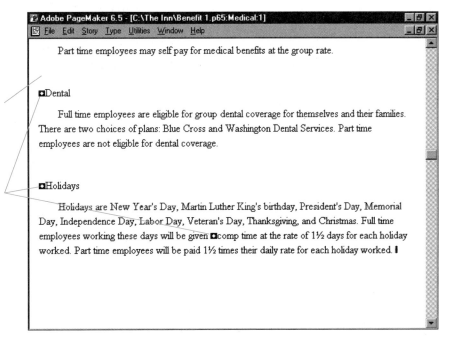

**4.** On your own, return to layout view.

Viewing the publication in story view allows you to look at the text from beginning to end and see which topics are indexed. This is useful when you are changing the index or editing the text.

## Show Index Command

The Show Index command allows you to review and edit the index prior to creating a final version. You'll review the index now.

**1.** Select Show Index from the Utilities menu.

The Show Index dialog box appears, as shown in Figure 11.13.

**Figure 11.13**
**Show Index dialog box**

Click Next section to proceed through the list

Shows cross-reference topic

First letter of index entries in this section

Shows page references for entries

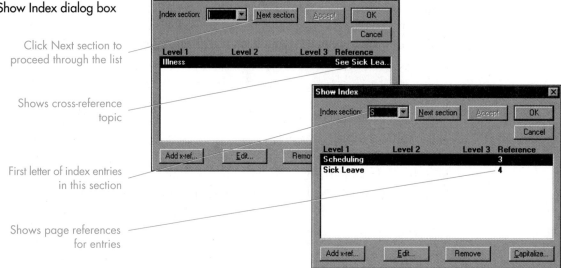

The options in this dialog box allow you to display the next alphabetical section having at least one entry (Next section), add a cross-reference (Add x-ref), change an index entry (Edit), delete index entries from an index (Remove), capitalize the selected entry (Capitalize), and accept changes while keeping the Show Index dialog box open (Accept). You won't do any of these right now, so you'll close the dialog box.

**2.** Click Cancel to exit the Show Index dialog box.

You can review your index at any time using either story view or the Show Index command.

## Saving the Indexed Publication

Before you continue, you will save this publication with all the index entries you marked with a different file name.

**1.** Select Save As from the File menu.

**2.** Type *Benefit 1 Indexed* as the new file name.

You have indexed one publication—Benefit 1 Indexed—which is open in your publication window.

The Employee Benefits book will also use a second publication (Benefit 2), which must also be indexed. You will open and index this file using the steps you learned in the first part of this chapter, without closing Benefit 1 Indexed.

With PageMaker you have the ability to **open multiple publications** at the same time. When you select the Open command in the File menu for a new publication, all other opened publications remain open.

You'll open Benefit 2, without closing Benefit 1 Indexed. Then you'll arrange the two publications on your screen.

CTRL O

1. Open Benefit 2.

2. Select Cascade from the Window menu.

Now you see two title bars, one for each open publication. Only one publication is active at a time, as indicated by the highlighted title bar. To switch from one publication to another, simply click the title bar or click within the publication you want to make active. To restore the cascaded configuration, again select Cascade from the Window menu. In the projects at the end of the chapter, you will experiment with multiple open publications.

Next, using Figure 11.14 and the steps you learned earlier as a guide, index Benefit 2 and save it with a new file name.

**Figure 11.14**
Benefit 2 with index entries highlighted

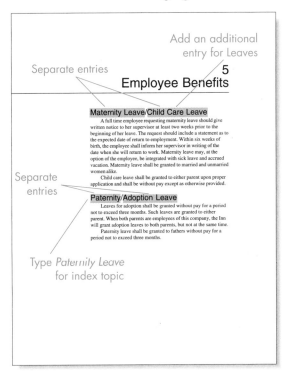
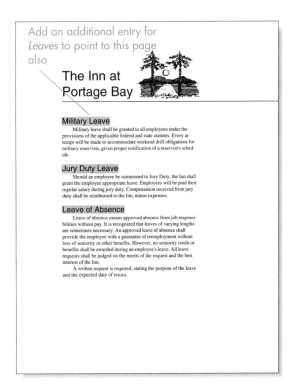

CTRL Y

3. On your own, create the index entries for Benefit 2 highlighted in Figure 11.14.

**4.** Save the indexed publication as Benefit 2 Indexed.

With all the index entries marked for the Employee Benefits book, you are ready to have PageMaker compile the index and table of contents.

## CREATING NEW PUBLICATIONS FOR THE INDEX AND TABLE OF CONTENTS

PageMaker will compile an index and a table of contents for you, but you first have to create empty publications so you have somewhere to put them. To create these two publications, start with the same template that was used to create the other Employee Benefits publications: Benefit Template. Because this is a short book, the table of contents and index will each be only one page.

CTRL O

**1.** Open a copy of Benefit Template.

Notice that the template has two pages, but the table of contents and index will each need only one. You will remove page 2.

**2.** Select Remove Pages from the Layout menu.

You want to remove pages 2 through 2.

**3.** Type 2 in the Remove page(s) box.

**4.** Press TAB once.

**5.** Type 2 in the through box.

**6.** Click OK.

PageMaker will ask if you want to remove the pages and their contents.

**7.** Click OK.

Now save the one-page publication twice, once for the table of contents and once for the index.

CTRL S

**8.** Save the publication as Benefit TOC.

The index will fit on one page only if the entries are placed in two columns, so you need to change the layout to a two-column page.

**9.** Click the page 1 icon (if necessary).

**10.** Select Column Guides from the Layout menu.

**11.** Type 2 in the Number of columns box.

**12.** Click OK.

Now you can save the modified file for the index with a new file name.

SHIFT CTRL S

**13.** On your own, save the publication as Benefit Index.

You've just created two new files, one for the one-page table of contents, and one for the one-page, two-column index.

PageMaker can do four tasks for a book: create an index, create a table of contents, update the page numbers, and print the book. Recall that a book is a set of related PageMaker publications, which you specify in a **book list**. You must create a book list in every publication from which you want to do any of these tasks. The simplest way to do this is to create the book list once, for example in the index, and copy that book list to all the publications inserted into the book list, for example to the Benefit TOC, Benefit 1 Indexed, and Benefit 2 Indexed publications. You can print the entire book from any publication that has the book list.

Typically, the page number of the index is listed in the table of contents. In order to have an Index heading to include in the table of contents, you'll create the index first and the table of contents second.

## Creating the Book List

Currently, the index, Benefit Index, should be the active publication window. If necessary, make that publication window active so you can create the book list in it.

1. Select Book from the Utilities menu.

The Book Publication List dialog box appears, as shown in Figure 11.15. Notice that the current publication is already part of the list.

**Figure 11.15**
**Book Publication List dialog box**

Insert these three files into the book list

Click to move selected file into the book list

Current publication is automatically included in the book list

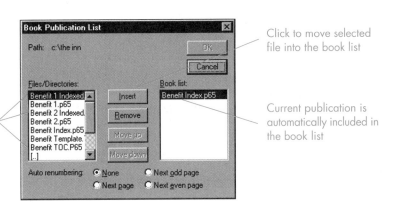

2. Click Benefit 1 Indexed in the Files/Directories box to select it if necessary.

3. Click Insert.

Notice that Benefit 1 Indexed becomes part of the book list.

4. On your own, insert Benefit 2 Indexed and Benefit TOC into the book list.

Your list should have four PageMaker publications in the book list, but they are not in the correct order for the book. The correct order is:

- Benefit TOC
- Benefit 1 Indexed
- Benefit 2 Indexed
- Benefit Index

The publications must be listed in the book list in the order in which you want them to print. This will ensure that PageMaker numbers the pages consecutively. You'll move the publications to the correct locations in the book list.

**5.** In the Book list box, click the name of the publication you want to move to highlight it.

**6.** Click Move up or Move down, as appropriate.

**7.** On your own, move publications up or down in the book list until your book list matches the one in Figure 11.16.

**Figure 11.16**
**Book list in correct order**

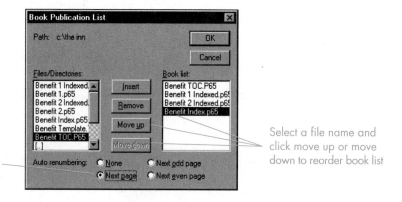

Select so PageMaker will number the book with consecutive page numbers

Select a file name and click move up or move down to reorder book list

PageMaker can number the pages from 1 through the last page of the book. You can tell PageMaker to do this from the Book Publication List dialog box.

**8.** Click the Next page option in the Auto renumbering section.

**9.** Click OK.

PageMaker will tell you that Auto renumbering is selected and ask if you want to update the page numbers of all publications in the book now.

**10.** Click Yes.

Now that the page numbers are updated, reflecting the order of the publications in the book list, you're ready to compile the index.

**Compiling the Index**

With all the entries marked and the book list in place, compiling the index takes just a few clicks of the mouse. PageMaker does the rest of the work.

CTRL + O

**1.** If necessary, adjust the view to Fit in Window.

**2.** Select Create Index from the Utilities menu.

You'll accept all the defaults in this dialog box.

**3.** Click OK.

PageMaker compiles the index. When it's done, a text icon appears so you can place the index story. Three new styles appear in the Styles palette—the default index styles. You will place the index and change the default styles to conform to those of the Employee Benefits book.

**4.** Position the text icon  at the 2½-inch mark on the vertical ruler, as shown in Figure 11.17.

**Figure 11.17**
Placing the text icon

Open publications are cascaded in publication window

Position the text icon at the 2½-inch mark on the vertical ruler

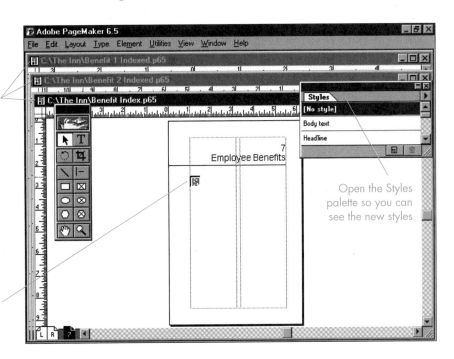

Open the Styles palette so you can see the new styles

**5.** Click to place the index.

The full index is about twice the length of the index from *A* to *L*. Breaking the columns after the *L* entries will make the two columns approximately the same length, as shown in Figure 11.18.

**6.** Drag the windowshade handle up to the bottom of the *L* entries.

**7.** Click the triangle symbol ▼ in the windowshade loop. A text icon appears.

**8.** Click the text icon at the top of the second column so it aligns with the *A* entries (refer to Figure 11.18).

The two columns of the index are placed. However, the Index heading is in the wrong style for the Employee Benefits book. You'll change the style of the word *Index*.

**9.** Double-click Index title in the Styles palette.

Notice that double-clicking a style name in the Styles palette is another way to open the Style Options dialog box.

**10.** Click Char, change the settings to Arial 24 point, Normal and click OK.

**Figure 11.18**
Completed index page

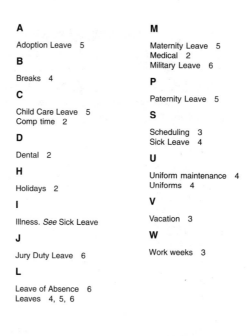

7
# Employee Benefits

## Index

**A**

Adoption Leave   5

**B**

Breaks   4

**C**

Child Care Leave   5
Comp time   2

**D**

Dental   2

**H**

Holidays   2

**I**

Illness. *See* Sick Leave

**J**

Jury Duty Leave   6

**L**

Leave of Absence   6
Leaves   4, 5, 6

**M**

Maternity Leave   5
Medical   2
Military Leave   6

**P**

Paternity Leave   5

**S**

Scheduling   3
Sick Leave   4

**U**

Uniform maintenance   4
Uniforms   4

**V**

Vacation   3

**W**

Work weeks   3

**11.** Click Para, change Alignment to Left, and click OK.

**12.** Click OK in the Style Options dialog box.

Because you've changed the size of the Index heading, which affects the placement of the entries in the first column, you need to verify the alignment of the entries in the two columns.

**13.** Pull a ruler guide from the horizontal ruler immediately below the title bar for Benefit Index to the baseline of the letter A in the first column.

**14.** Adjust the text block in the right column as necessary to align the baselines of the A and the M.

When you are satisfied with the placement of the index text, you should save the publication.

CTRL S

**15.** Select Save from the File menu.

When you save the index publication, you also save the book list. Whenever you open the index publication, you have the option of printing either the index alone or the entire book.

The steps to create the table of contents are similar to those used to create the index. First open the table of contents publication, and then make or copy the book list, create the table of contents, adjust the styles for some of the text, and, finally, save the table of contents publication.

Like an index, a good table of contents requires organization and planning. The organization for a table of contents is similar to an outline, where some topics are identified as major topics and others are subordinate topics. The planning is related to creating a Styles palette. As you define each style, such as Headline, Subhead 1, and Body text, you select whether to include any text tagged with that style in the table of contents. A good table of contents gives an overview of the publication and helps the reader navigate through the topics.

### Copying the Book List

PageMaker requires that a book list exist within every publication using a book feature. The table of contents and index are both book features, so they both need a book list. Rather than duplicate the steps to create the same book list in the table of contents as you created earlier in the index, you'll copy the book list from the index into all the publications in the book. This way, you can print the entire book from any publication, not just from the table of contents or index.

1. Press CTRL while you select Book from the Utilities menu.

PageMaker copies the book list into every publication in the list. Now you can open the Benefit TOC publication and have PageMaker compile the table of contents.

CTRL O

2. Open the Benefit TOC publication.

3. Select Create TOC from the Utilities menu.

The Create Table of Contents dialog box appears, as shown in Figure 11.19.

**Figure 11.19**
Create Table of Contents dialog box

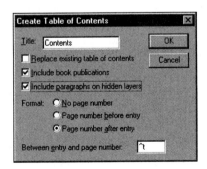

4. Click OK to accept the standard defaults.

The text icon appears and the Styles palette lists the default TOC styles.

**5.** Place the text icon ▤ at the 2½-inch mark on the vertical ruler, and click.

Next, you'll change the TOC title style to Arial Normal.

**6.** Double-click TOC title in the Styles palette to open the Style Options dialog box.

**7.** Click Char.

**8.** Change Type style to Normal.

**9.** Click OK to return to the Style Options dialog box.

**10.** Click OK to return to the publication window.

The last entry in the table of contents is the word *Index,* which is in a different style than the other entries. You'll change it to the TOC Subhead 1 style to match the other entries.

**11.** Click the text tool **T** in the Toolbox.

**12.** Click an insertion point in the word *Index.*

**13.** Click TOC Subhead 1 in the Styles palette.

All the entries in the table of contents now have the same style. The completed Contents page is shown in Figure 11.20.

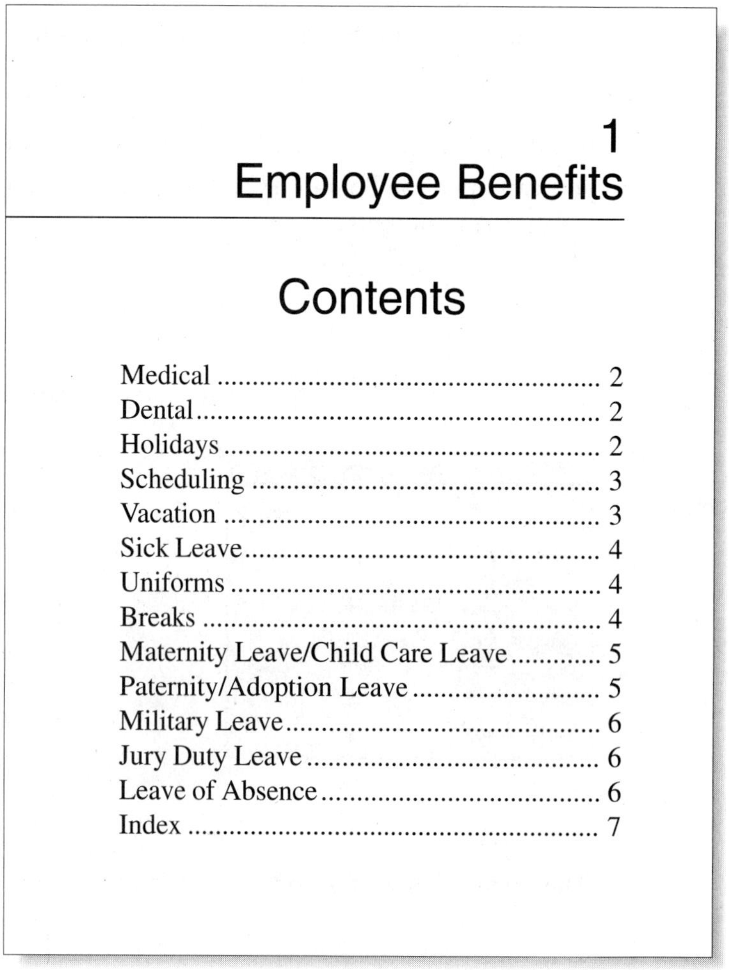

**Figure 11.20**
Completed Contents
page

Before printing the book, you should save the table of contents.

CTRL S

**14.** Select Save from the File menu.

Now that the Employee Benefits book is complete, you can print it.

## PRINTING THE BOOK

The last step is to print the book. This can be done from any publication in the book because they all have a book list. Because you have the table of contents publication open, you'll print the Employee Benefits book from there.

CTRL P

**1.** Select Print from the File menu.

The Print Document dialog box appears. It is set to print only the active publication. You'll change it to print the entire book.

**2.** Select the Print all publications in book option.

Your screen should match Figure 11.21.

**Figure 11.21**
**Print Document dialog box**

Select Print all publications in book

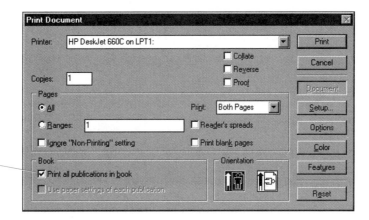

**3.** Click the Options button and select Printer's marks.

You want to print the book with printer's marks on the pages because the Employee Benefits publication is a nonstandard size. This way the printed copy shows the actual size of the final book. Your screen should match Figure 11.22.

**Figure 11.22**
**Print Options dialog box**

Select Printer's marks

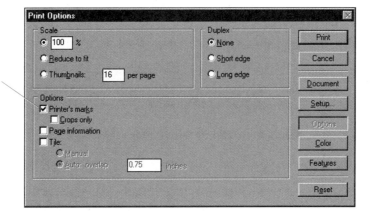

**4.** Click Print.

CTRL W

**5.** Close all your publications, saving each one.

Your finished, printed book should look like Figure 11.1.

## SUMMARY

Congratulations on publishing your first book! In the process of assembling a multiple publication into a book, you learned about the importance of planning for the book. In addition, you found out how PageMaker makes creating a book easier. PageMaker automates the process of creating an index and table of contents. You can check from the Styles palette whether a style is set to be included as a table of contents entry. You mark an index entry using the Index Entry command in the Utilities menu. Before creating an index or table of contents, you must create empty publications for each and assemble a book list. A book list contains all the PageMaker publications that will be included in a book. Printing an entire book is done from any publication that contains the book list.

## QUESTIONS

1. Why is it a good idea to plan before creating any documents for a book?

2. List the steps to follow to create a book.

3. How do you mark an entry for the table of contents?

4. Describe the process for marking an Index Entry.

5. The index you created has a page number after *Sick Leave* and a cross-reference after *Illness* (See *Sick Leave*). Why was *Sick Leave* chosen as the primary reference and *Illness* chosen as a cross-reference?

6. In cross-referencing, what is the indexer trying to do?

7. Explain the different things you can learn when you look at index entries in story view and with the Show Index command. When would you use the two options?

8. Why do you have to create an empty publication for the index and table of contents?

9. Why do you need to create a book list in both the table of contents and index?

10. From what publications can you print a book?

11. Using Help, answer the following questions.

    a. What does the ^t in the Create Table of Contents dialog box instruct PageMaker to do? (*Hint*: Select Create TOC from the Utilities menu. Write down the words to the left of ^t. In the Help menu, click Help Topics (or F1). Click the Find tab. Type the words. This hint gets you part of the way to the solution.)

    b. The maximum length of an index title is _____ characters.

    c. What is the maximum number of levels for cross-referencing a topic?

## PROJECTS

1. Use Benefit Template to create another two- to three-page publication to add to the book. Index the publication. Re-create the book with this additional publication.

2. Create a cover for the Employee Benefits book. Remember to use the Benefit Template, and print the publication using printer's marks.

3. This project illustrates the power of multiple open publications. Do the following.

    a. Open Benefit 1 Indexed and Benefit 2 Indexed.

    b. Tile (rather than Cascade) the two publication windows.

    c. Click the page 4 icon in Benefit 1 Indexed.

    d. Click the page 5 icon in Benefit 2 Indexed.

You are going to copy the Breaks section of page 4 to page 5. You will separate the Breaks section to make it a separate text block, using a technique you learned in Chapter 4.

    e. Using the pointer tool, click the text block on page 4.

    f. Move the windowshade up to the end of the Uniforms section.

    g. Click the triangle symbol in the windowshade loop.

    h. Place the text icon (containing the Breaks section) after the Uniforms section on page 4.

    i. Drag the Breaks text block from page 4 to page 5, placing it below Paternity/Adoption Leave.

Create a new index publication, including this altered Benefit 2 Indexed.

    j. Open Benefit Template.

    k. Remove page 2 of Benefit Template (this will be a one-page index).

    l. Create the index.

    m. Print the index.

    n. Save the index.

Look at the Breaks section of this index. Compare it to the one you created in the chapter. Notice in the new index that Breaks has two references: pages 4 and 5. Why?

4. Create one book made up of publications produced by a group of 3 to 5 students. Start by planning a book and creating a group template. Each student should create a one-page indexed publication for the book. Place all the PageMaker publications on one disk and copy the disk to a hard drive or file server. Create a table of contents and index for the book. Print the book.

# Using Adobe Table 3.0 and Linking Files

**Upon completion of this chapter you will be able to:**

- **Explain the purpose of the Adobe Table program**
- **Use Adobe Table to create, edit, enhance, and save a table**
- **Copy a table to a PageMaker publication**
- **Link a file to a PageMaker publication**

This chapter covers two separate but related skills: creating tables and linking files. Adobe Corporation provides an easy-to-use program, **Adobe Table 3.0**, that allows you to create tables for use in a PageMaker publication. Tables are effective ways to present such information as budgets, financial reports, schedules, price lists, directories, and invoices. You will also learn about linking external files to a PageMaker publication. Linking enables you to quickly and easily update text and graphics created with other programs.

Developing tables using Adobe Table is easier than using the publication window in PageMaker because you can have the program create the basic table structure. A **table** organizes information in **rows** and **columns**. The intersection of a row and a column is called a **cell**. Rows and columns can be inserted, deleted, and resized; numbers can be aligned on their decimal points; and text enhancements such as lines, colors, fonts, and type sizes can be used in Adobe Table. Figure 12.1 shows an example of a table.

**Figure 12.1**
**Example of a table**

| PORTAGE BAY PROPERTIES INCOME STATEMENT FORECAST | | | | |
|---|---|---|---|---|
| | 1998 | 1999 | 2000 | 2001 |
| Sales Revenue | 8,000,000 | 8,800,000 | 9,680,000 | 10,648,000 |
| Cost of Sales | 6,800,000 | 7,480,000 | 8,228,000 | 9,050,800 |
| Gross Profit | 1,200,000 | 1,320,000 | 1,452,000 | 1,597,200 |
| Expenses | | | | |
| Sales Commission | 410,000 | 451,000 | 496,100 | 545,710 |
| Operations | 220,000 | 242,000 | 266,200 | 292,820 |
| Administrative | 120,000 | 132,000 | 145,200 | 159,720 |
| Promotion | 300,000 | 330,000 | 363,000 | 399,300 |
| Total Expenses | 1,050,000 | 1,155,000 | 1,270,500 | 1,397,550 |
| Income Before Taxes | 150,000 | 165,000 | 181,500 | 199,650 |
| Income Taxes | 57,000 | 62,700 | 68,970 | 75,867 |
| Net Income | 93,000 | 102,300 | 112,530 | 123,783 |

Adobe Table is a separate program from PageMaker. In this way, Adobe Table is just like other spreadsheet, word processing, or paint programs used to create graphics or text that you place in a PageMaker publication. The difference is that Adobe Table comes packaged with PageMaker.

Another difference is that you cannot print from Adobe Table. Instead you must incorporate the table into a PageMaker publication. The process for incorporating a table into a publication is to load the Adobe Table program from the Windows screen and create the table. Then use either the Clipboard to copy the table to a publication page or the Place command to place the table on the page.

In this chapter you will use Adobe Table to create a table. Then you will copy it to a PageMaker publication.

**Getting Started with Adobe Table**

Because Adobe Table is a separate program from PageMaker, you can start it without having PageMaker open. The steps to start Adobe Table vary depending on the way your computer is set up.

1. Start the Adobe Table program.

When you start Adobe Table, the New Table dialog box appears because the program assumes you want to create a new table. For now, close this dialog box.

2. Click Cancel.

The Adobe Table window appears, as shown in Figure 12.2. If you see either the Text palette or Table palette onscreen, click the close button ☒ in the upper-right corner of the palette to hide it from view.

Figure 12.2
Adobe Table window

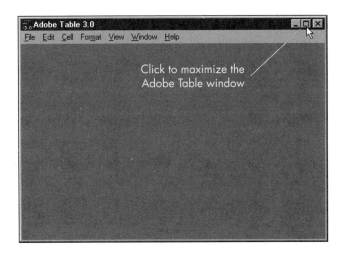

Click to maximize the
Adobe Table window

**3.** Click the maximize button to enlarge the Adobe Table window.

The components of the Adobe Table window are similar to the PageMaker publication window. A title bar shows the program name, Adobe Table 3.0, and a menu bar lists the seven menus. Take a moment to look at the contents of each menu.

**4.** Click each menu as you read the descriptions in Figure 12.3.

Figure 12.3
Adobe Table menus

| Menu | Description |
| --- | --- |
| File | Used to create new tables; open and close existing tables; import data into a table; and export the table to another program |
| Edit | Used to cut, copy, paste, clear, and select text and cells |
| Cell | Used to change column heights and row widths, insert and delete rows and columns, and group rows and columns |
| Format | Used to change fonts, type styles and sizes, leading, and text alignment, as well as the table layout, cell borders, and colors |
| View | Used to change the table view size and to turn on and off the display of screen components, such as rulers and tab markers |
| Window | Used to show and hide text and table palettes and change how windows are displayed. For example, if you have two tables open you can display them in a cascading arrangement |
| Help | Used to display Adobe Table Help screens |

Now that you know the basic components of Adobe Table, you can begin the table.

Just as planning makes creating a finished publication easier, planning streamlines the process of creating a finished table. Before starting a new table, you should take a moment to answer the following questions.

- **How many rows and columns are in the table?** The default settings are four rows and four columns. When you start a new table, you may want to change these settings. Later, when working on the table, you can insert and delete rows and columns as needed.

- **What is the overall table size?** The default settings are 4 inches for width and 2 inches for height. When you start a new table, you can change these settings. If you insert or delete rows or columns, the table size will increase or decrease accordingly. Changing the height of rows and the width of columns can also change the overall table size. Keep in mind the size of your publication page; the default PageMaker publication page, minus the margins, is 6¾ inches wide and 9½ inches high. You will want to keep your table smaller than the size of your publication page. However, you can also resize the table after you place or copy it to the publication page.

Figure 12.4 is a table, created in Adobe Table, that contains a one-month summary of the revenue for each department in the gift shop at The Inn at Portage Bay. As you can see, the table has six rows and three columns.

Figure 12.4
Table created in
Adobe Table

| Department | Revenue | Comments |
|---|---|---|
| Books, Mag, N/P | 3,015.25 | Business conference next month. Increase stock of WSJ |
| Novelty items | 6,476.40 | Start promotion of kites (eagle design) |
| Apparel | 4,511.74 | Need to develop a line of T-shirts with our logo |
| Food items | 1,209.54 | Chocolate ferry boats are a hit |
| Total | $15,212.93 | |

To create this table, you will specify these settings in the New Table dialog box. Now start a new table.

You start a new table by indicating the structure you want to use in the table.

CTRL N

1. Select New from the File menu.

The New Table dialog box appears with the default settings. Here, you can change the number of rows and columns and modify the table size. You can also alter the space (called the **gutter**) between the columns and rows. This is similar to changing the gutter space between columns in a multicolumn publication. You need to change the number of columns to three and the number of rows to six.

2. With the 4 highlighted in the Rows box, type 6.

3. Press TAB to move the highlight to the Columns box.

4. Type 3 and click OK.

The table you specified appears, as shown in Figure 12.5.

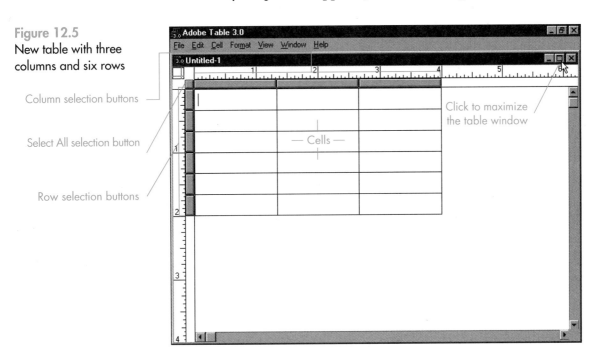

**Figure 12.5**
New table with three columns and six rows

Column selection buttons

Select All selection button

Row selection buttons

5. Maximize the table window.

You can change the view of the table using the View menu.

6. Click View in the menu bar.

CTRL 1

7. Verify that the table is Actual Size.

The components of the screen now include a table with three columns and six rows, vertical and horizontal rulers, scroll bars, and a Pasteboard. There are also selection buttons used to select all or part of the table. The table template is a grid with columns and rows. As mentioned earlier, the intersection of the rows and the columns form cells. You type information into a cell.

Figure 12.6 shows the completed template, which you will create.

Figure 12.6
Completed table
template

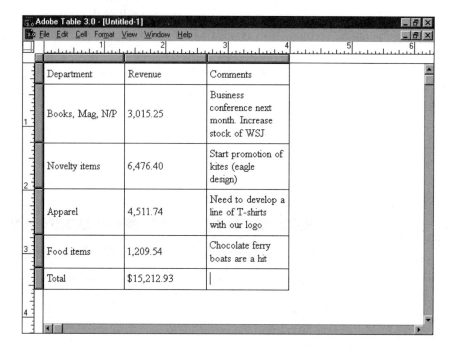

To duplicate the table in Figure 12.6, you click an insertion point inside a cell and then type the text. Figure 12.7 shows how to move within the table.

Figure 12.7
Ways to move insertion
point within a table

| Action or Key(s) | Results |
| --- | --- |
| Click in a cell | Moves insertion point in cell |
| TAB | Moves insertion point to next cell |
| SHIFT TAB | Moves insertion point to previous cell |
| ←, →, ↑, ↓ | Moves insertion point up, down, left, or right one cell (These keys also move the insertion point within a cell.) |
| HOME | Moves insertion point to upper-left cell of the table |
| END | Moves insertion point to lower-right cell of the table |

Depending on the font and font size you are using, your table might be slightly different than shown in Figure 12.6.

8. Verify that the insertion point is in the first cell (the upper-left corner of the table).

9. Type *Department*.

10. Press TAB to move the insertion point to the next column.

11. Type *Revenue*.

12. Press TAB to move the insertion point to the next column.

**13.** Type *Comments*.

**14.** Press (TAB).

Notice that the insertion point moves to the first cell of the next row.

**15.** Type *Books, Mag, N/P*.

**16.** Press (TAB) to move the insertion point to the next column.

**17.** Type *3,015.25*.

**18.** Press (TAB) to move the insertion point to the next column.

You will be entering several words in this column. They will not all fit within the current cell size. As you type and reach the right side of the cell, the words automatically wrap around to the next line. You do not have to press (↵ ENTER). Adobe Table will automatically increase the height of the cell to accommodate the text.

**19.** Type *Business conference next month. Increase stock of WSJ.*

**20.** Press (TAB) to move the cursor to the next row.

**21.** On your own, complete the table shown in Figure 12.6.

Before continuing, you should save the table.

**Saving the Table**

The process for saving a table is to select the Save as command from the File menu. Then specify a file name. Adobe Table adds a **.tbl** file extension to the name you specify. Save the table as Gift Shop Table.

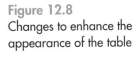

**1.** Select Save as from the File menu.

**2.** Save the table with the file name Gift Shop Table.

The basic table is complete, although there are several changes you can make to enhance its appearance, as shown in Figure 12.8.

**Figure 12.8**
Changes to enhance the appearance of the table

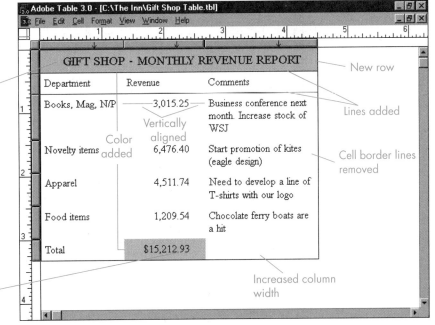

The enhanced table has the following changes:

- The width of the last column has been increased.

- A new row has been added at the top of the table.

- A title has been typed in the new row, enlarged, and centered.

- The numbers have been lined up on their decimal point.

- The cell borders have been removed.

- Lines have been placed above and below the second row.

- A color has been placed in the top row and in the cell displaying the total amount.

- The numbers and their row headings have been vertically aligned.

You'll start by increasing the width of the last column.

## Changing the Width of Columns

You can change the column width of a table in two ways. First, you can highlight the column(s), select the Row/Column Size command from the Cell menu, and type the width you want. Second, you can use the column boundary pointer ◄◆► to drag a column boundary to the width you want; this technique is shown in Figure 12.9.

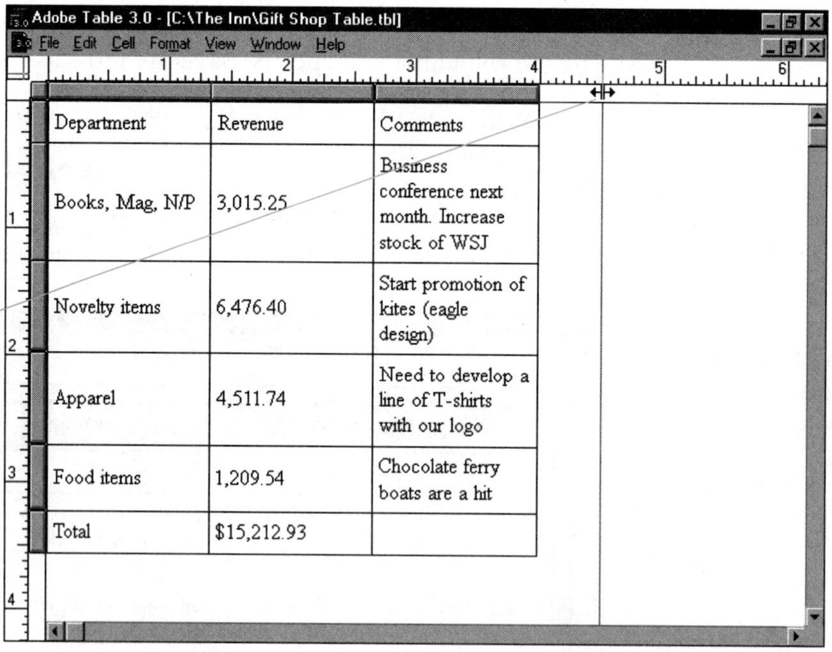

**Figure 12.9**
Dragging a column boundary to change the column width

Shows new column width

Use the second method to increase the width of the Comments column.

1. Point to the Comments column boundary (the right side of the column selection button).

2. When the pointer changes to ◄◆►, drag the boundary to the 4½-inch mark on the horizontal ruler.

3. Release the mouse button.

You can also use this drag technique to change row heights. Before making the other changes in the table, you need to understand how to work with a table by selecting rows, columns, and individual cells.

Working with Tables

Before you make changes to a table such as removing borders or adding colors, you must specify which part of the table you are working with. You can use the row and column selection buttons to select rows and columns and the arrow pointer to select individual cells. Figure 12.10 lists the ways to select cells. (Refer to Figure 12.5 if you need help finding the row, column, and Select All selection buttons.)

**Figure 12.10**

**Ways to select table cells**

| To select | Click |
| --- | --- |
| A row or column | Row or column selection button |
| A range of contiguous rows or columns | First row or column selection button and hold down (SHIFT) while you click last row or column selection button |
| A range of noncontiguous rows or columns | First row or column selection button and hold down (CTRL) while you click other row or column selection buttons |
| Single cell | Arrow pointer ▶ inside cell |
| A range of contiguous cells | Arrow pointer ▶ inside first cell of the range and hold down (SHIFT) while you click inside last cell of range |
| A range of noncontiguous cells | Arrow pointer ▶ inside first cell and hold down (CTRL) while you click inside other cells |
| All rows | Select All selection button or choose Select All from the Edit menu |

Take a few moments to practice selecting rows, columns, and cells in a table. You can remove a selection by clicking the Pasteboard.

1. Click the column selection button for the Department column.

Notice that all of the cells in the column are highlighted. If you were to make a change, such as adding a color, it would affect each highlighted cell.

2. Click the row selection button for the Department row.

3. Hold down (CTRL) while you click the row selection button for the Apparel row.

**4.** Hold down ⎡CTRL⎦ while you click the row selection button for the Total row.

The three nonadjacent rows are highlighted.

**5.** Click the Pasteboard to deselect the rows.

**6.** Click the row selection button for the Books row.

**7.** Hold down ⎡SHIFT⎦ while you click the row selection button for the Food row.

All of the rows between Books and Food are selected, along with the Books and Food rows.

**8.** Click the Pasteboard to deselect the rows.

Now you will select individual cells. When you point to a cell, either an I-beam pointer or an arrow pointer will be visible. The I-beam pointer is used to select text and click an insertion point in the cell. The arrow pointer is used to select the cell itself.

**9.** Point to the top of the Revenue cell. See Figure 12.11.

**Figure 12.11**
Selecting an individual cell

Point here

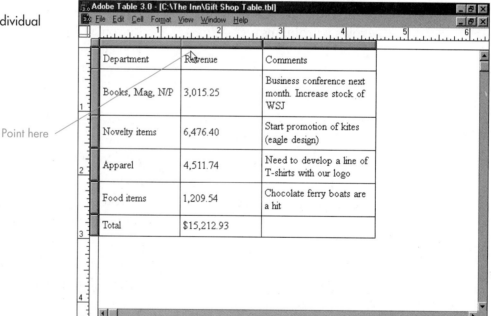

**10.** With the arrow pointer ➤ displayed, click the mouse button.

The cell is selected. You can select another cell at the same time even if it is not adjacent to the selected cell.

**11.** Hold down ⎡CTRL⎦ while you click the arrow pointer ➤ on the cell that displays the total revenue—$15,212.93.

Both cells are selected. Now you'll select a range of cells.

**12.** Click the Pasteboard to deselect the cells.

**13.** Use the arrow pointer ‣ to select the cell that displays 3,015.25 (Books, Mag, N/P revenue).

**14.** Hold down ⌈SHIFT⌋ while you click the cell that displays $15,212.93 (Total revenue).

All of the cells containing numbers are selected. Next try selecting the entire table.

**15.** Click the Select All selection button.

**16.** Click the Pasteboard to deselect the table.

Now that you can easily move around the table, you will duplicate Figure 12.8. Start by inserting a new row, grouping the cells, and entering and formatting the text.

---

## Inserting Rows

You can insert rows and columns into the table using the Cell menu. The process to insert a row is to select a row that will be adjacent to the new row. Then select the Insert Row Above or Insert Row Below command from the Cell menu. You need to insert a row above the Department row.

**1.** On your own, select the Department row.

**2.** Select Insert Row Above from the Cell menu.

A blank row with three cells appears at the top of the table.

---

## Grouping Cells

Because the title you will type in this row is longer than the width of one cell, you will need to combine, or **group**, the three cells into one. The process is to highlight the cells you want to combine and then select the Group command from the Cell menu. The gridlines and gutters disappear, so the grouped cells become a single cell.

 **1.** With the new row highlighted, select Group from the Cell menu.

Now enter a heading as the table title.

**2.** With the new cell highlighted, type *GIFT SHOP - MONTHLY REVENUE REPORT.*

Next you will center align the heading and change the type size. This can be done using the Format Text dialog box from the Cell menu, or the Text palette. The Text palette is similar to the Control palette in PageMaker. You can display this palette using the Window menu.

 **3.** Select Show Text Palette from the Window menu.

Notice that the Text palette is named Text Attributes.

**4.** Select the cell with the GIFT SHOP heading.

---

**5.** Move the Text palette below the table by dragging its title bar. See Figure 12.12.

**Figure 12.12**
Text palette positioned below the table

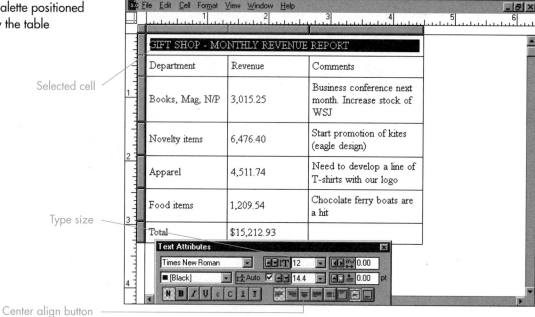

**Figure 12.12**
Text palette positioned below the table

Selected cell

Type size

Center align button

**6.** Click the center align button [icon] on the Text palette (refer to Figure 12.12).

**7.** On your own, change the type size to 14.

The table heading changes to a larger size and is centered in the cell.

## Aligning Numbers

To align numbers in a column you need to set a decimal tab marker, which aligns the numbers on the decimal point, and insert a tab before each number. The completed process is shown in Figure 12.13.

**Figure 12.13**
Tab markers used to align the numbers

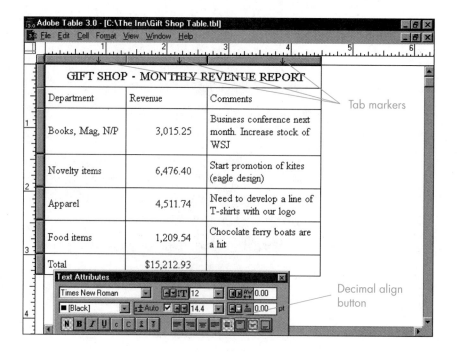

Tab markers

Decimal align button

You'll align the column of numbers so it matches the alignment shown in Figure 12.13.

1. Click the Revenue column selection button to select the column.

2. Click the decimal alignment button  on the Text palette (refer to Figure 12.13).

3. Select Show Tab Markers from the View menu.

Now insert a tab into each cell with a number. You cannot press TAB because it will move the insertion point to the next cell. You need to press CTRL . (a period). Start by moving the insertion point to the left of the number 3,015.25.

4. Position the I-beam pointer in front of the 3.

5. Click an insertion point.

6. Hold down CTRL while you press . (period).

The number moves to the right and the decimal point aligns on the tab marker. Continue with the other numbers.

7. On your own, insert tabs for the other four numbers.

With the dollar amounts aligned on the decimal points, it's much easier to read and compare the amounts.

## Working with Borders

The next enhancement you will make to the table is to change the border around the table and selected cells. If you look back at Figure 12.8, you'll see a border around the entire table and border lines above and below the Department row. You can use either the Format Cells dialog box from the Format menu or the Table palette to change border lines.

1. Click the Select All selection button to select the entire table.

CTRL A

2. Select Show Table Palette from the Window menu.

CTRL 8

3. Move the Table palette to the right of the table. See Figure 12.14.

Figure 12.14
Table palette positioned
to the right of the table

Borders proxy        Border line
                     point size

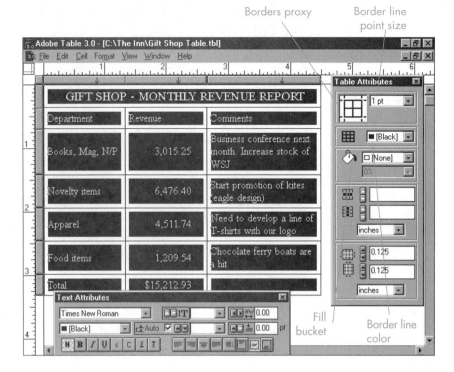

Fill
bucket

Border line
color

Figure 12.14 labels the parts of the Table palette (which is named Table Attributes). The borders proxy is used to select the borders you want to work with. The borders currently selected appear in bold. Because the entire table is selected, all of the lines of the proxy are bolded. Each border line has two attributes: line width (measured in points) and color. Currently, the line width is 1 pt and the color is Black. You can easily change these and view the results.

**4.** Click the down arrow next to the border line point size and select 4 pt.

**5.** Click the down arrow next to Black and select Blue.

**6.** Click the Pasteboard to deselect the table.

The table appears with the new line width and color. Now, you will remove all of the borders. You can do this by specifying None for the border color. Start by selecting the entire table.

 CTRL A

**7.** On your own, select the entire table.

**8.** Change the border line color to None.

**9.** Click the Pasteboard to deselect the table.

All of the borders disappear. Continue by specifying a 2 pt black border for the table, but not for the gridlines within the table.

CTRL A

**10.** On your own, select the entire table.

The borders proxy, as shown in Figure 12.15, indicates that the border lines that will be affected are on the outside edges of the table. If you were to click the lines inside the proxy, they would be selected. Then any change would affect the inside gridlines of the table.

Figure 12.15
Borders proxy showing
which border lines will
be affected

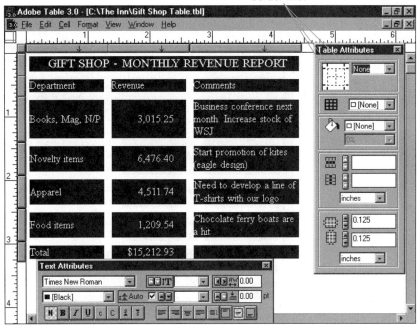

11. With only the outside border lines selected, select Black as the border line color.

12. Select 1 pt as the line width.

13. Click the Pasteboard to deselect the table.

You'll place lines above and below the Department row to help the column headings stand out more.

14. Select the Department row.

Notice that the borders proxy on the Table palette indicates border lines at either end of the row. The borders proxy also assumes that the top and bottom border lines are to be displayed for this row. Because the color is already set to black, you just need to change the border line width.

15. Set the line width to 1 pt.

16. Click the Pasteboard to deselect the row.

Next you will fill the top row and the total number cell with green color to distinguish the title and total revenue from the rest of the table cells.

17. Select the top row.

18. Click the down arrow next to the fill bucket and select Green.

19. Drag the I-beam across $15,212.93 to select the number and choose Green as the color.

The last change you will make to the table is to vertically align the headings and numbers for selected cells. You will use the Format Text dialog box to do this.

**20.** Select all the cells with numbers in the Revenue column and their corresponding labels in the Department column. See Figure 12.16.

Figure 12.16
Selecting a range
of cells

Selected cells to align
vertically

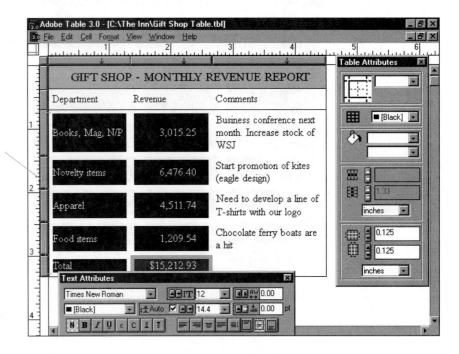

CTRL T

**21.** Select Format Text from the Format menu.

The Format Text dialog box appears with many of the same options that are available on the Text palette.

**22.** Change the Vertical alignment to Top.

**23.** Click OK.

**24.** Click the Pasteboard to deselect the cells.

You have finished adding enhancements to the table.

CTRL 6  and  CTRL 8

**25.** Use the Window menu to hide the Text and Table palettes.

CTRL S

**26.** Save the table with the same file name, Gift Shop Table.

## Copying a Table to PageMaker

You cannot print a table from Adobe Table. To print a table you must incorporate it into a PageMaker publication. There are two ways to incorporate a table, or part of a table, into a PageMaker publication. First, you can copy the table from Adobe Table to the Clipboard and then paste the table from the Clipboard to the publication page. Second, you can use the Export command to save the table as a graphics or text file. Then you can use the Place command to place the table on the publication page. Exporting a table as a graphic or text file allows other applications to read the file directly from disk. You will use the first method to incorporate the table into a publication.

The process for copying a table to a PageMaker publication page is to select the entire table. Then select the Copy command from the Edit menu. This places a copy of the table on the Clipboard. Next, you must start or switch to the PageMaker program and select the Paste command from the Edit menu. The table appears on the publication page.

Complete the following to copy the gift shop table to a PageMaker publication page.

1. Choose Select All from the Edit menu.

2. Select Copy from the Edit menu.

Now you need to start the PageMaker program. Because you are using Windows, you can keep Adobe Table running while you start PageMaker.

3. Minimize the Adobe Table program window.

4. Start the PageMaker program.

5. Start a new publication and accept the default settings.

With the publication page in view, you can copy the table onto the page.

6. Select Paste from the Edit menu.

Figure 12.17 shows the table pasted into the publication page. Notice that graphics handles surround the table. This is because the table is an object and can be resized, cropped, moved, or deleted just like any other object.

**Figure 12.17**
Table pasted into the publication page

Position pasted table here

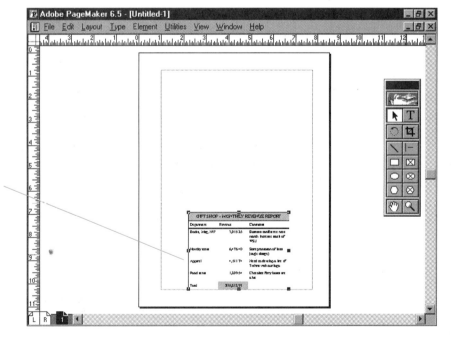

**7.** Drag the graphic to the bottom center of the page.

CTRL 7

**8.** Change the view to 75% Size and look at the table.

CTRL 0

**9.** Change the view to Fit in Window.

Next you will place a Microsoft Word document, called Gift Shop Memo, on the publication page with the table, as shown in Figure 12.18, to complete the PageMaker publication.

**Figure 12.18**
Document placed on the publication page

Place text here

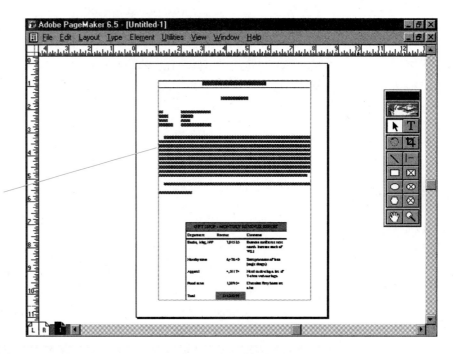

CTRL D

**10.** Select Place from the File menu.

**11.** Select the Gift Shop Memo document and click Open.

**12.** Position the text icon 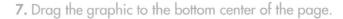 in the upper-left corner of the page.

**13.** Click the mouse button.

The text appears at the top of the publication. If necessary, you can reposition the text block or table object for better placement on the page. Before you close the publication, you will save and print it.

CTRL S

**14.** Save the publication as Gift Shop Memo Done.

CTRL P

**15.** Print the publication.

CTRL W

**16.** Close the publication.

Now that you know how to create a table in Adobe Table, you will learn about linking a file to a PageMaker publication.

As you have been working with PageMaker, you might have noticed that often a publication contains text and graphics created in another program, such as a graph developed using a spreadsheet program. But what if, for example, the graph changes, because of a change in the spreadsheet? Will you have to place the graph each time the spreadsheet changes? Fortunately, PageMaker provides a function that allows you to **link** a publication to an external file so that changes made in the original file (the spreadsheet) will appear in PageMaker (the placed graph).

Figure 12.19 illustrates this link function. A graph with the file name SALES was developed with the Excel spreadsheet program and placed in a PageMaker publication. A link was created between the graph file and the publication. Now, whenever the publication is opened, the most recent version of the graph is automatically placed in the publication. This process is called **Object Linking and Embedding** (OLE) and is common to Windows programs, such as PageMaker and Adobe Table.

**Figure 12.19**

Linking a publication to an external file

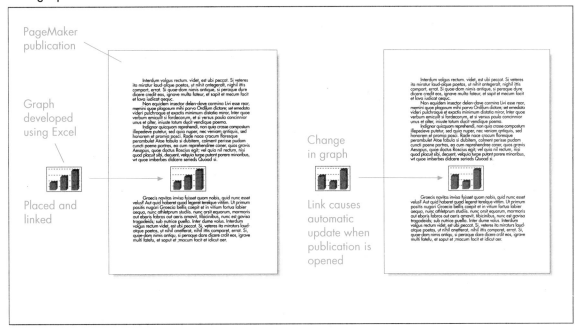

To practice this function, you will use the gift shop table you created in Adobe Table. First you will place the table in a publication and link the publication to the table file. Then you will make a change in the table and see how PageMaker automatically updates the publication. You use the Insert Object command from the Edit menu to link a file.

**1.** Start a new publication.

**2.** Select Insert Object from the Edit menu.

The Insert Object dialog box appears. You need to indicate that the object you want to insert is a file.

**3.** Click Create from File to select this option.

Also, you need to specify the file location and name and to indicate that the file will be linked. Figure 12.20 shows the completed Insert Object dialog box. (*Note*: The location for your file might be different than the one displayed.)

**Figure 12.20**
**Completed Insert Object dialog box**

Use Browse to locate Gift Shop Table file

Click to select link

Description of link function

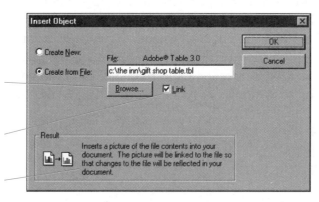

**4.** Use the Browse function to locate the Gift Shop Table file you created earlier.

**5.** Click Link to display a check mark.

**6.** Read the text in the Result box on the screen.

**7.** Click OK.

**8.** Position the table in the middle at the top of the publication page.

**9.** Change the view to 75% Size.

You use the Links Manager command from the File menu to complete the linking process.

**10.** Select Links Manager from the File menu. See Figure 12.21.

**Figure 12.21**
**Links Manager dialog box**

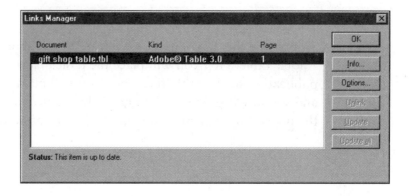

The Links Manager dialog box appears, showing that the Gift Shop Table file, which is an Adobe Table 3.0 table, is linked and up-to-date.

11. Click Options.

The Link Options dialog box allows you to indicate that you want the table in the publication to be updated automatically.

12. Click Update automatically to display a check mark.

13. Click Alert before updating to display a check mark.

14. Click OK in the Link Options dialog box.

15. Click OK in the Links Manager dialog box.

16. Save the publication with the file name Gift Shop Link.

17. Close the publication.

Now return to the Adobe Table program and make a change in the original gift shop table.

18. Display the Adobe Table program.

19. Change the novelty items number to 16,476.40 and the total to 25,212.93.

20. Select Save As from the File menu and save the table using the same file name, Gift Shop Table.

21. Return to the PageMaker program.

22. Open the Gift Shop Link publication.

A message appears indicating that the linked file (Gift Shop Table) has changed and asking if you would like to update the table in the publication.

23. Click Update.

The publication appears with the updated table.

This completes linking a file to a PageMaker publication. You can exit PageMaker.

24. Exit PageMaker without saving the publication.

25. Exit Adobe Table.

Object Linking and Embedding is a powerful feature that be extremely useful when you need to use different programs to create a publication, especially when some of the files you place might change.

In this chapter you learned how to use Adobe Table to create and edit a table. You also learned how to place a table into a PageMaker publication and how to link a file with a PageMaker publication. You saw how linking a file rather than just placing it can save you time if the contents of the file might change.

QUESTIONS

1. What is the purpose of the Adobe Table program?

2. Is Adobe Table part of the PageMaker program? Explain.

3. How is a table organized?

4. What is the process for selecting a group of noncontiguous cells?

5. What is the purpose of grouping cells?

6. What is the difference between the Text palette and the Table palette?

7. How is the borders proxy used?

8. Describe the ways to incorporate a table into a PageMaker publication.

9. What is the purpose of linking a file to a PageMaker publication?

10. Give an example of how a linked file would be used.

PROJECTS

1. Assume the role of the manager of the gift shop. Using a word processing program or PageMaker, write a memo to the employees that contains the revised schedule for Labor Day weekend. Save the memo as Schedule Memo. Use Adobe Table to create a table that contains the weekend schedule. The table will contain the information shown in Figure 12.22.

Figure 12.22
Project 12.1—
Weekend schedule
information

| Time | Sat | Sun | Mon | Hours |
|------|------|------|------|-------|
| 8–12 | Bob | Bob | Bob | 12 |
|      | Sue | Sue | Sue | 12 |
| 12–4 | Bob | Bob | Cary | 12 |
|      | Cary | Cary | Lee | 12 |
| 4–8 | Cary | Cary |  | 8 |
|      | Lee | Lee |  | 8 |
|      |  |  |  | Total: 64 |

Include a title for the table and enhance the table with such attributes as large type, color fills, column width adjustments, and so forth. Save the table as Schedule and copy it to the memo publication. Save and print the publication.

2. Develop a table using the Adobe Table program. Enhance the table using the features you learned in this chapter. Save the table. Then open PageMaker, start a new publication, and use the Import Object command to import the table and link it to the publication. Use the Links Manager command to specify an automatic update for the linked table. Save and close the publication. Then display the Adobe Table program and make a change in the table. Use the Save As command to save the table with the same name (and keep the file small). Return to the PageMaker program and open the publication.

3. Assume the role of finance manager for Portage Bay Properties. Using a word processing program or PageMaker, write a memo to the president of the company. The memo should include an introduction to the Income Statement Forecast shown in Figure 12.1 and indicate the highlights of the forecast. Use Adobe Table to create the Income Statement Forecast table shown in Figure 12.1. Enhance the table with such attributes as large type, color fills, column width adjustments, and so forth. Save the table as Forecast and copy it to the memo publication. Save and print the publication.

# Quick Reference

| To select | Press |
|---|---|
| Fit in Window | `CTRL` `0` |
| 50% Size | `CTRL` `5` |
| 75% Size | `CTRL` `7` |
| 100%/Actual Size | `CTRL` `1` |
| 200% Size | `CTRL` `2` |
| 400% Size | `CTRL` `4` |
| Entire Pasteboard | `SHIFT` `CTRL` `0` |

To switch between Actual Size and Fit in Window, point to the desired area of the page, and hold down `CTRL` while you click the right mouse button. To increase your view, select the zoom tool and click the left mouse button.

To decrease your view, select the zoom tool and hold down `CTRL` while you click the left mouse button.

| Selecting Text | Text block | Select the pointer tool ▲, point to the desired text, and click the left mouse button. |
| | Letter, word, paragraph, or any part of text | Select the text tool **T** and drag the I-beam I across the desired text. |
| | Word | Select the text tool **T** and double-click the I-beam I in the word. |
| | Paragraph | Select the text tool **T** and triple-click the I-beam I in the paragraph. |
| | Part of text | Click an insertion point at beginning of text, move the I-beam I to the end of text you want to select, hold down (SHIFT), and click the left mouse button. |
| | Entire text | Choose Select All from the Edit menu or press (CTRL)(A). |

| Selecting Text and Graphics | Single object | Select the pointer tool ▲ and click the text block or graphic. |
| | Multiple objects | Select the pointer tool ▲ and hold down (SHIFT) while you click each object. |
| | Stacked object | Select the pointer tool ▲, hold down (CTRL) while you click the top item to select it. Continue to hold down (CTRL) while you click each item until the entire object is selected. |
| | All objects | Choose Select All from the Edit menu or press (CTRL)(A). |

| Deselecting Text and Graphics | Click a blank area of the Pasteboard or document setup, select another object, or click another tool. | |
|---|---|---|

| Moving or Copying Text and Graphics | Select the text/graphic(s). | |
|---|---|---|
| | Select Cut (to move) or Copy from the Edit menu. | |
| | Select Paste from the Edit menu. | |
| | Drag the text/graphic(s) to the desired location. | |

| Deleting Text and Graphics | Select the text/graphic(s) object(s). | |
|---|---|---|
| | Select Clear from the Edit menu, press (DELETE), or press (← BACKSPACE). | |

| Altering Graphics | Trim an imported graphic | Select the cropping tool [icon], point to a handle, and drag it. |
|---|---|---|
| | Resize a graphic | Select the pointer tool [icon] and drag a handle. |
| | Proportionally resize a graphic | Select the pointer tool [icon] and hold down (SHIFT) while you drag a handle. |
| | Draw a circle | Select the ellipse tool [icon] and hold down (SHIFT) while you draw. |
| | Draw a square | Select the rectangle tool [icon] and hold down (SHIFT) while you draw. |
| | Draw an equilateral hexagon | Select the polygon tool [icon] and hold down (SHIFT) while you draw. |

Toolbox

| Tool | Icon | Function |
| --- | --- | --- |
| Pointer | ▶ | Selecting text blocks and graphics |
| Rotating | ✳ | Rotating text and graphics |
| Line | + | Drawing diagonal lines |
| Rectangle | + | Drawing rectangles and squares |
| Ellipse | + | Drawing ovals and circles |
| Polygon | + | Drawing polygons |
| Grabberhand | ✋ | Scrolling the page |
| Text | I | Selecting, entering, and editing text |
| Cropping | 🔳 | Trimming graphics |
| Constrained line | + | Drawing perpendicular lines |
| Rectangle frame | + | Creating rectangular placeholders for text and graphics |
| Ellipse frame | + | Creating elliptical placeholders for text and graphics |
| Polygon frame | + | Creating polygonal placeholders for text and graphics |
| Zoom | 🔍 | Magnifying or reducing view of the page |

Place

| Icon | Name | Function |
|---|---|---|
| | Text | Placing text—manual flow |
| | Text flow | Placing text—automatic flow |
| | Text flow | Placing text—semiautomatic flow |
| | Paint | Placing paint-type graphics |
| | Draw | Placing draw-type graphics |
| | TIF | Placing scanned image graphics in TIF, GIF, JPEG, and Photo-CD formats |
| | EPS | Placing graphics in Encapsulated PostScript format |

Other

| Icon | Name | Function |
|---|---|---|
| | Story view | Indicates story view |
| | Layout view | Indicates layout view |
| | Close | Closes a dialog box, window, or program |
| | Graphic boundary pointer | Moves a graphic boundary for text flow |
| | Index marker | Marks a word or words for inclusion in the index |
| | Left tab | Left-aligns text at tab |
| | Right tab | Right-aligns text at tab |
| | Center tab | Centers text at tab |
| | Decimal tab | Aligns numbers on their decimals |

| Example | Description | Keyboard shortcut |
|---|---|---|
| • | bullet | ALT 8 |
| © | copyright symbol | ALT G |
| … | ellipsis | ALT 0 1 3 3 |
| — | em dash | ALT SHIFT – |
| | em space | CTRL SHIFT M |
| – | en dash | ALT – |
| | en space | CTRL SHIFT N |
| LM,RM | page-number marker | CTRL ALT P |
| ® | registered trademark symbol | ALT R |
| ™ | trademark symbol | ALT 0 1 5 3 |
| " | typographer's open quotation marks | ALT SHIFT [ |
| " | typographer's close quotation marks | ALT SHIFT ] |
| ' | typographer's single open quotation mark | ALT [ |
| ' | typographer's single close quotation mark | ALT ] |

## PAGEMAKER MENUS

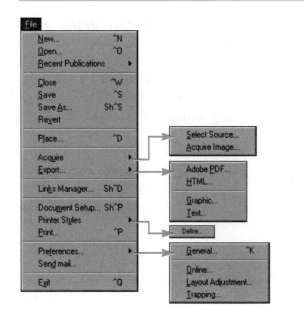

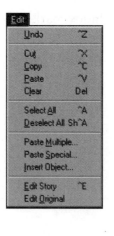

Appears only in layout view

Appears only in story view

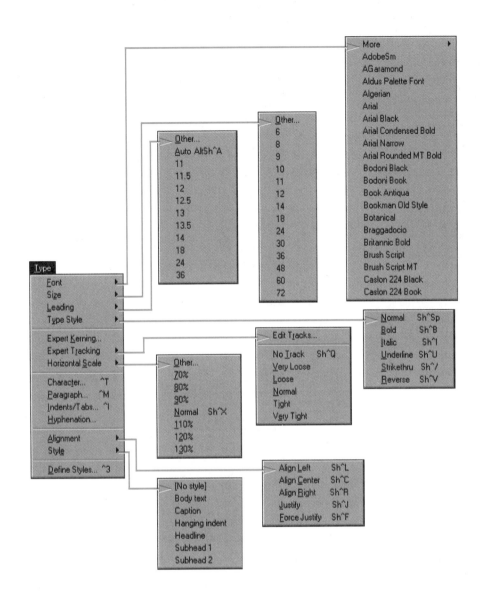

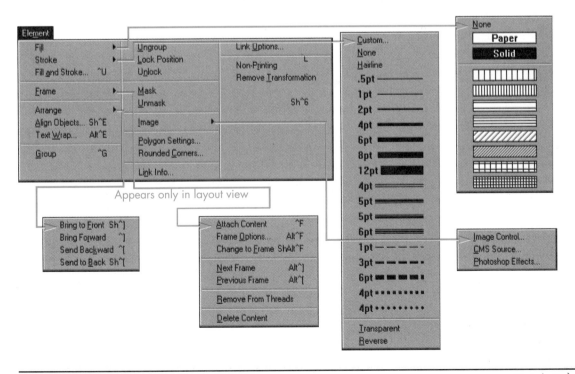

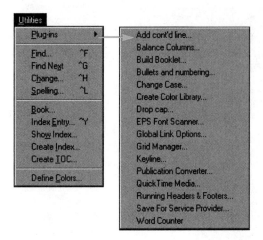

**Utilities**

Plug-ins ▶

Find... ^F
Find Next ^G
Change... ^H
Spelling... ^L

Book...
Index Entry... ^Y
Show Index...
Create Index...
Create TOC...

Define Colors...

Add cont'd line...
Balance Columns...
Build Booklet...
Bullets and numbering...
Change Case...
Create Color Library...
Drop cap...
EPS Font Scanner...
Global Link Options...
Grid Manager...
Keyline...
Publication Converter...
QuickTime Media...
Running Headers & Footers...
Save For Service Provider...
Word Counter

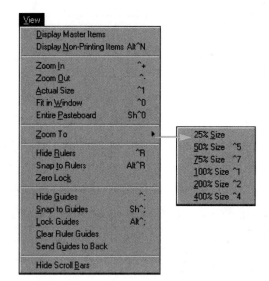

**View**

Display Master Items
Display Non-Printing Items Alt^N

Zoom In ^+
Zoom Out ^.
Actual Size ^1
Fit in Window ^0
Entire Pasteboard Sh^0

Zoom To ▶

Hide Rulers ^R
Snap to Rulers Alt^R
Zero Lock

Hide Guides ^;
Snap to Guides Sh^;
Lock Guides Alt^;
Clear Ruler Guides
Send Guides to Back

Hide Scroll Bars

25% Size
50% Size ^5
75% Size ^7
100% Size ^1
200% Size ^2
400% Size ^4

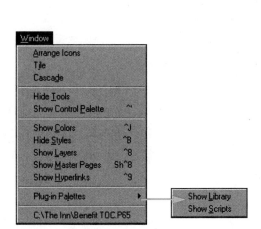

**Window**

Arrange Icons
Tile
Cascade

Hide Tools
Show Control Palette ^

Show Colors ^J
Hide Styles ^B
Show Layers ^8
Show Master Pages Sh^8
Show Hyperlinks ^9

Plug-in Palettes ▶

C:\The Inn\Benefit TOC.P65

Show Library
Show Scripts

**Help**

Help Topics... F1
Shortcuts...

About PageMaker®...